CRIME AND THE COMPUTER

Crime and the Computer

Martin Wasik

CLARENDON PRESS · OXFORD
1991

Oxford University Press, Walton Street, Oxford OX2 6DP
Oxford New York Toronto
Delhi Bombay Calcutta Madras Karachi
Petaling Jaya Singapore Hong Kong Tokyo
Nairobi Dar es Salaam Cape Town
Melbourne Auckland
and associated companies in
Berlin Ibadan

Oxford is a trade mark of Oxford University Press

Published in the United States
by Oxford University Press, New York

© Martin Wasik 1991

British Library Cataloguing in Publication Data
Wasik, Martin
Crime and the computer. – (Oxford monographs on criminal
law).
1. Great Britain. Computer crimes. Law. Reform
I. Title
344.105268
ISBN 0–19–825621–3

Library of Congress Cataloging in Publication Data
Wasik, Martin
Crime and the computer/Martin Wasik
(Oxford monographs on Criminal law and Criminal justice)
Includes bibliographical references (p.   ) and index.
1. Computer crimes—Great Britain.   2. Computer crimes.
I. Title.   II. Series.
KD7990.W37   1990   345.42'0268—dc20   [344.205268]   90–38538
ISBN 0–19–825621–3

Typeset by Hope Services (Abingdon) Ltd
Printed and bound in Great Britain by
Biddles Ltd, Guildford and King's Lynn

Undoubtedly computer-related crime will soon become one of the most important areas of legal study

(Kelman and Sizer, 1982)

The first myth about computer crime is that it exists . . .

(Ingraham, 1980)

Editor's Preface

Public interest in criminal law and criminal justice can rarely have been so great as it is today. News and discussion of crime fill a large part of the newspapers and appear on television screens daily. It is probable that never before has awareness of the problems of the application of the criminal law been so widespread. The complexity of the law has increased enormously. For the first half of this century Professor Kenny's famous *Outlines of Criminal Law* seems, in one short volume, to have satisfied the needs of the student not only of the law, but of criminal procedure, evidence, and sentencing. We have come a long way since then. Certainly the rate of change has never previously been so great. Fortunately all this has been matched by an increase in interest in these problems in the university, polytechnic, and professional law schools and among some members of the practising profession. Criminal law, once thought a not very respectable subject for academic study, is now among the principal interests of many of the very best legal scholars. Criminal procedure, evidence, and sentencing, which scarcely featured in the academic scene at all, have now become highly developed subjects of study. A vast amount of study of and research into these subjects is going on.

For these reasons, the time is ripe for the appearance of a new series of monographs on criminal law and criminal justice which will provide an outlet for the products of the study and research and encourage more of it. There could be no more appropriate subject for the first volume in the series than *Crime and the Computer*, dealing, as it does, with a completely new phenomenon which tests the adequacy of the traditional concepts of the criminal law, evidence, and procedure and raises questions as to the proper bounds of the criminal law. Martin Wasik is already well known for his writing on various aspects of the subject. In this work he has taken a comprehensive view of it which not only facilitates and improves understanding of the issues and provides a source of information but which may be expected to influence the development of the law and practice in the future.

Cambridge
6th July 1990

JOHN SMITH

Preface

Computer misuse has frequently been in the news over the past few years. Stories about computer fraud, especially those versions with exotic names like 'Trojan horse' and 'salami' frauds, have vied with descriptions of teenage 'hackers' breaking Pentagon computer access codes and nearly triggering World War III. Latterly, the malicious introduction of 'worms' and 'viruses' into computer systems, and the phenomenon of 'computer eavesdropping', have provided regular journalistic copy. Other concerns have been widespread computer software piracy and the unauthorized removal of confidential information held on computers.

It has been argued by some that many of these new 'technocrimes', often committed remotely and across national boundaries, are virtually undetectable and fall outside the scope of a criminal law largely drafted before the dawning of the information technology age and hampered by antiquated jurisdictional rules. Computers, unlike most crime victims, cannot be 'deceived' and intangibles like computer data and programs cannot be the subject-matter of theft or criminal damage laws. Yet until the mid-1980s there seemed to be no sense of urgency in Britain about these problems, and many lawyers still assumed that existing British law could, with a little stretching here and there, cater quite adequately for the commission of crimes involving computers: they were merely old offences appearing in a new guise. A change in the method of commission of an offence seemed not to require a reform of the substantive law, or an updating of evidential or procedural requirements. This view was adhered to in spite of important law reform developments taking place in many other jurisdictions, particularly the comprehensive 'computer crime statutes' in the United States, which were designed to tackle just those same problems encountered there a few years earlier.

Following the quashing of the convictions of the Prestel hackers Gold and Schifreen by the House of Lords in 1987, however, it became generally accepted that our criminal law was indeed in urgent need of reform. A Report on the matter from the Scottish Law Commission in the same year was followed in 1989 by a Private Member's Bill designed to outlaw hacking, subsequently withdrawn, and a carefully considered Report from the English Law Commission. That body, after receiving a record number of submissions in response to its earlier Working Paper on the subject, recommended the creation of three new criminal offences to cater for specific aspects of computer misuse. Although the Law Commission was placed under pressure to produce its Report quickly, with a view to government legislation on computer misuse in the next Parliamentary session, change of personnel following a government reshuffle apparently meant that computer misuse was dropped from the legislative timetable, and no mention was made of it in the Queen's Speech in November 1989. Its omission attracted almost as much interest as some of the legislation which was actually proposed. Soon afterwards, however, it became clear that there was to be full government support for a Bill sponsored by a Private Member, Mr. Michael Colvin, the terms of which were to be very much in accord with the Report of the English Law Commission. The Computer Misuse Bill received a favourable passage through Parliament during the Spring of 1990 and, somewhat amended, received the Royal Assent on 29 June. It will come into force on 29 August 1990. The passage of the first criminal statute in the United Kingdom to tackle the misuse of computers prompted several comments in Parliament to the effect that the rapid advance of technology, together with the ingenuity of the criminal, would mean that this Act was likely to be the first rather than the last word on the matter. At the time of writing, other law reform initiatives which impinge on computer misuse are pending, most importantly in respect of conspiracy to defraud.

It is these developments which form the main subject-matter of this book. In its preparation I have benefited throughout from the advice and encouragement of Professor J. C. Smith, who was also kind enough to read the whole book in draft. Manchester colleagues Rodney Brazier, Sean Doran, Tom Gibbons, Ken Pease, and Catherine Redgwell also kindly undertook to read and comment upon various draft chapters. I am also very grateful to Steven Saxby of Southampton University for his willing advice and assistance on several occasions, and in particular for allowing me access to the excellent Southampton collection of computer law materials. Needless to say, nobody but the author is responsible for errors or omissions in the final text. I am also grateful for the patience of the publishers since, in part due to the rapidity of change in the subject area, the book took rather longer to come to fruition than was at first anticipated. In preparing the text I have drawn upon a number of my own publications and I am grateful to the various publishers for permission to use them here: 'Surveying Computer Crime' (1985) 1 *Computer Law and Practice* 110 and 'Tackling Technocrime: The Law Commission Report on Computer Misuse' (1989) 6 *Computer Law and Practice* 23 (Frank Cass & Co.); 'Criminal Damage and the Computerised Saw' (1986) 136 *New Law Journal* and 'Computer Crime: Recent Legal Developments' (1987) 3 *Yearbook of Law, Computers and Technology* 195 (Butterworths Law Publishers Ltd); 'Law Reform Proposals on Computer Misuse' [1989] *Criminal Law Review* 257 and 'Crime', Chapter 12 in S. Saxby (ed.), *Encyclopedia of Information Technology Law*, 1990 (Sweet and Maxwell Ltd). The material contained in the Appendices of this book, including the text of the Computer Misuse Act 1990, is reproduced with the permission of the Controller of Her Majesty's Stationery Office.

M.W.

July 1990

Contents

Table of Statutes

OTHER JURISDICTIONS

Australia

Table of Statutes

Table of Cases

1

The Nature of Computer Misuse

1. MATTERS OF DEFINITION

'Computer crime' is a rather diffuse topic and it is hard to agree upon definitions. It is not, of course, a precise legal category. Theft or deception offences, for instance, may be committed with or without the use of a computer, and it is rare to find offences which are applicable solely in a computer environment.[1] It has often been pointed out, rightly, that generally the use of the computer in the commission of an offence in no way alters the fact that the offence has taken place, or affects the category of the crime committed, though it may well affect the actual or potential scale of the lawbreaking and make it more difficult to detect and prosecute successfully. A computer fraud is, in many cases, capable of being prosecuted in just the same way as a book or paper fraud would have been prosecuted before the advent of computers, and there is no special difficulty in establishing, say, the offence of criminal damage where the property happens to be computer hardware.

Computer crime is an artificial overlapping class of lawbreaking which is uncertain in scope. Some proposed definitions are narrow, insisting that the category of computer crime must involve the highly skilled operation of a computer in circumstances where the offence could not otherwise have been committed. Taber is perhaps the clearest exponent of this view, so that according to him the 'true' computer crime is almost mythical,[2] but Parker and Nycum have also defined computer crime narrowly as being 'any illegal act where a special knowledge of computer technology is essential for its perpetration, investigation or prosecution'.[3] Others take a broader view. Comer, in his book on corporate fraud, suggests that 'any financial dishonesty that takes place in a computer environment is a computer fraud',[4] arguing, perhaps rather oddly, that since computer manufacturers have claimed credit for the advantages of increased computerization, 'then all of the adverse

---

[1] Examples would be offences under the Data Protection Act 1984 and new offences under the Computer Misuse Act 1990. See, further, Chapter 3 and App. 4.

[2] J. K. Taber, 'On Computer Crime' (1979) 1 *Computer and Law Journal* 517.

[3] D. B. Parker, S. Nycum and S. Aura, *Computer Abuse*, Menlo Park, Calif.: Stanford Research Institute, 1973. This definition was adopted by the United States Department of Justice, *Criminal Justice Resource Manual*, Washington, DC: Federal Government Publication, 1979.

[4] M. J. Comer, *Corporate Fraud*, 2nd edn., London: McGraw-Hill, 1985, p. 141.

consequences must be accepted'.[5] The Audit Commission for Local Authorities in England and Wales, a body which has conducted a series of surveys of
computer fraud and abuse in this country, adopts a middle course, defining
computer fraud as 'any fraudulent behaviour connected with computerization
by which someone intends to gain dishonest advantage'.[6] The Law Commission, whilst declaring that finding an appropriate definition is impossible,
offers a rather similar assessment, where computer fraud is said to be 'the
manipulation of a computer, by whatever method, in order dishonestly to
obtain money, property or some other advantage of value, or to cause loss'.[7]
A more elaborate definition of computer crime in general is provided by
Mandell,[8] who asserts that computer crime consists of two kinds of activity:

(a) the use of a computer to perpetrate acts of deceit, theft or concealment that are
intended to provide financial, business-related, property or service advantages; and
(b) threats to the computer itself, such as theft of hardware or software, sabotage and
demands for ransom.

It will be seen that under the more generous of these definitions the role of the
computer may be strictly incidental to the offence, in that under (a) the act of
deceit could perhaps just as well have been committed in a non-computerized
environment and under (b) the theft of a computer rather than, say, a
television set, qualifies the offence as a computer crime. It is easy, therefore, to
deride such broad definitions, which imbue perfectly ordinary criminal
offences with the apparently rather mysterious mantle of 'computer crime'.[9]
Some of the compendious computer crime legislation adopted in other
jurisdictions has created computer-specific offences such as criminal damage
to computers, theft of semi-conductor chips,[10] and using a computer to cause
physical injury to a person, where in each case the ground was quite clearly
entirely covered by pre-existing general offences. These extreme legislative
responses have led some sceptics to the opposite extreme view that computer
crime is a complete myth, in the sense that it merely represents new ways of
committing old offences, and that existing criminal laws are more than

---

[5] M. J. Comer, *Corporate Fraud*, 2nd edn., London: McGraw-Hill, 1985, p. 141.

[6] A series of three Reports have been produced: Audit Inspectorate, *Computer Fraud Survey*,
London: Department of the Environment, 1981; Audit Commission for Local Authorities in
England and Wales, *Computer Fraud Survey*, London: HMSO, 1984; Audit Commission for
Local Authorities in England and Wales, *Survey of Computer Fraud and Abuse*, London:
HMSO, 1987.

[7] Law Commission, Working Paper No. 110, *Computer Misuse*, London: HMSO, 1988,
para. 2.2.

[8] S. L. Mandell, *Computers, Data Processing and the Law*, St Paul, Minn.: West Publishing,
1984, p. 155.

[9] Perhaps the best of the articles debunking the whole concept of 'computer crime' for this
reason is D. G. Ingraham, 'On Charging Computer Crime' (1980) 2 *Computer and Law Journal*
429, who comments at p. 438: 'Striking a watchman with a disk pack should remain the battery
that it is, and not be elevated to the status of a computer crime. There are enough red herrings in
our courts already.'

[10] Semi-Conductor Chip Protection Act 1984 (US).

capable of dealing with it, perhaps with a little stretching of the wording where necessary. A corollary of the latter view is that there is 'nothing special' about computers, and that it would be anomalous to create specific criminal law provisions to take account of them. This is simplistic, and a mistake. The adoption of a very rigorous and narrow definition of computer crime simply acts as a definitional stop to debate, and excludes from the scope of enquiry a range of difficult substantive, evidential, and procedural issues in the criminal law which tend to come to the fore when a computer is involved in the commission of the offence, or is itself the target of the offence.

One object of this book is to explore exactly those difficult criminal law issues, and so a broad approach to the subject of computer crime is adopted here. Indeed, for present purposes it is necessary to go wider still than Mandell's definition, to encompass not just 'computer crime' but 'computer misuse', which may be described as unethical or unauthorized behaviour in relation to the use of computers, programs, or data, in order to consider the extent to which such activities should properly be the subject of the criminal law. The notion of 'computer misuse' allows a wider variety of issues relating to computers to be addressed, where criminality is open to doubt. As the Law Commission has observed, to describe all such peripheral behaviour as computer crime is 'to prejudge the conduct in question'.[11] In short, whilst many writers have quibbled over the definition of computer crime, the matter is, in the end, somewhat beside the point. Nimmer[12] sums this up rather elegantly:

Although aspects of computer use in society create vulnerabilities or opportunities for abuse, these are not always qualitatively different from vulnerabilities that exist independently of computers. In many cases, however, the degree of risk and the nature of conduct are sufficiently different to raise questions about basic social decisions concerning levels of criminality for computer-related actions and the ability to discover and prosecute them under current law. Whether these are discussed under the heading of computer crime or merely as general criminal law problems is not important.

It is with these 'vulnerabilities' that the current enquiry is principally concerned, and for the purposes of further discussion the term 'computer misuse' is adopted in preference to 'computer crime'.

The secondary object of the book is to address the remarkable manner in which public and media attention has been gripped in recent years by the phenomenon of computer misuse. It is perhaps that form of offending which has most captured the modern imagination. There is already a substantial literature on computer misuse though, it must be said, a good deal of it is repetitious and ill-considered. Great fears have been engendered in computer users about the 'hacker lurking behind the screen', fears to some extent nurtured by computer security 'experts' anxious to sell their expensive

[11] Law Commission (1988), para. 1.5.
[12] R. T. Nimmer, *The Law of Computer Technology*, New York: John Wiley, 1985, p. 9.

products, fears which are often held largely in ignorance of the facts of computer misuse. Many different specialities lay claim to the area apart from the lawyers; computer scientists, computer security consultants, law enforcement personnel, sociologists, and psychologists have all advanced their varying accounts of computer misuse activity and motivation. The whole subject is pervaded by media hype. It is interesting that the effect of all this has been to deter virtually all serious criminological enquiry into the subject. It is as if the topic's very popular fascination has caused it to be shunned as a legitimate one for academic investigation. The secondary object of this book, then, is to make a start in remedying this by indicating the issues in this area which surely merit criminological attention: often these stem as much from the way computer misuse is perceived, reported, and reacted to, and the various myths built up around it, as from the details of the computer misuse itself.

There is also the matter of defining technical terms, particularly that of 'computer' itself, for the purposes of this book. Many different definitions have been suggested by writers, and some have been adopted into legislation. In the United States, where there has been by far the greatest development of statute law on the subject of computer misuse, the usual definition of 'computer' adopted by states is:[13]

an electronic device that performs logical, arithmetical, and memory functions by the manipulation of electronic or magnetic impulses, and includes all input, output, processing, storage, computer software, and communication facilities that are connected or related to a computer.

Comparable definitions of 'computer network', 'computer system', 'computer program', 'computer software', and 'data' have also been variously adopted, in the United States and elsewhere. The main difficulty with these definitions is that they are almost certain to become outdated very quickly through technological advances, such as through the development and introduction of non-electronic, optical computers which utilize light.[14] Also, their breadth is such that they certainly cover devices other than computers, such as calculators, digital watches, and automated traffic signals. Consequently, in federal legislation on computer misuse in the United States passed in 1984,[15] the definition of 'computer' has been amended, rather clumsily, to read as follows:

an electronic, magnetic, optical, electrochemical, or other high speed data processing device performing logical, arithmetic, or storage functions, and

[13] B. J. George, 'Contemporary Legislation Governing Computer Crimes' (1985) 21 *Criminal Law Bulletin* 389, at p. 402.

[14] R. Matthews, 'New Light on Problems', *The Times*, 13 July 1989.

[15] Counterfeit Access Device and Computer Fraud and Abuse Act, 1984, codified at 18 USC ss. 1029–30. For the definition see s. 1030(e)(1), and see J. B. Tompkins and L. A. Mar, 'The 1984 Federal Computer Crime Statute: A Partial Answer to a Pervasive Problem' (1985) 6 *Computer and Law Journal* 459.

includes any data storage facility or communications facility directly related to or operating in conjunction with such device, but such term does not include an automated typewriter or typesetter, a portable hand held calculator, or other similar device.

The issue of defining 'computer' has plagued the consideration of computer crime legislation since the early days in the United States and still gives rise to prolonged discussion in American legal journals.[16] In Britain and some other jurisdictions the approach has been not to define these terms for criminal law purposes at all. The relevant provisions in the Police and Criminal Evidence Act 1984 and the Criminal Justice Act 1988, dealing with computer-generated evidence, leave 'computer' undefined,[17] as does the Copyright, Designs and Patents Act 1988. Law Commission proposals on computer misuse in this country have favoured the same approach,[18] with the result that the term has been left undefined in the Computer Misuse Act 1990. That is also the line taken in this book.

While a definition of 'computer' will not be attempted, a brief description of the main features of computer operation is given here,[19] since familiarity with a number of technical computing terms is essential in understanding the material in later chapters of this book. A computer is a device for storing and processing 'data', a term which can be taken to include information of any kind. It is helpfully regarded as having a series of component parts, or 'stages'. The first stage of the computer is the 'input' device, which translates data into signals which the computer understands. Several different techniques are used, including computer keyboard, optical scanners, card readers, and magnetic tape units. A computer program, known as 'system software', or the 'operating system', acts as an interpreter between the input device and 'central processing unit' (CPU) of the computer, since the computer language employed on the machine, such as BASIC or COBOL, has to be translated into mathematical 'machine code' before the computer can process the instructions. This software acts, in effect, as the computer's housekeeper, and it is etched on a silicon or gallium semi-conductor ROM (Read Only Memory) 'chip' which is built into the CPU and which co-ordinates the working together of the various parts of the computer and 'peripherals', such as a printer or computerized cash-till, and controls the main disk drive. The

---

[16] See, for example, R. K. Kutz, 'Computer Crime in Virginia' (1986) 27 *William and Mary Law Review*, 783, at pp. 791–800.

[17] Though it is possible that the 1988 Act may have provided one unintentionally, incorporating by Schedule 2 the definition from the Civil Evidence Act 1968, s. 5; see D. J. Birch, 'Documentary Evidence' [1989] *Criminal Law Review* 15, at p. 30, and Chapter 6.

[18] Various definitions of 'computer' adopted or under consideration in other jurisdictions are listed in Law Commission (1988), pp. 126–8. The Commission concludes, however, that 'the word should be given its ordinary meaning' (para. 6.23). A fuller list is given in Tasmanian Law Reform Commission, Report No. 47, *Computer Misuse*, Tasmania: Government Printer, 1986, Appendix C.

[19] An excellent 'user-friendly' guide, to which the present author is greatly indebted is H. Cornwall, *Datatheft*, London: Heinemann, 1987.

chip dictates end results by regulating and redirecting electrical impulses which are passed through it. The second stage is programming, where the computer is given a set of logical instructions contained in a program or 'application software' for the performance of useful functions. The program completely controls the operation of the computer; the computer system can only use data and perform operations as directed by a program. Application software controls the tasks required, such as arithmetic calculations, word processing, stock control, or data management. These tasks take place within the third stage, which is the CPU hardware, the most prominent aspect of which is a screen or terminal, often a visual display unit (VDU). The machine follows instructions in the program, retrieves data from its 'memory', and performs functions such as altering or adding to or deleting this information as requested. Data 'files' contain the material upon which the applications programs work. The fourth stage is 'output', where data received from the CPU are translated into an intelligible form and displayed on the VDU or, if required, printed out. The final stage is 'data communication': telephone circuits used to transmit data back and forth between computers and remote terminals. The size and power of computers varies from the largest mainframe through the minicomputer to the microcomputer and the portable 'lap-top' computer. A large number of computer terminals may be connected to a central computer, and a network may be linked together through communication links within a building, or spread throughout the country or internationally. Many modern computer systems can therefore be 'accessed' from a remote location.

As we shall see, all of these various stages are susceptible to misuse and may be attacked or manipulated in various ways. In particular, data may be suppressed prior to entry into the computer, false data may be introduced, or the data may be altered, copied, removed, or destroyed subsequently, when held on file. Programs may be altered, copied, stolen, or erased. The CPU is vulnerable to damage, eavesdropping, and unauthorized access whether by someone such as an employee exceeding their normal authority to use the computer or by an outsider, by remote access. Chips may be copied. Computer output may be stolen, suppressed, or altered. Data communications may be penetrated, with secrecy or confidentiality infringed and data intercepted.

2. THE COMPUTER ENVIRONMENT

In understanding the phenomenon of computer misuse it is essential first to appreciate the extent to which computerization enters into so many different areas of life and forms a crucial aspect of business operation, both large and small, within the United Kingdom. Computers are now a central feature of the financial and insurance sectors, particularly in the stock markets, money markets, and electronic funds transfer, retail, and distribution markets, and the government sector, in defence, education, and health services. Domestic expenditure on hardware, software, and computer services accounts for an increasing proportion of total outlay in both the public and private sectors, representing about 3 per cent of total domestic expenditure in most European countries.[20] In Britain, the value of government computer assets exceeds £5 billion and government expenditure on computer systems exceeds £1 billion each year.[21] The number of computer systems installed in the United Kingdom is growing at a rate of about 25 per cent every year and is forecast to continue at the same rate.[22] Nearly one quarter of the gross national product is dependent upon the financial and insurance sectors, which in turn is dependant on computers. The extent to which the financial services sector has become reliant upon new technology is illustrated in the City since 'Big Bang', when the International Stock Exchange introduced its on-line computer system in October 1986, as a result of which the physical trading floor is a thing of the past. As the Audit Commission notes,[23] however, the commitment to new technology is such that when the computers fail through mechanical breakdown or power failure, there seems to be no possibility of the market being reconvened on the floor of the Stock Exchange. If the computers fail, the City shuts down. At the time of the stock market 'crash' of October 1987 some commentators expressed the view that the problems were caused or exacerbated by computer-assisted trading. The author of a comprehensive study of the stock market crash rejects the idea that computers caused the problem,[24] but concedes that reliance upon them could well have increased volatility in a falling market. Further computerization of the Stock Exchange, provided for in section 207 of the Companies Act 1989, will remove the need for physical evidence of transactions and stock ownership.

The professions now exhibit a similar degree of reliance upon computers to their colleagues in industry. Many solicitors' offices now have integrated computer systems, disruption of which would bring the practice to a standstill. One practitioner[25] explains how her firm utilizes computers through the practice to manage files on clients, precedents, legal research, document creation, and the allocation of the time of individual lawyers to particular tasks. Most accountancy firms require computing facilities to conduct audits. Many other groups, such as doctors, dentists, and estate agents, rely upon

[20] Organization for Economic Co-operation and Development (OECD), *Internationalisation of Software and Computer Services*, Paris: OECD, 1989.

[21] Public Accounts Committee, 25th Report, *Computer Security in Government Departments*, HC 291, London: HMSO, 1988, p. v.

[22] 1985 Report of the Quantum Science Corporation, cited in S. L. Everson, *Computer Crime*, London: ELS Services, 1987, p. 2.

[23] Audit Commission (1987), p. 5.

[24] J. Essinger, *Computers in Financial Trading*, London: Elsevier Advanced Technology Publications, 1988.

[25] D. C. Loeschmann, 'Computers and the Management of a Law Practice' (1987) 3 *Yearbook of Law, Computers and Technology* 68.

floppy disks for their records. It is important to understand how this reliance
has come about.

The earliest computers, designed just after World War II, were operated by
thermionic valves. They were very bulky and slow in operation. One famous
computer put into operation in 1946 in North America, known as ENIAC,
was described as being nearly 1,000 times faster in operation than any
predecessor, but suffered the disadvantages of weighing thirty tons, using
more than 18,000 vacuum tubes, requiring extensive air conditioning, and
occupying 1,500 square feet of floor space. Faults in early computers were
manifest. In the 1950s experts, including the first president of IBM, Thomas J.
Watson, Sr., forecast confidently that there would be no need for more than 'a
dozen or so' such computers operating throughout the world, and into the
1960s and 1970s computers were perceived generally as specialized instruments with very limited usefulness, primarily to improve upon manual
record-keeping functions. The replacement of valve systems by semi-conductor technology and the growth of micro-electronics have, of course,
transformed all that. A microprocessor would now carry all the power of one
of the early computers in a single silicon chip. Over only a very few years
computers have become much smaller, more efficient, more reliable, and less
expensive. The rapidity and irreversibility of the changes has been startling,
generating what has often been referred to as the Information Revolution and
the arrival of Bell's 'post-industrial society'.[26] In the words of one commentator,[27]

The information society . . . is a society where the economy reflects growth according
to technological advances. Just as machines are the tools of the industrial economy,
computing and telecommunications technologies are the tools of a new 'information'
economy. Industries directly specializing in information, including the production of
information technologies and services, constitute the primary sector of this economy.
The revitalization of traditional agrarian, extractive, manufacturing, transportation
and service industries through information technologies is a secondary sector. Another
component of the secondary sector is the use of information technologies to increase
productivity of services in the public area—education, health care and government . . .

According to a recent review of the importance of information technology to
the techniques of modern management in Britain, 'today IT is the very stuff
of management and tomorrow there may be little else that needs to be
managed'.[28] There is now an expectation that any business, large or small,
will make use of new technology to a substantial extent. Similar developments
have occurred outside the business world, where many non-profit-making

[26] D. Bell, *The Coming of Post-Industrial Society*, New York: Basic Books, 1976.
[27] F. Williams, 'The Information Society as a Subject of Study' in F. Williams (ed.), *Measuring
the Information Society*, Beverly Hills: Sage Publications, 1988, 13, at p. 15.
[28] Price Waterhouse, *Information Technology Review 1988/89*, London: Price Waterhouse
Publications, 1989.

organizations have also turned to information technology to modernize their work arrangements.

An important part of the shift seems to be that while computers were first installed into businesses and other organizations to carry out specific functions, such as order processing, payroll, or accounts, once this degree of computerization is achieved other managerial opportunities present themselves. The shift is from having computers installed in the workplace to having computers fully integrated into organizations in what are referred to as 'management information systems'. By combining together the computerized data obtained it is possible for management to gain an overview of company operations that would have been impossible to achieve by manual methods. As Cornwall[29] says:

Marry together the data from a warehouse inventory/stock control system with information from salesmen's orders and you can determine, among other things: what is selling where, what seasonal and regional sales patterns exist, how far the inventory needs to anticipate consumer demand, how late the purchase of raw materials and the commitment to manufacture can be timed and still please the consumer, how to manage the organization's working capital more effectively, and so on. The marginal cost of most of these extra items of information, once the basic systems have been installed, is often remarkably low. And once a company has come to rely for its decision-making on the availability of these answers, the word 'installation' is no longer adequate: the computers have become 'integrated' into the very fabric of the organization's existence.

Management information systems are set to expand into computer networks extending beyond the individual organization. The information contained within the computer then becomes crucial, and is as much an asset as the company's buildings. The more successful the computer system is, the greater the reliance upon it and the greater the potential losses if the system 'crashes'. Experience shows that it is very easy to underestimate the extent to which an organization becomes dependent upon the information contained in the computer. If the system fails, this can result in a complete closing down of operations. If the information is corrupted then, in the absence of comprehensive back-up arrangements, management will lose its ability to make proper decisions. If the information finds its way into the hands of a rival, then the company will lose its competitive edge. If the information can be altered so as to mislead and if the information is in the form of money, such as authorizations for payment or electronic funds transfer, then the opportunities for the operation of a company-crippling fraud are obvious.

Funds are transferred electronically within the international banking community through a computer network called SWIFT, first introduced in 1978. A new version of SWIFT is to be introduced in 1990, based on a more modern networking system adopting a transaction-processing approach, intended to increase the flexibility and message-handling capacity of the present system.

[29] Cornwall (1987), p. 8.

In the United States the four major electronic funds transfer networks carry the equivalent of the entire federal budget every two to three hours. Transactions worth $250 billion pass in and out of the City of London every day by electronic means. Automation of the banking industry at first mainly concerned internal operations, such as the development of electronic clearing houses, known by acronyms such as CHIPS, operational in New York since 1980, and CHAPS, in London. Latterly, though, customers have been offered a range of facilities utilizing modern banking technology. The 'cashless society' has been much talked about and although for the vast majority of small transactions cash will probably always offer outweighing advantages, for larger transactions the ubiquitous plastic card, and the 'application of electronic techniques to all parts of banking'[30] is clearly the way of the future, involving electronic links and interfaces between cash dispensers, automated teller machines (ATMs), point of sale systems, and home banking. Some home banking schemes are already operational, allowing customers to transfer money, ask for a statement, or pay bills using a screen linked to the Prestel network, or by telephone using a voice recognition system. The concept of a nation-wide system of Electronic Funds Transfer at Point of Sale (EFTPOS) has been developing over the last ten years and though still generally confined to trial operations in specific retail sectors, will surely soon become more generally available. The general manager of EFTPOS UK, the main organization involved, which is owned by thirteen banks and building societies, has confirmed the policy of a gradual build-up of terminals and transaction volume over the next few years. In September 1989 the largest scheme so far came into operation, involving terminals capable of handling any plastic card offered by customers in the outlets of 500 retailers in Edinburgh, Leeds, and Southampton.

The opportunities for the largest losses lie in the rapid growth of network and communication facilities between computers, particularly in banking and electronic funds transfer. During 1984 one of the major British banks lost £6 million when an employee, a data processor, diverted the first ten EFT payments of the day to his account in Switzerland.[31] In September 1987 two defendants of British nationality were given prison sentences of three years and eighteen months in the United States after admitting a conspiracy to defraud Prudential-Bache Securities of New York of £5.15 million by initiating the unauthorized transfer of eighteen Eurobonds through the Morgan Guaranty Trust's Euroclear account in London.[32] The crime was uncovered when a supervisor noticed that the wrong reference numbers for the transfers

---

[30] OECD, *Banking and Electronic Fund Transfers*, Paris: OECD, 1983, p. 30. This report provides an excellent overview, now together with OECD, *Electronic Funds Transfer: Plastic Cards and the Consumer*, Paris: OECD, 1989.

[31] S. Saxby, 'EFT Fraud Report' (1986–7) 3 *Computer Law and Security Report*, 2. See further J. Gait, 'Security of Electronic Fund Transfer Systems' (1981) 32 *Journal of Systems Management*, 6.

[32] Reported in *The Times*, 15 Sept. 1987.

had been keyed in. In England in 1988 a junior employee of the National Westminster Bank was caught using the bank's computers to transfer just under £1 million into a friend's bank account. Other examples are detailed in later chapters.

Computer security consultants emphasize that without careful security planning, back-up arrangements which will permit rapid reconstitution of data, and adequate computer insurance, few firms will survive a collapse of their computer networks. Whilst any immediate loss may prove substantial, experience shows that it will often be much less than the longer-term cost of reconstituting lost or damaged data and of restoring public and employee confidence. A complete collapse of a computer network, a 'computer disaster', which may be the product of computer misuse or other event, such as fire or flood, can be survived only by those firms having comprehensive disaster recovery plans. According to the security consultants, fewer than 20 per cent of firms are so equipped to survive a computer disaster. The sums involved can be massive. A breakdown of the computer system at the Bank of New York in 1985, which lasted 24 hours, for instance, resulted in no receipts being taken but $30 billion being paid out, a sum which had to be found subsequently by means of an emergency loan from the Federal Reserve. It was reported in the press in October 1989 that a British bank had lost £2 billion, more than the bank's annual profits, in 30 minutes after a software design flaw in the computing system resulted in the erroneous transfer of that sum into the accounts of various companies in Britain and overseas.

Reliance upon computers generates risks other than financial ones. Faults in computer systems or accidental misuse by operators have already created many situations of real physical danger. Where the computers affected regulate hospitals, air traffic control, or defence systems, for instance, the scale of such risks can be enormous. In a well-known incident which occurred in November 1979, a technician at the North American Air Defence command centre at Cheyenne Mountain, Colorado (NORAD), accidentally fed a test tape which simulated a Soviet missile attack into the central computer. In the six minutes which it took to detect and trace the error, strategic aircraft carrying nuclear weapons had been put on alert and ten tactical aircraft were airborne. In another incident, this time in 1980, a faulty microchip gave signals which implied that two submarine-launched nuclear missiles were approaching the United States, heralding a full-scale nuclear attack. Again the error was detected in minutes, but it took several days before the faulty component was identified. There are fears that equivalent Soviet computer equipment may be prone to more frequent errors, and Mr Gorbachev has publicly admitted his concern about the safety of the Soviet system. Numerous other incidents have been reported. The Los Angeles air traffic control computer apparently failed on numerous occasions in a single day in 1989. A defective printed circuit logic card in the auto-pilot software on British Airways jumbo jets, which malfunctioned on six separate occasions, cutting power to the aircraft throttle on all engines when near the top of its climb and approaching cruise altitude, was being investigated by the Civil Aviation Authority in April 1990. In 1988 it was reported that British government scientists are convinced that a serious accident caused by faulty microchips is 'inevitable' within the next few years. The prediction is based on research into the extent of design and production faults in microchips for military use, carried out by the Royal Signals and Radar Establishment at the Ministry of Defence. A design error in a microchip might only take effect in a combination of very particular circumstances, perhaps years after the chip is put on the market. According to Dr John Cullyer of RSRE, 'some time between 1991 and 1992 computers will start to kill human beings in a way that will be noticed by others'.[33] Standard methods of increasing safety are to install duplicate systems, either of which is capable of taking over if something goes wrong, and ordering software and computer chips from different manufacturers, in case one batch has a design flaw. Computer scientists are responding to the threat by developing microprocessors such as the 'Viper' chip, now in commercial production, which are capable of being proved mathematically to be free of design faults. During 1989, various groups including British Computer Society and the Institute of Electrical Engineers have asked the government to set up a special group to monitor those computer systems which threaten life if they go wrong. The Society has drawn attention to the critical role played by computers in various fields including water-treatment plants, the chemical industry, medical electronics, and motor-car manufacture as well as the nuclear industry and aviation. It emphasizes the importance of monitoring to ensure that safety is not compromised in order to save money. These groups have also argued that staff who use computers in areas that are of critical importance to safety or to business should hold specialized professional qualifications.[34]

Parallel to this vastly increased and now crucial reliance upon computers has been the 'democratization' of computer use within companies, whereby computing has gradually become removed from the Electronic Data Processing Department and has become, to a significant extent, the property of everyone within the organization. There has been a move away from large mainframe installations to widespread computing using minicomputers linked to intelligent terminals. In banking, for instance, in the 1960s the costs of installing computers meant that facilities were centralized, using mainframe computers, with each clearing bank setting up one or two such centres. The advance of technology over the last fifteen years, however, has resulted in at least a tenfold increase in computing power for the same cost outlay. Because of the greatly increased levels of computing and storage powers of microcomputers, in the future the banking system will continue the move away from centralization towards terminals at the branch counter and automated

[33] Quoted in *The Times*, 29 Jan. 1988.
[34] Institute of Electrical Engineers, *Software in Safety-Critical Systems*, London: IEE, 1989.

teller machines at more remote locations. Increasing computer literacy and user-friendly software has meant the arrival of 'end-user' or 'desk-top' computing.

The opportunities for computer misuse have thus ceased to be within the domain solely of computer operators and programmers. A central mainframe is a potentially vulnerable target for damage and immobilization through industrial action as well as through fraud. Any damaging event, especially when perpetrated by someone knowledgeable in computing, is likely to cause very substantial loss to the organization. In one sense, then, dispersal of computer facilities reduces the likely extent of losses caused by misuse. On the other hand it multiplies the points at which the system may be attacked. Whilst central control of computing facilities may create resentments elsewhere in the workforce at the emergence of a new centre of corporate power, dispersal increases the potential number of fraudsters within an organization, and increases the number of places at which the organization may be vulnerable to attack.

At the same time it seems that some senior management has failed to keep pace with events and has remained largely ignorant of computer development. The general tendency has been for computer staff to be isolated within the company. In a study[35] at the end of 1985 the management consultants Kepner Regoe Inc. asked the chief executive officers of the Fortune 500 companies about their attitudes towards computers. Fifty-two per cent said that they never used computers. Only 27 per cent of chief executives had a computer terminal in their offices. In a comparable survey[36] conducted in Britain in April 1987, a survey for the Institute of Directors by the software company Lotus Developments UK found that 50 per cent of directors believed that working a keyboard was 'beneath them' and that only 3 per cent of the companies surveyed had computer experts involved at board level. A later survey in 1989 by the PA Consulting Group found that fewer than half the companies surveyed had any formal plan for career development of their computer staff. One implication of this was that data-processing professionals did not feel confident in approaching senior management to discuss matters relating to technology within the company. As we shall see later, this may engender feelings of resentment among the staff, providing a breeding ground for fraud or sabotage. Another aspect of the problem is pressure within an organization to compete in the race to keep up with new developments in technology. The Audit Commission has warned that 'security blindness' is 'an unfortunate characteristic of many who lose no time in installing technology but are less committed to protecting the system from misuse'.[37] The lack of a comprehensive plan of computer security often means that statistically unlikely risks are guarded against but some more obvious loopholes in security are overlooked. In 1989 a MORI poll asked 500 senior managers about their views on information technology. Whilst almost all stressed the

---

[35] Cited by Cornwall (1987), p. 40.
[36] Reported in *The Times*, 24 Apr. 1987.   [37] Audit Commission (1987), p. 1.

importance of information technology to them, they were equally divided on the question of whether they were satisfied with their current arrangements for computer system security and data protection.

A British Institute of Management Survey in 1988 found that few organizations plan or manage rigorously their information technology training and education activities, leading to 'a failure to harness and exploit the investment in information technology'.[38] Yet the costs of competing in the technology race are high. In a review by Price Waterhouse, it was estimated that every United Kingdom company with a computer department employing five or more staff will have invested an average of £1.4 million in information technology during 1988 alone, an increase of 11 per cent over the previous year.[39] The larger solicitors' firms, especially those in London, started investing enthusiastically in computers in the mid-1970s, and it is estimated that around 30 per cent of law practices in the UK are now heavily computerized, but many of these systems have been bought piecemeal. The rapid obsolescence of computer systems and the search for integration of systems means that firms may be faced with complete renewal of an office system, which can cost in the order of £2 million. Cornwall summarizes the current situation as follows:[40]

The benefits of democratic information availability have been accompanied by corporate warfare for control over computer and systems resources, as departments old and new have fought to show that they alone have proved their right to be in command. Standing above them, but not really in control, are top management who, through a combination of fundamental computer illiteracy and a lack of awareness of the profound changes that the last ten years have brought about, seem unprepared for the vulnerabilities that their businesses face.

Outside the business environment, the computer revolution has meant new, faster, and better services for everyone. Computers automatically check out goods in the shops, maintain up-to-the-minute balances in bank accounts, transfer funds, and pay bills even when the bank is closed. There is increasing computer-literacy in the general population, particularly amongst young people, who seem to be more positive in their attitudes towards science and technology generally. The 'need to produce a computer-literate younger generation' is seen by some educationalists as being perhaps the greatest current educational challenge.[41] American figures[42] show that by 1985 the percentage of schools in the United States which used computers in the classroom had risen to 92 per cent, the number of computer science degree courses available had increased tenfold over ten years, and the percentage of

[38] British Institute of Management, *Managers and IT Competence*, London: BIM, 1988.
[39] Price Waterhouse (1989).
[40] Cornwall (1987), p. 40.
[41] Cited in N. Estes and V. Williams, 'Computers in Texas Schools' in F. Williams, 243 (1988), at p. 245.
[42] J. J. BloomBecker (ed.), *Computer Crime, Computer Security, Computer Ethics*, Statistical Report of the National Centre for Computer Crime Data, Los Angeles. NCCCD, 1986.

people who had regular access to computers and those who were in computer-related employment, whether in equipment, services, or programming, had also shown steady increases during the 1980s. In a MORI poll[43] conducted in Britain in 1989, it was found that pupils' use of computers in primary schools had risen from 12 per cent to more than 75 per cent from 1982 to 1989, and in secondary schools from 50 per cent to almost 90 per cent over the same period. One in five people in Britain now use a word processor or computer at work.

The majority of American homes which have televisions also have computers. Time now spent at the computer was formerly spent on leisure pursuits, most significantly watching television. One research project found an 80 per cent reduction in television viewing amongst home computer users. On the other hand, a recent study by the United States Census Bureau,[44] based on 1984 figures, indicates that 47 per cent of people aged eighteen and over who have computers at home never use them. Of the remainder, most use them primarily for playing computer games. Yet even the infrequent users, when asked, say that they intend to update the machine they have and buy a new one, because 'they are afraid of being left behind in a computerized world'.[45] The most up-to-date government figures in Britain show[46] that from 1984 to 1986 the percentage of homes here which had a computer had risen from 9 per cent, the year when the statistic first appeared, to 17 per cent, though the higher socio-economic groups were much more likely to have one. In fact there is now more recent evidence of a tailing off in the United Kingdom home computer market, with the MORI poll indicating a contraction in the home ownership of computers to 13 per cent by 1989, together with a narrowing of the gap between the number of middle-class and working-class people who had a computer at home. The same poll found that the 'fad for computer games' has tailed off, and that computers at home are being used more for word processing and financial spreadsheets.

Different aspects of the public attitude to computers and information technology is pointed up by surveys in the United States and Canada during the past decade which have shown that an increasing percentage of respondents think that computers represent a real threat to privacy, and although much of modern life has benefited from computers, people often react negatively to what is perceived as the impersonality and dehumanization of the technology. In a poll taken in Texas[47] in 1986, for instance, where at

[43] Reported in The Times, 29 Nov. 1989.

[44] United States Department of Commerce, Bureau of the Census, Computer Use in the United States, Washington, DC: Federal Government Publication, 1988.

[45] K. Christensen, 'Home PC: People Don't Need it, But they Fear Life Without it', Wall Street Journal, 13 Aug. 1985, cited in D. Hayes, Behind the Silicon Curtain, London: Free Association Books, 1989, p. 183.

[46] Central Statistical Office, Social Trends, vol. 19, London: HMSO, 1989, based on 1986 figures.

[47] J. Dyer, F. Williams, and D. Haynes, 'Gauging Public Attitudes Towards Science and Technology' in F. Williams (1988), p. 191.

that time one in five households had a computer and one in three members of the workforce used a computer in the course of their employment, three-quarters of those responding said that in their view computers had benefited society, while one quarter disagreed or strongly disagreed with that assessment. Forty-four per cent of respondents felt that modern technology was accompanied by 'greater risks for society that are difficult to overcome', including increased unemployment perceived as being a likely outcome of the changes. In a recent poll conducted on behalf of the OECD, respondents from several countries including the United Kingdom were unenthusiastic about further information technology developments in the banking field, expressing themselves relatively well satisfied with existing services.[48] Fifty per cent of people questioned, for example, preferred to deal with human tellers at the bank, rather than machines. Scepticism about the 'cashless society' is confirmed by a 1989 survey conducted on behalf of the Abbey National Building Society, which found that the majority of the sample of 2,000 people still chose to pay for food, clothes, shoes, petrol, and regular household bills with cash. Half still paid for their holidays in cash. The second preferred method of payment is cheque, whilst credit cards account for only 4 per cent of such transactions. Not surprisingly, those people least impressed by technological development came from those age groups and socio-economic groups who perceive themselves as least likely to be able to use it to their own advantage. The 1989 Report of the Data Protection Registrar,[49] which updates research carried out over the last few years, shows that British people are becoming increasingly concerned about the threat to privacy posed by computers. The percentage of the sample expressing concern about the way in which personal data about them is kept and used had increased from 62 per cent to 74 per cent. 'Keeping personal information or details private' is the aspect of privacy causing the most concern, and many also express worry about 'organizations building up files about me'. The 1989 MORI poll found that 25 per cent of those asked were suspicious of information technology, a significant increase over earlier figures, and more than one third of parents said that they felt 'left behind' by their children's familiarity with computers.

Whilst computers and those skilled in their operation are still held in awe or regarded with suspicion by many older people, most younger people have sufficient familiarity with what computers can do, and a degree of knowledge about computers, so that they regard the computer at least as a compliant games-playing machine, and in many cases as a helpful educational and career tool, rather than as a frightening spectre. But, for some, computer systems are still shrouded in a mystique and an impersonality that enhances

---

[48] OECD (1989).

[49] Data Protection Registrar, *Fifth Annual Report*, London: HMSO, 1989. See also the evidence collected by R. Wacks, *Personal Information, Privacy and the Law*, Oxford: Clarendon Press, 1988, ch. 4.

the intimidating effect of the technology. As Tapper says:[50] '. . . in the abstract [computers] seem to inspire in otherwise rational human beings feelings of such distrust, suspicion and awe as to subvert all sensible judgment'. Parker[51] goes so far as to devise a separate category of computer misuse for cases where the fraudster relies upon people's susceptibility to the mystique of computers to perpetrate the misuse. Here the computer is neither the tool nor the object of the crime, but is used 'symbolically'. Lawyers, government agencies, and other officials are perceived as using 'mounds of computer-generated data' to confound their audiences, and criminals can create a realistic-looking front to a fraud by churning out large quantities of computer print-outs. Parker cites as an example a rather trivial fraud involving a dating service which advertised itself as 'computerized', but which had no computer, and did its matching manually, using untrained clerical personnel. More generally, the fear of new technology undoubtedly runs very deep. There has always been, as Tapper puts it, 'a distrust, suspicion and awe' underlying attitudes to computer development; a sense that such changes are bound to occur at the expense of the individual; that the citizen will become subservient to the system, which is seen as an increasingly computer- and corporate-dominated society. In ideas perhaps best expressed by Marcuse,[52] the fear is that individuals' rights and liberties will be sacrificed at the altar of technological advancement. Weeramantry[53] is one lawyer who gives voice to these concerns and he claims that the law has been left well behind scientific development. He urges the law to awake from its 'slumber' and adapt itself quickly, to protect citizens from the worst excesses consequent upon these changes.

At the other end of the attitude scale, some people become so fascinated with information technology that they 'turn their talents for programming and engineering into a permanent love affair with the computer'.[54] A book[55] published in 1989 investigates 'computer tendency syndrome' and various suggestions that some people's obsessive use of computers harms their social and personal development and their mental health. The author, Shotton, found that a group of self-confessed 'computer addicts' was composed of people from well-educated backgrounds who had always had an enthusiasm for science and technology. Compared to a group of people who used computers but were not 'addicted' and a group who had never owned a computer, they tended to be shy and less able to form satisfactory human

---

[50] C. Tapper, 'Computer Crime: Scotch Mist?' [1987] *Criminal Law Review* 4, at p. 4.

[51] D. B. Parker, *Crime by Computer*, New York: Scribner, 1976, p. 21, citing *US* v *Curtis* 537 F 2d 1091 (10th Cir 1976).

[52] H. Marcuse, *One-Dimensional Man*, Boston: Beacon Press, 1964.

[53] C. G. Weeramantry, *The Slumbering Sentinels*, Middlesex: Penguin Books, 1983.

[54] J. D. Bolter, 'The Computer in a Finite World' (1985) 6 *Computer and Law Journal* 349, at p. 355.

[55] M. Shotton, *Computer Addiction? A Study of Computer Dependency*, London: Taylor & Francis, 1989.

relationships. They derived much of their self-esteem and confidence from their ability with computers. The author suggests that computer-dependent people tend to have had an upbringing which leads them to be 'object-centred' rather than 'people-centred'. She concludes, however, that far from harming addicts, in the main computers provide people of this type with an important outlet for their intelligence, curiosity, and originality, as well as improving their employment prospects.

Then there are the 'hackers'. The origin of the word is obscure, and the term has been used to mean rather different things.[56] Its first regular modern usage in the computer context was to mean a person who is an expert and enthusiastic programmer, who enjoys learning the details of computer systems and how to stretch their capabilities. By about 1981 or 1982, at the time of the great expansion in the personal computer market, media attention to the activities of those who accessed major computer systems through the communications networks, often using relatively simple and inexpensive computer equipment at home, altered the meaning of the term to one who is an inquisitive or perhaps malicious meddler, who tries to discover information about computers by gaining unauthorized access to them, and exchanging intelligence with other like-minded people. Commonly, and confusingly, the term is now also used to embrace fraudsters and spies who use their computer knowledge to enrich themselves. A considerable folklore has grown up around the 'hackers'. In 1976 Weizenbaum, a professor of computing at the Massachusetts Institute of Technology, drew attention to:[57]

... 'a mental disorder that, while actually very old, appears to have been transformed by the computer into a new genus: the compulsion to program'. He cited the programmers in the computer centres of which he had personal knowledge, remarking on 'bright young men of dishevelled appearance, often with sunken glowing eyes'. Working at a keyboard their attention is 'a riveted as a gambler's on the rolling dice', as they pore over printouts 'like possessed students of a cabalistic text'. These people, seemingly indifferent to personal appearance and normal preoccupation, 'exist . . . only through and for the computer'. They are, suggests Weizenbaum, 'computer bums, compulsive programmers . . . an international phenomenon'.

Numerous such accounts refer to the hacker's obsession with computers, likening it to an addiction, which induces the hacker to see every computer system as a challenge to be 'tested' or 'cracked'.

Public attitudes towards the misuse of computers seem to be varied and

---

[56] J. J. BloomBecker, 'Computer Crime Update: The View as we Exit 1984' (1985) 7 *Western New England Law Review* 627, offering at p. 629 the following alternative definitions: (1) A person who enjoys learning the details of computer systems and how to stretch their capabilities; (2) one who programs enthusiastically; (3) a person capable of appreciating 'hack' value; (4) a person good at programming quickly; (5) an expert on a particular program; (6) an expert of any kind; and (7) a malicious or inquisitive meddler who tries to discover information by poking around. See also Hayes (1989), p. 186.

[57] Cited in R. Doswell and G. L. Simons, *Fraud and Abuse of IT Systems*, Manchester: National Computing Centre Publications, 1986, p. 48.

complex. Some people exhibit a degree of amused tolerance towards it, which may well be an extension of the computer games-playing ethos. Some also express a degree of admiration for those perceived to be skilled enough to be able to manipulate computers to their own financial advantage. An image is presented, through popular films like *War Games*, television series, and novels, of the commission of fraud and other computer manipulation involving huge financial gain and minimal chance of detection, committed remotely by the highly intelligent manipulation of computers by romanticized heroes. As BloomBecker says:[58]

War Games took the NORAD malfunction, added teenage sex and heroism, threw in the 'everynerd'[59] element of personal computing, the far-out possibility of artificial computer intelligence deciding whether a nation goes to war, and the spice of 'hacking' . . . A spate of new shows asked: *War Games*—Could It Really Happen?

Other plots have included the United States selling a computer to the Soviet Union which contains a device within it so strong as to infect and corrupt data held on all computers within the Kremlin, and the hacking into national defence computers bringing about superpower nuclear confrontation. A whole area of science fiction writing has developed:[60]

Movies, videos and television programmes depict computer savants wielding exotic tools, committing or solving 'computer crimes'. Science fiction and suspense novels borrow props, idioms and plots from the electronics industry workplace. In adventure comics and cartoons, the appeal of the computer-aided hero rivals that of the wide-arm cowboy in the pulp genres of a century ago. The hacker, like the cowboy, is a lonely male drifter who stalks an expansive frontier.

These fictional escapades are committed remotely, often without violence, against unsympathetically portrayed government or corporate victims. An important element here is that computers give an impersonal 'clean quality' to crime,[61] which makes tolerance or even admiration for it more likely. Levi suggests that the computer now occupies a 'folk devil' role in crime and that 'this makes computer fraud into a kind of Chaplinesque morality play in which the little man humiliates and triumphs over those in authority'.[62] The very great skill which is demonstrated in some forms of computer misuse, and the barely concealed public admiration which surrounds it, is surely a phenomenon which deserves closer attention from criminologists. Most crime, however cleverly committed, would still attract condemnation, and it is difficult to think of other forms of deviance which are viewed in quite the same way as computer misuse. One example, perhaps, is fine art fraud, where disapproval may, for some, be outweighed by admiration for the skill and

[58] BloomBecker (1985), p. 630.
[59] A 'nerd' is 'an adolescent technical genius', according to Hayes, p. 186.
[60] Ibid., p. 91.
[61] M. Volgyes, 'The Investigation, Prosecution and Prevention of Computer Crime: A State-of-the-Art Review' (1980) 2 *Computer and Law Journal* 385, at p. 393.
[62] M. Levi, *Regulating Fraud*, London: Tavistock, 1987, p. 37.

audacity of the artist, as in the famous forgeries by Tom Keating of Samuel Palmer and Constable paintings, which came to light in 1976.

The impersonality of the computer tends to incite efforts to retaliate against it. Because of the hacker's abilities to subvert the computer, the symbol of power, authority, and technology, there has been much glamourizing of his activities:[63] 'The hacker's popularity stems from the credible belief that he is at the centre of a force that is clearly shaping the future . . . The hacker is at once an exciting and an ambiguous figure.' One of the best known of all the various hacking incidents which have come to light involved the Milwaukee 414 gang, a group of young computer hobbyists in the United States who admitted gaining remote unauthorized access to computer files at the Los Alamos National Research Center, a bank, a cement company, and a hospital. The trial was a great media event. One of the defendants appeared on chat shows and was featured on the cover of *Newsweek*. Twenty television cameras filmed the proceedings, and columnists condemned and applauded the gang's activities in about equal proportion.[64] In a more modest way, perhaps, the leading hacking case to be prosecuted in the United Kingdom has brought great publicity, not all of it adverse, to the defendants Gold and Schifreen.[65]

The press often has a field-day with 'computer crime'. Exaggeration and contradiction is common and Bequai[66] claims that 'to the news media and avid computer fans the hacker is a modern-day joy-rider, roaming the electronic highways'. Researchers have noted that crime tends to be reported in the press to a far greater extent when it is perceived as serious, unusual, and dramatic.[67] As well as being highly selective in the crime news which is reported, journalists tend to filter the facts through certain stereotypes in creating the story they write. An event is the more newsworthy if it can be described in personal terms, with 'human interest', and if well-known individuals are the perpetrators or the victims of crime. In general this means that white-collar crime is greatly under-reported in the press, because it lacks this necessary immediacy; the wrongdoing is less dramatic and less instant than, say, a crime of violence. Computer misuse, though, has the attributes to attract media attention. It also has the irresistible attractions of 'man against machine', sometimes very youthful defendants, and corporate victims being made to look foolish. The only element usually missing is that of the prominence of the perpetrator or victim, but in the Gold and Schifreen case even this was supplied by the fact that one of the electronic mailboxes accessed by the hackers belonged to the Duke of Edinburgh.

   [63] Hayes (1989), p. 92.
   [64] BloomBecker (1985), pp. 631–2.   [65] See Chapter 3.
   [66] A. Bequai, *Technocrimes*, Lexington, Mass.: D. C. Heath, 1987, p. 30.
   [67] See R. V. Ericson, P. M. Baranek and J. B. L. Chan, *Visualising Deviance*, Milton Keynes: Open University, 1987; H. J. Gans, *Deciding What's News*, New York: Pantheon Books, 1979, and essays in S. Cohen and J. Young (eds.), *The Manufacture of News*, London: Constable, 1981.

It is also well known that once attracted by an unusual or dramatic crime story, journalists will collect other examples, often generating a journalistic crime wave which may bear no relation to the true prevalence of that kind of incident.[68] Usually such a process follows a cyclical pattern, and once the new activity becomes familiar to journalists and to readers, they lose interest and it will no longer attract media attention. There does seem to have been some tailing off in media interest in incidents of computer fraud, perhaps because they seem to have become so commonplace.[69] In other areas of computer misuse, however, journalistic attention has been maintained by the appearance of regular new developments, in the form of stories about 'electronic eavesdropping' and, most recently, 'computer viruses', so that its newsworthiness has been retained to a large extent. Ambivalence towards, or outright glamourizing of, computer misuse in the media has led many more sombre commentators to agree with Parker that 'the harm of abusive acts has not been sufficiently perceived'[70] by the public, though Parker has stated recently that the extensive press coverage given to computer viruses means that computer misusers are now losing interest in viruses and turning their attention to new ideas. Mandell[71] asserts the power of the press, and claims that when the media portrays the computer fraudster 'as an eccentric genius engaged in a Robin Hood type operation, stealing from a large impersonal machine', this 'leads the public to ignore the high cost to society that such crimes exact'.

Yet attitudes to computer misuse, like public attitudes to white-collar crime generally, may well be far more complex than these last observations suggest. While it is true that computer technology has developed so rapidly in recent years that ethical attitudes to some forms of computer misuse have not caught up or have on occasions been suspended or ignored, most people are still perfectly capable of identifying dishonest conduct when perpetrated by way of a computer, even when this may on occasions be glamourized by the press. For instance, researchers in England conducting a survey of public attitudes to the seriousness of various crimes, found that those interviewed were consistently tough in their assessment of a case of computer fraud which netted £7,000, ranking it as being more serious than other examples put to them, including a case of domestic violence, a public house fight, and the setting of a dangerous booby-trap for a thief. The computer fraud was the only offence for which a majority of the sample surveyed recommended a custodial sentence.[72] Though there is little hard evidence of public attitudes

---

[68] Gans (1979), p. 170.

[69] So commonplace that a non-computer fraud becomes newsworthy: reported in the press in Oct. 1988 was an alleged trans-European share fraud, involving a total of $1 billion. Joint action by German, Swiss, and Spanish police forces resulted in the retrieval of 'several boxes of index cards'!

[70] D. B. Parker, *Fighting Computer Crime*, New York: Scribner, 1983, p. 23.

[71] Mandell (1984), p. 156.

[72] N. Walker and C. Marsh, 'Do Sentences Affect Public Disapproval?' (1984) 24 *British Journal of Criminology* 1.

towards computer misuse, it is often urged by reformers advocating tougher criminal laws in this area that there is a compelling need for the law to lead public opinion in recognizing the seriousness of computer misuse and that so far the public seems relatively unconcerned, or looks upon it with amused tolerance. The campaigning organization Federation Against Software Theft (FAST) has been especially prominent in raising public awareness of the implications of unauthorized copying of computer software,[73] and they certainly take the view that one effect of their publicity and law enforcement efforts has been to peg losses in the United Kingdom to a constant level since 1984 despite a growth in the turnover of the software industry in the United Kingdom of over 20 per cent each year since then. Levi[74] has analysed the studies of public attitudes towards fraud offences generally in some detail, and has found that public evaluations of seriousness depend primarily upon the perceived impact of the crime. In the United States, it seems that crimes committed by corporations are viewed more seriously than crimes committed against corporations, but that frauds by employees and by outsiders are regarded as more serious than some 'common' or 'street' crimes. Crucial is the amount of money involved. Wolfgang *et al.*[75] found that embezzlement of $1,000 by an employee was regarded as twice as bad as a burglary where the property loss amounted to $10. If, however, the sums involved were equal, the burglary was regarded as much more serious. Also important is the status of the offender. A fraud committed by a 'professional person', within management, was regarded as more serious than a fraud committed by an employee. British surveys produce comparable results.[76] Levi suggests that[77]

... these surveys reveal that the public is highly intolerant of commercial frauds of the kind examined ... One possible hypothesis to account for the high disapproval ratings for fraud is the psychological need for the public to adopt a 'just world' perspective where everyone gets rewarded according to their efforts. Deliberate fraud ... disrupts this sense of 'natural order' and therefore is a target for severe condemnation (tinged, at times, with envy and admiration).

This element of envy and admiration is certainly to be found in the public's attitude to computer misuse, and it may well be true that 'we are more

---

[73] Federation Against Software Theft (FAST), *Thou Shalt Not Cheat*, publicity material, London: FAST, 1986; FAST, 'Submission to the European Commission on the Software Piracy Implications of the E.C. Green Paper on Copyright' (1989) 5 *Computer Law and Practice* 94, at p. 95.

[74] Levi (1987), p. 60.

[75] M. Wolfgang, R. Figlio, P. Tracy and S. Singer, *The National Survey of Crime Severity* Washington, DC: Department of Justice, 1985; see also L. Schrager and J. Short, 'How Serious a Crime? Perceptions of Common and Organisational Crimes' in G. Geis and E. Stotland (eds.), *White Collar Crime: Theory and Research*, Beverly Hills: Sage Publications, 1980.

[76] R. Sparks, H. Genn, and D. Dodd, *Surveying Victims*, Chichester: John Wiley, 1977; M. Levi and S. Jones, 'Public and Police Perceptions of Crime Seriousness in England and Wales' (1985) 25 *British Journal of Criminology* 234; M. Levi, *The Incidence, Reporting and Prevention of Commercial Fraud*, Summary of Findings, Cardiff: Dept. of Social Administration, 1986.   [77] Levi (1987), pp. 61, 63.

tolerant of criminals who display panache',[78] but this is always provided that the respondents do not perceive themselves as likely to become the next victims. In a survey by the American Bar Association[79] of nearly 300 private organizations and public agencies, who probably did regard themselves as being at risk, respondents were given a list of other types of crime and were asked to indicate whether computer misuse was more or less 'important'. Respondents generally rated computer misuse as less important than most violent crimes, but perceived it to be equal to or more important than many other types of white-collar crime, such as antitrust violations, counterfeiting, consumer fraud, bank fraud, and insider trading. Computer misuse surveys in Britain indicate that business organizations take the matter very seriously, though most are primarily concerned about the possibility of fraud. Sixty per cent of the respondents to the Audit Commission[80] survey in 1987 said that they perceived fraud to be the greatest risk to them, though 38 per cent said that theft was the most important. Overall, however, hacking as such was not regarded as a very significant problem.

Once again, the ambiguity in these assessments of computer misuse emerges from a recent survey conducted by a computer magazine,[81] in which 25 per cent of the 540 computer professionals questioned, who all no doubt condemn computer misuse, admitted to having engaged in some form of computer hacking themselves. Eighty-seven per cent of those who made that admission claimed that they had never been discovered. Perhaps a distinction needs to be drawn between incidents like fraud, where condemnation of the activity is likely to be relatively unaffected by whether a computer is the instrument of fraud or not, and other more novel forms of misuse, such as hacking, unauthorized copying of computer materials, or the unauthorized use of an employer's computer, where ethical standards are unclear and may not yet have caught up with the technology or the full implications of the conduct. In a Canadian study[82] which is admittedly now over ten years old, the majority of a sample of senior computer science students could see nothing wrong in doing work for one employer or client using computer time supplied by another, and a substantial minority thought that it was acceptable to share with friends a password to a time-sharing system which had been accidentally discovered, to run personal programs after hours on an employer's computer, or to copy an employer's software and take it away when changing employment. These matters are, in any event, far from straightforward ethical problems. The extent to which hacking or computer

---

[78] Ibid., p. 74.
[79] American Bar Association, Task Force on Computer Crime, *Report on Computer Crime*, Washington, DC: Government Printer, 1984.
[80] Audit Commission (1987), p. 13.
[81] Survey conducted by *Computer Weekly*, reported in *The Times*, 7 Aug. 1989.
[82] 1978 study, carried out by Professor J. M. Carroll of the University of Western Ontario, cited in S. Schølberg, *Computers and Penal Legislation*, Norwegian Research Centre for Computers and Law, Oslo: Universitetsforlaget, 1983, p. 49.

'time theft' should arouse condemnation, or criminalization, is far from obvious. These issues are discussed further in subsequent chapters.

3. COMPUTER MISUSE AND WHITE-COLLAR CRIME

Most published discussions of computer misuse have made some reference to the existing body of research and writing on business crime or 'white-collar crime'. At first glance, there seems to be a substantial overlap between the two fields. If so, existing criminological research and analysis of white-collar crime should be useful in understanding the current topic. Writers on computer misuse seem, however, to be divided on its relevance, with some regarding computer crime simply as a subset of white-collar crime and others, such as Parker, stating that computer crime 'is as different from white-collar crime as white-collar crime is different from street crime'.[83] One important area of overlap is fraud. Levi[84] gives his book on regulating fraud, published in 1987, the subtitle 'white-collar crime and the criminal process', but deals with the body of learning on white-collar crime primarily in a short preface to the work, entitled 'The Academic Context of This Study'. On the other hand Comer,[85] in his book giving practical advice on counter-measures for dealing with corporate fraud, attempts to draw upon some insights emanating from white-collar crime research to underpin his recommendations for corporate defence against fraud committed by employees and outsiders. The contention in this book is that existing white-collar crime studies do contain helpful insights which assist in understanding some aspects of computer misuse. Other aspects of computer misuse, however, lie outside its scope. It must also be appreciated that research into white-collar crime is, in itself, controversial and subject to widely differing interpretations.

In his pioneering work on the subject in the 1940s, Sutherland[86] drew attention to what he termed 'white-collar crime' to expose the paucity of contemporary criminological explanation, which stressed the personality and background of offenders, and he showed that crime was also prevalent in the richer and more professional segments of society. He seems to have regarded these crimes as falling into two categories: those involving mis-representation of corporate assets and those involving the manipulation of power. From the beginning, however, the whole subject was diffuse, with Sutherland advancing numerous different definitions of white-collar crime, at times stressing the social status of white-collar offenders, sometimes the commission of crime within an occupational role, and sometimes crimes committed by individuals acting in organizational capacities. Later writers,

---

[83]   D. B. Parker, 'Computer-Related White-Collar Crime' in Geis and Stotland (1980), p. 200.
[84]   Levi (1987).   [85]   Comer (1985), ch. 2.
[86]   E. H. Sutherland, 'Is "White-Collar Crime" Crime?' (1945) 10 *American Sociological Review* 132; id., *White-Collar Crime*, New York: Holt, Rinehart & Winston, 1949.

such as Clinard and Quinney,[87] have distinguished two main types of white-collar crime: 'occupational crime', or crimes committed against business, and 'corporate crime', or crimes committed by business. Problems of definition have dogged the subject throughout, but the bulk of white-collar crime research has been focused on the commission of crime within an occupational role.

One of Sutherland's most important observations was to note that many white-collar offences are handled informally or administratively rather than through the courts, and that those who were prosecuted seemed to receive lenient sentences. He insisted that such crimes should be considered 'as cognate with other crime' but, ironically, his propagation of the term 'white-collar crime' lent support to the idea that white-collar criminality was something other than 'common' criminal activity. Sutherland included within the category of white-collar crime certain violations of administrative rules and breaches of the civil law. To those who protested that these were not crimes at all,[88] Sutherland replied that businessmen had the power and status to influence legislation and it was an example of their discriminatory treatment that such breaches were kept out of the criminal law. This has engendered a recurrent theme in writings on white-collar crime; whether criminologists should confine their attention to behaviour which is already legally stigmatized as criminal, or whether they should also consider other dubious commercial and corporate practices. The arbitrariness of too rigid adherence to legal categories is illustrated by the way these change over time, such as the fact that insider dealing is now a criminal offence carrying a maximum penalty of seven years' imprisonment in Britain,[89] yet prior to 1985 it was not a criminal offence at all. Hadden makes the point more generally:[90]

The boundaries between what is acceptable and unacceptable conduct in corporate and securities transactions are constantly changing. Practices which were commonly accepted in the latter part of the nineteenth century and the early years of the twentieth century are now regarded as unacceptable. Some but not all of these changes are reflected in extensions in the criminal law.

White-collar crime research has shown that there is little to mark the boundary between the acceptable and the unacceptable business practice and that many individuals find it easier to convince themselves that acts which would otherwise certainly be reprehensible and perhaps criminal are none the less ethically justifiable in a commercial context. Again, to quote Hadden:[91]

---

[87] M. B. Clinard and R. Quinney, *Criminal Behaviour Systems: A Typology*, New York: Holt, Rinehart & Winston, 1967, p. 131.

[88] e.g. P. Tappan, 'Who Is the Criminal?' (1947) 12 *American Sociological Review* 96.

[89] Company Securities (Insider Dealing) Act 1985; Criminal Justice Act 1988, s. 48.

[90] T. Hadden, 'Fraud in the City: The Role of the Criminal Law' [1983] *Criminal Law Review* 500, at p. 501.

[91] Ibid.

. . . there is a continuum between legitimate and illegitimate conduct. To this extent it is often not the substance of what is done but the manner in which it is done which matters. It may even be argued that a degree of deception is of the essence of the market system, in that profitable dealing in many spheres depends on the exploitation of information which is not generally available.

Ambiguity over the illegality or perceived wrongfulness of particular conduct lies at the heart of white-collar crime. This is also true of computer misuse. As we shall see, there is disagreement over whether particular forms of computer misuse should be criminalized. The white-collar crime literature provides insights into the ways in which the use of a label such as 'computer misuse' may be 'negotiated' by perpetrators, so as to argue that the misuse is within sharp though acceptable business practice, rather than clearly reprehensible or criminal.[92]

Most modern writers continue to accept a distinction between corporate crime and occupational crime.[93] The former deals with the setting up and running of businesses with the sole or subsidiary purpose of perpetrating fraud or other crime. Examples would include some securities and commodities fraud, merchandise fraud, large-scale insurance swindles, false financial statements by a company, deceptive advertising, corporate tax liability deception, and corporate-encouraged industrial espionage. Examples of the latter group would include theft by employees, embezzlement, insider dealing, and fraud perpetrated upon the firm or, through the firm, upon others. Within occupational crime, there has been a recognition that such offending is not confined to the wealthy or to people of high status. Finn and Hoffman[94] have shown that offenders may be salespersons, retail business employees, or private citizens, as well as high-salaried professionals.

The broadening out of the scope of enquiry of white-collar crime research was also accepted by Edelhertz,[95] who in 1970 provided the most widely accepted modern definition of white-collar crime when he described it as '. . . an illegal act or series of illegal acts committed by non-physical means and by concealment or guile, to obtain money or property, to avoid payment or loss of money or property, or to obtain business or personal advantage.' It will be seen that this definition focuses on 'means' and 'motivation'. It is a useful definition, but it is still prone to the same kind of ambiguity which has plagued the subject since the early days. In attempting to be exhaustive,

[92] e.g. D. Cressey, *Other People's Money*, New York: Patterson Smith, 1973; M. Levi, *The Phantom Capitalists*, London: Heinemann, 1981, and see Chapter 2 below.

[93] e.g. D. Smith, 'White-Collar Crime, Organised Crime and Business Establishment' in P. Wickham and T. Dailey (eds.), *White-Collar Crime and Economic Crime*, Lexington, Mass.: D. C. Heath, 1982; R. C. Kramer, 'Corporate Criminality' in E. Hochstedler (ed.), *Corporations as Criminals*, Beverly Hills, Calif.: Sage Publications, 1984, p. 13.

[94] P. Finn and A. R. Hoffman, *Prosecution of Economic Crime*, Washington, DC: Government Printing Office, 1976, p. 2.

[95] H. Edelhertz, *The Nature, Impact and Prosecution of White-Collar Crime*, Washington, DC: Government Printing Office, 1970, pp. 3, 73–5; H. Edelhertz and C. Rogovin, *A National Strategy for Containing White-Collar Crime*, Lexington, Mass.: D. C. Heath, 1980.

Edelhertz seems to have stretched the subject-matter of white-collar crime well beyond the problematic areas originally addressed by Sutherland. He regards 'petty theft' and the act of 'a housewife who orders books and records through the mail with no intention to pay' as constituting white-collar crimes. The 'outsider', then, can certainly qualify as a white-collar criminal. There is also the familiar problem that whilst his definition speaks of 'an illegal act or series of illegal acts' it is clear that some of the forms of behaviour Edelhertz identifies certainly need not involve conduct contrary to the criminal law. Industrial espionage, which he includes as a broad category, may well not infringe substantive criminal laws in Britain.[96] It is also unclear from the Edelhertz definition what is entailed by the requirement that white-collar crime be committed by 'non-physical means'. If this amounts merely to the exclusion of violence it may be acceptable, but in what sense is petty theft helpfully regarded as having been achieved by non-physical means?

How far does computer misuse fit within the kind of analysis outlined above? The issue may be addressed in the following way. Computer misuse may be regarded as taking place at three fairly distinct levels. The first is that of corporate crime, where the element of computer misuse is company policy, or is central to acts which are part of deliberate decision-making by people who occupy structural positions within the organization. As Clinard and Quinney put it,[97] these are 'offences committed by corporate officials for their corporation and the offences of the corporation itself'. Examples are industrial espionage involving computer misuse which is initiated and financed by one company directed against a rival company,[98] and corporate-sponsored business crime. An example of the latter is the well-known Equity Funding case,[99] where a massive fraud was perpetrated by the creation of fictitious insured lives, the deception being maintained by bogus records maintained on computer. It took place between 1964 and 1972 in the United States.

The Equity Funding Corporation was formed to sell unit trusts and linked life insurance policies. Customers bought unit trust shares and borrowed

---

[96] K. Hodkinson and M. Wasik, *Industrial Espionage: Protection and Remedies*, London: Longman Intelligence Reports, 1986. In a trial in 1988 of charges under the Interception of Communications Act 1985 where Dixons, the electrical retail chain, were alleged to have hired a private detective to spy on a former employee, the judge commented that companies have 'a legitimate right to protect their commercial interests by such methods as undercover surveillance work and electronic eavesdropping, so long as their agents do not actually resort to telephone tapping': reported in *The Times*, 12 Feb. 1988.

[97] Clinard and Quinney (1967), p. 132

[98] Such as the well-known FBI 'sting' operation in 1983 conducted on behalf of IBM to trap an agent from Hitachi who was attempting to gain access to valuable confidential information concerning the introduction by IBM of a new generation of computers; see BloomBecker (1985), pp. 641–2.

[99] This account is taken from A. R. D. Norman, *Computer Insecurity*, London: Chapman & Hall, 1983, p. 119. See also Parker (1976) and, for a book-length account, R. L. Soble and R. E. Dallas, *The Impossible Dream: The Equity Funding Story: The Fraud of the Century*, New York: Putnam, 1975.

money against the security of these shares to purchase a life insurance policy, on the basis that the gains in the shares would be high enough that the borrowed money and the policy would be paid for. The scheme was financially unrealistic and Equity Funding soon became short of cash. By 1968 the company started to buy, with its inflated shares or with money raised against them, genuine corporations with real cash income, trading these assets for the worthless, but apparently valuable, securities of Equity Funding. Still short of cash, the company began to sell some of the future income due on the life policies to co-insurance or re-insurance companies. Equity Funding began to run out of genuine lives to sell and so resorted to inventing fictitious ones. Computers were used to create the details of bogus insured lives. By the time the deception was uncovered 64,000 of the 97,000 policies which the company claimed to have in force were bogus ones. The computers were used to record cancellations, deaths, and lapses in the fictitious policies so that the computer output on these lives appeared authentic. The fraud came to an end after a tip-off by an employee and a snap audit was carried out. As a result of the fraud shareholders lost $600 million and insured persons lost policies with a total face value of $1 billion. Twenty-two convictions for fraud-related offences resulted. While it has been argued that the Equity Funding case was not a true computer fraud, and that 'while the computer may have generated a paper "screen" for some aspects of the fraud, in fact the role played in it was no bigger or more complicated than that played by the company's adding machines',[100] it remains the fact that such a massive fraud could not have been committed, or remained undiscovered for so long, without computing facilities to generate and keep track of all the bogus lives.

We may also include manipulation of computer-held records of revenue, accounts, balance sheets, and tax declarations. Erasure of stock-keeping records and balance sheets from the computer memory may be done to disguise business offences, committed at the expense of business rivals, consumers, investers, governmental, or funding agencies, or to remove evidence of the commission of such offences. This kind of activity is described in Vaughan's study of the Ohio Revco case of Medicaid fraud,[101] where a drugstore chain initiated a computer-generated double-billing scheme which cost $500,000 in Medicaid funds. According to the author:[102]

The tendency of accounting procedures to facilitate unlawful behaviour has been exacerbated by the advent of computer and other electronic equipment, which have come to dominate the daily operation of nearly all large organizations. While these new technologies complete and record transactions with increased speed and efficiency, they simultaneously offer faster and more efficient ways to gain resources unlawfully.

[100] R. Loeffler, *Report of the Trustee of Equity Funding Corporation of America*, Report to the United States District Court for the Central District of California, 1974, cited in L. H. Leigh, *The Control of Commercial Fraud*, London: Heinemann, 1982, p. 63.
[101] D. Vaughan, *Controlling Unlawful Organisational Behaviour*, Chicago: University of Chicago Press, 1983.   [102] Ibid, p. 77.

Corporations may be involved in defrauding customers in numerous ways, such as through automated record systems and electronic funds transfer. In such cases customers may fail to check invoices or financial statements, and either overlook discrepancies or assume that these are the product of computer or human 'error', rather than fraud. Computer-held information gained about customers, such as their credit-worthiness, may be misused and privacy breached.

The second level is that of occupational crime, described by Clinard and Quinney as 'offences committed by individuals for themselves in the course of their occupations and the offences of employees against their employers'.[103] Examples are theft of computer hardware and software, computer fraud, and theft of computer services committed against the employer, after the employee has taken advantage of his authorized access to computing facilities, or has gained unauthorized access to them. Numerous such examples are given in subsequent chapters of this book, but three recent instances which have come to light and been reported to the Audit Commission are fairly typical. In the first,[104] two perpetrators were involved, a management accountant and a purchases ledger manager. The former invented fictitious companies and set up dummy records on the computer. The two then used the accounting system to produce business credit invoices for existing valid customer accounts. The names and addresses of the suppliers were then altered to tally with the names of the bogus records, and cheques were then produced. The accountant, who incidentally had gained his position by falsifying his educational and professional qualifications, had earlier told the management of the security weaknesses in the system but, when nothing was done, took advantage of them himself. Management was alerted by a tip-off. The sum of £1,125,655 was obtained by this method over a one-week period. In a second case,[105] a computer operator in a local authority housing benefit department took advantage of the fact that there was no security check on operators' input to the computer and obtained £5,000 over three months by reactivating closed benefit claims on the computer and changing the addresses on file. There were four payments a fortnight to her address and four similar payments to a friend. The fraud was detected by internal audit, and security procedures were subsequently tightened. A third case[106] involved a clerk who was in sole charge of a branch bank computer linked to the central computer where statements were produced. She debited substantial sums from business accounts and hid this by intercepting the bank statements and sending out substitutes which she typed, omitting the fraudulent entries, on special stationery to which she also had access. The fraud, which lasted six years and netted £193,781, was discovered when a customer queried his account statement, which turned out to be understated by £15,000. Although the

---

[103] Clinard and Quinney (1967), p. 132.   [104] Audit Commission (1987), case 22.
[105] Ibid., case 26; on this and the following case see, further, Chapter 3.
[106] Ibid., case 34.

clerk's annual salary was £6,000 she took exotic holidays, bought expensive gifts, owned a shop, and was said to have lived a 'life of luxury', without her supervisors noticing anything amiss.

A variant of occupational misuse is where an employee may use his employer's computer to make a secret profit for himself, or even run his own business in his employer's time. Reported instances in the United Kingdom include one where a data-processing manager undertook to program and run a computer-based analysis for a firm of accountants.[107] The scheme lasted for 18 months and occasioned loss to the employer of £2,000. In another,[108] an energy management program purchased for use by the company to control energy costs of premises was used by an employee in the course of running his own business. He used the company's equipment and this software in office hours to provide energy surveys for other organizations. The surveys were sold as part of a consultancy business which he ran. A much larger scheme in the United States in 1976 involved two Philadelphia computer programmers employed by Sperry-Univac, who used the company's computer to run a music-arranging business.[109] They developed a program which turned out musical arrangements to run on the computer and also used the computer to maintain a record of their business transactions. The cost to the company was estimated at $144,000.

The third level is that of misuse committed by outsiders, which can take the form of unauthorized remote access to a computer, and may involve seeing sensitive or confidential material, the perpetration of fraud, or the infliction of damage to programs or data held on computer. As we shall see, although much of this remote access is merely preliminary to the main objective, which is some kind of theft or fraud, some hacking is said by the perpetrators to be done purely for reasons of curiosity, or as an intellectual challenge, to find out if the computer security measures in place can be avoided and to see how far it is possible to penetrate into the computer system which has been accessed. In a recent case,[110] a hacker aged 23 operating from the University of Surrey managed to gain access to numerous supposedly secure computers across the world, including NASA. When interviewed by the police he explained that there was no financial objective to the hacking activities, although he believed that he would have been able to transfer up to £5 million if he had wished to. He claimed that '. . . at every stage it's a purely intellectual challenge'. Several other cases are discussed in later chapters.

To come near to encompassing these three levels of computer misuse, the very broadest definition of white-collar crime would have to be adopted. Edelhertz's definition covers most aspects, such as theft, fraud, and deception at levels one and two, but his insistence upon an economic motive means that it

---

[107] Audit Commission (1987), case 48; and this and the following two cases see, further, Chapter 5.
[108] Audit Commission (1987), case 108.   [109] Norman (1983), p. 167.
[110] A. Moger, 'A Hacker's Electronic Voyage around the World', *The Times*, 28 Oct. 1988.

does not extend to computer misuse which is perpetrated for non-economic reasons, such as where it is done for an intellectual challenge or thrill. Gaining unauthorized access to information as such, without an economic motive, does not strictly qualify either, nor does the infliction of damage to computer hardware or software where this is a form of industrial sabotage or done for reasons of boredom, frustration, grievance, or revenge. All these are very important aspects of computer misuse, and are covered in detail in following chapters of this book.

It is significant that in the statistics on incidents of computer misuse which have come to light, reviewed in Chapter 2, fraud and misuse committed by individual employees and outsiders against firms dominate the picture to the extent of almost total exclusion of corporate computer misuse where individuals have been the victims. On reflection, this is hardly surprising, when virtually all surveys designed to address the issue of computer misuse take corporations as their sole respondents. The predominant picture presented by these surveys, then, is of corporate vulnerability to computer fraud, damage, and misuse and this portrayal is fostered by those who seek to sell corporations expensive computer security materials and computer insurance. Surely, though, the question of the extent to which corporations and those who act on their behalf are involved in the perpetration of computer misuse, rather than just being the helpless victims of it, deserves consideration. Yet this aspect is also almost wholly missing[111] from the academic discussions of the phenomenon of computer misuse. Thus in this book on white-collar crime,[112] Bequai deals in separate chapters with computer fraud and fraud committed upon consumers without mentioning any possibility of overlap between the two. The assumption is that computer fraud is committed by individuals against corporations. The question of individual victimization by corporate computer misuse would be difficult, though not impossible, to survey. Some information has been gleaned about incidents of breach of privacy over computer-held records, which have been referred on complaint to solicitors.[113] Other surveys have been conducted into the experiences of individual consumers who have reported errors in computerized systems and services, such as bank statements and computer-generated invoices, though of course it would be very difficult to determine what percentage of these can be attributed to accident and genuine mistake and what percentage to fraud. One Canadian survey of 500 households[114] found that no less than 40 per cent of those sampled had experienced at least one such error in the previous

---

[111] An important exception is the excellent article by R. Kling, 'Computer Abuse and Computer Crime as Organisational Activities' (1980) 2 *Computer and Law Journal* 403.

[112] A. Bequai, *White-Collar Crime: A Twentieth Century Crisis*, Lexington, Mass.: D. C. Heath, 1978.

[113] Wacks (1989), ch. 4.

[114] A 1979 survey, cited in Kling (1980), p. 416. More recently, the consumer magazine *Which?* has highlighted complaints of 'phantom withdrawals'. See, for example, the June 1989 and Sept. 1989 issues.

year and about 15 per cent reported two or more errors. In 1989, the Banking Ombudsman in Britain reported that 'phantom' cash withdrawals from automated cash dispensers, where customer accounts had been wrongly debited for using ATMs, was the public grievance which occupied the bulk of his staff's time. Complaints to banks are running in the region of 50,000 a year, nearly 3,000 of which come subsequently to the Ombudsman where customers feel dissatisfied with the bank's initial response. Figures discussed in Chapter 6 reveal the importance of customer complaint as a means of alerting investigators to incidents of computer fraud and misuse. It is disturbing, then, that in the Canadian study, 20 per cent of the complainants experienced great difficulty in persuading the relevant computer-using organization to rectify the error which had been made.

  Some may believe that it is possible to account for all the diverse forms of criminal or ethically suspect behaviour placed under the heading of 'computer misuse' by way of a single theory, which locates its source in the fundamental features of a capitalist political economy.[115] While overt political motivation seems to be rare among computer misusers,[116] recently there have been reports that a select minority of hackers is developing a more aggressive political stance. Some delegates at a so-called 'Hackers' Conference' in Amsterdam stated their intent to make all computers and the information they hold 'freely accessible to the people' and in the United States one hacker group, known as the Cyberpunks, has promoted a 'charter of irresponsibility' with regard to accessing and opening up computer systems. It is tempting to identify the computer as a potent symbol of economic and political power, and computer misuse either as the illicit exploitation of that power, particularly in corporate crime, or as an expression of subversion, where the computer becomes the target for damage or manipulation by the powerless. One commentator suggests that[117] '. . . employee computer crime quietly suggests something larger than petty electronic sniping and greed: a latent collective power available to millions of computer workers, a power that can press their political interests successfully against their employers everywhere'. Computer misuse reminds us that computers are the tools of the powerful, but also that the Establishment is vulnerable to attack from below. Political accounts have been advanced to explain some instances of embezzlement by employees; Mattera,[118] for example, asserts that employees' 'fiddles' against the firm 'are perhaps best viewed as a covert form of struggle by workers', or

[115] F. Pearce, *Crimes of the Powerful*, London: Pluto Press, 1976.
[116] Though see, on motivation for damage to computer systems, Chapter 2. Some self-confessed hackers express political motivations for what they do, though this is rare. See generally S. Levy, *Hackers: Heroes of the Computer Revolution*, New York: Doubleday,1984, Hayes (1989), pp. 95–6 and N. Nuttall, 'Idealistic Hackers: a Global Threat', *The Times*, 21 Sept. 1989.
[117] Hayes (1989), p. 96
[118] P. Mattera, *Off the Books*, London: Pluto Press, 1985, cited in Levi (1987), p. xxii.

industrial sabotage[119] which, according to Taylor and Walton, sometimes 'aims to restructure social relationships: in its most extreme form to establish workers' control'.

It is suggested, however, that the sheer diversity of behaviour within the context of computer misuse, where the computer may figure at one moment as the instrument of crime, and at the next as the target for crime, and given the apparent importance of non-economic motives in some forms of computer misuse, such as the unauthorized access of computer systems purely for intellectual challenge and some cases of computer sabotage, makes any monolithic explanation of this phenomenon quite implausible. It seems that while white-collar crime studies on motivation are likely to be very helpful in respect of the acquisitive aspects of computer misuse, such as computer fraud, we also must have regard to the quite distinct criminological studies of other forms of deviance, particularly those involving destruction and vandalism, and to forms of lawbreaking which involve the demonstration of particular technical skills on the part of the perpetrator.

[119] L. Taylor and P. Walton, 'Industrial Sabotage: Motives and Meanings' in S. Cohen (ed.), *Images of Deviance*, London: Pelican Books, 1971.

2

The Scale of the Problem

1. QUANTIFYING LOSSES

Estimates of the total losses involved through computer misuse vary very greatly. This is due partly to definitional problems, over which activities should properly be included within the category, and partly to the large penumbra of cases which are undiscovered or unreported by victims.

Many of the incidents described as computer crime or computer misuse have taken place in the United States, though a substantial body of recent European, Australian, and other examples has now come to light. Much of the information about these incidents, particularly the earlier ones, is, however, fragmented and anecdotal. A number of 'casebooks' recording incidents of computer misuse in this country and the United States have been produced. These contain reports culled from newspaper or computer trade journals, which tend to stress the sensational aspects of the case and often omit important details from a lawyer's point of view, such as whether prosecution was initiated, for what offence, and whether it was successful. Apparently the same incident is reported in significantly different ways in different books, casting doubt on the reliability of the story. Statistics using published accounts of such cases have been built up by Parker[1] in his famous continuing computer crime project at the Stanford Research Institute in California and, in Britain, Wong's casebooks[2] are based partly on similar sources and partly on private communications to the author.

These casebooks have proved extremely valuable in alerting us to the varieties of computer misuse in general terms, and in identifying new forms of misuse as they arise, but as an indicator of the typical nature or general extent of computer misuse they are unhelpful and may well be quite misleading. It is nevertheless upon such sketchy information that many of the assessments about the overall extent of the computer misuse problem have been made and, in turn, these have provided the impetus for making changes in the criminal law. In 1973, Parker claimed on the basis of cases collected in his study that the annual world-wide loss from computer misuse was $300

---

[1] D. B. Parker, S. Nycum and S. Aura, *Computer Abuse*, Menlo Park, Calif.: Stanford Research Institute, 1973. See also D. B. Parker, *Crime by Computer*, New York: Scribner, 1976, and id., *Fighting Computer Crime*, New York: Scribner, 1983.

[2] K. Wong, *Computer Crime Casebook*, London: BIS Applied Systems, 1983, 1987, and K. Wong and B. Farquhar, *Computer-Related Fraud Casebook*, London: BIS Applied Systems, 1983, 1987.

million and that the average loss per case was $450,000. These conclusions were roundly criticized by Taber, seven years later, who stated that Parker's assessment was 'based on poor documentation, unacceptable methods, and unverified (indeed unverifiable) losses'.[3] By that time, however, legislative moves to tackle computer misuse were well under way. Subsequently, Parker has emphasized on numerous occasions the limited usefulness of the statistics gathered in his SRI project.

An alternative and more rigorous approach to the measurement of computer misuse incidents is to exclude all material except that for which actual case transcripts are available for analysis. The National Center for Computer Crime Data (NCCCD) in the United States adopts this approach[4] though, of course, this also has its difficulties. Obviously, misuse which is not contrary to the criminal law is unlikely to figure in such cases. For various reasons, few prosecutions may be initiated and it may be difficult to obtain transcripts for those cases which are, particularly where tried in the lower courts. Prosecutors may choose to proceed under the ordinary criminal law rather than state computer crime legislation, so that the computer element in the offending is more likely to be missed by researchers. The resulting data are thin and may well be unrepresentative and misleading. In its first Annual Statistical Report, NCCCD published the result of a survey of 130 prosecutors' offices in 38 states for examples of computer crime prosecutions and could report only 75 cases. In Germany a research project based at Freiburg has concentrated on computer crime cases which have been prosecuted, and where court records have been obtained and verified. Again, relatively few cases have come to light.[5] As Sieber, a West German researcher in the field, says:[6] 'Worldwide, only a few empirical research studies provide reliable information. An exact comparison between these is not possible because of the different underlying definitions of the phenomena being investigated as well as the different research methods of selection and verification.'

Since, as we have seen, computer misuse is an artificial category of lawbreaking, the official crime statistics provide no separate information about its prevalence and, even if such a separate classification was feasible, it would reflect only those cases which had been reported to the police, rather than indicating the true level of offending. In principle, the best way of

---

[3] J. K. Taber, 'A Survey of Computer Crime Studies' (1980) 2 *Computer and Law Journal* 275. Parker's study is also discussed by S. Mandell, *Computers, Data Processing and the Law*, St Paul, Minn.: West Publishing, 1984, at p. 155: 'Despite the drawbacks, the study has generally been well received, since imperfect information may be better than none. Even fictitious accounts have some value as they allow us to study the feasibility of such a crime.' For Parker's own later assessment of his statistics see his 'Computer Abuse Research Update' (1980) 2 *Computer and Law Journal* 329.

[4] J. J. BloomBecker, *Computer Crime, Computer Security, Computer Ethics*, Los Angeles: NCCCD, 1986.

[5] U. Sieber, *The International Handbook on Computer Crime*, London: John Wiley, 1986.

[6] Ibid., p. 29.

investigating the extent of computer misuse is to undertake victim surveys.[7] These involve the sending of questionnaires to a large randomly selected sample of individuals and corporations to see whether they have suffered losses through computer misuse during a given period, and if so how frequently and to what extent. Positive responses may be followed up by personal interview. The regular repetition of such surveys permits more meaningful assessment of changes in offending patterns over time than official statistics, since variance there may merely indicate changes in reporting or recording practices. Victim surveys, however, also have their limitations. There may be a low response rate to the enquiries, misreporting of incidents, concealment or exaggeration, and genuine uncertainty over whether an incident qualifies to be reported or not. Individuals or corporations may not realize that they have been the subject of criminal attention. A number of such surveys have now been carried out in the computer misuse field, though the results obtained do not provide a very clear picture.

In the United States, the Task Force on Computer Crime of the American Bar Association[8] sent out 1,000 questionnaires in 1984. There were 283 responses, of which 160 stated that they had suffered some form of computer crime. The great majority of these victims had suffered losses of up to $100,000. There were 18 cases reporting losses in excess of this, in one a loss of between $100 million and $500 million. The Task Force's estimate for total annual computer crime losses in the United States was placed somewhere in the rather wide range between $145 million and $730 million. By contrast, in the same year, the American Institute of Certified Public Accountants[9] conducted a survey of 9,405 banks and 1,232 insurance companies and reported that only 2 per cent of the banks and 3 per cent of the insurance companies had found instances of computer fraud. After reviewing the details of these cases the AICPA determined that 85 of the cases submitted by the banks and 34 of the cases submitted by the insurance companies conformed to the study's working definition of computer fraud. The Fraud Division of the United States Department of Justice, having set up a Corruption Tracking system to record referrals of suspected fraud against the Federal government, found that less than half of 1 per cent of the referrals were computer-related.[10] These contrasting findings may be explained partly by the Task

---

[7] See M. Wasik, 'Surveying Computer Crime' (1985) 1 *Computer Law and Practice* 110. The first general crime surveys were carried out for the United States President's Commission on Crime, and as a result a full-scale programme of national and city-level surveys began in the United States in 1972. Other countries have mounted similar surveys. The first in Britain was the British Crime Survey, first conducted in 1983.

[8] American Bar Association, Task Force on Computer Crime, *Report on Computer Crime*, Washington, DC: Government Printer, 1984.

[9] American Institute of Certified Public Accountants, EDP Fraud Review Task Force, *Report on the Study of EDP Related Fraud in the Banking and Insurance Industries*, 1984, outlined in United States Congress, Office of Technology Assessment, *Management, Security and Congressional Oversight*, Washington, DC: Federal Government Publication, 1987, ch. 5.

[10] Cited by C. Tapper, 'Computer Crime: Scotch Mist ' [1987] *Criminal Law Review* 4.

Force's interest in other forms of misuse as well as fraud, but their conclusion that the need to introduce 'Federal computer crime legislation is fully supported by the results of the Task Force survey'[11] is debatable, and may owe more to the American Bar Association's own policy commitment to such a development five years earlier.[12]

In the United Kingdom, in a 1986 study sponsored by the Home Office of the incidence of commercial fraud generally,[13] which estimated that fraud was running at the rate of about £1 billion a year, it was found that computer fraud was mentioned only rarely by the 56 respondents, who were senior executives, when asked for details of frauds which their companies had actually experienced. Cheque or credit card frauds, expenses frauds, and embezzlement were far more commonly encountered in practice. On the other hand, when asked which specific type of fraud had become a particular problem over the last ten years, 45 per cent of respondents mentioned computer fraud. Levi[14] suggests, therefore, that fear of computer fraud outstrips its reality, and that the managers may have responded as they did because information technology is the area of their business that they feel they least understand.[15] The Audit Commission has conducted three surveys of organizations primarily in the local government, health, finance, and manufacturing sectors addressed to the issue of computer fraud, in 1981, 1984, and 1987, although other forms of computer misuse were also reported to them.[16] In the second of these in 1984, of the 943 replies received, 92 per cent of respondents said that they had not suffered a computer fraud in the last five years. Seventy-seven cases of computer fraud were notified, 13 of which had involved no financial loss. The total sum lost was £1,133,487. In 24 cases the loss was less than £1,000. There were three cases where losses were between £50,000 and £100,000 and a further three where the losses were between £100,000 and £250,000. In the 1987 survey, by comparison, again 8 per cent said that they had incurred a computer fraud, 118 cases being reported.

[11] American Bar Association (1984), p. 45.

[12] In August 1979 the ABA's policy-making House of Delegates approved a policy resolution to this effect. This is reproduced in Appendix II to the *Report on Computer Crime*. Federal legislation was introduced by the Counterfeit Access Device and Computer Fraud and Abuse Act, of 12 Oct. 1984, codified at 18 USC ss. 1029–30. The first prosecution was not brought under this law until 1989; see p. 59 below.

[13] M. Levi, *The Incidence, Reporting and Prevention of Commercial Fraud*, Summary of Findings, Cardiff: Dept. of Social Administration, 1986.

[14] M. Levi, *Regulating Fraud*, London: Tavistock, 1987, p. 41.

[15] See Chapter 1.

[16] Audit Inspectorate, *Computer Fraud Survey*, London: Department of the Environment, 1981; Audit Commission for Local Authorities in England and Wales, *Computer Fraud Survey*, London: HMSO, 1984; Audit Commission for Local Authorities in England and Wales, *Survey of Computer Fraud and Abuse*, London: HMSO, 1987. Levi (1987), at p. 40, criticizes the 1984 Survey on the ground of bias in that only 209 of the 943 repondents were private-sector institutions and suggests that computer-related fraud is much more likely to be encountered in the private sector. The Audit Commission (1987), at p. 8, explains that for the 1987 survey 1,000 public sector and 3,000 private sector organizations were invited to respond, prompting a response rate of 60 per cent and 20 per cent respectively.

Sixty-three of these involved no financial loss. The total sum lost was double the 1984 figure, at £2,561,351. In 18 cases the losses were less than £1,000. There were four cases where the losses were between £50,000 and £100,000, one where the loss was between £100,000 and £250,000, and two cases involving losses of more than £250,000.

Although the Audit Commission's reports have gained considerable currency, and they represent the most comprehensive attempt to investigate the prevalence of computer misuse in Britain, their figures have been described as a gross underestimate by other organizations. Some press reports have speculated over massive figures for computer misuse losses, one suggesting computer fraud losses running in the order of £2 million a day.[17] A study by the computer services division of Deloitte Haskins and Sells in 1986 reported that 'millions of pounds' had been stolen from City institutions by computer fraud during the previous two years,[18] the CBI estimate[19] for annual losses in 1987 was between £25 million and £30 million, and a comprehensive Report produced by the Risk Management Services Division of Hogg Robinson Ltd. into computer security measures in place in fifty British companies in 1986 estimated that known 'computer associated fraud and theft will probably cost United Kingdom companies £40 million this year'.[20] This last figure has been repeated in numerous articles and press reports since, together with the observation that actual losses may be anything up to ten times as large. The Audit Commission asked its survey respondents to estimate the total loss sustained through computer fraud and abuse during 1986, and a figure of £330 million emerged, though the figure of £200 million was the result of averaging out responses from 'the more considered assessment' of those who had actually suffered computer fraud or misuse during the relevant period. The Commission comments that even this lower estimate is 'higher than any evidence available would sustain'.[21] Yet, not to be outdone, a recent estimate from Coopers and Lybrand, the management consultants and chartered accountants, was that business losses through computer fraud and misuse was running in the region of £1 billion a year, and some computer security consultants are quoted as putting the figure at £2 billion a year.[22]

There have been some comparable surveys in other countries, though few very recent ones, as the enthusiasm for the survey approach in the early 1980s seems gradually to have tailed off. The most comprehensive continuing Australian survey has been carried out by the Caulfield Institute of Technology,

[17] Reported in *The Times*, 14 Mar. 1985.
[18] Reported ibid., 4 Sept. 1986.
[19] Reported ibid., 20 Jan. 1987.
[20] Hogg Robinson, *Computer Security in Practice*, London: Hogg Robinson, 1986.
[21] Audit Commission (1987), p. 12.
[22] Reported in *The Times*, 17 Oct. 1989, also citing a report by the London Business School which postulates British losses from computer fraud at the rather exact figure of £407 million annually and which also claims that 'as many as 17,000 of our 900,000 companies have been victims of computer crime'.

Computer Abuse Research Bureau[23] in Victoria since 1978, and they have compiled a casebook from answers to questionnaires sent to a large number of Australian computer users. In a report published in 1980, 123 cases had been reported to the organization, involving total losses of $A5.6 million, and it has produced updated research findings ever since. By 1986 they had collected 150 cases, 69 of which were classified as incidents of computer-related fraud. Total losses from computer fraud taken alone over the full period of operation of the survey amount to nearly $A5 million.[24] As may be expected, however, estimates of non-reported losses are very much higher. It has been suggested that some 900 computer crimes a year are taking place in Australia, and that total annual losses are of the order of $A40 million.[25] The picture in Canada is much the same, with high estimates of total losses but with relatively few actual cases unearthed by the research studies.[26] In Germany, the Institute for Criminology and Economic Penal Law at Freiburg has collected data on incidents of computer misuse since 1974. Nine or ten cases have been reported each year for the first few years, but numbers are now growing steadily, and 170 convictions in cases of computer-related crime were reported to the Institute in 1987. Other European countries have conducted smaller-scale surveys and unearthed a few cases. In Switzerland the police department of the Canton of Zurich reported the surprisingly modest total of fifteen cases of computer crime.[27] The European Community Information Technology Task Force[28] in 1984 discovered forty cases of computer-related theft or embezzlement, eleven of which originated in the United Kingdom, nine in France, seven in West Germany, six in Belgium, four in Italy, and three in Switzerland. Spain reported supposedly its first incident of computer misuse to reach the courts in 1989.[29] Once again, estimates of losses vary enormously. Although France, for example, has few fully documented cases of computer misuse, statistics published by the French insurance industry suggest that losses in France through computer 'incidents' in 1987

[23] Caulfield Institute of Technology, Computer Abuse Research Bureau (CIT/CARB), 'Computer Related Crime in Australia' (1984) 6 *Computer Fraud and Security Bulletin* No. 12, at p. 1.

[24] The CIT/CARB research is discussed in Tasmanian Law Reform Commission, Report No. 47, *Computer Misuse*, Tasmania: Government Printer, 1986, p. 15.

[25] C. Sullivan, 'The Response of the Criminal Law in Australia to Computer Abuse' (1988) 12 *Criminal Law Journal* 228, at pp. 228–9.

[26] A study by the Ontario Provincial Police in 1981 is discussed in C. Webber, 'Computer Crime or Jay-Walking on the Electronic Highway' (1984) 26 *Criminal Law Quarterly* 217. Although only 2 per cent of the sample had experienced a loss through computer misuse, 84 per cent of respondents nevertheless considered it to be a significant problem; see Tapper (1987), at p. 7.

[27] Sieber (1986), at p. 33.

[28] European Community Information Technology Task Force, *The Vulnerability of the Information Conscious Society: European Situation*, unpublished, 1984, cited in Levi (1987), at p. 39. The research mentions 3 cases of banking fraud, each of which netted over £5 million, 13 cases costing an average of £500,000 and 8 cases averaging over £20,000.

[29] Reported in *The Times*, 6 June 1989: two technicians are alleged to have infected municipal computers all over the country with a computer virus and then offered to sell town councils the programmed vaccine to cure it. On computer viruses, see Chapter 4.

amounted to £800 million or so. This figure represents an increase of 7 per cent over 1986, and 49 per cent of the total is attributed to misuse, mainly in the form of fraud or sabotage, rather than computer breakdown and disaster.[30]

It is impossible to square all this widely divergent information. In its assessment of criminal law reform options, the Scottish Law Commission admitted that[31] 'it is impossible to form any definite conclusions as to the present scale of computer crime', and that seems a correct assessment. While it is true that the number of perfectly verifiable incidents of computer misuse in this research material is not very high, the matter is complicated further by the problem of undiscovered and unreported misuse, which is generally supposed to be far higher. The OECD estimates that 75–80 per cent of computer misuse is not reported.

It is well known that crime victims often do not report offences to the police. Reluctance varies in extent from one crime to another. For some crimes, such as car theft, the non-reporting figure is small, since successful insurance claim requires notification of the incident to the police. The British Crime Survey[32] found that twice as many burglaries take place as are recorded by the police, nearly five times as much wounding and thirteen times as much vandalism. In general the under-reported crimes are the less serious ones, but this is not always the case. According to the British Crime Survey, the reasons why people do not report crimes to the police are, in order of importance, that they have suffered no actual loss or damage, the loss or damage is trivial, that the police could 'do nothing', that it is inappropriate for the police to deal with the matter, or that the police 'would not be interested'.

Economic crime, in general, is substantially under-reported. Levi notes that where organizations are victims, they perform a kind of cost-benefit analysis when deciding whether to report or not.[33] The literature on white-collar crime illustrates that there is always a good deal of discretion in the use by business of formal avenues of justice, with informal and internal methods of disciplining malefactors within the organization generally being the preferred approach. This was one of the differences between white-collar crime and 'street crime' noted in the early work by Sutherland. Of the perpetrators responsible for the 118 incidents of computer misuse reported to the Audit Commission in 1987, for example, less than one-third were prosecuted.[34] Most perpetrators were disciplined by the firm, dismissed, or had resigned after discovery. Some writers suggest that firms are far too ready to put their victimization down to experience and do nothing, or to resort to traditional

---

[30] Cited in (1988–9) 4 *Computer Law and Security Report* 21.

[31] See Scottish Law Commission, Consultative Memorandum No. 68, *Computer Crime*, Edinburgh: SLC, 1986, pp. 32–8.

[32] Home Office Research Study No. 76, *British Crime Survey*, London: HMSO, 1983.

[33] Levi (1987), pp. 124–36.

[34] Audit Commission (1987), p. 22.

informal methods, and that they should recognize a public obligation to expose and prosecute fraudsters who otherwise may be free to move to a different firm and perpetrate much the same form of crime again.[35] Many organizations seem to be as fearful of adverse publicity revealing that they have been the victim of fraud as they are of suffering the fraud itself. Damage may be done to the company's reputation and there may be loss of confidence in it on the part of investors, shareholders, and customers. Victims may perceive the costs of prosecution to be too high, in terms of disruption of business by investigative officers, use of staff time in appearing in court, and diversion of management effort.

It is likely that computer misuse is even less frequently brought to the attention of the police. Media fascination with computer misuse in recent years has produced a variation on the non-reporting theme, whereby businesses may be forced to concede that they have been the victims of fraud, but remain at pains to point out that such fraud was not connected with computers. An example is a widely reported fraud at Barclays Bank, where the bank subsequently issued a statement admitting that fraud had taken place but 'categorically denying' that the fraud was a computer fraud.[36] In his extensive research Levi found that there was variation in attitude amongst senior executives over the issue of fraud reporting, but that companies which had 'an American connection' had a much tougher line on reporting fraud than did the British companies:[37]

Indeed, one large bank which dealt with countries on both sides of the Atlantic stated that attitudes varied even within the bank: in the United States and Europe there is an attitude of prosecute and be damned; in the United Kingdom the attitude is rather different and there is much more of a dainty attitude towards prosecuting.

In part this rests on the well-established legal requirement in the United States that all incidents of fraud must be reported to the authorities. Whether such an obligation should be imposed in this country is discussed further below.

2. CATEGORIES OF COMPUTER MISUSE

Numerous different categorizations of computer misuse have been designed by different writers for their particular purposes, influenced by whether the issue is being addressed primarily in terms of describing the practical impact of the most prevalent varieties of misuse, or in terms of identifying specific legal issues. Cornwall,[38] for instance, writing for a non-specialist audience, uses the broad non-technical categories of 'datafraud', 'dataspying', and

---

[35] See M. J. Comer, *Corporate Fraud*, 2nd edn., London: McGraw-Hill, 1985, ch. 8.
[36] Reported in *The Times*, 23 Aug. 1986.
[37] Levi (1987), p. 31.
[38] H. Cornwall, *Datatheft*, London: Heinemann, 1987.

'datatheft'. Sieber,[39] however, a German legal expert, adopts a more comprehensive sixfold classification: (*a*) fraud by computer manipulation, (*b*) computer espionage and software theft, (*c*) computer sabotage, (*d*) theft of services, (*e*) unauthorized access to data processing systems, and (*f*) traditional business offences assisted by data processing. Most of the law reform bodies which have addressed the issue of computer misuse so far have proceeded by identifying those areas in which problems have already appeared to challenge existing criminal law definitions and assumptions.

In this book we are concerned both with describing various aspects of computer misuse and with identifying substantive criminal law issues, and so a mixture of approaches is adopted. The substantive criminal law which is or may become relevant to computer misuse is considered in the next three chapters under the following broad headings: (*a*) unauthorized access and unauthorized use, (*b*) fraud and information theft, and (*c*) associated offences. The issues addressed are similar to those considered by the Scottish Law Commission in its Consultation Paper on the subject of Computer Crime produced in 1986 and its subsequent Report[40] in 1987, and the Working Paper and subsequent Report on Computer Misuse produced by the Law Commission for England and Wales[41] in 1988 and 1989. Prior to a fuller discussion of the legal problems arising in these three areas, something needs to be said about each of the key issues by way of introduction.

(i) *Unauthorized access*

We are here concerned with the gaining of 'unauthorized access to data or programs held on a computer'. Whilst other writers have described this issue in terms of the 'unauthorized access to a computer',[42] the chosen terminology more accurately reflects the fact that we are not concerned here with unauthorized access to the computer hardware, but with the gaining of access to material held on the computer, such as programs or data. No special legal problems arise in relation to the gaining of unauthorized access to the hardware itself. Any criminal liability in such a case would depend upon the reason for gaining access. Theft or destruction of tangible computer materials can simply be charged as theft or criminal damage, and entry into a building, or part of a building, such as a computer room, will constitute the offence of burglary where it can be proved that the trespasser had the intention to steal or commit such damage. Similarly, unauthorized entry accompanied by theft constitutes burglary.[43] There is, accordingly, no need for a special offence to cover burglary of computer premises.

[39] Sieber (1986).
[40] Scottish Law Commission (1986) and Scottish Law Commission, *Report on Computer Crime*, Cm. 174, Edinburgh: HMSO, 1987.
[41] Law Commission, Working Paper No. 110, *Computer Misuse*, London: HMSO, 1988, and Law Commission, Report No. 186, *Computer Misuse*, Cm. 819, London: HMSO, 1989.
[42] e.g. Law Commission (1988), para. 1.16.   [43] Theft Act 1968, s. 9.

Existing criminal law may well not, however, extend to unauthorized access to computer-held programs or data. A person may obtain unauthorized access to such material by any one of a number of methods, but he will either be a person such as an employee of a company who normally has limited access to a computer for specific purposes or on specific occasions, but on this occasion does so without permission, or he will be an outsider. As was explained above, desk-top computers which are linked to a central computer provide more opportunities for unobserved unauthorized access of this kind by an employee than was the case when all computer hardware was housed in a central computer room. The unauthorized access may be merely for curiosity, perhaps in order to discover information held by the firm about the employee, or other employees, or other aspects of the firm's operations, with no further nefarious intent. This is primarily a matter of confidentiality, and we consider below how far it is appropriate to use the criminal law to protect confidential computer-held information. A particular problem which has received a good deal of attention, of course, is that of long-range hacking by computer enthusiasts, whose avowed purpose is the intellectual challenge of subverting the computer security access devices in place.

Many hackers use comparatively simple computing equipment, generally a microcomputer coupled to a 'modem', which allows the hacker to access the target computer via a communications link, such as the public telephone system. Most computers are protected by devices to limit access to those who are authorized users, requiring proof of identity by the more or less sophisticated keying in of a password. Unfortunately, computer security is often not as tight as it should be and in some cases is virtually non-existent. There may be no security in place at all (the equivalent, to the hacker, of leaving all doors unlocked) or, where passwords are required, they may, for ease of use by employees, be very simple and easy to guess, and infrequently or never changed. They may be written down by users in a place where they can be seen, such as pinned up on a board beside the computer terminal. Often, then, a hacker will be able to gain access because he already knows a password which allows him into the computer system. Otherwise, it may be possible for him to discover a password by trial and error, such as by using a program which generates random numbers or letters, until the correct one is found. Again, this should be avoided by basic computer security methods which prevent repeated attempts to log on. While it is true that some hacking techniques are much more ingenious than these, the evidence is that the vast bulk of cases of unauthorized access to a computer occur in circumstances where quite inadequate security precautions have been taken. It is relatively cheap and simple to install these defences, which will effectively deter the majority of attempts to gain unauthorized access. A highly skilled and experienced hacker, however, will regard it as a personal challenge to circumvent security devices which are in place, and it is very difficult if not impossible to be sure that a computer system is totally secure.

Some hacking of this type, where there is said to be no further malicious or nefarious intent, has been declared by one of its best-known proponents, Hugo Cornwall, to be no more than[44] 'an educational and recreational sport ... the process of "getting in" is much more satisfying than what is discovered in the protected computer files'. A network of information is available to hackers, giving hints on making unauthorized access to various computers, some of it held on computerized hacker bulletin boards in the form of useful telephone numbers, user identifications, passwords, and the like.

A key issue for the criminal law is whether such hacking, also described as 'computer trespass', should be outlawed. The arguments are considered fully in Chapter 3. Suffice it to say here that even the non-malicious hacker may gain access to confidential or sensitive information and although not motivated to make gain or cause damage through his activity may, through gaining access, accidentally damage computer-held programs or data, or activate the computer security system which is in place, causing the whole system to shut down, with resultant inconvenience, loss, or danger. Additionally, of course, it may be extremely difficult to distinguish the non-malicious hacker from the malicious. Cornwall says that his own motives have always been clear:[45]

I personally have always been quite sure about how far I am prepared to go in pursuing the hacking sport. For me, hacking is ... simply a natural extension of my fascination with computers, networks and new developments in technology ... Popping into people's computers to see what they are doing has always seemed to me little different from viewing those same machines on an exhibition stand ... Breaking into areas where I am supposed to be forbidden has always been part of testing the capability of a machine and its operators. But causing damage, wilfully or inadvertently, has never been part of this. Hackers like me—and the majority are—admire the machines that are our targets.

There are numerous well-documented accounts of incidents of computer hacking, and anecdotal evidence abounds. Hacking came to real prominence in the early 1980s, though there are some earlier incidents reported, such as one in 1974 where a 15-year-old Westminster schoolboy cracked the security system of a major London computer time-sharing service and gained access to user files.[46] It seemed to develop from the 'phone-phreak' craze, where long-distance telephone lines were explored for interest and challenge.[47] A few of the more spectacular and recent examples of hacking can be summarized here.

One of the best-known hacking incidents was that involving the '414 gang', a group of Milwaukee computer hobbyists who gained access to computers at a bank in Los Angeles, a cement company in Montreal, a hospital in New York, and a relatively low-security file at the Los Alamos

---

[44] H. Cornwall, *The New Hacker's Handbook*, London: Century Hutchinson, 1985, p. viii.
[45] Ibid., p. xii.
[46] A. R. D. Norman, *Computer Insecurity*, London: Chapman and Hall, 1983, p. 139.
[47] Ibid., p. 133.

National Research Center.[48] In 1985 seven schoolboy computer enthusiasts in New Jersey accessed a military communications system at the Pentagon.[49] In 1986 three young computer technology students in France admitted that they had managed to access fifteen of France's largest computer systems during their Easter holidays, including a Cray-One computer which handled material for the National Office of Aerospace Research and other government bodies, and stored top-secret defence and technological data.[50] They explained that their motive had been curiosity and 'to see how far they could get'. Towards the end of 1988 the press carried reports of the activities of a 23-year-old man working from the University of Surrey, who used the Joint Academic Network (JANET), a link-up between British and American Universities and the United States 'Telenet', one of the largest computer communication networks, to access some 200 official commercial and military computer systems, including computers at the National Aeronautics and Space Administration (NASA) and an American nuclear weapons research centre.[51] He claims to have read files held on highly sensitive matters including space research, defence supplies, and weapons systems. He also tried, unsuccessfully, to access the Government Communications Headquarters in Britain (GCHQ). In early 1989 in Los Angeles a hacker was given a prison sentence after running unsuccessfully a defence based on lack of criminal intent. The case attracted particular attention because the judge ordered that the defendant Mitnick be held without bail for three months before trial, and denied him all access to telephones or computers. The defendant had gained access on previous occasions to internal computer records of the Los Angeles Police Department, Pacific Telephone Inc., and several commercial organizations. He altered the computer-held credit information on several individuals, including his own probation officer. It was said that the damage caused by his unauthorized intrusions into Digital Equipment Corporation software and files cost the company more than $4 million to repair.[52]

The Audit Commission Report of 1987 outlines several more prosaic and surely more typical hacking cases. In some of these, the perpetrator was identified quite quickly and there was no proof of further criminal intent. In one case reported by central government, a 'highly inquisitive' programmer was detected probing parts of the computer system which were outside his responsibility and authority. On discovery, the programmer co-operated

---

[48] J. J. BloomBecker, 'Computer Crime Update: The View as we Exit 1984' (1985) 7 *Western New England Law Review* 627, at p. 630.

[49] T. Fishlock, 'Schoolboy Hackers Crack Pentagon Telephone Codes', *The Times*, 18 July 1985.

[50] D. Geddes, 'Computer Pirate Raid Stuns Paris', *The Times*, 19 July 1986.

[51] A. Moger, 'A Hacker's Electronic Voyage Around the World', *The Times*, 28 Oct. 1988.

[52] C. Bremner, 'Death to the Hackers', *The Times*, 16 Oct. 1989. Assuming the sign-on name of 'The Condor', Mitnick is described as 'wreaking a trail of mischief through the digital telephone systems and computer files. When arrested the police would not let him use the telephone because they feared he could dial up the FBI records and erase his own files.'

with the security administrator in pointing out security weaknesses.[53] A local government case involved an assistant storekeeper with an interest in computers, who made more than 2,000 attempts over a period of a month to gain unauthorized access to the computer system from a VDU situated at a vehicle maintenance depot.[54]

Where the unauthorized access is to achieve some further objective, this objective may be rather vaguely formulated in the mind of the hacker, or be quite specific. The hacker may be looking for weaknesses in the company's security and the chance to perpetrate fraud, willing to take advantage of any opportunity which presents itself. Where the person's intention is clear, the prosecution will often be able to rely upon standard theft, fraud, and deception offences, or the law of attempt where the objective is not realized, but only where the person has done an act which is more than merely preparatory to the envisaged offence. In most cases such offences can be established, and the fact that the offence is perpetrated by operation of the computer is quite irrelevant. Occasionally, however, these offences cannot be made out. When such problems occur, the advantages of criminalizing the initial access by the hacker are clear. In the United States, where there has been the greatest development of law in response to computer misuse, one important approach has been to criminalize the initial access.[55] Thus, regardless of what a defendant does after gaining unauthorized access to a computer, the access itself may constitute a criminal offence. The Scottish Law Commission, in the first comprehensive survey of this area of law in Britain, also focused on the initial question of unauthorized access:[56]

(I)t is as well to bear in mind that some form of unauthorized access may precede many of the other activities with which we are concerned . . . Accordingly, unauthorized accessing may be seen as a subject which merits particular attention when we come to consider possible reforms of the criminal law.

Until 1990 there was in Britain no criminal law dealing specifically with unauthorized access to computer held programs or data, including hacking. The English Law Commission joined with its Scottish counterpart in recommending that such conduct should be made an offence. The Computer Misuse Act 1990, which implements these proposals, is discussed in detail in Chapter 3 and Appendix 4 of this book.

A problem closely related to unauthorized access is that of 'computer eavesdropping', referred to in the United States as 'electromagnetic pickup'. It is technically quite possible to 'read' from outside a building information currently being relayed through a computer system inside the building, using a television receiver connected to a video recorder, to pick up the electromagnetic radiation surrounding the computer. The data can then be re-

[53] Audit Commission, *Survey of Computer Fraud and Abuse*, London: HMSO, 1987, case 82.
[54] Case 85.
[55] M. D. Scott, *Computer Law*, New York: John Wiley, 1985, para. 8.5.
[56] Scottish Law Commission (1986), para. 3.19.

created in readable text on the eavesdropper's monitor, and recorded.[57] The radiation emitted by computers is known as Radio Frequency Interference or Electromagnetic Radiation (EMR). Mainframes and minicomputers emit EMR from all sides of the terminal, including the screen display, as well as from printed circuit tracks and internal wiring. Some cables, particularly those connecting VDUs, disk drives, and printers, also emit the signals. Telex and facsimile machines are similarly vulnerable. The technology necessary to intercept EMR is similar to that used in television licence detector vans, and is relatively cheap and easy to assemble and operate. Electromagnetic radiation can generally be picked up within a range of 200 metres, though occasionally further. The effectiveness of the technique was demonstrated convincingly by a Dutch engineer, van Eck,[58] in 1985, though its potential had been discussed long before. With the move from traditional mainframe computers to mini-computers and personal computers the opportunities for eavesdropping have increased. As an espionage device computer eavesdropping is rather hap-hazard, since the eavesdropper has no way of determining what material will be intercepted, but there is always a chance that useful information will be obtained, perhaps data being entered into the computer prior to encryption. It may also provide a means of obtaining access to passwords. There is plenty of advice from the computer security industry about protecting computer installations from eavesdropping.[59] Computer manufacturers are investig-ating the possibility of producing equipment which does not emit EMR, but this development is still some way off. The most effective interim solution appears to be to limit the emission of EMR, by radio frequency filtering techniques, or the shielding of equipment or parts of the building itself, so that it does does not pass beyond the building and cannot be intercepted externally.[59a] Some military and governmental installations have been protected for some time by a system called Tempest, which provides complete screening, but this is expensive and is not regarded as being generally commercially viable.

Whilst computer eavesdropping has received a good deal of attention in the press and computer journals, the extent of the problem is unclear. The computer crime surveys do not disclose examples but, if the technique is pursued effectively, it is likely to remain undiscovered. As we shall see, the main legal problem in this area is whether a justification can be found for criminalizing computer eavesdropping where exactly the same spying, but without the use of such a technical device, would not be criminal. To read someone's papers, or read their computer screen, by looking through their office window with binoculars is no offence in English law. If no special case

[57] For accounts of computer eavesdropping see I. Beale, 'Computer Eavesdropping: Fact or Fantasy?' (1986–7) 4 *Computer Law and Security Report* 14, Sieber (1986) and Cornwall (1987).

[58] W. van Eck, *Electronic Radiation from Video Display Units*, Netherlands: PTT dr Neher Laboratories, 1985.

[59] e.g. R. Potts, 'Emission Security' (1988–9) 3 *Computer Law and Security Report* 27.

[59a] In April 1990 Pilkington announced the development of eletronically leak-proof glass.

for criminalizing computer eavesdropping can be made out, the issue then is whether it can be dealt with in some other way, or whether the whole area of the law relating to privacy and 'spying' should be considered afresh. A criminal offence of 'surreptitious surveillance by a technical device' was proposed back in 1972 by the Younger Committee,[60] but was never acted upon.

(ii) Computer Fraud

Incidents of fraud form the largest proportion of reported incidents of computer misuse. The Caulfield Institute of Technology's survey in Australia has found that various forms of computer fraud made up 60 of the 123 incidents of computer abuse so far identified.[61] Other surveys are broadly in line with this. In the majority of computer fraud cases the object of the fraud is the assets represented by the data held in the computer system. These may be intangible, in the form of deposit money, credit balances, and credit ratings. Fraudsters will manipulate data representing salaries, invoices, pensions, welfare benefit payments, and bank accounts. Clearly, as the trend towards a cashless society increases, these methods of fraud will become much more prevalent, largely replacing paper and ledger frauds. A particular risk here is the massive sums of money which are transferred in this way through electronic funds transfer. In other cases, however, the object of the computer fraud is to remove tangible assets such as cash or cheques, taken away after the computer has been manipulated into providing them. Examples are the manipulation of cash dispensers and electronic vending machines.

Computer-related frauds may be perpetrated in many different ways and by authorized or unauthorized users of the computer. Probably the best way to subdivide such frauds is in terms of the stage at which the computer was involved in the perpetration.[62] First, input to the computer may be tampered with, by falsification, addition, or removal of information prior to or during its introduction into the computer. Such alterations, known as 'data-diddling', may be designed to cause the computer to generate payments to the fraudster's own bank account, or to that of an accomplice, or it may be to delete or suppress evidence of other illegal activities. Fictitious favourable credit information may be added or unfavourable information deleted from computerized files. Data such as purchase transactions or sales credits may be inflated, or subtracted, as where sales data or purchase returns are suppressed. Payrolls are also vulnerable to this kind of fraud. Such fraud is typically committed by clerks, data-typists, and operators responsible for the collection, checking, transmission, and input of data to be processed.

---

[60] Younger Committee, *Report of the Committee on Privacy*, Cmnd. 5012, London: HMSO, 1972. See, further, p. 89 below.

[61] Caulfield Institute of Technology (CIT/CARB), (1984).

[62] For comprehensive accounts of computer fraud techniques and countermeasures see J. Krass and A. MacGahan, *Computer Fraud and Countermeasures*, New York: Englewood Cliffs, 1979, and Comer (1985).

Second, the operation of the computer itself may be affected directly by the fraudster, by altering computer codes or operational programs on the computer. Programs may be introduced by the fraudster which operate to channel funds to a specified account, the program subsequently wiping itself out. Third, the computer output may be suppressed or altered to commit or cover up the fraud. These divisions are not watertight and frequently more than one of the methods will be involved in any one fraud, such as where input is tampered with and output is adjusted to conceal resultant losses. A further distinction may be drawn between the regular siphoning off of small amounts, perhaps together with efforts to cover up the fraud, with the intention of ensuring that the losses remain unobserved and the fraudster remains in place, and the much larger one-off fraud committed with little attempt at concealment but in the expectation that by the time of discovery the fraudster will have collected the proceeds and disappeared.

In their survey of computer fraud and abuse in 1987, 118 incidents were reported to the Audit Commission.[63] Sixty-one of these were classified as fraud, of which 57 were designated input frauds, three were program frauds, and one was an output fraud. This great predominance of input fraud mirrors the figures obtained by the Audit Commission in its earlier surveys in 1981 and 1984, and it is confirmed by research surveys elsewhere. Input fraud probably represents an area of such high risk, because it is the stage in the computer processing cycle at which manual effort is required. Often relatively little computer knowledge is required to perpetrate such frauds. The Audit Commission has noted in its Reports in 1984 and 1987 that the input frauds which have come to light were not particularly sophisticated, but took advantage of inadequate security controls. In particular, there was insufficient division of staff duties, which is a basic security requirement, inadequate training and supervision of staff, and an absence of controls at the input stage where transactions were not authorized or checked.

In one case of input fraud noted by the Audit Commission,[64] a company payments officer created unauthorized payments by submitting dummy invoices to the computer she was responsible for, having previously set up a dummy creditor's reference number. Cheques produced by the computer were sent to an address which was used to pick up mail. Over a five-month period £14,000 was obtained. In another,[65] involving £80,000 over eighteen months, the fraud was based on feeding spurious purchase invoices into the accounts department to the computerized purchase ledger system. The sales manager was able to authorize the opening of new supplier accounts on the purchase master file, originate purchase orders, authorize the completion of receipts for goods received, and approve invoices for payment. Cheques, automatically produced by the computer and signed using a cheque-signing machine, were sent to fictitious addresses created by the sales manager. Stock

[63] Audit Commission, (1987).   [64] Case 4.   [65] Case 9.

figures were amended in an attempt to cover up the fraud. In a third case,[66] a clerk in a housing benefits department prepared and input to the computer fraudulent claims in respect of his brother-in-law. Payments totalling £12,000 were made to various building society accounts. The perpetrator then moved on to another organization and used a similar scheme to produce twenty-nine further claims worth, in total, over £11,500.

The second major category of computer fraud is program fraud. Though these have attracted media attention there is little evidence that they occur very frequently. Since they involve manipulation of software programs they require substantial ability in computing. Three techniques in particular have been identified and have been given exotic names.[67] The 'Trojan horse' fraud requires that the perpetrator adds to or modifies instructions in the computer software before the program is run. When it is run the effect of the modification, or 'patch', is to channel funds into the fraudster's account. The program may be written in such a way as to become operational only after a certain triggering device is operated and so as to erase itself leaving no trace once the fraud has occurred. The 'trapdoor' refers to a variety of programming methods which allow the fraudster to gain access to portions of the computer to which he would not have authorized access.

One technique is to write a program which duplicates the normal logging-on procedure. When an authorized user logs on he is presented with the substituted program and, when requested, supplies his password, which is recorded by the fraudster for his own subsequent use. As this log-on will fail, the authorized user will try again, successfully this time, and not question the initial failure. The 'salami' type fraud refers to a method of fraud which involves inserting a program patch which removes very small sums of money from a large number of accounts so that users do not notice anything missing. A typical example is the 'round down fraud', where the computer rounds down any fractions of a penny on interest payments and diverts these to the fraudster's account. An almost certainly apocryphal case centres on the fraudster who opened an account in the name Zwana (or, according to another version of the story, Zzwicke) and programmed the computer to transfer small fractions from all other customer accounts to the last named file on the customer list. The fraud was detected by a snap audit of a number of customer accounts, including the first and last accounts alphabetically. According to Comer's detailed analysis of the techniques of corporate fraud,[68] 'The hub of all programming frauds is a trigger, or conditional jump, which diverts transaction data from a genuine routine into a fraudulent one . . . (H)igh levels of skill and almost unrestricted access are necessary to patch programs.' One case where these necessary conditions obtained is mentioned by Norman.[69] A computer programmer working for a service bureau was employed on computerizing the cheque handling system of the bank where

---

[66] Case 20.   [67] See Krauss and MacGahan (1979) for details.
[68] Comer (1985), p. 178.   [69] Norman (1983), case 66,010.

his own account was held. He wrote the program in such a way that it would ignore any overdraft on his own account. This was later discovered by accident when the computer system broke down and manual account processing turned up his overdraft, then standing at $1,357.

A variation on the program fraud theme occurred in an unreported English case[70] in 1987, where an accountant and a systems analyst had formed a company which developed and marketed a software package aimed at video recording hire shops. The package gave shops a system for keeping stock records, monitoring the hiring of videos and the hire income. Within the program was a hidden 'patch' which, when activated by the input of a password, allowed a shopkeeper to conceal part of his earnings each day, so that his statement of earnings for VAT purposes could be reduced. The software package had been sold to 120 retailers but apparently only 12 of these were party to the agreement to defraud the Customs and Excise. Tax underpaid as a result of the scheme amounted to £100,000.

The object of output fraud may be to distort the computer output in order to perpetrate or conceal a defalcation, or it may be to steal the output. The output of the computer is generally based upon the input, so that pure output frauds which do not also involve input fraud are rare. In several cases the defendant's accomplice, by tampering with the computer input, has caused the computer to print negotiable cheques in the defendant's name, which the defendant has then cashed. Two such cases are noted by the Audit Commission[71] in 1984, one involving theft of cheques to the value of £229,185. One of the best-documented incidents of computer misuse, the Flagler Dog Track case,[72] is probably best described as an output fraud. The facts were that the dog track accepted bets on a totalizer system. Bets would be placed on dogs at a number of ticket machines around the course. The fraudulent computer manipulation concentrated on the trifecta winners pool. A winning trifecta wager required correct prediction of first and second placed dogs in three consecutive races. All trifecta wagers went into a pool which, after track and state fees were deducted, was divided amongst the winners. A winning bet of $2 would often have a pay-off of several thousand dollars or more. For other wagers the pay-off amounts were displayed on boards around the course, but this was not the case for trifectas. The trifecta pay-off was derived by the track computers and displayed only after the completion of the last three races. The fraudsters manipulated the system, closing down one computer and causing the other to issue additional winning tickets immediately the races were over. Each legitimate winner received a lower pay-off than they should have received since the pool had to be divided amongst more winners. The fraud

---

[70] *IRC* v *Atkinson and Allsop*, Derby Crown Court; Audit Commission (1987), case 59; discussed further in Chapter 5.

[71] Audit Commission (1984), cases 59 and 60.

[72] M. Hochman, 'The Flagler Dog Track Case' (1986) 7 *Computer and Law Journal* 117; Norman (1983), case 77.090; Krauss and MacGahan (1979), p. 6.

involved six people, continued for five years, and netted some $1 million. It was uncovered by an auditor for the State Gambling Commission on a chance enquiry.

(iii) *Unauthorized Removal of Data or Programs*

Information in intelligible form can be taken and used by any person who gains access to it, by committing it to memory, noting it down, photographing it, or otherwise recording it. In each of these cases there need be no physical interference with the medium in or on which the information is stored. This is a principal objective of the industrial spy, who wishes the victim firm to remain in ignorance of the loss for as long as possible.[73] Increasingly, information of great commercial value or information containing sensitive personal data is held on computer files. Computer espionage may be particularly lucrative for the industrial spy, whose target may be development, research or production data, cost accounts, balance sheet and customer addresses, or confidential in-house computer programs themselves. Since unauthorized access to this kind of material and information is potentially very damaging it should be guarded against by appropriate security measures, particularly physical security and computer access control such as the use of passwords and data encryption. In 1982 the Security Commission, in a Report to the British Government, noted the risks involved and commented that,[74]

The amount of data that is capable of being stored upon a single disc or magnetic tape and the rapidity approaching instantaneity with which the data can be retrieved means that any vulnerability to access by hostile intelligence services of material stored in computers or word processors could be a major disaster to this country and in particular to the efficacy of those involved in secret intelligence work.

Unauthorized access to the information may be achieved by a number of methods. It may be read off a VDU linked to the computer where the data is stored, either by an unauthorized person gaining physical access to the computer itself, or by the implantation of a listening device, a remotely operated camera, or the recreation of the data from electromagnetic radiation emitted by the computer equipment. Standard techniques of industrial espionage[75] include the corruption or blackmail of employees, the infiltration of employees from rival companies into the organization for a short period (the 'hello-goodbye' method), and the formal or informal interviewing or

---

[73] K. Hodkinson and M. Wasik, *Industrial Espionage: Protection and Remedies*, London: Longman, 1986.

[74] Home Office, *Statement on the Recommendations of the Security Commission*, Cmnd. 8539, London: HMSO, 1982.

[75] See P. Hamilton, *Espionage and Subversion in an Industrial Society*, London: Hutchinson, 1967; R. Farr, *The Electronic Criminals*, New York: McGraw-Hill, 1975; M. Saunders, *Protecting Your Business Secrets*, London: Gower, 1985; Hodkinson and Wasik (1986).

entertaining of key workers from a rival organization in order to extract information about research and development. It may be obtained by temporary removal of a disk or tape with a view to copying and returning the physical object once the information has been copied. Or it may be obtained by an unauthorized user accessing the computer directly or from long range, through hacking, reading the relevant information or transferring a copy of it to the accesser's own files. A wide range of electronic devices is now available to improve upon the traditional techniques of the industrial spy or eavesdropper. Micro-transmitters can be placed in rooms where sensitive information is to be discussed. Such transmitters are commonplace and easy to obtain. Most of them transmit continuously once installed but some can be activated and de-activated by remote signal. These transmitters are very difficult to detect by physical search since they are so small and may be concealed in furnishings, light fittings, desk equipment, behind pictures, or even plastered into a wall. Silent and invisible flashlight photography can be achieved in darkness and cameras can be adapted to focus and take pictures through minute holes drilled in walls or furniture. Laser beams generated from outside a building can be reflected off the window of a room in which sensitive information is being discussed. Because speech sound-waves cause the window pane to vibrate very slightly, it is possible to record a signal from the reflected beam and re-create the speech.

Quite apart from data contained on the computer, some computer programs may themselves be extremely valuable, being the product of expensive and protracted research and design effort. Secret programs are a primary target for computer espionage. In one case[76] reported to the Audit Commission in 1987, a contract systems programmer had privileged access to the computer system and he used this to remove tapes out of hours and copy them. The copying came to light when he offered to sell the copies to his next employer. In another case[77] a computer operator, after resigning from his job, took with him a copy of a magnetic tape containing utility programs, which he thought might gain him credibility with new employers. The broader issue of the clandestine copying of commercially available computer programs requires special mention here. The West European software market is estimated to be in the order of £10 billion. A great deal of revenue, perhaps £1 billion per annum, is lost through software piracy, much of it the routine copying of software within commercial organizations.[78] Such copying is generally very easy to do, since most users will have copying facilities in their existing hardware. A first copy of the software will be bought, and then copies will be made for the tens or perhaps hundreds of personal computers within

[76] Audit Commission (1987), case 67.
[77] Case 65.
[78] Federation Against Software Theft, 'Submission to the European Commission on the Software Piracy Implications of the E.C. Green Paper on Copyright' (1989) 5 *Computer Law and Practice* 94. See further M. Dunning, 'Some Aspects of Theft of Computer Software' (1983) *Auckland University Law Review* 273.

the company. The copyright legislation is obviously of particular importance here, and the question of the role of the criminal law in the context of this legislation is discussed in Chapter 4.

Many cases of computer espionage have come to light, and there is no doubt that far more have not been publicized by their victims. In 1982 an attempted espionage attack on IBM by twenty individuals working for Hitachi was thwarted by an FBI 'sting' operation.[79] In 1984 twenty-five computer disks containing instructions for glass-cutting machines went missing from Waterford Crystal in the Republic of Ireland. Although they were eventually recovered, it seems clear that they had already been copied by an industrial rival.[80] On the industrial cases Cornwall comments:[81]

What is unusual about these cases of computer-assisted industrial spying and piracy is not that they happened but that they were fairly fully reported . . . Giants in information technology and the pharmaceutical industry have, for the last thirty years at least, been prime targets for concerted industrial espionage activity. Computer companies, together with defence industry concerns, have been the targets not only of spies employed by their rivals, but also those supplying the needs of foreign intelligence agencies.

In the most serious case yet to come to ight, it was alleged in 1989 that a group of West Germans, some of them computer hackers and the rest contact persons and espionage agents, managed to gain access to highly sensitive data on nuclear research and defence industries in Europe, the United States, and Japan using Milnet, a computer network linking defence plants, laboratories, and military installations.[82] All this information was, apparently, subsequently sold to the KGB over a period of fours years, who paid for it in cash and hard drugs. The KGB were reported to be prepared to pay large sums of money for information about hacking techniques, passwords, and security systems, information about silicon chip construction, software, and data files about military and scientific projects. The hacking activity came to light fortuitously when Clifford Stoll, a Harvard scientist and computer security expert working in San Francisco, noticed a discrepancy in a time-sharing bill and devoted considerable time and energy to tracking down the hackers. The defendants were charged with various offences including an offence of computer hacking which was introduced into West German law in 1985. One of the hackers committed suicide prior to the start of the trial, which is now due to start early in 1990, after some of the charges were dropped by the prosecutor towards the end of 1989.

[79] BloomBecker (1985).
[80] Cornwall (1987), p. 102.
[81] Ibid., p. 103.
[82] Reported in *The Times*, 4 March 1989; see also U. Wuermeling, 'New Dimensions of Computer Crime: Hacking for the KGB' (1989–90) 4 *Computer Law and Security Report* 20, and C. Stoll, *The Cuckoo's Egg*, London: The Bodley Head, 1990.

(iv) *Unauthorized Use of Computer Time or Facilities*

A frequently encountered form of computer misuse involves the accessing of the computer in order to make use of computer time or facilities to which the person making access is not entitled. Such misuse, often referred to as 'theft of services' or 'time-theft' may, once again, be committed by a person who has authorization to use the computer at other times or for other purposes, or by an outsider, by hacking. The objects of the activity are the processing, storage, and transmission services of the computer hardware and often also programs and data, which are used by the unauthorized operator for his own purposes.

Some of the earliest reported hacking cases involved enthusiasts, often university students, managing by illicit means to gain time on campus mainframe computers in order to learn how to use them. Now it is much more likely that an employee will be involved, using his employer's computer for purposes other than the job in hand. Large multi-user time-sharing systems are also targets for unauthorized use, either through authorized users exceeding their entitlement or unauthorized users posing as authorized ones. Some of this misuse is relatively trivial, as where an employee uses his employer's computer to play computer games, or to design programs for his personal use in the firm's time. Other cases are more serious, where the employee may effectively be running his own business through misuse of his employer's facilities. In one of the more spectacular cases[83] two Philadelphia computer programmers employed by Sperry-Univac used the company's computer to run a music-arranging business. Working on the company's computer, the two programmers spent three years developing a program for rewriting music into different styles, selectively editing it and printing out scores. It seems that they misused $144,000 worth of computer time. Eventually, and particularly in a case like this, significant unauthorized use of the computer will have a discernible effect on the time taken for legitimate tasks to be completed by the computer. Norman observes that while the computer operating system may maintain a constant log of machine use, 'in practice nobody ever looks at it'.[84]

In the computer fraud survey conducted by the Audit Commission in 1984, 17 of the 77 cases uncovered involved this kind of misuse.[85] The majority did not involve large losses, but the Audit Commission felt it appropriate to comment that[86] 'Forecasts of the future risks of fraud and abuse emphasise that the misuse of resources is likely to present the greatest problems for management.' Similarly, the authors of the Computer Crime Survey of the American Bar Association[87] identified cases of theft of resources as being the most frequently encountered in their survey and predicted that it was the area most likely to expand in the future. Thirty of the 123 cases in the Australian

[83] Norman (1983), p. 167.   [84] Ibid., p. 276.   [85] Audit Commission (1984).
[86] Ibid., p. 18.   [87] American Bar Association (1984).

survey were of this type,[88] though many were not particularly serious. In their 1987 Report, the Audit Commission reported 13 cases of 'unauthorized private work'. These involved no direct financial loss to the victims, though the Commission points out that there are often substantial costs involved in investigating the incidents, and in one of their cases these totalled £5,000. In one reported case,[89] a progam purchased for use by the company to control energy costs of premises was used by an employee in the course of running his own business. He used the company's equipment and software in office hours to provide energy surveys for other organizations. These surveys were sold as part of a consultancy business which he ran. In another case[90] an accountant in a senior post used his micro after hours in connection with a relative's business, for purposes of stock evaluation.

   In general, a fairly tolerant attitude is taken towards most incidents of this type. Many of those involved see little wrong in what they do, and some employers turn a blind eye or permit limited private use of desktop computing facilities. In the second case cited the individual involved said that the work had taken up no office time, no stationery, and a minuscule amount of electricity. As we shall see, misuse of computer time or facilities rarely infringes the criminal law, and in practice the only sanction available, even in blatant cases, is that of disciplinary measures or dismissal by an employer. Cornwall comments:[91]

Sensible managers will take a pragmatic view of each situation: in one sense the modest use of a computer for private applications could be considered a perk of many computer-orientated jobs ... Again, some exploratory activity can be seen as a form of self-training by employees and so to the benefit of the company's management.

Levels of tolerance differ, however, and there are many who take the view that certainly the more serious forms of 'time-theft' should attract the attention of the criminal law. In a memorandum to the Law Commission on the subject of computer misuse the CBI, for example, asserts that 'serious, dishonest acts of private use should be brought within the criminal law'.[92]

(v) *Destruction or Damage*

Many reported incidents show that computer installations and computer hardware represent attractive targets for the infliction of deliberate damage, though some writers understandably exclude accounts of damage to hardware from their 'computer crime' data. The practical and perhaps the symbolic importance of computer installations has meant that they have on occasions become the subject of malicious, sometimes terrorist attack. Deliberate

   [88] CIT/CARB (1984).
   [89] Audit Commission (1987), case 108.
   [90] Case 113.   [91] Cornwall (1987), p. 26.
   [92] CBI, 'Submission to the Law Commission on Working Paper No. 110 on Computer Misuse' (1989–90) 1 *Computer Law and Security Report* 14.

damage may be perpetrated by employees, as a form of industrial sabotage.[93] In one case a computer operator over a two-year period persistently short-circuited an internal disk drive by jamming a metallic object between the computer circuits.[94] Extremist European magazines recommend various techniques for damaging computers, for use in pursuit of labour conflicts within a company,[95] including pouring saline solution or caustic cleaning agents into the operating console, blowing smoke or hair spray into the computer, putting a container of hydrochloric acid in front of the air-conditioning induction pipe, interfering with power lines, and even placing mice under a raised floor where they can gnaw through electric wires.

The Stanford Research Institute study[96] of 1975 unearthed no fewer than 66 cases reported in the American press and elsewhere of physical attacks upon computers, including four cases of computers being shot by their operators! Student unrest in the United States at the time of the Vietnam war resulted in several attacks on computer centres.[97] Towards the end of the 1970s and into the 1980s, there were terrorist attacks by the Red Brigade on computers in Italy, and in France by hitherto unknown terrorist groups, who declared themselves to be challenging 'the present and future dangers of computer systems' and 'capitalist data processing'.[98] In 1983 there was a bomb attack on a West German computer centre, committed by a group protesting against the participation of the computer company in the production of nuclear missiles.[99] In San Francisco in 1988 a woman described in the press as a 'peace activist' was jailed for five years and ordered to pay $500,000 after attacking a computer system, which she believed was designed to launch a nuclear attack, at Vandenberg Air Force Base with a crowbar, electric drill, and bolt cutter and emptying the contents of a fire extinguisher into the computer.[100] Amongst the burgeoning literature now available on computer security, one aspect is defence of tangible computer assets against damage or theft. One writer advocates the adoption of 'a combination of methods such as receptionist control, closed circuit television, guard surveillance, combination or uniquely keyed locks and identification cards and pictures'[101] as necessary to achieve physical security of a computer installation.

While some countries have adopted computer crime legislation which specifically outlaws criminal damage in respect of computer installations or

---

[93] L. Taylor and P. Walton, 'Industrial Sabotage: Motives and Meanings' in S. Cohen (ed.), *Images of Deviance*, London: Pelican Books, (1971), 219.
[94] Norman (1985), p. 106.   [95] Sieber (1986), p. 15.
[96] D. B. Parker, Stanford Research Institute Report, *Computer Abuse Assessment*, Menlo Park, Calif.: Stanford Research Institute, 1975.
[97] Scott (1985), para. 8.10.   [98] Norman (1983), pp. 185, 229.
[99] Sieber (1986), p. 15.
[100] *US v Komnaruk*, unreported, California, 1988, cited in R. Bigelow, 'Computer Security, Crime and Privacy—US Status Report' (1988–9) 6 *Computer Law and Security Report* 10.
[101] V. P. Lane, *Security of Computer-Based Information Systems*, London: Macmillan, 1985. See also R. Sizer and J. Clark, 'Computer Security: A Pragmatic Approach for Managers' (1989) 11 *Information Age* 88.

computer hardware this seems quite unnecessary where generally applicable existing laws cover such situations. These developments probably reflect the extremity of the view that computer materials represent a particular temptation to crime, and that specific computer crime legislation is needed to provide a special deterrent effect.

More difficult, however, are cases where the form of damage which occurs is damage to computer programs or data. Again, there are numerous well-documented cases where, for instance, programs have been deliberately erased or magnets have been used to wipe information from computer tapes, sometimes for political reasons, sometimes as the result of an employee's grudge. In other cases manipulation or destruction of data has been achieved by remote terminal, sometimes as a prank, sometimes for commercial reasons. The vulnerability of industry to interference with computing facilities makes the threat of corruption of programs or data a very serious one. A common method of causing such damage is by the introduction of a 'crash program' or 'logic bomb', which can erase a large volume of data within a very short time. Such a program, once inserted, may be activated at a later date, long after the perpetrator has left.[102]

Most recently, a variation of sabotage techniques has developed, whereby 'cancer' or 'computer virus' programs have been created and deliberately introduced into computer networks.[103] While it has been suggested that it is possible for a computer virus to arise spontaneously from existing computer code, the evidence for this is thin. It is clear that the vast majority of such programs are deliberately created with mischievous intent. Virus programs have been known about in the United States since the early 1980s, but recently they have spread world-wide. These are relatively simple purpose-built programs which, when introduced into a computer, are self-reproducing, contaminating other programs and data files. They may be introduced through using a computer disk which already contains an infected program or through a computer communications link. If computer security arrangements can be bypassed, a virus can be inserted or transferred from another computer via the link. Of similar impact are computer 'worms' which, when introduced, replicate themselves rapidly, filling up the computer's disk storage devices with unwanted files so that the machine eventually shuts down from overloading. Of course where the computer is connected by telephone line, it may be accessed from anywhere in the world.

During 1988, a so-called Amiga virus was found to have caused considerable damage to research holdings at the Hebrew University in Jerusalem.[104]

---

[102] e.g. Norman (1983), p. 81.

[103] There is now a massive literature on this topic. For a comprehensive treatment see P. Fites, P. Johnston, and M. Kratz, *The Computer Virus Crisis*, New York: Van Nostrand Reinhold, 1989.

[104] B. Zajac, 'Computer Viruses: The New Global Threat' (1988–9) 1 *Computer Law and Security Report* 3, 31; C. Bremner, 'Virus Plague Wreaks Havoc with Computers', *The Times*, 1 Jan. 1988.

This virus was started up on the Commodore Amiga 500 machine, but soon spread to Amiga business computers. In the United States the 'Lehigh' virus,[105] emanating from a university in Pennsylvania, destroyed numerous files by propagating itself via a particular named file on personal computers. The virus was designed to hide in a file which would be accessed regularly by users. Each time it was accessed, the virus would infect another file. When the disk was introduced into a different machine the infection would spread there too. Also in 1988 a worm, apparently introduced by a postgraduate student at Cornell, infected the Arpanet (Advanced Research Projects Agency) System run by the Department of Defense at the Pentagon.[106] It was transmitted from computer to computer through electronic mail provided by Arpanet. The rogue program was discovered by a scientist working at a nuclear weapons research laboratory in California, who noted exceptionally heavy use of the computer system. It brought 6,000 computer terminals to a standstill for a day and a half, but apparently the disruption could have been much worse since the *New York Times* reports that as many as 60,000 computers are tied in to the Department of Defense network and were at risk of contamination. In Britain in October 1989 great media attention was given to the impending impact of the Friday 13 viruses Datacrime 1 and Datacrime 2, but when the 13th of October arrived there was relatively little disruption, apart from a chastened *Times* correspondent[107] in the United States who reported suffering erasure of a story on which he was working—about computer crime!

The most effective defence to computer viruses or worms lies in security precautions against unauthorized access and, in particular, not using unknown or suspect software. Once a virus or worm has been introduced it may be very difficult to eradicate, requiring expert assistance. It is likely that a further program, specifically written and designed to 'kill off' the virus, will have to be introduced. There are now some general 'vaccination' software packages available,[108] which can cure the computers by checking for and eradicating the suspect code in the system, but these will not always be effective. Just before Christmas 1988 the internal computer network of IBM was affected by a virus which proliferated yuletide greetings accompanied by a picture of a Christmas tree which appeared on screens. This virus proved relatively easy to deal with, and in-house experts eradicated it within a couple of hours. In early 1989 it was reported that Digital Equipment, the world's second largest

---

[105] B. Zajac, 'Computer Viruses: Can They Be Prevented?' (1989–90) 1 *Computer Law and Security Report* 18.

[106] J. Bone, 'Computer Virus Invades Pentagon', *The Times*, 5 Nov. 1988. In Jan. 1990 it was reported that Robert Morris, aged 24, and the son of a government adviser on computer security, was convicted under the Computer Fraud and Abuse Act in the United States in respect of this incident. M. Wines, 'FBI Investigates Network Crash', *The Times*, 9 Nov. 1988; Zajac (1988–9).

[107] N. Nuttall, 'Fear Proves More Infectious Than Software Disease', *The Times*, 14 Oct. 1989; C. Bremner, 'Friday 13 Virus Bugs The Times', ibid.

[108] Zajac (1988–9).

computer company, had discoverd a worm computer program, codenamed 'jig', which had been introduced to its computer network, originating at the company headquarters in Boston. Apparently the worm was identified quickly, some parts of the computer network were uncoupled to reduce its spread, and a vaccine program was written to eradicate it.

3. THE PERPETRATORS

According to Mandell:[109]

The popular view of the successful computer criminal is interesting and somewhat unsettling. Most companies would be eager to hire personnel who fit this description. Often such people are young and ambitious with impressive educational credentials. They tend to be technically competent and come from all levels of employees, including technicians, programmers, managers and high-ranking executives.

To what extent is this picture borne out by the evidence? Once again, there is some information to be gleaned from the computer misuse surveys.

One hundred and sixty participants responded to the American Bar Association survey[110] questions about the identity of the perpetrators of the crime. Nearly 40 per cent of perpetrators had not been identified. Of the remainder, programmers tended to predominate, and then there was a fairly even balance of executives, computer operations supervisors, workers, outside consultants, and individuals having no prior link with the organization, though more (125 cases) came from within the organization suffering the loss than from outside it (73 cases). In the NCCCD computer crime census[111] of computer crime cases processed through courts in the United States, a more detailed breakdown of perpetrators was made. The percentages obtained were: programmer (21 per cent), student (14 per cent), input clerk (14 per cent), bank teller (10 per cent), accomplice (10 per cent), unskilled (7 per cent), unemployed (7 per cent), employee with access (6 per cent), computer executive (5 per cent), and miscellaneous (6 per cent). In the Audit Commission survey[112] in 1987, where 118 cases were identified, the great majority of frauds seem to have been perpetrated by persons within the organization defrauded, though the identity of 14 fraudsters was unknown. The fraudsters were categorized as clerk/data processing operator (33 per cent), supervisors (17 per cent), director/management (8 per cent), programmer/analyst (8 per cent). There was also a large 'other' category (17 per cent). The losses produced by those in positions of higher authority tended to be larger. The Commission commented that 'As in the 1984 survey it remains a worrying feature that around a quarter of the cases were committed by individuals holding posts of responsibility'.[113] In the Australian study[114] 16 per cent of

---

[109] Mandell (1984), p. 155.   [110] American Bar Association (1984).
[111] BloomBecker (1986).   [112] Audit Commission (1987).   [113] At p. 21.
[114] CIT/CARB (1984): in fewer than half the cases was the employment of the perpetrator known.

perpetrators were not identified, 70 per cent were employees, and 14 per cent were outsiders. Of the total of 123 cases, 18 per cent were perpetrated by programmers, 8 per cent by customers, 8 per cent by operators, 7 per cent by input clerks, and 7 per cent by students. Empirical studies in West Germany show that the vast majority of detected computer manipulations were committed by employees.[115] The proportion of employee to outsider in all of these studies is fairly consistent and seems to be broadly in line with Levi's survey on commercial fraud in general,[116] which found that in three-quarters of the cases analysed, the offender was an employee. The percentage they obtained were manager (29 per cent), accounts official (19 per cent), sales-person/shopfloor (13 per cent), director/partner (10 per cent), distributor/driver (6 per cent), and computer operative (3 per cent).

Consistent in all these studies is that the great bulk of computer misuse which has come to light is committed by individual employees within the company which becomes the victim. Those employees who have regular and unimpeded access to computers clearly pose a risk, but fraudsters and other misusers are certainly not confined to the computer specialists within the company. This pattern must be seen in the context of the general background of computerization which was described in some detail in Chapter 1. According to Norman:[117]

Computer people must have enquiring minds, which are frequently associated with a taste for mild mischief. They are likely to see a computer system's security measures as a personal challenge, and will set about defeating them. In the course of such an exercise, they are likely to find their way through the flaws in the defences and put themselves in a position to exploit them for other reasons than harmless fun.

While this is certainly true, the phrase 'computer people' must now be expanded substantially to take account of the increasing numbers of computer-aware employees who have legitimate access to desk-top micros. This is borne out by the Audit Commission survey, for instance, where one-third of input frauds, the largest category, were committed by clerks in the user departments. As we have seen, the input frauds generally require little specialized technical know-how. Similarly, in the West German studies it has been found that 90 per cent of perpetrators detected were employees of the victim firm and that 60 per cent, particularly in the field of input manipulation, did not have specialist skills.

By far the most important motive for the commission of computer fraud is surely the same motivation that there has always been for fraud: financial gain. In his discussion of motivation of white-collar criminals generally, Stotland[118] observes that

[115] Sieber (1986), p. 11.
[116] Levi (1986).
[117] Norman (1983), p. 17.
[118] E. Stotland, 'White Collar Criminals' (1977) 33 *Journal of Social Issues* 179 at p. 185. See also S. Box, *Power, Crime and Mystification*, London: Tavistock, 1983.

... some analyses go as far as to state simply that it is all a matter of greed. In more psychological terms, the greed can be translated into some theoretical conception such as relative deprivation, of not having as much money as some group that one perceives as being a relevant standard. This group standard may take the form of certain luxurious forms of living commensurate with a high status in society.

Studies of white-collar crime have discovered a range of particular triggering factors, which tend to distinguish the dishonest from the honest employee, and which are likely to be relevant to computer misuse also. One is financial difficulty which an employee finds himself in: the temptation to take advantage of the employer's funds to tide him over what is seen as a temporary problem. Another is seeking a lifestyle which is beyond the salary legitimately available. An employee may feel envious and resentful at the financial success of the company and believe that his own contribution is worth more than is represented by his salary. A whole range of personal difficulties may underlie the money motivation, such as crises in marriage or sexual life, gambling, alcoholism or drug dependence in the family. An actual or perceived lack of interest by management in the staff fosters resentment and increases the risk of fraud. There is also the matter of loyalty to a firm. It has been argued that the employee's sense of loyalty to his employer has weakened considerably in recent generations,[119] and that this is particularly so of computer staff who change employment regularly. The lack of a feeling of loyalty makes frauds by employees more likely. Frauds are not limited to recently recruited staff. In the Audit Commission survey in 1987 there were a number of incidents reported where employees had been in the post for upwards of ten years and had worked in the particular organization for twenty years or more. Yet at higher management levels individuals may adhere to a subverted sense of corporate loyalty in the wish to secure and hold down positions of responsibility and influence within huge corporations. In a corporate computer crime, such as the Equity Funding case, many employees were involved in the conspiracy, although some knew only of part of the deception. Stotland suggests that[120] 'Some were recruited because they had committed small crimes, which made it easier to get them to commit larger ones. The strength of the group pressures is suggested by the fact that the conspiracy went on for several years without a meaningful leak.' The Equity Funding case should remind us, however, that it is a mistake to assume that computer misuse is always committed by individuals against corporate victims. This assumption is inherent in most of the computer crime surveys which have so far been conducted, which target corporations as the victim population. Corporations, or at least their controlling officers, are computer misusers, too.[121]

As we have seen, it is characteristic of white-collar criminals to persuade themselves that their depredations are not really crimes, particularly where

[119] Norman (1983), p. 22. [120] Stotland (1977), p. 190.
[121] See R. Kling, 'Computer Abuse and Computer Crime as Organisational Activities' (1980) 2 *Computer and Law Journal* 403.

no discernible individual has suffered, but rather a corporate enterprise. This again eases the passage into dishonesty, with typical 'justifications' such as 'This is really a perk', 'Everyone else does it', 'They owe it me anyway', 'No one is really losing', and 'The insurance will pay'.[122] Another factor mentioned by Stotland is the relative sense of superiority with respect to their victims often displayed by white-collar criminals. He remarks that while often the original motivation for crime may have been economic, secondary satisfaction is obtained by the knowledge that they have fooled the victim:[123]

In a competitive, open society this respect for intelligence is inevitable. Yet intelligence is in danger of becoming a golden calf. Our admiration of intellectual acuity may give the intellectually acute implicit permission to feel so superior that they feel that they have a right to rise above ordinary concerns such as right and wrong.

This sense of superiority may be fuelled to some extent by the perception of a degree of public toleration for some computer misuse though, as we have seen, this argument has often been exaggerated, particularly in respect of lucrative fraud.

This intellectual challenge is fired in the computer environment by the need to overcome security devices and so on, but again this aspect should not be overstated since the evidence shows that most computer fraud, certainly that which comes to light, is actually quite simple in conception and operation. It is clear that in computer fraud as well as in fraud generally the greatest losses occur through fairly obvious opportunities and utilize quite simple methods. Fraud is one of the clearest examples of rational choice offending,[124] where the risk of being caught can be controlled to a significant extent by planning and rational decision-making. Employees take advantage of opportunities presented to them where the temptation is for some particular reason greater than usual, security is slack, and the chance of detection seems slim. Computer security experts emphasize the overwhelming importance of 'people risks' and Comer,[125] among others, has stressed the importance of staff training in basic company computer security procedures to restrict the opportunity for fraud.

The motivations underlying other forms of computer misuse, such as the deliberate corruption or destruction of data or software, are in general distinct from those which underlie fraud. Here the key factors seem to be three: boredom, dissatisfaction, or malicious intent.[126] In the case of boredom the act is usually committed by a skilled computing professional who thinks that his abilities are not being used to the full and who feels undervalued. Corrupting the system is a way of 'making a mark', which may also provide

---

[122] Cornwall, (1987), p. 144.   [123] Stotland (1977), p. 187.

[124] See e.g. D. B. Cornish and R. V. Clarke (eds.), *The Reasoning Criminal*, New York: Springer-Verlag, 1986.

[125] Comer (1985).

[126] D. Davies, 'Computer Losses During 1988: A Review' (1989–90) 1 *Computer Law and Security Report* 2.

an opportunity to demonstrate a degree of computer skill which may be far in advance of that shown by senior managers in the company. Such professionals may be primarily interested in developing new computer systems and applications and feel frustrated if this aspect of their employment has dried up. Disaffection or the harbouring of some grievance against the firm has often been noted as a motivating force, whether for physical damage or more insidious corruption of the system. A computer security consultant speaking at a conference recently suggested that psychological tests at the staff recruitment stage could weed out potential employees who were likely to cause problems. He suggested that there was a need to take precautions against 'mischief makers, grudge holders and loners'.[127] There seems to be a particular risk from employees who have just left a company's employment, who may corrupt or erase information stored on computer as a parting gesture. This may not be effective immediately, but involve the placing of an instruction to the computer to wipe out certain files at some time in the future. Much of this behaviour seems to have the same complex roots as vandalism or its more specialized form, industrial sabotage. According to Cohen,[128] vandalism can be vindictive, where it is done as an emotionally satisfying form of direct or indirect revenge, tactical, done as a means to achieve some particular result, or malicious, where the action is done as a kind of practical joke, very much for its own sake and for the enjoyment to be derived from it. Each of these forms have their expression in computer-related damage. The first is seen in numerous cases where the employee has harboured a grudge against the company and leaves a mark on the computer system to gain revenge; the second is neatly illustrated by a West German case where the computer operator repeatedly disabled the computer he was working on in order to enjoy an amorous rendezvous with the wife of the repairman in charge of the computer.[129] The third seems likely to be the main motivation for the creation and introduction of computer viruses, since the extent of the resultant damage and the identity of the range of victims is generally unpredictable.

There can be overlap with fraudulent motives where the damage or destruction merely paves the way for financial gain, perhaps by way of blackmail. In a case[130] which occurred in Britain in 1977, a computer operations supervisor and a systems analyst removed 48 disk packs and 540 tapes, including back-up copies, from their employers ICI, and demanded £275,000 for their return. Much of this information was vital to ICI, who estimated that it would take six years' work to recreate the data. The blackmailers partially erased one of the files and sent it to ICI, and threatened

---

[127] Y. Henniker-Heaton, 'The Human Risks: An Auditor's Point of View' (1986–7) 3 *Computer Law and Security Report* 21; R. Matthews, 'Psychology to Beat the Hackers', *The Times*, 2 Feb. 1989.

[128] S. Cohen, 'Property Destruction: Motives and Meanings' in C. Ward, *Vandalism*, London: The Architectural Press, 1973. [129] Sieber (1986), p. 17.

[130] *Cox and Jenkins* (1979) 1 Cr App R (S) 190; Norman (1983), p. 178.

to destroy all the material if the money was not paid. The scheme failed when the defendants were arrested when they tried to collect the ransom money. Another motivation for destruction or damage, aimed at computer hardware or software, is political protest or terrorism. The actual and symbolic importance of computers makes them a target not only for individuals within the company who have a political grievance, but also for terrorist attack, as has already been demonstrated by the Red Brigade in Italy and by terrorist organizations in West Germany and France. In one of the French incidents,[131] the terrorist group Action Direct destroyed computer programs and data valued at £250,000 during a raid on the offices of the Philips company in Toulouse, claiming that this material was for the use of the armed forces and the French counter-espionage service. The destruction appeared to have been the work of people with specialist knowledge of computers.

4. THE VICTIMS

It seems that no sector of society is exempt from the risks associated with computer misuse. In the NCCCD computer crime census the bulk of victims were described as commercial users, banks, telecommunications authorities, and government. Losses were also incurred by individuals, computer companies, retail firms, and universities.[132] The 1987 Audit Commission survey uncovered computer fraud incidents within the previous three years in the central government, local government, public utilities, communications, manufacturing, finance, health, food, retail, and education sectors.[133] Again, of course, in all of these cases the targeted population was that of computer users, so the surveys have nothing to say about the extent of corporate misuse of computers in the process of business crime, such as consumer fraud, where members of the public or corporations may be characterized as the ultimate victims.

The Audit Commission Report in 1984 stated that[134] 'none of the cases appeared to demonstrate any ingenious application of technological skills: indeed the majority took advantage of inherent weaknesses in particular procedures'. They also noted that the general survey finding, that the majority of reported computer misuse takes the form of fraud involving manipulation of input data, 'serves to emphasize that the absence of basic controls provides opportunities which some feel unable to resist'. It is clear that improvements in fundamental controls and safeguards could reduce the risk and numbers of occurrences quite significantly. The Audit Commission says:[135]

The risks of fraud and abuse will be all the greater if internal controls are inadequate. Poor supervision and ineffective audit will almost certainly encourage the opportunity

---

[131] Norman (1983), p. 229.　　[132] BloomBecker (1986).
[133] Audit Commission (1987), p. 8.　　[134] Audit Commission (1984), p. 14.
[135] Ibid., p. 15.

for large scale and long-running losses. Where the organization sustains such an environment and still encourages the widespread introduction of computing the risks will be considerable.

Once again, the 1987 Report suggests that 'the risk of fraud and abuse would have been minimized' if 'fundamental internal controls had been imposed and adhered to'.[136]

The Data Protection Act 1984 requires that 'appropriate security measures shall be taken against unauthorized access to, or alteration, disclosure or destruction of, personal data and against accidental loss or destruction of personal data'.[137] Whilst this applies solely to personal data held on computer, it is not unreasonable for these principles to extend to all data. In the United States, Congress has established the Small Business Computer Security and Education Act of 1984, a computer security and education programme to provide small business concerns with information about the management of computer technology, computer misuse, and computer security, and to provide those concerned with training on computer security techniques. An advisory group has been established to assist the executive in implementing the statute.[138]

The duty of the employer must surely be to encourage responsible computer use amongst employees. According to the Audit Commission, however, the drive and determination of many organizations to promote a better understanding of computers amongst its staff may well result in an attitude that encourages games-playing, developing programs to satisfy personal rather than corporate needs, and using the desk-top micro at home to continue the education process.[139] This has also certainly been the case within universities, where numerous examples have come to light of students being encouraged by their teachers to devise procedures to bypass security devices. In 1973, for instance, there was a sponsored student contest at the Massachusetts Institute of Technology to find the cheapest and most effective technique for circumventing the security of magnetic-stripe cards.[140]

In writings on white-collar crime, part of the ambivalence toward the perceived seriousness of the offence has been the role of the victim. Criminal law is almost exclusively concerned with the conduct and culpability of the offender rather than with victim conduct and does not find it difficult to sanction the burglar even though the victim left the house unlocked. In academic writing, however, there has been some interest in the role of the victim in 'precipitation' of crime.[141] It is a characteristic of white-collar crime that the offence is often seen to turn upon the conduct of the victim as much as

---

[136] Audit Commission (1987), p. 15.

[137] Data Protection Act 1984, Principles of Data Security No. 4.

[138] See, for detailed discussion, B. J. George, 'Contemporary Legislation Governing Computer Crimes' (1985) 21 *Criminal Law Bulletin* 389; M. D. Scott, *Computer Law*, New York: John Wiley, 1986.

[139] Audit Commission (1987), p. 18.   [140] Norman (1983), p. 131.

[141] D. Miers, *Responses to Victimisation*, London: Professional Books, 1978.

that of the offender. Edelhertz has noted the importance in this kind of lawbreaking of 'reliance by the perpetrator on the ignorance or carelessness of the victim'.[142] The negligence of the victim can, in an extreme case, be used as an argument to shift some of the blameworthiness from the offender. One explanation for non-reporting of white-collar crime is a kind of embarrassment on the part of the victims at their own negligence, rather than indifference to victimization. As Walsh and Schram[143] suggest, in some cases 'the fact of victimization may reflect more negatively on the victim than on the offender'. Similarly, in the complex commercial world, some view the victims of white-collar crime merely as losers, outsmarted in 'a game among sharp practitioners',[144] and incidents of computer misuse as 'routinized occurrences in criminogenic environments'.[145] Traditional victimology has concentrated upon crimes committed between individuals, and we have more difficulty in perceiving organizations as being the victims of crime. Perhaps the answer is to view the crime as committed against the employees, customers, and shareholders of the company. Victimization is, none the less, indirect and diffuse.

Based upon the view that computer crime is substantially under-reported, and that police action on fraud tends to be reactive rather than proactive,[146] relying on the initial reporting to them of such offences, it has been suggested that victims should be placed under a statutory duty to report to the police any incidents of computer crime of which they become aware. Some of the state computer crime laws in the United States contain such an obligation, and this mirrors a more general obligation in that country placed upon victims to report financial crime. The Criminal Code for the State of Georgia,[147] for instance, imposes a duty on 'every business, partnership, college, university, person, governmental agency or subdivision, corporation or other business entity having reasonable grounds to believe a computer crime has been committed to report a suspected violation promptly to law enforcement authorities'. The Society of Conservative Lawyers and the British Computer Society are among those groups on record as supporting the introduction of comparable laws here, placing a duty upon computer users to disclose incidents of computer crime of which they have been the victim, but both the Scottish and English Law Commissions have decided against recommending it, although a number of respondents were strongly in favour.[148]

---

[142] H. Edelhertz, *The Nature, Impact and Prosecution of White-Collar Crime*, Washington, DC: Government Printing Office, 1970; see, further, Chapter 1.

[143] M. E. Walsh and D. D. Schram, 'The Victim of White-Collar Crime: Accuser or Accused?' in G. Geis and E. Stotland (eds.), *White-Collar Crime*, Beverly Hills, Calif.: Sage Publications, 1980.

[144] Levi (1987), p. 136.

[145] Kling (1980), p. 407.

[146] Levi (1987), p. 136.

[147] Ga Code Ann s. 16–9–95.

[148] Scottish Law Commission (1987), paras. 5.8–5.11; Law Commission, Report No. 186 (1989*b*), para. 4.14.

The arguments in favour of introducing such a duty are that non-disclosure conceals the true extent of the computer crime problem, so that potential victims are less alive to the risks than they should be, perpetrators are encouraged to commit fraud, or not deterred from continuing, and shareholders are kept in ignorance of the true situation and are unable to review the adequacy of management strategy. The objections, which the two Law Commissions found more persuasive, are ones of principle and of practice. The main objection of principle is that, with very few exceptions, such as the special case of road traffic accidents,[149] there is no duty on the public to disclose or report any crime committed in the United Kingdom. Indeed, the Criminal Law Act 1967 abolished the offence of misprision of felony, which had penalized an omission to report any felony to the police.[150] It would, therefore, be anomalous to create a duty in respect of computer crime where it did not exist for business crimes generally or, indeed, for offences such as murder or rape. The Commission questioned exactly who would be subject to such a duty, and how it would be enforced. Should all crimes be reported, regardless of the seriousness of the loss involved, and to whom should the loss be reported? There is also the familiar difficulty of defining 'computer crime' for this purpose and the difficulty of enforcing any such duty. Singling out computer-related crime for the obligation of reporting does seem inappropriate. Perhaps, however, there is a more coherent case to be made out for an obligation placed upon key officials in respect of business crime generally. Company liquidators, for example, are already under a statutory obligation[151] to report to the Official Receiver and/or the Director of Public Prosecutions every case where it appears to them that a criminal offence has been committed by any past or present officer or member of a company which they are involved in winding up. There is also the issue of the proper role of the auditor in reporting fraud. This is discussed in Chapter 6, in the context of the problems of detection and prosecution of cases of computer misuse.

---

[149] Road Traffic Act 1988, s. 170.
[150] In its place the Criminal Law Act 1967, s. 5(1) creates a much more restricted offence.
[151] Insolvency Act 1986, s. 218.

3

Unauthorized Access and Unauthorized Use

In those jurisdictions where there has been the greatest development of the criminal law in response to computer misuse, particularly the United States, the most important approach has been to criminalize the initial unauthorized access of the computer. Some computer crime statutes penalize 'computer trespass', whatever the motivation or reason for that intrusion. Often there are also aggravated forms of the offence, turning upon proof of an intent to defraud, steal, or embezzle, or upon proof of harmful results following the unauthorized access.[1] Thus, according to Scott,[2] regardless of what a defendant does after gaining unauthorized access, the access itself may well constitute a criminal offence under United States federal or state legislation if the defendant (i) gains access by false pretences, such as by using another's password or a false password to gain access, (ii) gains access for the purpose of committing a criminal act, such as theft, often regardless of whether the goal is actually achieved or (iii) gains access by improper means, such as by wiretapping.

The choice of this avenue for law reform reflects a decision by law reform agencies to tackle computer misuse in terms of the initial wrongful access, rather than addressing the range of property offences which the person gaining unauthorized access may have in mind at the time of access, and which may all require redrafting to take account of the computer dimension. There is also a ready, though inexact, parallel between gaining unauthorized access to material held on a computer and existing criminal offences, particularly burglary. In short, criminalizing the initial act of unauthorized access offers the simplest route for law reform in that it removes, or at least postpones, the need to criminalize the 'theft of information' or the gaining of other intangible benefits by the accesser. It may be characterized by the reformer as a necessary updating of the criminal law, rather than a significant extension of its boundaries. The popular equation of computer misuse with 'hacking' from a remote terminal tends to promote the same solution. The American approach has been followed in several other jurisdictions, and it has now been adopted in Britain, with the passing of the Computer Misuse Act

---

[1] B. J. George, 'Contemporary Legislation Governing Computer Crimes' (1985) 21 *Criminal Law Bulletin* 389; G. Thackeray, 'Computer Related Crimes' (1985) 25 *Jurimetrics Journal* 300.
[2] M. D. Scott, *Computer Law*, New York: John Willey, 1985, para. 8.5.

1990. While there is much to recommend this strategy, and it seems the best approach overall, objection may be levelled at criminalizing and recommending a heavy punishment for what is essentially a preliminary act of 'trespass'. Trespass into someone's home is ordinarily a civil rather than a criminal wrong and it seems anomalous that trespass should amount to a criminal offence merely because a computer is involved.

The Scottish Law Commission,[3] in the first comprehensive survey of this area of law undertaken by a law reform body in Britain, proposed law reform broadly along these lines, recommending the creation of two offences, which would cater for the obtaining of unauthorized access to a program or data stored in a computer, where a specific further criminal purpose could be proved, but they stopped short of proposing that unauthorized access *per se* should be an offence. A Private Member's Bill,[4] sponsored by Emma Nicholson MP, which was introduced in summer 1989 but withdrawn on the understanding that the government would introduce its own legislation in due course, took a similar line. The English Law Commission then produced a Report[5] which went further than did its Scottish counterpart, in proposing the creation of a basic offence of 'unauthorized access to a computer', punishable in a magistrates' court, and an 'ulterior intent' offence, where the unauthorized access was accompanied by an intent to commit or facilitate the commission of a serious crime. In the event, the government did not find time in its legislative programme for a Bill to criminalize computer misuse, and it was left to a Private Member, Mr Michael Colvin, to sponsor a Bill which reflected closely the English Law Commission proposals. This Bill became the Computer Misuse Act 1990, and its provisions are considered in this Chapter and in Appendix 4 below, where the full text of the Act is set out, together with a commentary.

1. HACKING

It became quite clear after the decision of the House of Lords in *Gold and Schifreen*[6] that there was no specific criminal offence in England which could be used to deal with the unauthorized use of a legitimate user's password or the use of a false password to gain access to information stored in a computer. There is no general offence of impersonation in English law and none of the traditional property offences in the Theft Acts 1968 and 1978 can be made out on these facts. It had been thought by some[7] that an offence under the Forgery and Counterfeiting Act 1981 might be utilized in such a case, but a

---

[3] Scottish Law Commission, *Report on Computer Crime*, Cm. 174, Edinburgh: HMSO, 1987.
[4] Set out in App. 2, below.
[5] Law Commission, Report No. 186, *Computer Misuse*, Cm. 819, London: HMSO, 1989.
[6] [1988] 2 WLR 984 (HL).
[7] e.g. R. A. Brown, 'Crime and Computers' (1983) 7 *Criminal Law Journal* 68.

prosecution under this statute, while proving successful at trial, ultimately resulted in the convictions being overturned on appeal. This meant a substantial limitation on the prospects for successful prosecution of the hacker or other computer misuser, where no dishonest or malicious intent at the time of access could be proved, and where no offence consequent upon access had been committed. Some hackers at least are, as we have seen, motivated solely by curiosity, admiration for computers, and the intellectual challenge of overcoming computer security devices in place. Their activities were found to be outside the ambit of English criminal law.

In *Gold and Schifreen*, by taking advantage of some slack security procedures, the defendants, a freelance computer journalist and an accountant, were able to gain unauthorized access to material contained in the Prestel computer system, a public information service, and to user files containing all the identification numbers and passwords of subscribers. According to various accounts of the background to the case Schifreen, who was a subscriber to Prestel, came across a supposedly secure identification code when testing new computer equipment and used it to access the system. By keying in a very simple set of numbers (eight 2s) and a very obvious password (1234) he obtained access to the account of a British Telecom employee, which contained confidential numbers of Prestel computers not available to the public. By using those numbers he was accepted by the system as an authorized user of the passwords. Schifreen passed on the computer information to Gold, who also accessed the computer. They altered files. They also found codes belonging to the Duke of Edinburgh, amongst others, and used the Duke's number to access his private electronic mailbox, leaving the message 'Good afternoon, HRH Duke of Edinburgh'. The identity of the hackers became well known when Gold and Schifreen talked of their exploits on a BBC television programme and were interviewed by the computer news magazines. Schifreen gave a demonstration of the method of computer access to one reporter after which, apparently, he encouraged the reporter to inform British Telecom of the security lapse. Even after Prestel had been informed, the defendants continued with their unauthorized accessing of the system. Clearly, they did not expect to be prosecuted but, in the event, they were charged with forgery. Section 1 of the Forgery and Counterfeiting Act 1981 provides:

A person is guilty of forgery if he makes a false instrument, with the intention that he or another shall use it to induce somebody to accept it as genuine, and by reason of so accepting it to do or not to do some act to his own or any other person's prejudice.

There is a twin offence of using a forged instrument, by section 3 of the Act:

It is an offence for a person to use an instrument which is, and which he knows or believes to be, false, with the intention of inducing somebody to accept it as genuine, and by reason of so accepting it to do or not to do some act to his own or any other person's prejudice.

Nearly all cases of forgery can also be prosecuted as obtaining either services or property by deception, or as an attempt to do so. In such cases the courts have said that a forgery charge is unnecessary and should not be pursued.[8] On the present facts, though, a deception-based offence would not have availed the prosecution, because apparently only the computer, and no human mind, was deceived by what the defendants did.[9] Moreover, section 1 does require that 'somebody' accepts the false instrument as genuine. This potential difficulty is anticipated in the Act and catered for by section 10(3):

> In this Part of this Act references to inducing somebody to accept a false instrument as genuine . . . include references to inducing a machine to respond to the instrument . . . as if it were a genuine instrument . . .

In fact all nine counts brought against the defendants were under section 1, five against Schifreen and four against Gold. The prosecution's argument was that the 'false instrument' was 'made' by entering the customer identification number (CIN) and password of a genuine subscriber into the user segment of the computer by electronic means with the intention of making a Prestel computer accept it as genuine, to the prejudice of British Telecom PLC. The company was said to have been prejudiced because it was thereby induced to provide the defendants with Prestel services without charge, the sum involved being some £379.[10] At trial the defendants were convicted on all counts, in six cases on majority verdicts. They were fined £750 and £600 respectively and each ordered to pay £1,000 costs. The judge commented that normally forgery would attract a prison sentence but that this was an exceptional case. It should not thereby be assumed, he said, that subsequent similar cases would also be dealt with leniently.[11]

The real difficulty with this decision was to determine what exactly constituted the 'false instrument'. While the statutory offence prior to 1981 spoke of forging a 'document',[12] the 1981 Act prefers 'instrument', defined by section 8(1) to be:

(a) any document, whether of a formal or informal character;
(b) any stamp issued or sold by the Post Office
(c) any Inland Revenue stamp
(d) any disk, tape, sound track or other device on or in which information is recorded or stored.

The Law Commission said of its own draft provision, which although not reproduced in identical terms in the Act, was very similar in its effect, that:[13]

---

[8] _per_ Lord Ackner in _More_ [1987] 3 All ER 825; R. Rowell, _Counterfeiting and Forgery_, London: Butterworths, 1986.   [9] See further Ch. 4.

[10] In fact, s. 10(4) indicates that no 'prejudice' need be proved beyond the misleading of the machine itself.

[11] Trial unreported; see reports in _The Times_, 8 Dec. 1984, 13 June 1985, 16–25 Apr. 1986.

[12] Forgery Act 1913, s. 1(1).

[13] Law Commission, Report No. 55, _Forgery and Counterfeit Currency_, London: HMSO, 1973, para. 36.

'The increasing use of more sophisticated machines has led us to include within "instruments" capable of being forged the disks, tapes and other devices . . . which may cause machines into which they are fed to respond to the information or instructions upon them.' As far as the requirement of 'falsity' is concerned, section 9 of the Act provides an exhaustive definition, the central notion of which is said to be that the document must tell a lie about itself:[14] the document itself must be false, not merely the information contained within it. The unauthorized use of a Prestel subscriber's password was, then, argued by the prosecution to be similar to signing a cheque in someone else's name. The instrument would be a forgery because it would tell a lie about itself and would be tendered with the intention of inducing a person to accept and act upon the message contained in it, in this case by allowing access to material held on and services provided by the computer.

On appeal, Lord Lane C.J. said that to secure a conviction the prosecution had to prove that the appellants made a false instrument, and that whether they had done so was the central issue in the case. There were two possible candidates to qualify as the false instrument: (*a*) the electronic impulses and (*b*) the user segment of the computer. The Court soon reached the view that the electronic impulses could not themselves constitute the instrument, since they were intangible and all the examples given in section 8 of the Act were tangible: the impulses 'were not of the same genus as disk, tape or sound track'.[15] The prosecution placed more reliance upon the second option. Their argument was that the user segment of the computer received the information (the CIN and password) and retained or stored it for a period which was required to verify it against user files held in the computer memory. For that brief moment the user segment became a false instrument made by the appellant who had keyed in the CIN and password. This argument was rejected by the Court, on the basis that the Act was not designed to deal with a situation where information was held for a fleeting moment while automatic checking took place and then expunged: such a process was not one to which the words 'recorded or stored' in section 8(1)(d) could properly be applied, suggesting as they did a degree of continuity. A further difficulty was that under section 1 of the Act it had to be shown that the appellants intended that someone should be induced to accept as genuine the false instrument they had made, and it was contended that it was the machine which had been induced to respond. This, according to the Court of Appeal, entailed finding that:[16] 'the user segment, which was intended to be induced seemed to be the very thing which was said to be the false instrument, that is, the user segment which was inducing the belief. If that analysis was correct, the prosecution case was reduced to an absurdity.' A further appeal to the House of Lords was unsuccessful,[17] Lord Brandon endorsing the views of the Court of Appeal. He

[14] Ibid.; confirmed in *More* [1987] 3 All ER 825.
[15] [1987] 3 WLR 803, at p. 808.
[16] At p. 809.   [17] [1988] AC 1063.

agreed with the Lord Chief Justice that there was no reason to regret the failure of the prosecution, which had been a procrustean attempt to force the facts of the case into the language of an Act not designed to fit them.[18]

The case has been the focus of much subsequent discussion,[19] and the Law Commission delayed the production of their Working Paper on computer misuse to take account of the decision of the House of Lords. Surely, with respect, the House of Lords was entirely right to reach the view which it did. The wording of the offence simply did not fit the facts and it is appropriate for Parliament rather than the judges to make the kind of extension to the criminal law which would have been required to produce convictions in this case. While the central issue is whether the gaining of unauthorized access to the computer should be criminalized or not, it is sometimes overlooked that the defendants might well have been guilty of the offence of criminal damage in altering data once they had accessed the system. This possibility is discussed further in Chapter 5.

If, however, we envisage a person such as a hacker, working entirely from motives of curiosity, and merely inspecting data without changing anything, such accessing of the computer was not, prior to the Computer Misuse Act 1990, a criminal offence. Should it be? There are strongly held views on this matter, and sometimes they come from surprising quarters. Some argue that 'pure' hacking is harmless, indeed even socially desirable, in that it may point up security weaknesses in computer systems which can be remedied before being exploited by less well-intentioned individuals. Alistair Kelman,[20] a barrister specializing in computer law, takes this view:

I don't want to see curious hacking made a criminal offence. We get a lot of useful information about gaps in the security of computer systems from hackers, which are often suppressed by manufacturers. Hackers are being made the whipping boys for generally lax computer security. The moment it is criminalized, manufacturers can start saying it is not a matter we need to worry about because it is a criminal activity.

The Data Protection Registrar, Eric Howe, has also voiced concern that criminalizing hacking may encourage system managers to be less vigilant and computer security conscious. It has even been suggested that making hacking

---

[18] At p. 1069.

[19] Law Commission, Working Paper No. 110, *Computer Misuse*, London: HMSO, 1988, I. Lloyd, 'Computer Abuse and the Law' (1988) 104 *Law Quarterly Review* 203; D. I. Bainbridge, 'Hacking: The Unauthorized Access of Computer Systems: The Legal Implications' (1989) 52 *Modern Law Review* 236. A stern critic of the decision is Tapper, who argues that it is 'unfortunate that their Lordships should baulk in this way at extending the meaning of words such as "recording" or "storing" when used in the context of the computer. It seems immaterial whether a piece of false information requires to be stored for a short or a long period to accomplish its object. If words in common usage cannot be adapted to deal with modern technology, the terminology of the law will have to become even more curious and jargon-ridden than it is at present.' See C. Tapper, *Computer Law*, 4th edn., London: Longman, 1989, p. 292.

[20] Cited in M. May, 'How a Hacking Law Could Weaken Security', *The Times*, 20 Apr. 1989.

a crime will attract further attention to it and might thereby encourage others to try.

On the other hand Steven Gold, one of the defendants in the case, argued subsequent to his acquittal that 'computer trespass' should be criminalized:[21]

If Schifreen or I had been aware that our activities were illegal—and not just a process of investigative journalism—it is unlikely that we would have pursued our activities in the manner in which we did. By informing British Telecom of our discoveries, we felt that we were doing them a service. We were therefore astonished when we were charged with forgery in March 1985. If the law relating to computer misuse remains unchanged . . . then the hapless DP manager will remain unprotected against computer hackers, unless they cause damage or deprive him of money.

The arguments on both sides were very well marshalled by the Law Commission in its Working Paper on Computer Misuse.[22]

The main arguments in favour of creating a specific offence of 'computer trespass' are that, given the great and increasing importance of computers in modern society, it is in the public interest that those who use and rely upon computers should not be hampered by the fear that others may gain un-authorized access to material held on the computer, particularly where that information is sensitive or confidential. While this is primarily a matter of confidentiality, concerns are not confined to this. The great dangers posed by hackers disrupting the operation of computers in fields such as defence, nuclear power, air traffic, or the health service were outlined in Chapter 1. The hacker may accidentally corrupt or destroy information held on the computer, even apart from any malicious intent. In-built computer security measures may respond to attempts to access the system by closing the system down, causing inconvenience and expense. On the other hand, as we have seen, some people argue that hacking is a relatively harmless recreation and may even provide positive benefits to computer users by indicating security weaknesses. Additionally, arguments against the creation of such an offence are that it would to a large extent criminalize an invasion of privacy in respect of computer-held information, which would be anomalous where no general right of privacy is recognized by the criminal law. Why should obtaining unauthorized access to confidential material held on computer be an offence where if the same material were retained on a card index no offence would be committed? Further, to create an offence of 'computer trespassing' would be anomalous where trespass in the sense of unauthorized entry into a person's house, is not generally a criminal matter.[23] The response to the argument from anomaly, however, is that special treatment is already accorded to

---

[21] S. Gold, 'Hackers: Are They a Threat to World Peace?' *Computer Talk*, 28 Nov. 1988.
[22] Law Commission (1988), Pt. VI.
[23] Proposals for the introduction of a general offence of trespass were mooted in a Home Office Consultation Paper, *Trespass on Residential Premises*, London: HMSO, 1983, though not acted upon. See also Criminal Law Act 1967, s. 9 (trespass on a diplomatic mission).

computer-held data by the Data Protection Act, though the statute is largely concerned with civil rather than criminal remedies, and the reassertion that the great social and economic importance of the computer makes it a 'special case'.

In its Report on Computer Misuse, issued in September 1989, the Law Commission recommended the creation of three new offences, one of which was the 'basic unauthorized access' or 'basic hacking' offence.[24] Because of the speed with which the Report was published, in response to government pressure to produce recommendations which could be acted upon without delay, the Report had no Draft Bill attached to it and consequently no precise definition of the proposed offences. It is clear, however, that the offences in the Computer Misuse Act 1990 are squarely based upon the wording in the Law Commission's Report.[25] By section 1 of the Computer Misuse Act 1990:

> 1(1) A person is guilty of an offence if—
>   (a) he causes a computer to perform any function with intent to secure access to any program or data held in any computer;
>   (b) the access he intends to secure is unauthorized; and
>   (c) he knows at the time when he causes the computer to perform the function that that is the case.
> (2) The intent a person has to have to commit an offence under this section need not be directed at—
>   (a) any particular program or data;
>   (b) a program or data of any particular kind; or
>   (c) a program or data held in any particular computer.

A marginal note describes this offence as being one of 'unauthorized access to computer material'. Section 1(3) provides that the offence shall be summary only and punishable with imprisonment for a term not exceeding 6 months, a fine not exceeding level 5 on the standard scale (currently £2,000), or both. Before the application of this offence is considered in detail, two points should be made about the meaning of key terms.

The Law Commission, in its earlier Working Paper on Computer Misuse, relied heavily on the phrase 'unauthorized access to a computer',[26] but this term is potentially misleading, as it may be taken literally to cover unauthorized access to the computer hardware itself. The Law Commission stated that 'obtaining access to a computer' was not meant to include 'the obtaining of physical access thereto',[27] but in the absence of a definition of 'access', the term would have covered the case of a person who manufactures and uses a skeleton key to enter the computer room. There is room for confusion

[24] Law Commission (1989*b*), paras. 3.4 et seq.
[25] Ibid., para. 3.14. See App. 3, below.
[26] Law Commission (1988), criticized by M. Wasik, 'Law Reform Proposals on Computer Misuse' [1989] *Criminal Law Review* 257 at p. 263.
[27] Law Commission (1988), para. 1.16.

between the general term 'access' and the computer-specific derivative 'accessing'.[28] In the United States, the term 'access' is also used in this context as a verb, and it occurs in many State computer crime laws, most frequently broadly defined as[29]

> to instruct, communicate with, store data in, retrieve data from, or otherwise obtain the ability to use the resources of a computer, computer system, computer network, or any part of a computer system or network.

Other states have preferred the term 'use', though it is very similarly defined.[30] It may be noted that the Scottish Law Commission adopted the term 'access' after rejecting the alternative 'to communicate with' on the basis that the latter presupposed a two-way interchange which, on the facts, may not occur. Further, they decided not to define the term.[31] While it has been argued that 'access' 'carries within it an element of purpose',[32] there is a danger that without qualification by an appropriate fault element on the part of the accesser, accidental or inadvertent accessing of the computer would be included. Nobody suggests that inadvertent accessing of a computer should be a crime.[33] The difficulties over the meaning of 'access' are neatly avoided in the Computer Misuse Act, where the term is not used as a verb. The Act provides[34] that the securing of access to a program or data is established where the defendant, by causing the computer to perform any function, alters or erases the data or program, copies it, moves it, uses it or displays it.

The question of when an access is 'unauthorized' has been little discussed in the United States. The Scottish Law Commission thought that the term 'probably requires no further explanation',[35] but in any event suggested that it meant 'not having authority granted by the person or persons entitled to control access to the program or data in question'.[36] This presents no difficulty where the access is by an outsider, but it may be more contentious where the access is made by an employee who has limited permitted access to the computer but on this occasion does so without permission, or acts in excess of that permission. In this case of 'partial authorization', the Scottish Law Commission suggested that any new offence should apply where the

[28] It is interesting to note that the latest edition of the *Oxford English Dictionary* now accepts that 'access' may be used as a verb, and defines 'to access' as 'to gain access to data etc. held in a computer or computer-based system, or the system itself'.

[29] e.g. Alaska Stat s. 11.46.99(1); Cal Penal Code s. 502(a)(1); Idaho Code s. 18–2201(1); Ill Ann Stat ch 38 s. 16–9(a)(7). For others see George (1985), p. 406.

[30] e.g. Colo Rev Stat Ann s. 18–5.5–101(1); Va Code s. 18.2–152.2(4).

[31] Scottish Law Commission, Consultative Memorandum No. 68, *Computer Crime*, Edinburgh, 1986, para. 4.10.

[32] George (1985), p. 406.

[33] See Scottish Law Commission (1987), para. 4.10 and CBI, 'Submission to the Law Commission on Working Paper No. 110', summarized at (1989–90) 1 *Computer Law and Security Report* 14.

[34] By s. 17(2). See App. 4, below.

[35] Scottish Law Commission (1987), para. 4.16.

[36] Ibid.

person gains unauthorized access not just to a program or data but also to any part of a program or data to which the person concerned is not authorized.[37] The Law Commission's Report on Computer Misuse made very similar proposals, and these are incorporated into the Computer Misuse Act. By section 17(5) access is defined as 'unauthorized' if the defendant is not himself entitled to control access to the program or data and he does not have the necessary consent from any person who is entitled to give it. Further, section 17(10) explains that for the purposes of the Act any reference to a program includes a reference to part of a program. While lack of authorization will generally be clear beyond doubt where remote hacking is concerned, there may be practical difficulty where unauthorized access is alleged against an insider such as an employee, and it is unclear who had the necessary authority to grant access. In large commercial organizations which have perhaps hundreds of computer terminals, it may be difficult to prove that the defendant knew that his access was in fact unauthorized. This places an onus on computer users to improve the standard of authorization procedures in computer security management.[38]

The term 'computer' is left undefined in the Act, endorsing the Law Commission's view that it would be 'unnecessary' and 'foolish' to provide a definition. An attempt at a comprehensive definition would produce something very complex and quite possibly flawed. Technological advances might soon render a precise definition inaccurate. This matter was discussed in Chapter 1.

We can now turn to consider the new basic hacking offence in more detail. The central phrase in the offence is 'causes a computer to perform any function'. The effect is to impose liability on a defendant at a rather earlier stage than might otherwise have been possible, to include the person who 'knocks on the door' of the target computer but who is denied access by a security device, as well as the person who manages to evade the security device and succeeds in penetrating the system. In a standard log-on procedure, the computer user enters some form of identity code and password. If verified by the computer access device, and perhaps subject to further checks, the user is then offered some sort of menu of available functions. Whilst a person could not be said to have 'accessed' the computer until he had been presented with that menu and invited to proceed, the ingenious drafting of the Act means that where the computer security device operates to deny access the defendant has 'caused a computer to perform any function' and, if the necessary *mens rea* can be proved, the offence is made out. This wording seems likely to

[37] Ibid., para. 4.18, and see below.
[38] The English Law Commission makes precisely this point, at Law Commission (1989*b*), para. 3.37: 'We think there is some importance in requiring the court, in a case where there is a dispute about authorization, to identify, and to be clear about the status of, the person alleged to have authority to control the access which is in issue. In our view (and consultation has confirmed the point) such regulations should be laid down as a matter of good management practice . . .'.
[39] Unless special statutory provision were made: Criminal Attempts Act 1981, s. 3(1).

remain effective in the event of more advanced identification procedures becoming commonly available, such as voice or print recognition. Whatever the form of identification, the computer would still have to perform some function in response to the attempt to log on.

Another way of designing a hacking offence would be to define it in terms of 'unauthorized access' and then to rely on the law of attempt to cater for the unsuccessful hacker. One difficulty with that approach is that where the offence is a purely summary one, there can be no liability to attempt to commit it.[39] A second is that even if the law of attempt did apply, it is limited by statute to instances where the defendant, with the necessary intent, performed an act which was 'more than merely preparatory' to the offence. It is not entirely clear that this would always cater for the unsuccessful hacker.[40] On the other hand, the breadth of the unauthorized access offence would also cover some perhaps surprising cases, such as the employee who, knowing that he is not authorized to view particular data, switches on the computer on his desk in order to try to do just that. If intent can be proved, by switching on the machine the employee has 'caused a computer to perform any function' and he would, without more, be guilty of the offence.

The offence requires proof of two *mens rea* elements: that the defendant 'knew' that his intended access was unauthorized and that he 'intended' to secure access to or obtain information about a program or data held in a computer. Careless, inattentive, or even reckless accessing of computer-held material is not sufficient to establish this offence, though recklessness would have been a sufficient fault element under Miss Nicholson's Bill.[41] The wording might well cover a case, though, where the defendant gained access, without the necessary intent but, on realizing that he was now being offered, say, a chance to peruse confidential data, he took advantage of that opportunity by pressing a key. Once the defendant knows he is unauthorized, he would commit the offence as soon as he 'causes the computer to perform any function' with intent. Insistence upon proof of intent and knowledge on the part of the defendant before liability may be incurred is entirely in accord with criminal law principle, though some critics have argued that practical problems of proof in this area dictate that the prosecution's burden should be eased somewhat. They point, for example, to extended criminal provisions in the Copyright, Designs and Patents Act 1988 which, by section 107, extend liability to a person who 'knows or has reason to believe' that an article is an infringing copy of a copyright work. It is submitted, however, that the Act, based on the Law Commission's approach, is entirely sound in this respect. Questions of proof are discussed in Chapter 6.

The Law Commission intended that computer eavesdropping should fall

---

[40] Criminal Attempts Act 1981, s. 1(1). Under the Act, proximity is a question of fact for the jury. A judge may, however, withdraw the issue from the jury on the ground of insufficiency of evidence.
[41] See Appendix 2, below.

outside the scope of this offence, and envisaged that the misuse of computer time and facilities would only occasionally be punishable by virtue of it. These matters are discussed further below.

The punishment of hacking, or the unauthorized accessing of material held on a computer, may be achieved under laws now in force in several other countries.[42] Most of these create summary offences, which exist alongside the equivalent of indictable offences, made out when a further criminal intent or consequent loss or damage is established. Within Europe, the Swedish Data Act of 1973, generally regarded as being the earliest computer misuse legislation, as amended in 1982, contains in section 21 a broad 'data trespassing' offence, covering anyone who unlawfully procures access to computer-stored data. In Denmark the Penal Code Amendment Act of 1985 has reformed section 263(2) of the Penal Code, making it a crime to 'obtain access to another person's information or programs which are meant to be used in a data processing system'. Similar law has been introduced in France in January 1989. Elsewhere, the Australian Victorian Crimes (Computers) Act 1988 provides in section 9 for a new summary offence of 'computer trespass', carrying a maximum penalty of six months' imprisonment:

> A person must not gain access to, or enter, a computer system or part of a computer system without lawful authority.

In line with several other American state jurisdictions, Pennsylvania's computer crime statute provides a two-tier offence structure, the lower tier being a misdemeanour akin to trespass, covering unauthorized access, and the higher tier being a felony covering similar acts with intent to defraud.[43]

A variation upon these laws, found in other jurisdictions, is to criminalize the unauthorized access where it involves the overcoming of a computer security device. Provisions in West Germany and Norway are to this effect, the former punishing 'any person who obtains without authorization, for himself or for another, data which are not meant for him and which are specially protected against unauthorized access'[44] and the latter anyone who 'breaks a protection' in order to gain access to data.[45] The effect of this is to confine the attention of the criminal law to cases where the victim has a security device in place and the defendant uses guile to overcome it. Thus such a law discriminates against victims who have no such devices in place, and switches attention to the victim's carelessness rather than the defendant's intentions. The approach has been rejected by British law reform bodies. The Scottish Law Commission, for instance, rejected it on the basis that:[46] '(J)ust

---

[42] U. Sieber, *The International Handbook on Computer Crime*, New York: John Wiley, 1986, OECD, Information Computer Communications Policy No. 10, *Computer-Related Crime: Analysis of Legal Policy*, Paris: OECD, 1986.
[43] 18 Pa Stat Ann s. 3933.
[44] West German Penal Code, s. 202.
[45] Norwegian Penal Code, s. 145.
[46] Scottish Law Commission (1987), para. 4.15.

as the law of theft does not distinguish between householders who lock all their doors and those who do not, so too, in our opinion, it would be inappropriate to distinguish between owners with and without security devices or systems.' Perhaps the anomaly would be reduced if computer owners were obliged by law to adopt prudent computer security measures. The Data Protection Act 1984 does require this to some extent already, but only in respect of certain classes of data. The eighth Data Protection Principle,[47] set out in the Act, requires of data users, individuals, corporations, or other agencies that control the automatic processing of data, that 'appropriate security measures shall be taken against unauthorized access to . . . personal data'. The extent of such security measures must have regard to the degree of harm which could result from unauthorized access to the data and to the ease with which security can be incorporated into the system. If this principle is breached, the Data Protection Registrar has powers of enforcement which he may exercise supported by criminal sanctions.[48] The Act, however, creates no criminal offences in relation to those who obtain unauthorized access to computer held material, whether in the form of personal data or not.

2. HACKING FOR A FURTHER PURPOSE

The second type of legislative initiative has been to criminalize the gaining of unauthorized access to a computer where some further nefarious purpose can be proved. Most computer crime legislation in the United States takes this general form.[49] At federal level, part of the Counterfeit Access Device and Computer Fraud and Abuse Act 1984 prohibits activities in relation to certain information (national security, foreign relations, financial, credit) on certain computers (operated for or on behalf of the federal government).[50] The statute makes it an offence to gain unauthorized access to, or use beyond authorized access, a computer to gain classified information related to national security, financial information protected from disclosure by the Right to Financial Privacy Act,[51] or where the user knowingly uses, modifies, destroys, or discloses information in, or prevents authorized use of, the computer.

The computer crime legislation which now exists in a majority of the states[52] is also of this type. The California Penal Code contains the following provisions, upon which the legislation of several other states is based:[53]

(b) Any person who intentionally accesses or causes to be accessed any computer system or computer network for the purpose of (1) devising or executing any scheme or artifice to defraud or extort or (2) obtaining

---

[47] Data Protection Act 1984, Sched. 4.
[48] Ibid., s. 10, s. 19, Sched. 4.
[50] 18 USC, ss. 1029–30.
[52] Thackeray (1985).

[49] Scott (1985), ch. 8.
[51] 12 USC, ss. 3401–22.
[53] Cal Penal Code s. 502(1).

money, property, or services with false or fraudulent intent, representations or promises shall be guilty of a public offence

(c) Any person who maliciously accesses or causes to be accessed any
computer system or computer network for the purpose of obtaining
unauthorized information concerning the credit information of another
person or who introduces or causes to be introduced false information
into that system or network for the purpose of wrongfully damaging or
wrongfully enhancing the credit rating of any person shall be guilty of a
public offence

(d) Any person who maliciously accesses, alters, deletes, damages, or
destroys any computer system, computer network, computer program,
or data shall be guilty of a public offence.

It will be seen that these provisions combine two approaches in outlawing
unauthorized access *per se* in (d) as well as unauthorized access with a further
purpose in (b) and (c). The latter is seen as an aggravated version of the
former, attracting higher penalties. As far as other states are concerned, the
most commonly specified further purpose in these statutes is an intent to
defraud, steal, or embezzle[54] once unauthorized access to the computer has
been obtained. Otherwise, more serious offences or higher penalties are
triggered by what results from the unauthorized access. Specified consequences include the planting of false or misleading information in a
computer system,[55] obtaining[56] or disseminating[57] information to which the
accessor is not entitled, or causing damage or destruction to computer
systems, data, or software.[58]

A number of European countries have followed a similar line in their own
computer-specific criminal law or reform proposals. In Denmark, an aggravated form of computer trespass is made out by proving 'the intention to
procure or make oneself acquainted with information about trade secrets of a
company'[59] and the French law incorporates an aggravated version of
computer trespass, where the purpose is to defraud or secure other advantage.
Recent reform of the Criminal Code of Canada incorporates a comparable
provision dealing with 'unauthorized use of computers',[60] which penalizes
the use of a computer system to commit various specified offences. An
amendment to the law of the Australian Capital Territory entitled 'dishonest

---

[54] e.g. Cal Penal Code s. 502(b); Colo Rev Stat Ann s. 18–5.–102(2); Fla Stat Ann
s. 815.06(b); Minn Stat Ann s. 609.88(b), Nev Rev Stat s. 205.4765(4).
[55] Alaska Stat s. 11.46.740(a)(2), Fla Stat Ann s. 815.04(1), Minn Stat Ann s. 609.88(b), Wis
Stat Ann s. 943.70(2)(1).
[56] Iowa Code Ann s. 716A.9, Nev Rev Stat s. 205.4765(1)(e), Wis Stat Ann s. 943.70(2).
[57] Conn Gen Stat Ann s. 53a–251(e)(4), Fla Stat Ann s. 815.04(3), La Rev Stat Ann
s. 14:73.1(A)(2), Mo Ann Stat s. 569.095(1)(3).
[58] Cal Penal Code s. 502(d), Colo Rev Stat Ann s. 18–5.5–102(2), Conn Gen Stat Ann ss.
53a–253–53a–256, Idaho Code s. 18–2202(2), Wis Stat Ann s. 943.70(3)(2).
[59] Sieber (1986), p. 88.
[60] Canadian Criminal Code, s. 301.2(1); Criminal Law Amendment Act 1985, s. 46.

use of computers' outlaws a person's use of a computer 'with intent to obtain by that use a gain for himself or herself or another person or to cause by that use a loss to another person'.[61]

Both the Scottish and English Law Commissions have proposed that it should be made a criminal offence to obtain unauthorized access to material held on a computer, where a further nefarious intent on the defendant's part can be proved. The former Commission formulated the terms of such an offence in a Draft Computer Crime (Scotland) Bill, annexed to their Report.[62] The proposed penalty, on indictment, was to have been 5 years imprisonment or an unlimited fine, or both. The Commission felt on principle that the securing of unauthorized access to programs or data should only constitute a criminal offence where the prosection could prove that the defendant had the intention thereby to procure an advantage for himself or another person, or to damage another person's interests. This would have continued to exclude from the scope of criminal liability cases of hacking *per se*, or computer trespass, where no such further harm was envisaged or committed. Although the policy arguments for criminalizing hacking *per se* were discussed in the Scottish Consultative Memorandum and Report, the eventual stated reason for not recommending a computer trespass offence was the rather unconvincing claim that if all varieties of hacking were outlawed under the umbrella of one offence, it would be difficult for courts to distinguish serious from trivial breaches of the law, when sentencing.[63] Surely this problem could have been surmounted by adequate fact-finding at the sentencing stage or, better still, by the creation of an additional offence with a lower maximum penalty covering such conduct, as has been done in many American jurisdictions and has now been adopted in the Computer Misuse Act 1990, which applies to Scotland.

The English Law Commission Report, as we have seen, went further than that of their Scottish colleagues, by recommending the creation of a summary 'basic hacking offence'. They also proposed the enactment of a second tier 'ulterior offence'.[64] This proposal has now found its way into the Computer Misuse Act 1990, section 2 of which provides:

2(1) A person is guilty of an offence under this section if he commits an offence under section 1 above ('the unauthorized access offence') with intent—
    (a) to commit an offence to which this section applies; or
    (b) to facilitate the commission of such an offence (whether by himself or by any other person);

---

[61] Crimes Ordinance 1983 (ACT), 1983.
[62] See App. 1, below.
[63] Ibid., para. 4.6. See M. Wasik, 'Scottish Law Commission: Report on Computer Misuse' (1987–8) 4 *Computer Law and Security Report* 20, at p. 22.
[64] Law Commission (1989), para. 3.49. See App. 3, below.

and the offence he intends to commit or facilitate is referred to below in this section as the further offence.

By section 2(2) the further offence is defined to extend to any offence the sentence for which is fixed by law (in practice, only the offence of murder has a fixed sentence), or any offence which carries a maximum sentence of at least 5 years imprisonment on indictment. It is provided by section 2(5) that the 'ulterior intent offence' created by section 2 should itself be triable either way, punishable on summary conviction with imprisonment not exceeding 6 months, a fine not exceeding the statutory maximum (currently £2,000) and on conviction on indictment to imprisonment for a term not exceeding 5 years, a fine, or both. The ulterior intent offence under section 2 is an aggravated form of the basic hacking offence, which was discussed above. Where tried on indictment, it is open to a jury to convict of the basic hacking offence as an alternative.[65]

It will be seen that the section 2 offence would be complete whether or not the further offence was committed. It may be envisaged by the defendant that the further offence will be committed at virtually the same time as the hacking, such as where the defendant gains access to material held on a computer in order to divert funds electronically to his own bank account, or on a later occasion, such as where the defendant obtains confidential information about a person held on a computer with a view to blackmailing him in the future. The relationship between the basic hacking offence and the law of attempt was discussed above. The same issue arises here. It is clear that a conviction could be obtained for the ulterior intent hacking offence in some circumstances where the defendant would not yet have performed an act 'more than merely preparatory' to the commission of the further offence itself, so as to render him guilty of an attempt to commit that offence. In the blackmail example, just given, it is very unlikely that a prosecution for attempted blackmail would succeed where the defendant had obtained the confidential information but had taken no steps to make use of it. In theory, liability could arise at an even earlier stage, for it seems that an attempt (or a conspiracy, or an incitement) to commit the ulterior intent hacking offence could be brought by the prosecution. If, for example, a person encourages a hacker to obtain password details which are held on computer, with a view subsequently to using that information to access another computer and commit theft, liability for incitement or conspiracy would lie where the hacker was aware of that person's ulterior purpose.[66]

The Computer Misuse Act provides no list of 'further' offences beyond the general limitation that they must carry a penalty of 5 years' imprisonment or

---

[65] Computer Misuse Act 1990, s. 12.

[66] Agreement would have to be established for the purposes of a conspiracy charge, and in the case of incitement it seems that it must be proved that the person incited possessed the necessary *mens rea*: *Curr* [1968] 2 QB 944. See, however, J. C. Smith and B. Hogan, *Criminal Law*, 6th edn., London: Butterworths, 1988, pp. 255–6.

more. It is difficult to think of any important offence that this would leave out of account and, of course, even if the envisaged offence was punishable with less than 5 years, the basic hacking offence would still be available to the prosecution. The statute also makes it clear that the ulterior intent hacking offence should stand even where it can be shown that, on the facts, it would have been impossible to commit the further offence.[67]

While the details differ from one jurisdiction to another, the drift of these various new offences which outlaw hacking for a further purpose is very similar. Instead of, or in addition to criminalizing 'computer trespass' as such, they focus upon what might loosely be termed 'computer burglary'. Currently under English law the offence of burglary is established by proof of the commission of a particular offence consequent upon the initial trespass upon the premises, or on proof of ulterior intent at the time of the trespass.[68] Although the trespass itself is not criminal, it becomes so by virtue of the associated criminal purpose or the further offence. Prior to the implementation of the Computer Misuse Act, where the defendant accessed a computer with the intention of committing an offence such as theft, or the obtaining of property or services by deception, such conduct had to be prosecuted by way of the subsequent offence committed, or an attempt to commit such an offence. As we shall see in Chapter 4, the interposing of the computer in the chain of these events can sometimes render such prosecution ineffective. The difficulty of establishing liability for the further offence has, then, led the majority of jurisdictions down the road of criminalizing the initial unauthorized accessing of the computer.

3. WIRETAPPING AND EAVESDROPPING

In the United States, use of wire, telephone, or television communication facilities for the purpose of executing a scheme to defraud or obtain money or property by false pretences is a federal offence[69] even where the underlying fraudulent activity is strictly not a federal or state offence.[70] Such use must be proved to be in furtherance of the scheme and not merely incidental to it.[71] The wiretapping laws predate and hence were not designed to deal with the problem of unauthorized access to a computer, and whether they apply in a given case is inevitably somewhat arbitrary. In *US* v *Seidlitz*,[72] the use of telephone wires to copy computer software led to a wire fraud conviction and

---

[67] Computer Misuse Act 1990, s. 2(4); a rule parallel to that contained in Criminal Attempts Act 1981, s. 1(2).

[68] Theft Act 1968, s. 9.

[69] 18 USC, s. 1343.

[70] *US* v *Kelly* 507 F Supp 495, 498 n6 (ED Pa 1981), *US* v *Gallant* 570 F Supp 303 (SDNY 1983).

[71] *US* v *Alston* 609 F 2d (DC Cir 1979), cert denied 445 US 918 (1980).

[72] 589 F 2d 152 (4th Cir 1978), cert denied 441 US 992 (1979).

in *US* v *Rifkin*[73] there was a conviction for fraudulent wire transfers. On the other hand in *US* v *Alston*,[74] where the defendant used keys on a computer to alter personal credit files, thereby enabling unqualified persons to gain cars and other items on credit, the legislation was held not to apply. This is an example of the fortuitous application of existing criminal offences to a new problem, and it cannot be regarded as an appropriate solution to the question of unauthorized access to the computer.

The wiretap statutes current in many other jurisdictions refer expressly to the interception of oral communications or conversations and hence these statutes are inapplicable to the accessing of computers. Section 617 of the Italian Penal Code, for instance, refers to communications 'between persons', as does section 201 of the German Penal Code.[75] In the important Canadian case of *McLaughlin*,[76] this type of legislation was found to be inadequate in a case of unauthorized access to a computer.

The defendant was a student at the University of Alberta, and he was convicted at trial on a charge that he fraudulently, without colour of right, used a telecommunication service facility, the property of the University of Alberta, contrary to section 287(1)(b) of the Canadian Criminal Code. McLaughlin had made unauthorized use of the university computer by gaining access to the central processing unit from one of the 300 remote terminals situated around the University. Section 287 provides:

(1) Every one commits theft who fraudulently, maliciously, or without colour of right,
. . . (b) abuses any telecommunication facility or obtains any tele-communication service.
(2) In this section . . . 'telecommunication' means any transmission, emission or reception of signs, signals, writing, images, sounds or intelligence of any nature by radio, visual, electronic or other electro-magnetic system.

The appeal against conviction was allowed by a majority of the Alberta Court of Appeal and the Crown's appeal to the Supreme Court of Canada was dismissed. Laskin C.J.C. said that the computer, the central processing unit and the terminals taken together, was a data processing facility rather than a telecommunications facility. Esty J. added[77]

The term 'telecommunication' as defined in the Criminal Code connotes a sender and a receiver. The computer, being a computing device, contemplates the participation of one entity only, namely, the operator. In a sense, he communicates with himself, but it could hardly be said that the operator by operating the terminal or console of the

---

[73] Unreported; see J. J. Becker, 'Rifkin: a documentary history' (1980) 2 *Computer and Law Journal* 471.
[74] 609 F 2d (DC Cir 1979), cert denied 445 US 918 (1980).
[75] Sieber (1986), p. 86.   [76] (1980) 53 CCC (2d) 417.   [77] At p. 425.

computer is thereby communicating information in the sense of transmitting information and hence it stretches the language beyond reality to conclude that a person using a computer is thereby using a telecommunication facility in the sense of the Criminal Code.

By the Canadian Criminal Law Amendment Act 1985, such conduct would now be an offence, though under section 301.2 of the Code, which proscribes unauthorized use of computers and was introduced in 1985, rather than section 287.

In Britain there is the Interception of Communications Act 1985, which is designed to create a statutory framework for the authorization, by the Secretary of State, of interception of communications sent through the post or a public telecommunications system. Although it was not designed for this purpose, it has been suggested on occasion that it may have some application in relation to computer misuse. Section 1(1) of the statute creates a new offence of unauthorized interception, punishable on indictment with a maximum prison term of 2 years:

> ... a person who intentionally intercepts a communication in the course of its transmission by post or by means of a public telecommunications system shall be guilty of an offence ...

No offence is committed if the Secretary of State has issued a warrant authorizing the interception.[78] There would appear to be two main difficulties in applying this wording to the gaining of unauthorized access to material held on a computer. First, 'communication' would have to be interpreted by an English court so as to include communications between computers or between a mainframe and remote terminal, an approach contrary to the inclination of the Supreme Court of Canada in *McLaughlin*. Second, there is the question of whether unauthorized access involves 'interception'. It would seem that where a hacker accesses the computer, he 'initiates' rather than 'intercepts' the communication, and so the statute almost certainly would not apply. Third, the statute cannot apply to 'in-house' communications which do not make use of a public telecommunications network, and so would exclude most cases of unauthorized access by employees. Exactly the same limitations would seem to apply to comparable statutes elsewhere, such as the Australian Telecommunications (Interception) Act 1979.[79]

None of the statutory provisions in the Telecommunications Act 1984 or the Copyright, Designs and Patents Act 1988, dealing with varieties of misuse of telecommunications systems, are likely to be directly applicable in this

---

[78] Section 1(2)(a).
[79] Telecommunications (Interception) Act 1979 (Cth), s. 6(1); R. A. Brown, 'Computer-Related Crime under Commonwealth Law, and the Draft Federal Criminal Code' (1986) 10 *Criminal Law Journal*, 377 at p. 388.

context.[80] An offence is committed where non-approved apparatus, such as a listening device, has been connected to a public telecommunications system,[81] but this would rarely be an appropriate charge to bring in a case of unauthorized access.

A final possibility of establishing that the unauthorized access to the computer may itself be contrary to criminal law lies with the offence of abstraction of electricity, under section 13 of the Theft Act 1968. This provides:

A person who dishonestly uses without due authority, or dishonestly causes to be wasted or diverted, any electricity shall on conviction on indictment be liable to imprisonment for a term not exceeding five years.

Electricity does not constitute 'property' for the purposes of theft[82] and English law, in common with many other countries,[83] makes express provision for the unique nature of this kind of property. There is very little authority on the scope of this offence in England, but it is clear that the offence may be committed by an employee who dishonestly uses his employer's electrically operated machinery without authority or permission or, probably, his telephone.[84]

The possibility of using the offence to prosecute computer-related crime is obvious, though no successful prosecutions in England are reported. In one Hong Kong case,[85] however, the defendant gained access to a computer system after accidentally coming across passwords to an electronic mailbox data system operated by Cable and Wireless PLC. His access was, apparently, motivated by curiosity rather than gain. The defendant was charged with abstracting electricity under section 15 of the Theft Ordinance and he was found guilty. The magistrate, however, discharged the defendant absolutely and ordered that no conviction be returned, adding that the prosecution should never have been brought. This seems to have been because of the very small amount of electricity proved to have been used (valued at less than one eighth of a Hong Kong cent). While there may be some problems in prosecuting successfully under section 13 which did not emerge in the Hong Kong case,[86] the real objection with bringing such a charge is its artificiality, for the

[80] Telecommunications Act 1984, s. 42(1): fraudulent use of public telecommunications system (covering only the use of such a system with intent to avoid payment) and s. 43(1): improper use of public telecommunications system (covering grossly offensive, indecent, obscene or menacing calls, or making false messages to cause annoyance etc.).

[81] Telecommunications Act 1984, ss. 4, 5.

[82] Theft Act 1968, s. 4(1); *Low* v *Blease* [1975] Crim LR 513.

[83] Sieber (1986), p. 82.

[84] *Scottings and Rasjke* [1957] Crim LR 241; J. C. Smith, *The Law of Theft*, 6th edn., London: Butterworths, 1989, paras. 304 et seq. For misuse of a public telephone the appropriate offence is British Telecommunications Act 1981, s. 48.

[85] *Sui Tak-Chee*, unreported, Hong Kong, Aug. 1984; see Tasmanian Law Reform Commission, Report No. 47, *Computer Misuse*, Tasmania: Government Printer, 1986, p. 23.

[86] Brown (1983); A. Tettenborn, 'Some Legal Aspects of Computer Abuse' (1980) 2 *Company Lawyer* 147.

mischief which it seeks to counter is quite different from the substance of the offence.

The technique of computer eavesdropping, whereby information currently being relayed through a computer system may be 'read' by a spy outside the building by picking up electromagnetic radiation surrounding the computer and converting this to a visual image, was described in Chapter 2. Whilst there is no doubt of the viability of the technology, very few cases have so far come to light. It is, of course, not clear from this whether the technique is little used or rarely detected. Nicholson[87] reports one recent case of a bank suffering eavesdropping on electronically transmitted financial transactions. Apparently, although the material was encrypted, the eavesdropper managed to break the code. He successfully blackmailed the bank and several customers, obtaining £350,000 in this manner, 'by threatening to reveal certain transactions to the tax authorities'. While in this example a prosecution for blackmail would clearly lie, the issue is to what extent the initial computer eavesdropping is or should be proscribed by the criminal law. This is controversial, with different law reform proposals taking rather different lines.

In England, the criminal law position seems to be exactly the same as obtains where use is made of a powerful telescope to read someone's private papers lying open on a desk, and this would not constitute a criminal offence in itself. While some forms of eavesdropping once constituted a criminal offence in England, this was abolished[88] in 1967 and under current law the traditional eavesdropper, like the 'peeping Tom', commits no criminal offence as such, but may commit some other offence in the course of his activity, or be arrested with a view to being bound over to keep the peace.

A criminal offence of 'surreptitious surveillance by means of a technical device' was proposed back in 1972 by the Younger Committee on Privacy,[89] though not in the context of computer eavesdropping, which is a more recent phenomenon. The offence was to have comprised the following elements:

(a) a technical device (defined to mean 'electronic and optical extensions of the human senses');
(b) surreptitious use of the device;
(c) a person who is, or his possessions which are, the object of surveillance;
(d) a set of circumstances in which, were it not for the use of the device, that person would be justified in believing that he had protected himself or his possessions from surveillance whether by overhearing or observation;
(e) an intention by the user to render those circumstances ineffective as protection against overhearing or observation, and
(f) absence of consent by the victim.

---

[87] E. Nicholson, 'Hacking Away at Liberty', *The Times*, 18 Apr. 1989.
[88] Criminal Law Act 1967, s. 13; R. Wacks, *Personal Information, Privacy and the Law*, Oxford: Clarendon Press, 1988, at p. 250.
[89] Younger Committee, *Reporting on the Committee on Privacy*, Cmnd. 5012, London: HMSO, 1972.

This proposal has not been acted upon. The Committee also noted the existence of criminal provisions in other countries dealing with the manufacture, import, and sale as well as the use of surveillance devices. Their view on this, however, was that to prohibit or restrict such devices would be 'unduly cumbersome and probably ineffective'[90] and would place an unjustifiable burden on industries dealing with devices such as specialist cameras which might be used for surveillance purposes but which also have perfectly legitimate uses. This would be true of the equipment used for computer eavesdropping. The same view was expressed by the Home Office Minister Mr John Patten in a Parliamentary debate in March 1989 on the issue of electronic surveillance devices, when he stated that the government was 'not persuaded that it is practicable to extend the criminal law to cover electronic or other surveillance or eavesdropping, objectionable though such activities can undoubtedly be'.[91]

It has been suggested on occasions that computer eavesdropping might fall within the provisions of the Interception of Communications Act 1985.[92] This was certainly never intended by Parliament. Indeed the Home Secretary commented during the passage of the Bill through Parliament that it was not envisaged that its provisions would reach any form of surveillance or eavesdropping apart from telephone tapping. Whether the statute would so apply would depend upon the interpretation given by the courts to the wording of section 1(1) of the Act. Can the computer eavesdropper really be described as having intercepted 'a communication in the course of its transmission'? This seems very hard to square with the facts and the ordinary meaning of 'intercept', which surely involves seizing and diverting from the intended destination, rather than 'listening in' to a message *en route* to that destination. It is interesting to note in passing, however, that in the view of the European Court of Human Rights,[93] on appeal by the plaintiff in *Malone*,[94] a decision which necessitated the passage of the 1985 Act through Parliament, Judge Pettiti said that 'bugging and long distance listening techniques' constituted just as much of an interference with the applicant's rights under Article 8 of the European Convention on Human Rights as did the telephone tapping which was the actual subject of the Court's decision. It may be, then, that further progress could be made under the Convention, but it seems very unlikely that the Act, as it stands, would encompass computer eavesdropping.

It could, however, be reached under existing criminal law elsewhere, such as the Canadian Criminal Law Amendment Act 1985, which creates in section 46 a new offence of unauthorized use of a computer. 'Intercept' is

---

[90] Ibid., para. 570.
[91] *Hansard*, 13 Mar. 1989, col. 187
[92] In notes at (1986) 2 *Computer Law and Practice*, pp. 13, 165.
[93] European Commission: *Malone Report* No. 8691/79; European Court of Human Rights Series A, vol. 82 (2 Aug. 1984); Wacks (1989), p. 284.
[94] *Malone* v *MPC* (No. 2) [1979] 2 All ER 620.

there defined to include 'listen to or record a function of a computer system, or acquire the substance, meaning or purport thereof'.[95] The compendious computer crime statutes in the United States do not refer specifically to computer eavesdropping, and there appear to be no reported prosecutions, but would seem to cover it, given the breadth of the definition of 'access', which is to include 'to retrieve data from, or otherwise obtain the ability to use the resources of a computer'. On the other hand, in the recent Queensland Green Paper on computer-related crimes,[96] there was said to be 'clearly no need to criminalise such action', the robust view being taken there that 'if the document is of some sensitivity those careless in maintaining its security should suffer the appropriate consequences' of espionage.

The offences proposed by the Scottish Law Commission, and set out at Appendix 1, below, were not designed to extend to computer eavesdropping, but the Commission conceded that the width of the term 'obtains unauthorized access' would include at least some cases of computer eavesdropping. Apart from this, however, the Commission proposed that there should be no new offence directed at computer eavesdropping.[97] The English Law Commission stated that any new offence of obtaining unauthorized access to a computer should not extend to computer eavesdropping,[98] because of the anomaly of creating a special offence in relation to computers where spying and surveillance generally does not come within the criminal law. Whether such conduct in general should fall within the law was, of course, a matter well outside the remit of their discussion. The Commission specifically excluded 'listening in' to a computer from a distance from the scope of their proposed 'basic hacking offence' and 'ulterior intent offence', with the additional argument that the kind of conduct involved in electronic eavesdropping does not pose a threat to the operational integrity of the system concerned in the way that hacking does, but is aimed more specifically at the confidentiality of the information which it contains. The Commission's view was, in turn, criticized as being too narrow an approach, with critics urging a definition of 'access' broad enough to cater for 'the emergence of this new threat'.[99] On balance, though, it is difficult to refute the Law Commission's argument and, with one possible exception, their proposed offences, as adapted and defined in the Computer Misuse Act 1990, would seem to exclude criminal liability for computer eavesdropping. The only situation where such conduct might fall within the terms of the basic hacking offence is where the monitoring device used by the eavesdropper can itself be regarded as a 'computer'. If it were to be so regarded in law, then the eavesdropper would be guilty of the basic hacking

[95] Criminal Law Amendment Act, s. 46(2).

[96] Queensland Government Department of Justice, *Green Paper on Computer-Related Crime*, Queensland: Government Printer, 1987, p. 47.

[97] Scottish Law Commission (1987), para. 3.20.

[98] Law Commission (1989*b*), para. 3.25.

[99] e.g. the CBI (1989), commenting on the Law Commission's provisional view in its Working Paper No. 110.

offence where he causes (his) computer to perform any function with intent 'to secure access to any program or data held in (the target) computer'.[100]

4. DATA PROTECTION OFFENCES

There is great concern over privacy issues in relation to the volume of sensitive personal data which can be held in computer databanks, the speed with which such information can be cross-matched, and the number of individuals and organizations who may gain authorized or unauthorized access to such material.[101] In most countries computer-related infringements of privacy have primarily attracted the attention of the civil law, though there has been some criminal law development in protecting some rights related to privacy, such as in trade secrets and the interception of communications, or by the creation of special data protection and privacy statutes.[102] These laws are often complex in operation and vary considerably from one jurisdiction to another. In the United States civil remedies form the basis of the balance sought to be achieved between the government's need for information and the individual's privacy in the context of computerized records. There is a complex interrelation between the Privacy Act of 1974 and the Right to Financial Privacy Act of 1978, violation of which is a criminal offence, and the Freedom of Information legislation.[103] Section 552a of the Privacy Act regulates how federal agencies subject to the Freedom of Information Act maintain records, both paper and computerized. Most recently Congress has passed the Computer Matching and Privacy Protection Act 1988 as an amendment to the 1974 Act. This new law[104] controls the use of computerized techniques by federal and state authorities to cross-check records of benefits and payments made to individuals by different agencies.

Many European privacy laws catering for data protection, however, involve the criminal law to a much greater extent, and include comprehensive lists of criminal offences with high maximum punishments. These cover such matters as the unauthorized collection, recording, and storage of data,[105] the unauthorized obtaining of or access to or disclosure of data,[106] or the unauthorized use of data.[107] Some also extend to the unauthorized entering,

---

[100] I am grateful to Professor Brian Napier for drawing this to my attention. The main difficulty would lie in showing that the defendant had 'secured access' to the program or data, within the meaning of s. 17(2) of the Act. See App. 4, below.

[101] See, e´ Scott (1985), ch. 7.

[102] See, e. ., the penal provisions of the French Act No. 78–17 of 6.1.1978, on Data Processing, Data Files, and Individual Liberties, ss. 30, 31, and 42. For discussion of comparative European approaches see Sieber (1986), pp. 94–110.

[103] Scott (1985), paras. 7.47 et seq.

[104] Effective from July 1989.

[105] e.g. French Act on Data Processing, Data Files, and Individual Liberties, s. 26.

[106] Austrian Data Protection Act, ss. 48, 49; Swedish Data Act, ss. 20, 21.

[107] Austrian Data Protection Act, s. 48.

modification, and/or falsification of data with the intent to cause damage,[108] which may overlap with more general computer misuse legislation. Some countries have made it an offence to neglect appropriate security measures in relation to data.[109] In Sweden, the country generally cited as the first to legislate on computer-related crime, the law on unauthorized access is part of a whole scheme dealing with rights of privacy in relation to computer-held information.

In contrast, in other countries, including the United Kingdom, the criminal law is not widely used in the Data Protection Act 1984 or indeed in the protection of privacy generally.[110] The Lindop Committee proposed that a breach of the data protection Code of Practice should be a crime triable either way,[111] but this proposal was not adopted in the legislation. Very occasionally, however, as the Law Commission points out,[112] the holding of personal data, as opposed to the obtaining of unauthorized access to it, may constitute an offence under the Data Protection Act. The offences under the Act are 'last resort' remedies, which can only be initiated by the Data Protection Registrar, or with the consent of the Director of Public Prosecutions.[113] Section 5 of the Act provides that a person shall not hold personal data on computer unless registration in respect of that person as a data user, or as a data user who also carries on a computer bureau, is made under the Act. Section 1(5) makes it an offence, apparently of strict liability, to contravene this registration requirement. Section 1(5) also makes it an offence in respect of any person who is so registered, knowingly or recklessly to hold personal data of any description other than that specified in the register, to hold it for any purpose or purposes other than is specified in the register, to obtain the data from any source not specified in the register, to disclose the data to any unauthorized person, or to transfer data outside the United Kingdom unless specified in the register. The Law Commission postulates that where a person who is not registered under the Act, such as a hacker[114]

. . . obtains access to personal data stored on another computer, records that information as data on his own computer and intends to extract the information constituting the data (for example, by displaying it on a VDU screen), that person may commit the offence of holding personal data without having registered as a data user.

If the person is registered under the Act, he may commit an offence under section 5(2), such as knowingly or recklessly obtaining personal data from a

---

[108] Austrian Data Protection Act, s. 49; Swedish Data Act, s. 21; West German Data Protection Act, s. 41.

[109] Danish Private Registers Act, s. 27; French Act on Data Processing, Data Files and Individual Liberties, s. 29.

[110] Wacks (1989).

[111] Lindop Committee, *Report of the Committee on Data Protection*, Cmnd. 7341, London: HMSO, 1978, para. 19.91.

[112] Law Commission (1988), paras. 3.58 et seq.

[113] Data Protection Act 1984, s. 19.   [114] Law Commission (1988), para. 3.59.

source which is not described in the entry, or knowingly or recklessly holding personal data of any description other than that specified in the entry. No prosecutions seem to have been brought in the situations envisaged and, as the Law Commission says, the Act provides only 'limited and complex criminal sanctions'[115] in the field of computer misuse.

Section 15(3) criminalizes the knowing or reckless disclosure of personal data by a person carrying on a computer bureau without the prior authority of the person for whom the services are provided. Section 6(6) makes it an offence for any person who applies for registration under the Act knowingly or recklessly to furnish the Registrar with information which is false or misleading. Further, under section 10 of the Act, the Data Protection Registrar, where satisfied that a registered person has contravened or is contravening one or more of the eight data protection principles[116] under the Act may serve upon him an 'enforcement notice' requiring him so to comply. Under section 10(9), failure to comply with such a notice is a criminal offence. There is a defence of due diligence, but the burden of proof is on the defendant. Similarly, under section 12 the Registrar may serve upon a person registered under the Act a 'transfer prohibition notice' prohibiting transfer of data in certain defined circumstances. Contravention of such a notice is a criminal offence, but again there is a defence of due diligence with the burden of proof placed on the defendant. All offences created under the Act are punishable by way of fine, apart from the offence under section 6, which may render the data user liable to forfeiture, destruction, or erasure of any data material connected with the commission of the offence.

One of the suggestions in the Law Commission's Working Paper on Computer Misuse was that any proposed offence of obtaining unauthorized access to a computer might be limited to the obtaining of access to certain kinds of information, such as personal data of the type already the subject of legislation in the Data Protection Act.[117] There was some discussion along similar lines in Australia where it appeared at one time that the law in Victoria would introduce such an offence.[118] In the event, however, the Victoria Crimes (Computers) Act created instead a general offence of 'computer trespass'.[119] The Law Commission also rejected this approach in their subsequent Report and proposed the creation of a general hacking offence, irrespective of the nature of the data held.[120]

---

[115] Ibid., para. 3.60. See further Tapper (1989), p. 309.
[116] Data Protection Act 1984, Sched. 1, Part 1. Principle No. 8 provides that: 'Appropriate security measures shall be taken against unauthorized access to, or alteration, disclosure or destruction of, personal data and against accidental loss or destruction of personal data.'
[117] Law Commission (1988), para. 6.25, 'Option A'.
[118] J. Chapman, 'Computer Misuse: A Response to Working Paper No. 110' (1989) 5 _Computer Law and Practice_ 115, citing Attorney-General Kennan.
[119] By s. 9.
[120] Law Commission (1989b); for discussion of the basic hacking offence see Section 1 above.

5. MISUSE OF COMPUTER TIME AND FACILITIES

A common form of computer misuse involves the accessing of a computer in order to make use of computer time or facilities to which the person making access is not entitled. This may be done either by a person who has authorization to use the computer at other times or for other purposes, or by an outsider, by hacking. Employees who are computer users will be tempted to use the computer for purposes other than the job in hand, and such misuse is known to be widespread. Large multi-user time-sharing systems, including computer bureaux, are also targets for unauthorized use, either through authorized users exceeding their entitlement or unauthorized users posing as authorized ones.

As we will see, this kind of conduct generally falls outside the scope of existing criminal law in England. Neither the Scottish Law Commission nor the English Law Commission have proposed any new offence in this regard and, indeed, both stated that they would regard it as anomalous so to do. On the other hand, it is apparent that sometimes cases of misuse of computer time or facilities will fall within the scope of the new offences in the Computer Misuse Act 1990. In what follows the possible application of more well established criminal offences is examined first, and then the implications of the 1990 Act for these cases is considered.

A first possibility to establish liability is prosecution for theft. The relevance of this offence to computer misuse is discussed in more detail in Chapter 4. Suffice it to say here that the English law of theft clearly does not cover the abstracting of intangibles such as computer time or facilities.[121] A theft charge would only be effective where tangible property was removed consequent upon the misuse of the computing facility, as in one case described in the 1985 Audit Commission survey. There,[122] the defendant was convicted of theft of computer print-outs and fined £1,200. The case is interesting because he was also ordered to pay £2,000 in compensation to the firm, the sum being an assessment of the value of the computer time lost to the firm through his unauthorized use. Theft would also be available in cases such as those where an employee was using his employer's computer to print out cartoons or tickets or 'biorhythm charts',[123] where the material on which they were printed was the property of the employer. Here, however, the charge would simply reflect pilfering and would not be directed towards the computer misuse itself. Problems over the non-applicability of theft to

---

[121] Despite the inclusion of 'other tangible property' within Theft Act 1968, s. 4(1); Smith (1989), para. 92.

[122] Audit Commission for Local Authorities in England and Wales, *Computer Fraud Survey*, London: HMSO, 1984, case 64; see also case 67.

[123] As in cases cited in Audit Inspectorate, *Computer Fraud Survey*, London: Department of the Environment, 1981, Appendix B.

unauthorized use of computer time or services have been fully discussed in the United States and most states now have specific provisions in their Codes to cover it. Some of these developments are worth outlining here.

In the 1977 case in Virginia of *Lund* v *Commonwealth*,[124] Lund was a graduate student who obtained access to a computer by using passwords provided by his friends. He was accused, under the general theft statute, of stealing the passwords, as well as the computer cards and print-outs, and of using the school's computer without authorization. A guilty verdict was overturned on appeal on the grounds that the mere 'use' of a computer was not theft under Virginia law, and that the print-outs were worth no more than scrap paper. In the wake of this decision the Virginia state legislature passed a statute[125] which explicitly described computer services as an item which could be stolen, thereby putting Lund's act within the State's general theft statute. In *US* v *Sampson*,[126] however, the outcome was different. The defendant was charged with theft of 'a thing of value' belonging to the United States, a federal crime. The defendant was an employee of a computer service company under contract to NASA. He was discovered using the computer, which he accessed by using his home telephone, for his own personal gain, for an average of six hours per week for thirty-two weeks. Some $1,924 was said to be involved. The court found that unauthorized use of a government computer was a violation of the federal theft law which provides that:[127]

> Whosoever embezzles, steals, purloins or knowingly converts to his own use or that of another, or without authority sells, conveys or disposes of any record, voucher, money or other thing of value of the United States shall be guilty of an offence . . .

since[128]

(t)he consumption of computer time and the utilisation of its capacities seem to the court to be inseparable from the physical identity of the computer itself. That the computer is property cannot be doubted. Thus the uses of the computer and the product of such uses would appear to the court to be a 'thing of value'.

This is clearly a very broad and rather strained interpretation of the wording of the statute.

---

[124] 217 Va 688, 232 SE 2d 745 (1977); see also *People* v *Kunkin* 9 Cal 3d 245, 507 P 2d 1392 (1973).

[125] Va Code, paras. 18.2–152.1 (1983); '(C)omputer time or services or data processing services or information or data stored in connection therewith is hereby defined to be property which may be the subject of larceny . . .'. See *Evans* v *Commonwealth* 226 Va 292, 308 SE 2d 126 (1983).

[126] 6 Comp L Serv Rep (Callaghan) 879 (ND Cal 1978); to the same effect is *State* v *McGraw* 459 NE 2d 61 (Ind App 1984); A. C. Hansen, 'Criminal Law: Theft of Use of Computer Services' (1985) 7 *Western New England Law Review* 823.

[127] 18 USC s. 641 (1982).

[128] *per* Ingram D.C.J., at p. 883.

[129] Model Penal Code, s. 223.7 (Proposed Tentative Draft 1982).

Prosecutions have also been brought in the United States under provisions for 'theft of services'. In general terms, a person is guilty of theft of services if 'he obtains services, which he knows are available only for compensation, by deception or threat or by false token or other means to avoid payment for the service'.[129] In *People* v *Weg*,[130] however, a prosecution under the precise terms of a New York theft of services law was unsuccessful. The defendant was a computer programmer employed by a board of education. He was charged with theft of services for allegedly using the board's computer without permission for various personal projects, including calculating a racehorse handicapping system and tracing the genealogy of horses that he owned. The statute was held by the court to apply only to computers used for profit in trade or commerce, but not to a computer used by a public agency for internal administration.

So, prior to the flurry of legislative activity which saw many states enacting specific computer crime legislation, it is fair to say that the outcome of prosecutions for this form of computer misuse was rather haphazard. Tapper notes that prosecutors were 'forced back into reliance upon such inherently implausible applications as forged telephone messages, general forgery or credit card crimes'.[131] In Senator Ribicoff's Bill, which was widely discussed but never became law,[132] it is clear that unauthorized use of computer time or services would have been made a serious offence. According to section 2(b) of that Bill:

> Whoever intentionally and without authorization, directly or indirectly accesses, alters, damages, destroys, or attempts to damage or destroy any computer, computer system, or computer network . . . or any computer software, program or data contained in such computer . . .

shall be guilty of an offence. The Bill was subject to fierce criticism, not least from the American writer John Taber,[133] on the ground that it would include within these provisions many very minor cases of computer users who 'on occasion use their employer's computer to play games like tic-tac-toe or Star Trek'. The California Penal Code, which broadly adopts the Ribicoff wording, does amend it so as apparently to restrict liability to cases where 'access' was either 'malicious'[134] or done 'for the purpose of . . . obtaining money, property or services with false or fraudulent intent, representations or promises'.[135] How far this could be stretched to cover minor cases is as yet unclear, for there appear to have been very few prosecutions under these laws.

Accepting the general inapplicability of a charge of theft to unauthorized

---

[130] 113 Misc 2d 1017, 450 NYS 2d 957 (1982).
[131] C. Tapper, *Computer Law*, 3rd edn., London: Longman, 1983, p. 108.
[132] Senate Bill S. 240.
[133] J. K. Taber, 'On Computer Crime' (1979) 1 *Computer and Law Journal* 517.
[134] Cal Penal Code, s. 502(d).   [135] Section 502(b)(2).

use of computer time or facilities in England, more promising perhaps, on the face of it, is a prosecution for obtaining services by deception, under section 1 of the Theft Act 1978. It provides that:

(1) A person who by any deception dishonestly obtains services from another shall be guilty of an offence.

(2) It is an obtaining of services where the other is induced to confer a benefit by doing some act, or causing or permitting some act to be done, on the understanding that the benefit has been or will be paid for.

Section 1 replaced in part section 16(2)(a) of the Theft Act 1968, which Tapper suggested might be useful in prosecuting cases of unauthorized use of computer time or facilities.[136] Several fact situations may be distinguished. First, the defendant may gain access by pretending to be an authorized user. He may have obtained an authorized user's password, or he may 'piggyback' on an authorized user's line. If permission to access the system is obtained via the computer's electronic access control, then the difficulty is that no deception has operated on a human mind. As we shall see in Chapter 4, this effectively rules out liability for any crime based on 'deception'. It is possible to imagine a case where this difficulty is avoided, as where the person contacts a computer bureau and pretends to be an authorized user, deceiving a human operator into allowing him to log on. Provided, as is likely to be the case, that there is an understanding that the computer time will be paid for, a charge under section 1 should succeed. It is important to note that liability does not turn on the question of whether the user is willing to pay.[137] Second, the defendant may be an employee of the computer owner, who normally has access to the computer but who on this occasion uses it outside working hours in order to develop or run his own programs. Again, the unauthorized access would presumably involve no deception of a human mind and so the charge would fail. Further, the employer could not be regarded as having 'permitted' the use of the computer without knowledge that it was being so used.[138] As one commentator on the 1978 Theft Act has aptly put it:[139] 'The gist of the offence is lying to others to persuade them to render a service. It was not intended to cover "stealing" services—simply helping oneself to them when no one is looking and no mind has been deceived.' The third situation is where the employee uses the computer for his own purposes during normal working hours. There is still the problem of absence of deception and no 'permission'. Also, in both this case and the last one, there is a lack of any understanding between the employer and the employee that the 'benefit' will be 'paid for'. This last difficulty could be circumvented, in a case where a computer owner regarded his computing facilities as being seriously at risk from unauthorized

---

[136] Tapper (1983), p. 109.   [137] J. C. Smith (1989), para. 236.
[138] *Souter* [1971] 2 All ER 1151.
[139] J. R. Spencer, 'The Theft Act 1978' [1979] *Criminal Law Review* 24, at p. 26.

use by employees, by the owner making it clear to them that any computer use outside the scope of normal employee duties was to be paid for.

The possibility of bringing a charge under section 13 of the Theft Act in respect of the dishonest use of electricity was discussed in a different context, above. The possibilities of using such an offence to prosecute unauthorized use of computer time or facilities is clear but there are no successful cases reported. Professor Smith provides the colourful example[140] of a wood-working company which allows sea scouts to use their electrically operated machinery. Where the defendant obtains the use of the machinery by falsely stating that he is a sea scout, the author thinks that this would constitute an offence under section 13.

A potential difficulty is suggested in a discussion on the point by Brown.[141] He says that in the situation where the defendant accesses the computer by use of a remote terminal he has dishonestly 'caused electricity to be used' by the computer, but this is not strictly within the wording of the section. The defendant does not himself appear to have 'used' the electricity, and so successful conviction under section 13 would depend upon the court being prepared to interpret 'uses' to include 'causes to be used'. His argument rests on the assumption that the machine is using the electricity rather than the person operating the machine, but of course electricity can only ever be used in this indirect way. It is impossible, in this respect, to distinguish the hacker from the employee who exceeds his authorized use. Since the latter would seem to be covered, surely the courts would interpret the section in such a way as also to convict the former. As was indicated earlier, the real drawback to using this offence is that it bears no real relation to the mischief involved.

In many countries the unauthorized use of computer time or services is not covered adequately by criminal law and other jurisdictions have been busy in recent years to tackle the problems. Some penal codes already contain provisions against the unauthorized or illegal use of another person's property,[142] which can be applied to the misuse of computers. Many other legal systems, including the English,[143] do not make criminal the unauthorized use of another's property. The point is clear from the old case of *Cullum*.[144] Unauthorized use will not ordinarily constitute an intention to deprive the owner of the property permanently, so such conduct does not amount to theft. There are certain exceptional cases provided for by statute, such as the unauthorized use of a vehicle, under section 12 of the Theft Act 1968, and it is argued by some that a further exception to the general rule ought to be made in respect of computers. The Law Reform Commission of Tasmania, for example, has advocated the creation of 'a furtum usus

[140] Smith (1989), para. 307; the example was first coined by Lord Airedale.

[141] Brown (1983).

[142] e.g. Belgian Penal Code, s. 461; Danish Penal Code, s. 293.

[143] See discussion in Law Commission (1988), para. 3.67; for the position in Scotland see *Strathern v Seaforth* (1926) JC 100 and Scottish Law Commission (1986), paras. 3.50–3.57.

[144] (1873) LR 2 CCR 28.

provision in relation to computers',[145] by analogy with an existing motor vehicle joyriding offence. The Commission argues that in many cases the unauthorized use of the computer is 'a far greater invasion of proprietary rights than the illegal use of a car'.[146]

One of the problems with proposals to criminalize unauthorized use of computer time and services is that the great majority of such behaviour which occurs is very trivial and hardly justifies the use of the criminal law. It is the kind of matter which is better dealt with by way of warning or other disciplinary action taken by an employer. The question is how to distinguish these cases from the few serious cases where the defendant may be running his own profitable business in his employer's time, using his employer's computing facilities. The Audit Commission has argued that a distinction must be drawn between 'instances of "playing" with the computer, and those activities which affect working patterns or are deliberately deceitful',[147] and this view has been echoed by the CBI.[148] One way of achieving this would be to criminalize profit-making by a defendant using another's property without authority. At one time it was thought that in such a case the employee could be treated in law as a constructive trustee of the profits and could be convicted of their theft if they were not made over to the employer.[149] However attractive this argument may seem to be, it has now been decisively rejected by the Court of Appeal in *Attorney-General's Reference No. 1 of 1985*.[150] The defendant was the salaried manager of a tied public house. He admitted that he had bought beer from a wholesaler and intended to make a secret profit by selling it to customers in the public house. The Attorney-General sought to rely on section 5(1) of the Theft Act 1968 to show that the defendant was a constructive trustee and was guilty of theft of the secret profits, assuming that dishonesty on his part could be shown. The Court disagreed, saying that section 5 dealt with the misappropriation of specific property and that if the draftsmen of the 1968 Act had intended to make such conduct criminal they would have used explicit words to do so. Lord Lane C.J. said that the argument to the contrary was 'abstruse' and 'so far from the understanding of ordinary people as to what constituted stealing (that) it should not amount to stealing'.[151] In their Working Paper on Conspiracy to Defraud, the Law Commission points out that where two or more defendants are involved in such an activity, they can be convicted of conspiracy to defraud.[152] This is anomalous where no offence is committed by an individual

---

[145] Tasmanian Law Reform Commission (1986), p. 24.

[146] Ibid., p. 24, proposing that the offence should be worded: 'Any person who without authority, knowingly uses a computer, is guilty of a crime.'

[147] Audit Commission (1987), p. 4.   [148] CBI (1989–90).

[149] Argued in G. Williams, *Textbook of Criminal Law*, 2nd edn., London: Stevens, 1983, para. 33.10.

[150] [1986] QB 491.   [151] Ibid., p. 503.

[152] Law Commission, Working Paper No. 104, *Conspiracy to Defraud*, London: HMSO, 1987, paras. 10.49 et seq.; *Cooke* [1986] AC 909.

on the same facts, and the Commission considers whether a new offence should be created to cover the situation if conspiracy to defraud is abolished. Their provisional view is that no offence is needed, largely because of the availability of civil remedies, but they express some interest in a new offence formulated in terms of an employee or agent using his position for gain without the consent of his employer or principal, with the result that the latter suffers a loss.

In the United States, as we have seen, many states have enacted new laws which include provisions against unauthorized use of computer time or services, though these are less comprehensive than in some other areas of computer-related crime. At the federal level it remains unregulated, since the Counterfeit Access Device and Computer Fraud and Abuse Act of 1984 does not extend to this activity. Most directly in point is the Canadian Criminal Law Amendment Act of 1985 which by section 46 adds a new section 301.2 to the Criminal Code, punishing, *inter alia*, 'anyone who fraudulently and without colour of right (a) obtains, directly or indirectly, any computer service . . .'. It is also an offence under the section to use, directly or indirectly, any computer system with intent to commit such an offence. In Britain the conclusion of the Scottish Law Commission was that no new offence directed to cover this form of computer misuse would be proposed, because it would be unjustifiable to create an offence of unauthorized use of another's computer where unauthorized use of virtually every other item of property remained unregulated by the criminal law.[153] An additional argument advanced by the Commission was that where the person making unauthorized use of the computer is an employee, he will be subject to internal disciplinary controls which will normally be sufficient for deterrence and punishment. It was accepted, however, that in some cases a person accessing the computer to make use of computer time or facilities would be guilty of the Commission's proposed unauthorized access offence.[154] A similar picture emerges from the recommendations of the English Law Commission, which commented that[155] '. . . our view remains that there is nothing to distinguish the misuse of an employer's computer from the misuse of the office photocopier or typewriter, and that it is therefore inappropriate to invoke the criminal law to punish conduct more appropriately dealt with by disciplinary procedures'. Again, however, the new offences proposed by the English Law Commission which, with some amendment, have been adopted in the Computer Misuse Act 1990, could on occasions extend to cases where the defendant's object was the obtaining of computer time or resources. Clearly, if an employee without permission accesses a program on his employer's computer for his own personal use, that conduct would fall within the basic hacking offence under section 1 of the Act.[156] There might also be an offence of 'unauthorized

---

[153] Scottish Law Commission (1987), para. 3.13(5).
[154] Ibid. See App. 1, below.
[155] Law Commission (1989*b*), para. 3.38.   [156] See above, and App. 4, below.

modification of computer material' committed under section 3 of the Act. This offence is dealt with fully in Chapter 5. Suffice it to say here that one situation envisaged by that offence is where the defendant without authorization modifies material held on a computer with intent to impair the operation of the computer or to impair the reliability or accessibility of data stored there. This might sometimes cover the case of an employee running his own business on his employer's computer. Where the unauthorized use was heavy, other people seeking access to the computer might well be prejudiced, but to obtain a conviction the prosectuion would have to prove that the defendant by his own access thereby intended to impair the reliability or accessibility of data for others.

4

Fraud and Information Theft

As was explained in Chapter 1, there are great difficulties in agreeing upon a definition of computer-related fraud. Suggestions have ranged from the narrow, with an insistence upon clear evidence of technical manipulation of the computer to perpetrate the fraud, to the broad, such as the commission of any financial dishonesty which takes place in a computer environment. For the reasons outlined there, the approach of this book is a fairly broad one. The object is to identify those cases where new and significant substantive criminal law problems arise through the fact that a computer was instrumental at some stage in the operation of the fraud. The concept of fraud is also difficult to define. In one case it was said by Shaw L.J. that[1] 'where a person intends by deceit to induce a course of conduct in another which puts that other's economic interest in jeopardy he is guilty of fraud'. This summary, while helpful, conceals a diversity of different criminal offences which together constitute the existing law on fraud. There is no single offence of fraud in English law; there is a patchwork of large and small offences, which overlap and interrelate with one another in complex and sometimes unpredictable ways.

1. ASPECTS OF FRAUD

Computer-related frauds may be perpetrated in several different ways and by authorized or unauthorized users of the computer. It was suggested in Chapter 1 that the best way to subdivide computer frauds is in terms of the stage at which the use of the computer is relevant in the perpetration of the fraud. Firstly, the input to the computer may be tampered with, by falsification, addition, or removal of information prior to or during its introduction into the computer. Such alteration may be designed to cause the computer to generate payments to the fraudster's own bank account, or to that of an accomplice, or it may be to delete or suppress evidence of illegal activities. Fictitious favourable credit information may be added or unfavourable information deleted from computerized files. Secondly, the operation of the computer itself may be affected directly by the fraudster, by the alteration of computer codes or operational programs on the computer. Programs may be

---

[1] *Allsop* (1976) 64 Cr App R 29, at p. 32.

introduced by the fraudster which channel funds to a specified account, the program subsequently wiping itself out. Thirdly, the computer output may be suppressed or altered to commit or cover up the fraud. Even so, these divisions are not watertight and frequently more than one of the methods will be involved in any one fraud, such as where input is tampered with and output is adjusted to conceal resulting losses.

Most of the computer frauds which have so far come to light are, in fact, fairly simple in conception and very similar to the equivalent activities in pre-computer times. Some could have been perpetrated in just the same way by taking advantage of an unquestioning human cashier. Others require computing ability only to the extent of creating spurious files on the computer in a manner comparable to that in which they might formerly have been created in a ledger. It is clear beyond doubt that the majority of cases of computer fraud fall well within established criminal law offences designed to combat fraud, such as theft, obtaining property by deception, and false accounting. This is to be expected, since in most computer fraud offences the object of the offence is to acquire a tangible benefit, generally money, and the computer is being used as a tool to perpetrate or conceal the fraud. In general the criminal law is addressed to, and defined in terms of, the objective of the dishonest conduct rather than the fraudster's precise *modus operandi*, so the computer manipulation ought, in principle, to be irrelevant to liability. Indeed, the policy behind the Theft Act 1968, in contrast with earlier legislation, was to create broadly drafted offences, defined to include a range of conduct and factual circumstances.

As we shall see, however, there are some problems stemming from the fact that most of the law of fraud was drafted at a time before computers were commonplace, and sometimes the use of a computer may place the fraudster outside the scope of the criminal law. Many criminal law jurisdictions have been grappling with similar problems, and much may be learned from the study of case-law and legislative developments elsewhere. Several other countries have seen the need to reform various aspects of their law of theft and related offences. These changes have been made or proposed as an additional or alternative response to the criminalizing of the initial unauthorized access of the computer. The first few state jurisdictions to legislate in this area in the United States did so largely by reforming their theft laws; subsequently that approach has been overtaken by the criminalizing of the unauthorized access.

2. DECEPTION

At first sight, the offence of obtaining property by deception under section 15 of the Theft Act 1968 might appear to be as appropriate a charge to bring in cases of computer fraud as it is in fraud generally. This offence provides that:

(1) A person who by any deception dishonestly obtains property belonging to another, with the intention of permanently depriving the other of it, shall on conviction on indictment be liable to imprisonment for a term not exceeding ten years.

(2) For purposes of this section, a person is to be treated as obtaining property if he obtains ownership, possession or control of it, and 'obtain' includes obtaining for another or enabling another to obtain or retain . . .

(4) For purposes of this section 'deception' means any deception (whether deliberate or reckless) by words or conduct as to fact or as to law, including a deception as to the present intentions of the person using the deception or any other person.

For the purposes of section 15, 'property' is widely defined, and the limits put upon the meaning of property for the purposes of theft are inapplicable to deception.[2] Land, for example, cannot in general be stolen but it may be obtained by deception. It should also be noted that the offence under section 15 requires a causal connection between the deception and the obtaining of the property: the property must be obtained 'by' the deception. So in a case where the fraudster obtains the property first, and then falsifies computer input as a means of covering up the obtaining, the charge would be ineffective, though in some cases an alternative charge, such as theft of the property, would be likely to succeed. The requirement that the conduct be 'dishonest' is discussed below.

Whilst subsection (4) of section 15 provides a definition of 'deception', the concept is further refined in the cases. There is a particular and well-known problem in applying this offence, and any other offence which turns on the idea of 'deception', in the context of computers because of a number of decisions which indicate that such deception must influence a human mind. The dictum of Buckley J. in *Re London and Globe Finance Corp.*[3] that 'to deceive is . . . to induce a man to believe a thing which is false, and which the person practising the deceit knows or believes to be false' has been applied in later cases, and Lord Morris commented, *obiter* in *DPP v Ray*,[4] that 'for a deception to take place there must be some person or persons who will have been deceived'. In these cases, however, computers were not in issue. Apparently the first case in this country in which the issue of deceiving a computer arose directly was *Moritz*,[5] a decision at first instance in June 1981. It was

---

[2] See J. C. Smith, *The Law of Theft*, 6th edn., London: Butterworths, 1989, para. 203, and further, below.

[3] [1903] 1 Ch 728, at p. 732.

[4] [1973] 3 All ER 131. See also J. C. Smith, 'Some Comments on Deceiving a Machine' (1972) 69 *Law Society Gazette* 576. See *Davies v Flackett* [1973] RTR 8.

[5] Unreported, 17–19 June 1981, Judge Finestein, Acton Crown Court. It is possible that the defendant might have been found guilty of the common law offence of cheating the public revenue, which requires no element of deception and which was broadly interpreted in *Mavji* [1987] 1 WLR 1388.

held in that case that there was no evidence to go to the jury that false Value Added Tax returns, which had secured unwarranted repayments, had 'deceived' in the required sense, given the computer-assisted nature of the processing of VAT returns.

The position, then, is that where the fraud operates by way of causing the computer to be misled by, say, tampering with the input, and where no human mind is deceived, the offence of obtaining property by deception is ineffective. This could occur where the computer was accessed by the defendant and misled into printing out cheques in the fraudster's name. If, as is often the case, however, the computer output is processed by a human operator, then it is likely that a conviction could be returned on the basis of the deceiving of that person. These contrasting outcomes are indefensible, because they turn on the matter of chance of whether there is a human operator who may be said to have been deceived. Nevertheless, there seem to be few problems encountered in practice in relation to cases of 'pure' computer deception. In some situations prosecutors may anticipate the difficulty and bring a charge of theft instead, but deception-based offences are still regularly and effectively used in cases such as obtaining social security payments by deception, even though a computer is instrumental in the production of the girocheques.[6] Successful prosecution will result either where an official, already having been deceived by a representation made by the fraudster, inputs material which is the product of that deception to the computer or where an official, acting in reliance on the computer's output, authorizes the sending of the cheques to the fraudster. Although it must strictly be shown by the prosecution that the fraudster's activity actually deceived the official, proof that he was ignorant of the truth and had relied on the representation, or upon the output, would suffice.[7] This would surely be clear where there was no other reason for the making of the payment than the official's reliance upon the accuracy of the representation or the output.[8]

If the opportunity arose, an appellate court might be prepared to take a fresh line and further extend the generous interpretation which the House of Lords has already given to the notion of deception. As Arlidge and Parry indicate, 'it is not self-evidently absurd to suggest'[9] that a computer can be deceived. To hold that a machine may be deceived would be to downplay further the requirement of the victim's 'belief' in the truth of the representation, a requirement already greatly attenuated by the decision in *MPC* v

---

[6] See, e.g. *Bogdal* v *Hall* [1987] Crim LR 500, and the comments of the Law Commission in their Report No. 186, *Computer Misuse*, London: HMSO,1989, para. 2.4, that the Commission has 'received little evidence of cases where a conviction for a fraud offence was lost because of that problem'.

[7] *MPC* v *Charles* [1977] AC 177; *Lambie* [1982] AC 449.

[8] *Etim* v *Hatfield* [1975] Crim LR 234; *Lambie* [1982] AC 449, *per* Lord Roskill at p. 461.

[9] A. Arlidge and J. Parry, *Fraud*, London: Waterlow, 1985, para. 2.30. The authors also state that, on the other hand, it would be possible in law to deceive a company, by imputing to that company the mental state of those who control it.

Charles.[10] While a machine cannot be said to 'believe' a representation made to it, it does not seem to stretch language too far to say that the machine is capable of being 'misled' or 'deceived'.

Some other jurisdictions have encountered similar problems in applying their deception offences to computer-related fraud. The traditional definitions of fraud in, for example, Austria, Denmark, and West Germany all require that a 'person' be deceived.[11] Other Code provisions, such as the Belgian and Canadian,[12] are more flexible, and do so extend. Some jurisdictions have legislated on the matter. The law in West Germany was updated in 1986, with a new provision on computer fraud removing the requirement that a person be deceived. Similarly the amended Criminal Code of Alaska provides that where 'deception' must be proved as an element of an offence 'it is not a defence that the defendant deceived or attempted to deceive a machine'.[13] It is unusual to find such an amendment in American state legislation, and generally the issue of whether a computer can be deceived does not seem to have been a problem in the United States, probably because the question is less likely to arise where the original unauthorized accessing of the computer is criminalized. In one case, however, said to be out of line by American commentators, a Californian judge dismissed a prosecution based on tampering with a computerized ticket machine used by the Bay Area Rapid Transit System by stating, rather elliptically, that the computer could not be the subject of deception since it was 'nothing more than a big Coke machine'.[14] The Scottish Law Commission thought that Scottish common law's use of the term 'false pretence' rather than 'deception' would avoid such difficulty, since that wording concentrates on what the offender does rather than the precise effect upon the person deceived.[15] A similar view has been reached by the Court of Criminal Appeal of Queensland in *Baxter*,[16] where it was held that a 'false representation' under section 29B of the Crimes Act 1914 could be made by the defendant to the bank via an automatic teller machine, the broad wording of the section not requiring that the representation be made to a 'real person'.

In England, a statutory amendment has been made to deal with the specific lacuna exposed in *Moritz*.[17] The relevant statute, the Value Added Tax Act

[10] [1977] AC 177.

[11] See Austrian Penal Code, s. 146; Danish Penal Code, s. 279; German Penal Code, s. 263.

[12] Belgian Penal Code, s. 45; Canadian Criminal Code, ss. 338, 387, 388; see *Kirkwood* (1982) 148 DLR (3d) 323, *Fitzpatrick* (1984) 11 CCC (3d) 46.

[13] Alaska Stat s. 11.46.985.

[14] *People* v *Moore*, Alameda County Superior Court (Cal) No. 71976 (1981).

[15] Scottish Law Commission, Consultative Memorandum No. 68, *Computer Misuse*, Edinburgh: SLC, 1986, paras. 3.8–3.9. English law previously took this form: Larceny Act 1916, s. 32(1).

[16] Unreported, CA No. 67 of 1987 (July); see G. Hughes, 'Mindless Computers in Australia' (1987–8) 2 *Computer Law and Security Report* 25.

[17] Finance Act 1985, s. 12(5), amending s. 39 of Value Added Tax Act 1983. See also Keith Committee, *Enforcement Powers of the Revenue Departments*, Cmnd. 8822, London: HMSO, 1983.

1983, was amended in 1985 so as to define 'intent to deceive' in terms of 'intent to secure that a machine will respond to the document as if it were a true document'. This legislative change may tempt the sceptic to observe the speed with which a gap in the revenue laws was closed whilst the general problem remains open. There are in fact one or two other criminal offences designed to deal with the 'deception of machines' in particular contexts.[18] In its Working Paper on Computer Misuse the Law Commission proposed to deal with the issue of machine deception by what it regarded as a 'largely technical and . . . relatively uncontroversial extension of the criminal law'[19] by extending the definition of 'deception' in all relevant Theft Act offences[20] to include 'inducing a machine to respond to false representations which the person making them knows to be false, as if they were true'.[21] 'Machine' would obviously include a computer, but would go much wider than that, so that it would become the offence of obtaining property by deception, as well as theft, to obtain goods from a slot machine by inserting a washer or a foreign coin.[22] In his text on the Theft Acts, Professor Griew[23] had warned that care would have to be taken to avoid linguistic oddity if such reform was undertaken, particularly in respect of the offences under sections 1 and 2 of the Theft Act 1978, which are worded in a way that cannot happily apply to a machine. The Law Commission did not note these problems specifically in the Working Paper, but did draw attention to them in the wider context of their Working Paper on Conspiracy to Defraud.[24] In its Report on Computer Misuse, however, the Law Commission has reassessed the drafting difficulties, now describing them as 'complex'.[25] While the matter has, therefore, been shelved for the moment, and forms no part of the changes made by the Computer Misuse Act 1990, it may well be that the Commission will return to the issue of 'deceiving a machine' when its final Report on Conspiracy to Defraud is published.

3. THEFT

As an alternative to obtaining property by deception, in many cases of computer fraud a charge of theft under section 1 of the Theft Act 1968 is

---

[18] e.g. Road Traffic Regulation Act 1984, s. 52, making it a summary offence to interfere with a parking meter with intent to defraud. See also *Clayman* (1972), *The Times*, 1 July.

[19] Law Commission, Working Paper No. 110, *Computer Misuse*, London: HMSO, 1988, para. 5.5.

[20] Theft Act 1968, ss. 15, 16, and 20(2); Theft Act 1978, ss. 1 and 2.

[21] Law Commission (1988), para. 5.3; compare to the language of the Forgery and Counterfeiting Act 1981, set out in Chapter 1.

[22] *Hands* (1887) 16 Cox CC 188.

[23] E. Griew, *The Theft Acts 1968 and 1978*, 5th edn., London: Sweet and Maxwell, 1986, para. 6.15.

[24] Law Commission, Working Paper No. 104, *Conspiracy to Defraud*, London: HMSO 1987, para. 10.7.   [25] Law Commission (1989*b*), para. 2.6.

likely to prove to be effective. The decision of the House of Lords in *Lawrence*[26] confirmed the existence of a substantial overlap between the fraud and theft provisions in the Act, though their Lordships did not seem to agree with the Court of Appeal's view that all cases of obtaining property by deception could be prosecuted in the alternative as theft. The basic theft provision is:

1(1) A person is guilty of theft if he dishonestly appropriates property belonging to another with the intention of permanently depriving the other of it, and 'thief' and 'steal' shall be construed accordingly.

So, in those cases where a charge under section 15 will fail for the reasons described above, there may well have been a dishonest appropriation of property, and a theft charge will succeed instead.

The case of *Morris*[27] holds that a defendant cannot be said to have 'appropriated' property where the owner has in fact authorized what the defendant has done, but this would not avail the defendant in the typical case of computer fraud since his conduct, such as the creation of dummy files on the computer, even where his initial access to the computer was authorized, clearly goes well beyond what the owner has agreed to. There is, however, some difficulty in establishing that, where a person by deception dishonestly causes another to transfer his entire interest in property, rather than just possession of it, this amounts to theft. Ordinarily, such a case would be covered by section 15 and, indeed, it was the intention of the draftsmen of the 1968 Act that such conduct should be deception rather than theft but, as we have seen, this is problematic where a computer is used as the instrument for the fraud. Some jurisdictions have experienced great difficulty here in relation to the misuse of automated cash dispenser machines (ATMs), where it has been questioned whether the money can properly be said to have been taken against the owner's wishes.

Where the defendant uses a stolen or forged card to obtain the cash, or where he uses his own card to obtain more cash than he is authorized to withdraw, there can be no liability under section 15 because the dispenser is automated and no human mind has been deceived. In English law, however, this seems to be a straightforward case of theft[28] of the money. Some countries have also managed to avoid this problem and the ordinary pro-

---

[26] [1972] AC 626.
[27] [1983] 3 All ER 288.
[28] *Hands* (1887) 16 Cox CC 188; J. C. Smith and B. Hogan, *Criminal Law*, 6th edn., London: Butterworths, 1988, p. 661. According to Law Commission (1989*b*), para. 2.4, 'Convictions for theft have been obtained . . . where forged cash point cards (or cards stolen from someone else) have been used to obtain money from a cash dispensing machine. In . . . these types of cases, and in most, possibly in all, others which initially appear to involve some kind of "deception" of a machine, the manipulation involves an appropriation of money or other property, sufficient to constitute theft.'

visions of theft have been applied to cash dispenser manipulations.[29] Others
have legislated to deal with the problem. The Criminal Law Amendment Act
of 1985 in Canada, for example, amends the Criminal Code to cover
fraudulent access to 'an automated teller machine, a remote service unit or a
similar automated banking device to obtain any of the services offered
through the machine, unit or device'.[30] The argument used in other jurisdictions to resist liability for theft, particularly where a legitimate card holder
exceeds his authorized withdrawal limit, is that the bank has consented to the
passing of the entire interest in the money to the defendant, and so there is no
appropriation of 'property belonging to another'. In the absence of legislation
in Australia, a series of decisions there now seems to have scotched that
argument.

In *Kennison* v *Daire*,[31] the defendant was the holder of a cash card, which
enabled him to use ATMs of the Savings Bank of South Australia to withdraw
money from his account with that bank. Before the date of the alleged offence
the defendant had withdrawn the balance and closed his account but had not
returned the card. He then used the card to withdraw $200 from the machine
at the Adelaide branch of the bank. He was successful because the machine
was off-line and was programmed to allow the withdrawal of up to $200 by
any person who placed the card in the machine and gave the corresponding
PIN. When off-line, the machine was unable to check whether the card-
holder had an account with the bank or whether the account was in credit.
There was no doubt that the defendant had acted dishonestly, but he argued
that the bank had consented to the transfer of property in the money. The
judgment of the High Court of Australia, Gibbs C.J. presiding, was, however,
that on these facts the proper inference was that the bank had consented only
to the withdrawal of up to $200 by a card-holder who held an existing
account with the bank. It was 'unreal', it was said, to infer that the bank
consented to a withdrawal by a card-holder whose account had been closed,
and so the defendant's conviction was upheld. Unfortunately, the High Court
chose not to consider what the position would have been if the defendant's
account had still been open but had insufficient funds in it to meet the
withdrawal. Subsequently, however in *Evenett*,[32] the Queensland Court of
Criminal Appeal approved the earlier decision and in addition ruled that
funds obtained by a card holder contrary to the instructions of use (i.e. in

---

[29] OECD, Information Computer Communications Policy No. 10, *Computer-Related Crime: Analysis of Legal Policy*, Paris: OECD, 1986, p. 30; U. Sieber, *The International Handbook on Computer Crime*, New York: John Wiley, 1986, pp. 9–11. A decision of the French Supreme Court, 24.11.1983, No. 82, however, holds that where a legitimate card holder exceeds his credit limit this is a breach of contract but not theft, or any other offence.

[30] Section 43, amending s. 282 of the Code.

[31] (1986) 60 ALJR 249.

[32] (1987) 2 Qd R 753; see, further, Hughes (1987–8), and Queensland Government Department of Justice, *Green Paper on Computer Related Crime*, Queensland: Government Printer, 1987.

excess of the permitted withdrawal limit) remain the property of the financial institution, as there is neither express nor implied consent for their removal.

The definition of 'property' in England for the purposes of theft is now quite broad. It is set out in section 4 of the 1968 Act, the relevant part of which is as follows:

(1) 'Property' includes money and all other property, real or personal, including things in action and other intangible property.

The other provisions of section 4 deal with questions over theft of land or things forming parts of land, theft of certain plants, and theft of wild animals. Prior to the Theft Act 1968, intangibles could not be stolen, since theft required a physical removal or 'asportation' of the property.[33] The category of 'thing in action' in section 4(1) covers personal rights of property which can only be enforced by a legal action rather than by taking physical possession. It includes bank debts and overdraft facilities, company shares, rights under trusts, trade marks, and copyrights.[34] If the defendant purports dishonestly to sell another's copyright in a book, this is theft of that copyright, the thing in action. Theft of copyright must, however, be distinguished from breach of copyright, and this distinction is discussed further, below. Patents are declared by statute not to be things in action, but count as 'other intangible property'[35] as, apparently, do export quotas.[36] The fact that intangible property can be stolen does not, however, mean that anything which is intangible can be stolen, for the item in question may not qualify as 'property'. 'Information' cannot, in general, be owned, so the definition of property in section 4 does not extend to information, even where that information is valuable, perhaps confidential or in the form of a trade secret. Since such information is often held in a computerized form, this is an important limitation to the law of theft in the context of computer misuse in English criminal law. This issue is also considered further, below.

Prosecution for theft of a bank debt is likely to become of increasing importance in the context of computer fraud, where the computer manipulation involves the transfer of a credit from the victim's account to the fraudster's own, followed by a transfer of funds to the fraudster. In the important case of *Kohn*[37] it was agreed by the Court of Appeal that a company accountant was guilty of theft of a thing in action, being the amount outstanding in his company's bank balance, when he wrote cheques upon the company's bank account for his own unauthorized purposes. Where the bank account is in credit the bank stands to the account holder in the relation of debtor to creditor. Thus the defendant in *Kohn* appropriated the debt owed by the bank to the company. The case was followed by the Privy Council in

---

[33] See *Kidd* (1907) 72 JP 104.   [34] Griew (1986), para. 2.11.
[35] Patents Act 1977, s. 30(1).
[36] *A-G of Hong Kong v Nai-Keung* [1988] Crim LR 125.
[37] (1979) 69 Cr App R 395; see also *Navvabi* [1986] 3 All ER 102.

Chan Man-Sin,[38] a case involving very similar facts. If the account in question is not in credit, the account holder may have an overdraft facility. If so, this facility is also a thing in action and may be stolen. Where the account is not in credit and there is no overdraft facility, there can be no theft.

In *Thompson*,[39] the defendant was a computer programmer employed by a bank in Kuwait. He opened savings accounts at Kuwaiti branches and programmed the bank's computer to credit those accounts with amounts debited from other customers' accounts. This action was not detected. Subsequently he returned to England and arranged through his bank for this fictitious balance to be telexed to his account in England. The problem with convicting the defendant of theft on these facts lies in identifying the property which is the subject of the theft. In this case there actually was no bank credit, merely the appearance of one, created by the defendant's manipulation of the computer. This may be contrasted with the situation in *Kohn*, where there was a credit balance in the company's account which was capable of being stolen. A further difficulty in establishing theft lies in proving that the property belonged to another. When the supposed balance was transferred to England any intangible property acquired by the defendant had surely never belonged to anyone except him. In the event, the defendant was convicted of obtaining property by deception rather than theft, and this was upheld on appeal. It seems that the court took the view that the manager at the Kuwaiti branch had been deceived by the defendant's communications to him into telexing the balances,[40] so that the difficulty of computer deception was avoided, but the problem of identifying the 'property' obtained by the deception remains as acute in the deception offence as it would have been for theft itself. The case has been criticized by a number of commentators,[41] and seems unlikely to be the last word on the subject. The case also raises jurisdictional problems, which are discussed in Chapter 7.

Several other jurisdictions have found themselves unable to treat the appropriation of bank balances as theft, since deposit money has been considered in law to be a civil claim rather than an item of property, but some have now amended their laws to include deposit money within their definitions of theft, deception, and embezzlement. In the Tasmanian case of *Hollingsworth*,[42] a bank's computer systems manager reprogrammed the bank's computer to inflate depositors' accounts, and then transferred the excess amounts to his own account, also through manipulation of the computer. The defendant was originally charged with theft, but the charges

---

[38] [1988] 1 All ER 1; see also *Tai Hing Cotton Mill* v *Lin Chong Hing Bank* [1986] AC 80.
[39] [1984] 3 All ER 565.
[40] The point is not clear from the report of the case.
[41] e.g. Professor J. C. Smith's commentary on the case at [1984] *Criminal Law Review* 428; E. J. Griew, 'Stealing and Obtaining Bank Credits' [1986] *Criminal Law Review* 356, and Law Commission, Report No. 180, *Jurisdiction Over Fraud Offences of Fraud and Dishonesty with Foreign Element*, London: HMSO, 1989a, para. 2.9.
[42] Unreported, Supreme Court of Tasmania, Sept. 1983; see Hughes (1987–8).

were dropped by the prosecutor when it emerged that nothing tangible had been taken from the bank, as required by Tasmanian law. The defendant subsequently pleaded guilty to a deception offence instead, but the Law Reform Commission of Tasmania expresses doubt whether on the facts the prosecution could have proved that any person had been deceived by what the defendant had done.[43]

In the United States, similar problems were encountered a decade ago. Judicial decisions varied in the extent to which they were prepared to depart from the traditional view of theft requiring an asportation of tangible property.[44] Some states have in consequence greatly expanded the definition of property so as, for example, to include:[45]

electronic impulses, electronically processed or produced data or information, commercial instruments, computer software or computer programs, in either machine or human readable form, computer services, any other tangible or intangible item of value relating to a computer, computer system, or computer network, and any copies thereof.

In contrast, in English law it is established that 'words transmitted by electronic impulses' do not attain the status of property,[46] nor does information, whether held on computer or not.[47] The question of the unauthorized use of computer services was considered in the last chapter.

4. FALSE ACCOUNTING AND FORGERY

A further possible option for the prosecutor in some cases of computer fraud is the offence of false accounting, under section 17 of the Theft Act 1968. This provides:

(1) where a person dishonestly, with a view to gain for himself or another or with intent to cause loss to another
   (a) destroys, defaces, conceals or falsifies any account or any record or document made or required for any accounting purpose; or
   (b) in furnishing information for any purpose produces or makes use of any account, or any such record or document as aforesaid, which to his knowledge is or may be misleading, false or deceptive in a material particular;
         he shall, on conviction on indictment, be liable to imprisonment for a term not exceeding seven years.

[43] Tasmanian Law Reform Commission, Report No. 47, *Computer Misuse*, Tasmania: Government Printer, 1986, p. 14.

[44] *Lund* v *Commonwealth* 217 Va 688, 691, SE 2d 745 (1977), reversed by Va Code s. 18.2–98.1; *People* v *Home Insurance Co.* 197 Colo 260, 591 P 2d 1036 (1979); *Ward* v *Superior Court*, unreported, 3 Comp L Serv Rep 208 (1972).

[45] Mont Code Ann s. 45.2.101(54)(k) (1981).

[46] *Malone* v *MPC* [1979] 1 All ER 620.

[47] *Oxford* v *Moss* (1978) 68 Cr App R 183.

(2) For purposes of this section a person who makes or concurs in making in an account or other document an entry which is or may be misleading, false or deceptive in a material particular, or who omits or concurs in omitting a material particular from an account or other document, is to be treated as falsifying the account or document.

This broadly drafted offence would seem to be applicable to many cases of fraud where computer input is tampered with, and convictions have indeed been returned on this basis.[48]

It has been held to be sufficient that accounting is only one of the purposes for which the record or document is required, so that a hire-purchase agreement fell within the ambit of the section.[49] The misleading or deceptive element does not have to be connected with the accounting purpose: it is sufficient that it is 'false in some respect that matters'.[50] It is clear that the courts will interpret 'record' to include 'computerized record',[51] as where the fraudster creates spurious files on the computer with accompanying addresses to which cheques will be diverted, and where the false account is typed directly into a computer terminal, the computer files would be the account or record that would have been falsified. There is in this respect an overlap between the offence of false accounting and forgery. As we saw in Chapter 3, the making of a false instrument constitutes forgery, and records kept in mechanical or electronic form are expressly included.[52] The offence is, however, crucially limited by the requirement not only that the instrument tells a lie, as by containing a false statement, but also tells a lie about itself, as by purporting to have been made or altered in circumstances in which it was not made or altered. The creation of dummy files on a computer, for example, may amount to the offence of forgery, but only where the entries purport to be made or authorized by someone who did not make them. A bank teller is not guilty of forgery merely by causing false entries to be made in the bank's computer any more than he would have been guilty of forgery in making false entries in the bank's ledgers.[53] A charge of false accounting will, however, extend to a number of cases where a forgery charge is inapplicable on the ground that the instrument does not tell a lie about itself. Judicial comments in *Hopkins and Collins*[54] to the effect that any case of false accounting could be prosecuted as forgery were disapproved in *Dodge and Harris*.[55]

[48] e.g. A. R. D. Norman, *Computer Insecurity*, London: Chapman and Hall, 1983, case 78.054.

[49] *Mallett* (1978) 66 Cr App R 239.

[50] *A-G's Reference No. 1 of 1980* [1981] 1 All ER 366.

[51] *Edwards v Toombs* [1983] Crim LR 43, where a turnstile recording the number of people passing through it was held to a record made for an accounting purpose; also *Solomons* [1909] 2 KB 980 (a taxi-meter).

[52] Forgery and Counterfeiting Act 1981, s. 8(1)(d).

[53] Smith and Hogan (1988), p. 649; *Windsor* (1865) 6 B & S 522.

[54] (1957) 41 Cr App R 231.

[55] [1972] 1 QB 416; though see *Donnelly* [1984] 1 WLR 1017, criticized by Arlidge and Parry (1985), p. 176.

Tampering with input may be done to generate the fraud or to cover up a fraud already committed. It may be questioned whether the defendant has a view to gain or an intent to cause loss under this section where he falsifies input in order to conceal a fraud. However, by section 34(2)(a), an interpretation section which applies to section 17:

(i) 'gain' includes a gain by keeping what one has, as well as a gain by getting what one has not; and
'loss' includes a loss by not getting what one might get, as well as a loss by parting with what one has.

This makes it clear that such a case would be covered, apart perhaps from the very rare situation where the sole reason for tampering with the record is to avoid detection for a fraud committed some time previously.[56] It was said by the Court of Appeal in *Eden*[57] that where theft was the essence of the alleged misconduct, it should be prosecuted as such and not as false accounting. In general, however, false accounting will cover any case where, in pursuance of a fraud, the defendant dishonestly causes records made or required for an accounting purpose and held in computerized form to be erased or falsified. The defendant in *Thompson* could have been convicted on such a charge.

5. CONSPIRACY TO DEFRAUD

The offence of conspiracy to defraud offers another possibility for the prosecutor in the area of computer-related fraud. Conspiracy to defraud is a common-law conspiracy which, anomalously, remains outside the main grouping of conspiracies, which are conspiracies to commit substantive criminal offences, under section 1 of the Criminal Law Act 1977. The long-term law reform objective was said by the Law Commission to be that the crime of conspiracy should be limited to agreements to commit crimes.[58] The 1977 Act, however, left conspiracy to defraud untouched, because it was thought that to abolish it at that stage would leave an unacceptably large gap in the criminal law. The abolition or replacement of conspiracy to defraud is still the subject of law reform attention,[59] but the offence itself has been much affected by case-law since 1977.

Of course, a statutory conspiracy, such as conspiracy to steal or conspiracy

---

[56] J. C. Smith (1989), para. 264; see *Eden* (1971) 55 Cr App R 193.

[57] Ibid.; perhaps the defendants might be guilty of evading liability by deception under Theft Act 1978, s. 2(1)(b).

[58] Law Commission, Report No. 76, *Conspiracy and Criminal Law Reform*, London: HMSO, 1976.

[59] Law Commission (1987); specific problems associated with the decision in *Ayres* [1984] AC 447 were dealt with by the Criminal Law Revision Committee, 18th Report, *Conspiracy to Defraud*, Cmnd. 9873, London: HMSO, 1986.

to obtain property by deception, may be an appropriate charge in a given case of computer-related fraud, where two or more persons agree that[60]

> a course of conduct shall be pursued which, if the agreement is carried out in accordance with their intentions . . . will necessarily amount to or involve the commission of any offence or offences by one or more of the parties to the agreement . . .

Many cases of fraud involve more than one defendant, and such a charge would be appropriate where the agreement had been reached but not put into effect.[61] The likely difficulty for the prosecution would be to establish that the specified substantive offence would in fact have occurred if the agreement had been carried through.[62] This takes us back to the questions, discussed above, of whether theft or obtaining property by deception would actually be committed in the course of a particular computer-related fraud. Conspiracy to defraud, on the other hand, not being tied to any substantive offence, offers a potentially very broad and flexible crime to cater for agreements to commit computer-related fraud.

It was stated by the House of Lords in *Scott* v *MPC*[63] that:

> . . . it is clearly the law that an agreement by two or more by dishonesty to deprive a person of something which is his or to which he is or would be or might be entitled and an agreement by two or more by dishonesty to injure some proprietary right of his, suffices to constitute the offence of conspiracy to defraud.

This is a very broad definition, but it has been further extended to cover cases where a person dishonestly misleads another into acting contrary to his public duty.[64] One of the difficulties in the substantive law is, as we have seen, the impotence of the notion of 'deception' in computer-related fraud. In *Scott* the House decided that deception was not an essential element of a conspiracy to defraud. There, the defendant agreed with certain cinema employees that, in return for payment, they would remove feature films without permission, in order that the defendant might make copies and distribute them for profit. It was held that the parties were guilty of conspiracy to defraud. It is implicit in this decision that the offence extends to agreements to commit fraud which are not offences under the Theft Acts, since the borrowing of the films would not amount to theft or obtaining property by deception, because of the lack of an intent to deprive the owner of the property permanently.[65]

---

[60] Criminal Law Act 1977, s. 1(1).

[61] Where the contemplated offence is actually committed, a conspiracy charge should not be brought: *West* [1948] 1 KB 709.

[62] Though the impossibility, in fact, of committing the contemplated offence is irrelevant: Criminal Law Act 1977, s. 1, as amended by Criminal Attempts Act 1981, s. 5.

[63] [1975] AC 819, 840 *per* Viscount Dilhorne.

[64] *Terry* [1984] AC 374, following *Welham* v *DPP* [1961] AC 103.

[65] *Lloyd* [1985] 2 All ER 661. In *Scott*, the defendant also pleaded guilty to conspiracy to contravene s. 21(1)(a) of the Copyright Act 1956. See further, below.

Following the 1977 Act there was uncertainty over the precise relationship between statutory conspiracy and conspiracy to defraud, and this matter was the subject of a number of appellate decisions, most notably *Duncalf*[66] in the Court of Appeal and *Ayres*[67] and *Cooke*[68] in the House of Lords. Fortunately it is not necessary here to describe all these developments since the matter has now received the attention of Parliament, in the form of section 12 of the Criminal Justice Act 1987. This section provides that the prosecutor has a discretion either to charge a statutory conspiracy or a conspiracy to defraud in cases where the conspiracy took the form of an agreement to commit a substantive offence. This follows the recommendation of the 18th Report of the Criminal Law Revision Committee[69] and is accompanied by guidelines issued by the Director of Public Prosecutions under section 10 of the Prosecution of Offences Act 1985 on the exercise of the prosecutorial discretion. The Act provides a maximum penalty of ten years' imprisonment for the offence.

The implications of these developments for the prosecution of computer-related crime are significant, for their effect has been to reinstate a broad 'fall-back' offence, 'an available option in almost every case where there has been an agreement to cause economic loss by dishonest means'.[70] The availability of the offence may be objected to on principle, in respect of its vagueness and the anomaly that some of the conduct encompassed by conspiracy to defraud is criminal only by virtue of its being committed in concert with others. On the other hand, a powerful argument may be made out that the simple abolition of conspiracy to defraud would be likely to leave loopholes and necessitate unmeritorious acquittals, or require the unreal stretching of existing statutory offences. Leigh has claimed[71] that the 'piecemeal' law reform which produced the Theft Act 1968 'left contemporary problems unrecognised and untouched' and that without a widely based offence of conspiracy to defraud, 'the system, bereft of reserve powers, would have broken down'.

In a Working Paper issued at the end of 1987 the Law Commission has set out a number of options for further law reform in this area.[72] The first option is to keep conspiracy to defraud as it is and the second is to reduce the existing law to statutory form. More likely options, however, are the third, which proposes abolition of the offence with replacements where necessary by adjusting the existing law, and the fourth, which is abolition of the offence together with replacement by a widely drafted statutory offence. In considering the third option, the Law Commission identifies no fewer than eleven

[66] [1979] 2 All ER 1116. [67] [1984] AC 447. [68] [1986] AC 909.
[69] Criminal Law Revision Committee (1986).
[70] G. R. Sullivan, 'Fraud and the Efficacy of the Criminal Law: A Proposal for a Wide Residual Offence' [1985] *Criminal Law Review* 616; economic loss is widely construed in this context: *Allsop* (1976) 64 Cr App R 29.
[71] L. H. Leigh, *The Control of Commercial Fraud*, London: Heinemann, 1982, p. 9.
[72] Law Commission (1987), Pt. X.

possible areas where the criminal law would probably no longer extend if conspiracy to defraud were abolished without replacement or amendment of existing laws. A number of these areas impinge upon the issue of computer misuse. The question of deceiving a machine has already been described, above. Other matters include possible criminal liability for the temporary deprivation of another's property, the making of a secret profit, commercial counterfeiting, the manufacture of goods designed to defraud, and the dishonest acquisition of confidential information. Each of these areas is considered in its appropriate place in this book. The Commission's fourth option raises squarely the problem of having a broad fall-back offence in the area of fraud. The advantages claimed for such an offence are its generality and flexibility, which allows the prosecution to present the essence of the wrongdoing which has occurred, and makes the presentation of the case simpler for prosecution, judge, jury, and defendant.[73] The drawbacks are that this leaves too much to the discretion of the courts, when the proper ambit of the law really should be declared in advance by Parliament, through legislation. In each of the problem areas identified by the Commission, the courts would eventually have to determine its legality or otherwise. As Smith points out,[74] the proposal involves creating a serious offence, carrying a penalty of ten years' imprisonment, 'when nobody can identify what it might be used to punish'. A final Report on Conspiracy to Defraud is expected from the Law Commission in the near future.

6. ESTABLISHING DISHONESTY

Most of the offences discussed in this chapter possess the common element of a requirement of 'dishonesty' on the part of the defendant. This is true of theft, obtaining property by deception, false accounting, and conspiracy to defraud.[75] The concept of dishonesty, even more than that of deception, lends a semblance of unity to the multitude of types of conduct which may constitute fraud.[76] Occasionally, in cases of computer-related fraud, there may be argument whether the defendant acted dishonestly and it is appropriate to say something on the point here.

The term 'dishonestly' is partly defined in section 2 of the Theft Act 1968, and while this strictly only applies to the offence of theft itself,[77] it would be strange if the concept were to be construed differently in respect of the other offences.[78] It is unlikely that the terms of section 2 could provide the basis of

[73] See Sullivan (1985).
[74] A. T. H. Smith, 'Conspiracy to Defraud' [1988] *Criminal Law Review* 508, at p. 515.
[75] And other offences, e.g. Theft Act 1968, s. 13 (abstracting electricity); see *Boggeln* v *Williams* [1978] 2 All ER 1061 and s. 16 (obtaining a pecuniary advantage by deception).
[76] Arlidge and Parry (1985), p. 3.
[77] Theft Act 1968, s. 1(3).
[78] See *Woolven* (1983) 77 Cr App R 231; *Melwani* [1989] Crim LR 565.

any unusual defence in a case of computer-related fraud. An appropriation of property is there declared not to be dishonest where the taker believes,[79] however mistakenly, that he had a proprietary right to the property. Similarly, he does not act dishonestly where he believes that he had or would have had the owner's consent to the taking, or that the owner cannot be discovered by taking reasonable steps. An appropriation may be dishonest even where the defendant is prepared to pay for the property. Since section 2 offers only a partial definition of dishonesty, the defendant may dispute the matter without asserting that he held any of the beliefs there set out. If so, the issue of dishonesty may be described as being 'at large' and is a matter for the tribunal of fact to determine the acceptability or otherwise of the defendant's conduct. The Court of Appeal in *Feely*[80] held that it was for the jury to determine not only what the defendant's state of mind was but also whether such state of mind is to be categorized as dishonest, applying the standard of 'ordinary decent people'. The test, as more recently elaborated in *Ghosh*,[81] is twofold:

(1) Was what was done dishonest according to the standards of ordinary decent people? If the answer is no, the defendant should be acquitted; if it is yes, then the second question also needs to be answered.

(2) Did the defendant realize that his conduct was contrary to such standards? If the answer is yes, the defendant should be convicted, if no, he should be acquitted.

This test would seem to be appropriate to all offences requiring proof of dishonesty, including conspiracy to defraud.[82]

Two points arise here. The first relates to the appropriate standard. Where dishonesty is alleged to have occurred in a business environment, should normal business practice be taken into account? In a case involving a charge of fraudulent trading,[83] Maugham J. expressed the view that:[84] '. . . the words "defraud" and "fraudulent purpose" . . . are words which connote actual dishonesty involving, according to current notions of fair trading among commercial men, real moral blame.' In *Sinclair*,[85] however, Lord Widgery L.J. said that the normality or otherwise of the business transaction involved was not the relevant standard, and recent cases confirm that the appropriate test is 'the ordinary standards of reasonable and honest people' rather than the accepted practice of commercial men.[86]

The second point relates to the application of that test, which may well give rise to difficulty in complex fraud cases, particularly those involving the use of computers. Such activities fall outside the experience of many people who are

---

[79]   *A-G's Reference No. 2 of 1982* [1984] QB 624 suggests that the belief must be 'an honest belief', but that appears to add nothing to the meaning of the provision.
[80]   [1973] 1 All ER 341.   [81]   [1982] 2 All ER 689.
[82]   *Ghosh* [1982] 2 All ER 689 is to be preferred in this respect to *McIvor* [1982] 1 All ER 491, which suggested a different test for conspiracy to defraud.
[83]   See below.
[84]   *Re Patrick and Lyon Ltd.* [1933] Ch 781 at p. 790.
[85]   [1968] 1 WLR 1246.
[86]   *Lockwood* [1986] Crim LR 244; *Re E B Tractors* [1986] 3 NIJB 1.

called to serve on a jury. The issue of dishonesty was problematic in *Greenstein*,[87] where the jury rejected a defence of honesty on a charge of obtaining property by deception, where the defendant, who was involved in 'stagging'[88] operations in the share market, claimed that he had arranged his financial affairs in such a way that the person deceived would not be financially disadvantaged. In *Tarling* v *Republic of Singapore*[89] the members of the House of Lords differed amongst themselves as to whether a clandestine transfer of shares, probably owned by the company, to directors in pursuance of a concealed share incentive scheme, amounted to dishonesty for the purposes of theft or conspiracy to defraud.

In the Roskill Fraud Trials Committee Report[90] the Committee noted a number of difficulties with the use of juries in complex fraud cases, including the application of the dishonesty standard, and suggested that such cases should be tried without a jury. The government adopted many of the Committee's recommendations in the Criminal Justice Acts of 1987 and 1988, but this particular suggestion has not been acted upon.

7. FRAUD: OTHER OFFENCES

In addition to the main fraud offences already discussed, there are many other related offences having more restricted application. Some of these might well be applicable in an individual case to prosecution for computer-related fraud. It would be pointless in this book to detail all these available offences, and for further information reference should be made to a specialist work on the law of fraud. All that will be attempted here is a summary of a few of them.

There are several offences of fraud within the modern Companies Act legislation. They overlap substantially with the main fraud offences already discussed. The offence of fraudulent trading, under section 458 of the Companies Act 1985, is made out where a person is proved to have been carrying on a company's business with intent to defraud its or another person's creditors, or for any other fraudulent purpose. In *Kemp*[91] this was held to extend to an intent to defraud the company's own customers or potential creditors. Such a prosecution may be brought whether the company is being or has been wound up or not, and the offence is punishable with up

---

[87] [1975] 1 All ER 1.
[88] The defendant and others applied for large numbers of shares and with each application they enclosed a cheque to cover the purchase price. They knew that they did not have the funds in the bank to meet the cheque at the time the application was made but they knew from experience that they would be allocated only a proportion of the shares applied for, a cheque refunding the difference being paid promptly to the defendant. Once this cheque was presented, the defendant's cheque would be met on the first, or, at worst, second presentation.
[89] (1980) 70 Cr App R 77. This issue, amongst others, is discussed by J. C. Smith, 'Theft, Conspiracy and Jurisdiction: Tarling's Case' [1979] *Criminal Law Review* 220.
[90] Roskill Report, *Report of the Fraud Trials Committee*, London: HMSO, 1986.
[91] [1988] QB 645.

to seven years' imprisonment. Dishonesty must be proved.[92] Other relevant offences under the Act are the falsification of company accounts and accounting records;[93] falsification or suppression of company records,[94] and making a false statement to an auditor.[95] Offences under the Theft Act 1968[96] and the Perjury Act 1911[97] may also extend to instances where company records are tampered with. Since many records are now held on computer, it is a matter for decision in each case whether a computer file would constitute an 'account', a 'record', or a 'document' for the purpose of these offences. There is no general provision to this effect in the substantive law, though the rules of evidence provide for the admissibility of statements contained in documents, including those produced by a computer.[98]

Offences relating to insolvency, including falsification of documents, can be found in the Companies Act 1985.[99] There are specific criminal offences available relating to fraud committed against investors, again overlapping with the main Theft Act offences. Deception of investors may be prosecuted under the Companies Act 1985[100] and the Financial Services Act 1986. Insider dealing is now prohibited by the Company Securities (Insider Dealing) Act 1985, and the Financial Services Act 1986 has conferred new powers on the Secretary of State to investigate insider dealing. These powers require a person under investigation to produce any relevant 'document', defined for these purposes as 'information recorded in any form'.[101] An insider is a person who is connected with a company and holds unpublished price-sensitive information in relation to any securities of a company. It is an offence for such a person to deal with those securities or communicate the information to any other person. The offence is confined to dealings in listed and advertised securities and, therefore, in effect, dealings on the Stock Exchange and the Unlisted Securities Market. Direct personal dealings remain unregulated. It must be proved that the individual's conduct was intentional or reckless with regard to all elements of the offence, which carries a maximum penalty of seven years' imprisonment.

8. UNAUTHORIZED REMOVAL OF INFORMATION

Increasingly, much commercially valuable and personally sensitive information is stored on computer. A common form of computer misuse is the unauthorized obtaining of that information, for one of a variety of purposes. Computer-held material such as development, research, or production data

---

[92] *Cox and Hedges* (1982) 75 Cr App R 291.
[93] Companies Act 1985, s. 221, amended by Companies Act 1989, s. 2.
[94] Ibid., s. 450(1), amended by Companies Act 1989, s. 66.
[95] Ibid., s. 389A inserted by Companies Act 1989, s. 120.
[96] Theft Act 1968, ss. 18, 19.   [97] Perjury Act 1911, s. 5.
[98] See Chapter 6.   [99] Companies Act 1985, ss. 626, 627.   [100] Ibid., s. 70(1).
[101] Financial Services Act 1986, s. 177(10). Under s. 200 of the Act it is an offence to knowingly or recklessly furnish information to an investigator which is false or misleading.

may be the target for an industrial spy. The special nature of the computer risk here lies in the sheer volume of data which may be accommodated within a single disk and the virtually instantaneous retrieval or copying of that data which can be achieved. Information can be taken and used by anyone who gains access to it, whether by committing it to memory, noting it down, printing it out, or otherwise recording it. Apart from data, computer programs themselves may represent very valuable assets, being the product of expensive and protracted research and design effort. Computer software is very expensive to develop and costs have been increasing steadily in contrast to hardware costs, which have been decreasing in recent years. New and customized programs are a key target for the industrial spy and, as is well known, there is large-scale copying by businesses and by individuals of commercially available software, which is estimated by the Federation Against Software Theft to cost the software industry in the region of £150 million a year. Total losses in Western Europe of the order of £1 billion have been estimated. Much of this copying takes place within commercial organizations and is easy to do, since most computer users will have software copying facilities within existing hardware. While the user of a sound recording will require just one copy for his own purposes, a commercial organization with perhaps hundreds of personal computers will often want to have copies of certain software packages for all, or most, of its terminals.

A variety of legal issues arise from the unauthorized removal of computer-stored material, data or software. It is clear in English law that information as such, even if commercially valuable or personally sensitive, does not achieve the status of 'property' to bring it within the law of theft, though on occasions the activities of the commercial spy may infringe other aspects of the criminal law. Other approaches to the problem are through the laws on copyright and trade secrets. The criminal law aspects of these areas are now discussed in turn.

The definition of 'property' for the purposes of the Theft Act 1968 covers 'money and all other property, real or personal, including things in action and other tangible property'.[102] It is clear that if the obtaining of the information involves the printing out of that information in tangible form then the removal of the print-out is theft of the paper itself. One such example appears in the 1981 Audit Commission report,[103] where a programmer and a computer operator sold the results of a program run on the company's computer to a third party. Although, in fact, this case did not result in prosecution, bringing a charge of theft would present no difficulty in England. Greater problems have emerged elsewhere, however.

In the American case of *Hancock* v *State*,[104] the issue was whether the defendant had stolen property of a value in excess of $50, making the crime a

---

[102] Theft Act 1968, s. 4, and see above.
[103] Audit Inspectorate, *Computer Fraud Survey*, London: Department of the Environment, 1981, p. 31.
[104] 402 SW 2d 906 (Tex Crim App 1966).

felony rather than a misdemeanour. In United States legislation theft is generally categorized either as grand larceny, a felony punishable with imprisonment not exceeding ten years, or petit larceny, a misdemeanour, a categorization based entirely upon the value of the property involved. The defendant was employed by Texas Instruments as a computer programmer. He suggested to his room-mate, who worked for the company Texaco, that Texaco might be interested in buying some of Texas Instrument's programs. A meeting was arranged and the defendant offered 59 programs to a man he believed to be a Texaco representative, for $5 million. This man was in fact an investigator and the defendant was arrested and indicted for theft. At trial it was argued on his behalf that he had committed a misdemeanour rather than a felony in that he had stolen property valued at about $35, the worth of the paper on which the programs were printed. The vice-president of Texas Instruments testified that the market value of the programs was about $2.5 million. The state court noted the existence of competitors in the same programming field, the existence of a ready market for the software, and the superiority of the software giving Texas Instruments a competitive advantage, and heard evidence of the unique nature of the software. The defendant's argument was rejected and the court held that the value of the property was determined by the information printed on it.[105] Clearly this was enough to dispose of this particular case but, as Tapper points out, in another case, where the precise value of the information was in issue, matters might be more difficult:[106] 'The seller might never have contemplated selling, or there might be no market for the programs. In such a case the value of the programs might plausibly be regarded as equivalent either to the commercial advantage of the victim in having them kept secret or perhaps to the cost of preparing them.'

On appeal,[107] the Fifth Circuit Court of Appeals denied Hancock's petition for a writ of habeas corpus, stating that the Texas court's construction of the relevant statute was not so unreasonable or arbitrary as to violate procedural due process.

Apart from the issue of quantifying the value of the loss, which does not have any comparable effect in England upon the offence of theft, this case illustrates the fortuitous aspect of the defendant's removal of tangible photo-copies of the information. If, for instance, he had memorized the programs for transcription elsewhere,[108] clearly there could have been no conviction on this basis.

Another technique of the spy is to remove temporarily a tangible item, such as a computer disk or tape, in order to copy the information, subsequently

---

[105] Compare *Lund v Commonwealth* 217 Va 688, 232 SE 2d 745 (1977) with *Evans v Commonwealth* 226 Va 292, 308 SE 2d 126 (Va 1983).
[106] C. Tapper, *Computer Law*, 3rd edn., London: Longman, 1983, p. 101.
[107] *Hancock v Dexter* 379 F 2d 552 (5th Cir 1967).
[108] *Commonwealth v Engleman* 142 NE 2d 406 (Mass 1957).

returning the original. The immediate difficulty in convicting the spy of theft of the disk or tape is that the offence of theft requires the prosecution to establish 'the intention of permanently depriving' the owner of the property. Section 6(1) of the Theft Act, which deals with this issue, provides that:

> A person appropriating property belonging to another without meaning the other permanently to lose the thing itself is nevertheless to be regarded as having the intention of permanently depriving the other of it, if his intention is to treat the thing as his own to dispose of regardless of the other's rights; and a borrowing or lending of it may amount to so treating it if, but only if, the borrowing or lending was for a period and in circumstances making it equivalent to an outright taking or disposal.

Professor Smith has argued[109] that the kinds of borrowings which will amount to theft under this provision are those where the taker intends not to return the article until the 'virtue' has gone out of it, such as where the defendant takes the victim's season-ticket, intending all along to return it when the season is over. The merits of this argument have received attention from the Court of Appeal in *Lloyd*.[110]

In this case a cinema projectionist clandestinely removed films from the cinema where he worked so that they could be copied, and pirated versions thereafter marketed. The films were only out of the cinema for a few hours for this purpose, and were returned in time for advertised film showings. The defendant projectionist and two others were convicted of conspiracy to steal the films. The Court of Appeal quashed the convictions, holding that section 6(1) had a very limited ambit and should be referred to in exceptional cases only. The Court was inclined to agree with academic writers that section 6 was one which 'sprouts complexities at every phrase',[111] but said that it should be construed so as to ensure that nothing constituted an intention permanently to deprive which would not have done so prior to the 1968 Act. An intention permanently to deprive could only be established by a temporary 'borrowing', where the defendant's intention was to return the thing in such a changed state that *all* its goodness or virtue had gone.[112] On the facts of *Lloyd* this was not so, since the films themselves had not diminished in value and the film performances had been unaffected. Professor Smith's example of the season-ticket would fall within this rule, but the decision raises difficult questions of degree, for instance where the defendant's intention was to return the season-ticket when a few matches were still left to play. It is such matters of degree which tend to arise when information is removed. Such removal clearly prejudices the owners, but only rarely could it be said that the

---

[109] J. C. Smith (1989), para. 140.

[110] [1985] 2 All ER 661.

[111] J. R. Spencer, 'The Metamorphosis of Section 6 of the Theft Act' [1977] *Criminal Law Review* 653.

[112] *Per* Lord Lane C.J. at p. 667. See, further *Bagshaw* [1988] Crim LR 321.

information was thereby rendered completely valueless.[113] The facts of *Lloyd* are very similar to those of *Scott* v *MPC*.[114] In that case the defendants pleaded guilty to conspiracy to contravene the copyright legislation and were also convicted of conspiracy to defraud. At the time of Lloyd's case, however, a charge of conspiracy to defraud was probably not open to the prosecution, as a result of the decision of the House of Lords in *Ayres*.[115] The reversal of that decision by statute now means that the defendants in *Lloyd* could be prosecuted successfully for conspiracy to defraud, or conspiracy to contravene the now amended copyright laws.

While the requirement of proof of an intention to deprive permanently is a cornerstone of the existing law of theft, as well as other offences within the Theft Acts,[116] it is a requirement not present in a number of other jurisdictions, such as Canada.[117] There is uncertainty whether the Scottish law of theft may extend in some situations to temporary deprivations.[118] The Law Commission gave consideration to the general issue of temporary deprivation of property in their Working Paper on Conspiracy to Defraud,[119] but are unlikely to recommend any change without a thorough review of the Theft Acts themselves.

The examples discussed so far have involved the removal of some tangible item. Where information is held on a computer, however, only that information itself may be taken. It is well established in English law, however, that 'information' is not property and so cannot be the subject-mater of theft. The authority for this proposition is the case of *Oxford* v *Moss*.[120] There, an undergraduate acquired the proof of an examination paper. He noted down the contents and returned it. He was charged with stealing certain intangible property, namely, confidential information the property of the University Senate. The Divisional Court upheld the dismissal of the charge on the ground that there was no property in the information capable of being the subject of theft. The case was followed in *Absolom*,[121] where a geologist was acquitted of a charge of theft after he had obtained and tried to sell to a rival company details of Esso Petroleum's oil exploration off the Irish coast, information which was valued in evidence as worth between £50,000 and £100,000. It can be appreciated that information is in fact a quite different type of commodity from the forms of intangible property which are capable of being stolen, such as a bank credit. Information is not a legal right or a

[113] Unless perhaps the copier had flooded the market with so many copies that it was no longer possible to sell the material at all: G. L. Williams, *Textbook of Criminal Law*, 2nd edn., London: Stevens, 1983, p. 718.

[114] [1975] AC 819. See above.   [115] [1984] AC 447.

[116] See G. Williams, 'Temporary Appropriation Should Be Theft' [1981] *Criminal Law Review* 129, Law Commission (1987), Pt. XIII.

[117] Canadian Criminal Code, s. 283; for the relevant provision see p. 127 below.

[118] Scottish Law Commission (1986), paras. 3.36–3.49; *Milne* v *Tudhope* (1981) JC 53; *Sandlan* v *HMA* (1983) SCCR 71.

[119] Law Commission (1987), Pt. XIII.

[120] (1979) 68 Cr App R 183.   [121] *The Times*, 14 Sept. 1983.

claim. It does not exist by virtue of a relationship between the owner of the commodity and the person against whom it can be enforced. Information, in this general sense, can be 'owned' by very many people quite independently of one another, and so the notion of personal ownership is very problematic.[122] To provide information generally with the status of property would be a very bold step to take and would be 'likely only to create conceptual confusion'.[123] Parliament rejected any such idea while the Theft Act was in the process of becoming law, and the Younger Committee on Privacy[124] resisted the suggestion that there should be a crime of theft of information. Clearly, the competing notion of freedom of access to information is also a very important principle. As Lord Upjohn said on one occasion,[125] 'in general, information is not property at all; it is normally open to all who have eyes to read and ears to hear'. On the other hand some information is commercially very valuable, the product of painstaking research or intellectual breakthrough. Such information can be bought and sold and may attain the status of property for civil law purposes.[126] Although there is certainly a strong argument based on commercial reality for according at least some forms of information property status, to do so in English law 'would involve reading the [Theft] Act in a very robust way for the purposes of producing a dramatic new offence'.[127] The Law Commission proposals on computer misuse in this country have not advocated such a change, and clearly any development along these lines would have implications extending far beyond the special difficulties of computer misuse.

In the United States there have been contrasting decisions on the status of computer programs and computer data as constituting the subject-matter of theft. Traditionally, in the United States as well as in England, the crime of theft was developed to protect tangible property. Many state statutes addressing theft required a physical taking and an asportation of tangible property from the possession of the owner. Thus in *Ward v Superior Court*,[128] an unreported but much discussed Californian case, the defendant gained unauthorized access to a computer program by using a remote terminal and a legitimate user's password and instructed the computer to print out a copy of a company's sophisticated remote-plotting program. He did so at the request of a rival company, which wanted the software, valued at $5,000, in order to

---

[122] G. Hammond, 'Theft of Information' (1984) 100 *Law Quarterly Review* 252; D. G. Johnson, 'Should Computer Programs be Owned?' (1985) 16 *Metaphilosophy* 276; E. Weinrib, 'Information as Property' (1988) 38 *University of Toronto Law Journal* 117.

[123] R. Wacks, *Personal Information, Privacy and the Law*, Oxford: Clarendon Press, 1988 at p. 44.

[124] Younger Committee, *Report of the Committee on Privacy*, Cmnd. 5012, London: HMSO, 1972.

[125] *Boardman v Phipps* [1967] 2 AC 46, 127.

[126] Ibid., and cases cited at n. 138, below.

[127] E. J. Griew, *The Theft Acts 1968 and 1978*, 5th edn., London: Sweet and Maxwell, 1986, para. 2.21.

[128] Unreported, 3 Comp L Serv Rep 208 (1972); see Tapper (1983), pp. 102–3 for details.

avoid having to purchase expensive equipment. The defendant was charged with theft of a trade secret, but the judge found that the only theft which had taken place was of the electronic impulses which produced the defendant's copy of the program, and that these impulses were not sufficiently tangible to constitute an 'article' within the meaning of the statute. The defendant was, none the less, convicted, on the basis that the print-out of the program which he had obtained did constitute a tangible article which could be stolen. A very similar issue arose in *People v Home Insurance Co.*,[129] where the defendant gained remote access to a hospital computer and copied confidential hospital records regarding insurance claims. The Colorado court followed *Ward* and, since nothing tangible had been taken, the charge was dismissed. These decisions would now be different, following the introduction of comprehensive computer crime statutes in both states.[130] At the federal level, the offence of theft of goods in interstate commerce was held not to extend to the copying of computer software by the use of a remote terminal and the transmission of electronic signals from one state to another, since no transportation of property had occurred.[131] On the other hand, convictions have been returned under a broadly drafted federal statute which penalizes the theft of 'anything of value' belonging to the United States, its departments, and agencies and to those under contract to such agencies.[132] Theft of information stolen from a Drug Enforcement Administration computer was covered by this statute, although no actual documents were taken,[133] as was the theft of FBI records.[134] Following these various decisions, some states have legislated to expand the definition of 'property' for the purposes of theft, so as to include:[135]

electronic impulses, electronically processed or produced data or information, commercial instruments, computer software or computer programs, in either machine or human readable form, computer services, any other tangible or intangible item of value relating to a computer system or computer network, and any copies thereof.

States which have taken this line have not, generally, opted for the more comprehensive computer crime statutes. In those statutes the focus is mainly upon the issue of gaining unauthorized access to the computer, and it has not been necessary to devise broader definitions of property for that purpose.

[129] 197 Colo 260, 591 P 2d 1036 (1979).
[130] Cal Penal Code, s. 502; Col Rev Stat Ann, s. 19–5.5–101, 18–5.5–102.
[131] *US v Seidlitz* 589 F 2d 152 (4th Cir 1978), cert denied, 441 US 992 (1979); the relevant provision was 18 USC para. 659 (1982).
[132] 18 USC, para. 641.
[133] *US v Lambert* 446 F Supp 890 (DC Conn, 1978); *US v Girard* 601 F 2d 69 (2d Cir 1979), cert denied, 444 US 871 (1979).
[134] *US v DiGilio* 538 F 2d 972 (3d Cir 1976), cert denied; *Lupo v US* (1977) 429 US 1038.
[135] Mont Code Ann, s. 45.2.101(54)(k) (1981).

The issue of theft of information was also discussed extensively in the Canadian case of *Stewart*.[136] The defendant was a self-employed 'consultant'. He was approached by someone associated with a trade union, seeking to form a bargaining unit in a large hotel complex employing about 600 people, and asked to obtain the names, addresses, telephone numbers, and any other relevant information of the employees of the hotel. This information, regarded by the hotel as confidential, could be obtained only through the personnel files or a computer print-out used for the payroll. These documents were protected by the hotel's security arrangements and would not have been disclosed to the union. The defendant approached an employee of the hotel in an attempt to obtain this information and was prepared to pay $2 for each employee's name, address, and telephone number. The defendant and his union contact were each to receive the same sum, so that the overall payment for the list, had the attempt been carried out, was $3,600. The information was to be copied by hand or photographed from confidential records without removing or affecting the physical records themselves. The defendant was charged with counselling theft, but was acquitted at trial. The Crown appealed to the Ontario Court of Appeal, where the decision was reversed by Holden J.A. and Cory J.A., Lacoucière J.A. dissenting. A further appeal to the Supreme Court of Canada resulted in a reversal of the Court of Appeal's decision. It should be noted that the definition of theft under section 283(1) of the Canadian Criminal Code is different in a number of respects from its English counterpart. It provides that:

> Everyone commits theft who fraudulently and without colour of right takes, or fraudulently and without colour of right converts to his own use or to the use of another person, anything whether animate or inanimate, with intent
> (a) to deprive, temporarily or absolutely, the owner of it or a person who has a special property or interest in it, of the thing or of his property or interest in it,
> (b) to pledge it or deposit it as security
> (c) to part with it under a condition with respect to its return that the person who parts with it may be unable to perform, or
> (d) to deal with it in such a manner that it cannot be restored in the condition in which it was at the time it was taken or converted.

In the Court of Appeal, Houlden J.A. said that the word 'anything' in section 283(1) was restricted to anything capable of being property, and the issue was whether information could constitute property. He said[137] 'While clearly not all information is property, I see no reason why confidential information that has been gathered through the expenditure of time, effort and money by a commercial enterprise for the purposes of its business should not be regarded

---

[136] (1983) 5 CCC (3d) 481 (CA); rvsd (1988) 1 SCR 963 (SC).
[137] At p. 492.

as property and hence entitled to the protection of the criminal law.' His Lordship then cited a number of cases in support of his view, all of which were English or American civil cases,[138] arguing that if a thing could constitute property for civil law purposes then it should also be property for the purposes of the Criminal Code. Further, he said:[139]

The last half of the twentieth century has seen an exponential growth in the development and improvement of methods of storing and distributing information. I believe that section 283(1) of the Code is wide enough to protect the interests of those who compile and store such information and to restrain the activities of those who wrongfully seek to misappropriate it. I appreciate that this conclusion is not in accord with the decision of the Divisional Court in *Oxford* v *Moss* . . .

In the Supreme Court of Canada, however, this view was rejected. In line with a number of critical comments made on the Court of Appeal's approach, it was accepted that, whatever its merits, such a 'wholesale revision of the law'[140] was properly a matter for Parliament rather than the judges.

9. TRADE SECRETS

Because of the problems involved in extending traditional theft laws to cover information, many jurisdictions have adapted their theft statutes to extend to the theft of 'trade secrets' and then to extend to unauthorized removal of computer-stored information where that information constitutes such a secret. Trade secret protection initially provides for a civil remedy, but in recent years criminal provisions have also developed. In the United States some statutes, such as California's, are broadly drafted:[141]

Every person is guilty of theft who, with intent to deprive or withhold from the owner thereof the control of a trade secret, or with an intent to appropriate a trade secret to his own use or to the use of another does any of the following:

(1) steals, takes or carries away any article representing a trade secret . . .
(2) having unlawfully obtained access to the article, without authority makes or causes to be made a copy of any article representing a trade secret . . .

---

[138] *Exchange Telegraph* v *Gregory* [1896] 1 QB 147, *Exchange Telegraph* v *Central News* [1897] 2 Ch 48, *Board of Trade of Chicago* v *Christie Grain and Stock* (1905) 198 US 236, *Hunt* v *New York Cotton Exchange* (1907) 205 US 322, *Boardman* v *Phipps* [1967] 2 AC 46 *per* Lords Hodson and Guest. [139] At p. 495.

[140] See D. Magnusson, 'Using the Criminal Law Against Infringement of Copyright and the Taking of Confidential Information' (1983) 35 CR (3d) 129 (Criminal Reports: Canada), Hammond (1984); F. R. Moskoff, 'The Theft of Thoughts: The Realities of 1984' (1985) 27 *Criminal Law Quarterly* 226; G. Hammond. 'Electronic Crime in Canadian Courts' (1986) 6 *Oxford Journal of Legal Studies* 145. The Supreme Court decision has, in its turn, been criticized: G. Doherty, '*Stewart*: When is a Thief not a Thief? When he steals the Candy but not the Wrapper' (1988) 63 *Criminal Reports* 3d 322.

[141] Cal Penal Code, s. 499c(b).

The American Restatement of Torts defines a trade secret as 'any formula, pattern, device or compilation of information which is used in one's business, and which gives an opportunity to obtain an advantage over competitors who do not know or use it'. Other state legislation covers a more limited range, such as secret scientific material,[142] and is inapplicable to intangibles. There is also a federal Trade Secrets Act.[143] In general, in the United States 'trade secrecy is and always has been, the overwhelmingly preferred method of protection for computer software'.[144] This is because trade secrecy laws protect the underlying ideas and design concepts of the computer program so long as the owner implements reasonable measures to maintain the trade secret in confidence. In spite of this, there seem to have been few cases in which such statutes have been used to prosecute persons charged with theft of computer-held trade secrets. There seems to be no obvious reason for this, but it may have something to do with the ready availability of punitive damages in civil trade secret litigation and the fear of trade secret owners that they will have less influence over the course of criminal litigation, perhaps resulting in further breaches of secrecy in the course of a contested criminal trial.

There is no special criminal legislation in England in the field of protection of trade secrets. Trade secrets are not 'property', and hence cannot be stolen. Similarly, in 1988 it was confirmed in Scotland that there is no crime in that country of the dishonest exploitation of the confidential information of another,[145] but most other European countries do have such laws. Many of these have been modernized to accommodate the misappropriation of secrets held in the form of computer programs or computer data, providing penal provisions in addition to civil remedies. Sieber[146] states that the criminal provisions of European trade secrets law represent an effective weapon against 'traitors and users who act in bad faith'. Legislative reform is pending in several countries. In Canada, for instance, a current Draft Bill seeks to criminalize the fraudulent acquisition, use, or disclosure of a trade secret.[147] It may be noted that the information which was the subject of the decision in *Stewart*[148] would not come within most of the widely used definitions of a trade secret, since the information was not actually used in commerce, nor did it give the hotel a commercial or competitive advantage over rival concerns. It would probably not come within the proposed Canadian legislation, either, which requires that the secret 'is or may be used in a trade or business'.

---

[142] e.g. New York Penal laws, s. 150.00(6); for a full list see M. D. Scott, *Computer Law*, New York: John Wiley, 1985, para. 5.28, n. 65.

[143] 18 USC, s. 1905 (1982).

[144] See C. M. York, 'Criminal Liability for the Misappropriation of Computer Software Trade Secrets' (1986) 63 *University of Detroit Law Review* 481, at p. 483.

[145] *Grant* v *Procurator Fiscal* [1988] RPC 41.

[146] Sieber (1986), p. 57.

[147] See Edmonton Institute of Law Research and Reform, Report No. 46, *Trade Secrets*, Edmonton: Government Printer, 1988; A. Coleman, 'Trade Secrets and the Criminal Law: The Need for Reform' (1989) 5 *Computer Law and Practice* 111.

[148] (1988) 1 SCR 963 (SC).

10. COPYRIGHT

It is important to distinguish copyright infringement, with its attendant criminal penalties, from theft. Copyright is the right to do and to authorize certain acts, particularly publication and reproduction, in respect of literary works, or other works similarly treated in law. As was mentioned earlier, English law accepts the possibility of theft of intangibles, including copyright. Factually, such a theft would arise only rarely, as where a person such as a trustee wrongfully sold the beneficiary's copyright in a book for his own benefit. If, much more commonly however, another person copies the author's work without permission, he infringes the author's copyright, but does not steal the work, or the copyright itself. The distinction was stressed by members of the House of Lords in *Rank Film Distributors* v *Video Information Exchange*.[149] It would seem that for the purposes of theft no property has been appropriated, but even if it has, no intention permanently to deprive the copyright owner can be proved.[150] In *Stewart*, discussed above, one judge in the majority in the Court of Appeal argued that the relevant property constituting the subject-matter of theft in that case was the copyright existing in the confidential list of names and addresses,[151] but this seems clearly to be wrong and was disapproved by the Supreme Court.

In common law countries in the past copyright law has resorted only infrequently to penal sanctions, and these have been fairly mild. Increased concern about music, video, and computer program piracy has altered this, however, and many countries have created more powerful deterrents against copyright infringement.[152] Essentially these criminal sanctions are parasitic upon the ambit of the civil law. It is only comparatively recently that it has been recognized that computer programs may be the subject of copyright.[153] In the United States this was achieved by the Computer Software Protection Act 1980, which resolved a string of conflicting judicial decisions. In the United Kingdom, the passage of the Copyright (Computer Software) Amendment Act in 1985, which was originally a Private Member's Bill initiated by a campaign by the Federation Against Software Theft, provided that copyright law should apply in relation to a computer program 'as it applies' in relation to a literary work, and made computer software piracy a criminal offence.

---

[149] [1982] AC 380, *per* Lord Wilberforce at p. 443.

[150] Griew (1986), para. 2.83; see Professor Smith's commentary on *Storrow and Poole* [1983] Crim LR 332, suggesting that infringement of copyright could be an appropriation after *Morris* [1983] 3 All ER 288.

[151] (1983) 5 CCC (3d) 481 at pp. 500–1; the decision was not followed in *Offley* (1986) 28 CCC (3d) 1.

[152] Sieber (1986), pp. 65–72.

[153] Important overseas decisions on copyright in computer programs are *Apple Computer Inc.* v *Mackintosh Computers Ltd.* [1986] 28 DLR (4th) 178; *Computer Edge Pty Ltd.* v *Apple Computer Inc.* [1986] FSR 537.

The Copyrights, Designs and Patents Act 1988 has now replaced previous criminal provisions in this area, by virtue of the entire repeal of earlier legislation, including the 1985 Act. Section 107(1) of the 1988 Act reforms and extends the criminal law and provides that:

A person commits an offence who, without the licence of the copyright owner—
(a) makes for sale or hire, or
(b) imports into the United Kingdom otherwise than for his private and domestic use, or
(c) possesses in the course of a business with a view to committing any act infringing the copyright, or
(d) in the course of a business—
   (i) sells or lets for hire, or
   (ii) offers or exposes for sale or hire, or
   (iii) exhibits in public, or
   (iv) distributes, or
(e) distributes otherwise than in the course of a business to such an extent as to affect prejudicially the owner of the copyright, an article which is, and which he knows or has reason to believe is, an infringing copy of a copyright work.

Generally, 'possession' of such an article is punishable, by subsection (5) of section 107, on summary conviction with up to six months' imprisonment and a fine of up to £2,000 or both, and the other forms of infringement are punishable, by subsection (4) of section 107, on indictment with a prison term not exceeding two years and an unlimited fine or both.

Whilst these changes represent a reinforcement of the criminal law in this area, there still remains a substantial gap between the penalties available here and those which are available under the Theft Acts. In principle, it seems that a person who gains unauthorized access to a computer and thereby obtains a copy of a program in which copyright subsists, will be guilty of an offence under the 1988 Act if, in particular, he makes that copy in order to sell it, or possesses it in the course of a business with a view to infringing the copyright, or sells, offers for sale, or distributes it in the course of a business. There are some important limitations and difficulties, however, in the use of these criminal copyright provisions in respect of computer misuse.

First, the information removed must, of course, be the subject of copyright. Copyright subsists in any original literary work recorded in writing or otherwise. These requirements should present no difficulty in respect of computer programs since the requirement of originality is not very stringent,[154] literary works are now defined in section 3(1) of the Act so as to

---

[154] 'Originality' merely means that there must be a direct causative link between the author's idea and the work itself: *University of London Press v University Tutorial Press* [1916] 2 Ch 601. It is a much less stringent requirement than that of novelty in patent law.

include computer programs, and 'writing' is defined by the Act to include 'any form of notation or code, whether by hand or otherwise and regardless of the method by which, or medium in or on which, it is recorded'. Dworkin and Taylor,[155] however, question whether a computer program may properly be regarded as 'recorded' when it is stored in a computer memory rather than held on a disk. It will be recalled that when interpreting the words 'recorded or stored' in section 8(1)(d) of the Forgery and Counterfeiting Act 1981, the House of Lords in *Gold and Schifreen* said that the words implied a degree of continuity,[156] so that the Law Commission has now recommended that the phrase 'stored or otherwise held in' should be included in the definition of one of their proposed offences, to cater for material housed temporarily in a computer memory.[157] None the less, the facts of the House of Lords case involved the information in the log-on procedure being held for only a fraction of a second and then expunged, and it would certainly be open to the courts to distinguish that case and find that a computer program was 'recorded' in the memory of the computer where its retention there was somewhat less transitory. It seems that where, after gaining access to the program, the program is run or displayed on the screen of the person making access, this is sufficient to constitute a copyright infringement, since section 17(2) of the Act declares 'copying' to include 'storing the work in any medium by electronic means' and, by section 17(6), copying 'includes the making of copies which are transient'.

Second, in general the Act's provisions extend only to copyright infringements committed in the course of business, unless the infringement is to such an extent as to 'affect prejudicially the owner of the copyright'. It follows from this that the commercial copying of computer software falls within the offence, whilst persons who copy data or programs for their own personal or domestic use may incur civil liability but will rarely infringe the criminal law. In *Reid* v *Kennet*,[158] for example, a private individual who purchased video cassettes from somebody whom he knew to be in the trade of buying and selling pirate video tapes was held to be not guilty of the offence of possessing by way of trade an infringing copy under the Copyright Act 1956 because 'by way of trade' meant 'in the course of trade'. This position is unaffected by the 1988 Act.

Third, while it is now clear that the Act protects the unauthorized copying of computer programs, to what extent does it protect computer-held data? It seems that data will qualify for protection provided that the data constitutes an original literary work, as outlined above. If so, any unauthorized accessing of a computer which results in the production of an unauthorized copy of material which is protected by copyright will be an offence, where it fulfills

---

[155] G. Dworkin and R. Taylor, *Blackstone's Guide to the Copyright, Designs and Patents Act 1988*, London: Blackstone Press, 1989, at p. 182.
[156] [1988] AC 1063; see Chapter 3.
[157] Law Commission (1989*b*), para. 3.67.   [158] [1986] Crim LR 456.

the requirements of section 107(1). The means of obtaining access, whether by an employee exceeding authorization, remote hacking, or electronic eavesdropping, is immaterial. The 1988 Act does not tackle directly the problem of the ownership of copyright in a database, 'a problem of great difficulty and immense practical significance',[159] on which judicial development is awaited.

Fourth, a traditional limitation of copyright as compared to trade secret protection is that copyright protects against the verbatim copying of the data or the program, but does not protect the underlying idea, design, concept, or discovery inherent in the data or program. American courts have recently been prepared to extend copyright protection in this way,[160] but it is unclear in English law to what extent 'non-literal' copying may constitute a copyright infringement, or an offence. If copyright law were to be extended in this context in England it would fill a gap, since the alternative approaches of trade secret law or patent protection are rarely available. As was explained, above, trade secrets law is little developed in England, and patent protection for computer programs is explicitly barred by statute.[161]

Section 107(2) of the 1988 Act provides for an offence of making or being in possession of an article specifically designed or adapted for making copies of a particular copyright work, where the copies are to be used in the course of a business. This is a new offence, and the issue is dealt with in Chapter 5.

---

[159] J. Phillips, *An Introduction to Intellectual Property Law*, London: Butterworths, 1986, para. 23.10; see further C. Tapper, 'Copyright in Databases' (1988) 5 *Computer Law and Practice* 20.

[160] *Whelan Associates Inc.* v *Jaslow Dental Laboratory Inc.* [1987] FSR 1.

[161] Patents Act 1977, s. 1(2); though a computer which has been programmed in a particular manner to perform a particular task may be the subject of a patent: *Re Slee and Harris's Application* [1966] RPC 194.

5

Associated Offences

Apart from those cases which come under the umbrella of fraud, a person who gains unauthorized access to a computer or material held on a computer may have one of a range of other criminal offences in mind. In many cases it will be irrelevant that a computer is selected to be the target of the offence or the tool for commission of that offence. Sometimes, however, it may make a difference. Such cases are examined in this chapter.

1. DESTRUCTION AND DAMAGE

Questions of destruction or damage in relation to computers may conveniently be divided into two; first the damage or destruction of the computer itself or tangible assets associated with it, such as disks or tapes, and second the damage, destruction, or interference with programs or data stored on those disks or tapes. The first category gives rise to no novel substantive criminal law problems, whilst the second is capable of doing so primarily because of questions over the applicability or otherwise of the concept of 'property' to intangibles. Accordingly, the former requires only a passing reference here whilst the latter needs more expansive treatment.

(i) *Tangible Assets*

In some circumstances computers present an attractive target for the criminal. There are well-documented cases involving organized attacks upon European computer centres by extremists such as the Red Brigade in Italy and CLODO in France[1] and the destruction of computers by anti-Vietnam War demonstrators in the United States.[2] Probably the most significant motivation is grievance by employees.[3] As we saw in Chapter 2, computers are vulnerable to physical attack, and numerous incidents have been reported where they have been destroyed or damaged in various more or less sophisticated ways, including being smashed or shot by their operators. This raises important

---

[1] A. R. D. Norman, *Computer Insecurity*, London: Chapman and Hall, 1983, case 77.318; case 80.050.
[2] M. D. Scott, *Computer Law*, New York: John Wiley, 1985, para. 8.10.
[3] Norman (1983), case 72.030.

issues of the physical security of computers and the vetting of employees but no substantive criminal law problems.

Apart from particular criminal laws in England designed to deal with the use of explosives, and anti-terrorist legislation, in general the relevant provision here would be the Criminal Damage Act 1971. By section 1(1) of the Act:

A person who without lawful excuse destroys or damages any property belonging to another intending to destroy or damage any such property or being reckless as to whether any such property would be destroyed or damaged shall be guilty of an offence.

By section 4, the offence is punishable by imprisonment for ten years. The application of this law to cases involving deliberate physical damage to computers is unlikely to cause any problems. It should be noted that while ordinary carelessness is insufficient fault to bring a person within the section, following the decision of the House of Lords in *Caldwell*[4] the term 'reckless' has been reinterpreted to cover cases where there was a serious and obvious risk that property would be damaged or destroyed, whether or not the perpetrator specifically adverted to that possibility.

It may seem superfluous to create criminal damage provisions related specifically to physical damage to computers, but the compendious computer crime legislation of, for instance, the California Penal Code s. 502 does just this, providing that

. . . (d) Any person who maliciously . . . damages or destroys any computer system, computer network, computer program or data shall be guilty of a public offence.

As we have seen, many of the other current state computer crime laws are identical to, or at least patterned upon, the Californian statute.

(ii) *Intangible Assets*

More difficult cases arise where the form of damage which occurs is the erasure or alteration of programs or data. Traditionally there has been no requirement for criminal damage provisions to extend to intangible property, and section 10(1) of the 1971 Act provides that 'In this Act "property" means property of a tangible nature, whether real or personal, including money . . .'. This will be seen to be narrower than the definition of property in section 4 of the Theft Act 1968, discussed at length in Chapter 4.

Again there are several well-documented cases where, for instance, magnets have been used to erase information from computer tapes,[5] sometimes for political reasons, sometimes because of a grudge. In other cases manipulation

---

[4] [1981] 1 All ER 961.
[5] Norman (1983), case 69.050; Scott (1985), para. 8.10.

or destruction of data has been the objective of unauthorized access by an employee or by using a remote terminal, sometimes as a prank, sometimes for a commercial reason. More recently the advent of the computer 'worm' and computer 'virus', in addition to the 'logic bomb', has meant that massive disruption may be caused to computer systems through the passing on of 'infected' disks. These phenomena were described in Chapter 2.

Prior to the Computer Misuse Act 1990, case law in England suggested that most instances of erasure or damage of computer-related intangible property could be brought within the Criminal Damage Act. In the first case, *Talboys*,[6] in May 1986, the defendant pleaded guilty to the charges and so no legal argument was heard. As a practical joke he reprogrammed his employer's computer to display a farewell message to his colleagues every time they entered his leaving date on the computer. In fact the effect of the program was to blank the screen entirely, and it cost his employers £1,000 to investigate and put it right. Talboys was conditionally discharged and ordered to pay £1,000 compensation to the firm. In *Cox* v *Riley*,[7] however, the issue was contested and went on appeal to the Divisional Court, and this is now the leading case on the point in England.

The defendant was employed to work on a computerized saw, which relied for its operation on a printed circuit card being inserted into it. This contained programs which enabled the saw to be operated to cut window frame profiles of different designs. He deliberately blanked the card of all its sixteen programs by repeatedly operating the program cancellation facility. This rendered the saw inoperable apart from limited and rather slow manual operation. The defendant appealed against his conviction for criminal damage to the Divisional Court where Stephen Brown L.J. and McCullough J. gave 'the quite emphatic answer, yes' to the question whether the erasing of the programs could constitute criminal damage under the 1971 Act, the former saying that 'it seems to me to be quite untenable to argue that what this appellant did on this occasion did not amount to causing damage to property'. At first sight this decision appeared to remove any potential problems in this area, and in their Working Paper on Computer Misuse the Law Commission stated that:[8]

In essence, any interference with the operation of a computer or its software which causes loss or inconvenience to its legitimate users can probably now be charged as criminal damage . . . The law of criminal damage now seems to extend to persons who damage a computer system, without the need for any further reform of the law.

As we shall see in a moment, however, the Law Commission subsequently revised its view.

---

[6] *The Times*, 29 May 1986.

[7] (1986) 83 Cr App R 54; M. Wasik, 'Criminal Damage and the Computerised Saw' (1986) 136 *New Law Journal* 763.

[8] Law Commission, Working Paper No. 110, *Computer Misuse*, London: HMSO, 1988, paras. 3.35, 3.68.

After *Cox* v *Riley* it seemed that the great majority of cases of deliberate or reckless deletion of programs or data would fall within the existing offence of criminal damage. The rather trivial nature of the two English cases cited should not mislead us, for very considerable damage may be occasioned by the deletion or corruption of computer-held material. In an American case[9] in 1988 the defendant, after being dismissed from the brokerage firm where he worked, activated a logic bomb which destroyed 168,000 payroll records. In an earlier logic bomb case a defendant in France[10] had been working with a program which kept all his employer's records systematically updated on an annual basis. After having been given notice and during his last few days with the company he added to the program an instruction to destroy all records two years later. The bomb operated on New Year's Day as instructed and all data held on the computer were erased.

The criminal damage laws might also be used, however, where the deletion or alteration of material held on computer is part of a scheme to defraud or commit some other computer misuse. Thus in *Selvage*,[11] where a woman clerk employed at the Driver and Vehicle Licensing Centre at Swansea, where endorsements of convictions for driving licences are recorded, used her position to alter computer records by deleting four endorsements from a friend's driving licence, a prosecution for criminal damage might well, at that time,[11a] have succeeded. In fact she was charged, together with the friend, with conspiracy to pervert the course of justice. This charge failed, it being held that such conspiracy could only be made out where proceedings of some kind were imminent, or an investigation was in progress which might bring about proceedings, so that a course of justice had been embarked upon. In cases where students have gained access to university records and altered their marks,[12] or where credit ratings have been altered, the defendants may not have done enough to be guilty of an offence of deception or even an attempt to commit such an offence, but their liability for criminal damage would have seemed clear. The defendants in *Gold and Schifreen*[13] might have been convicted of criminal damage, since they altered files and left messages after having gained access to the Prestel computer system. It would also seem to cover cases where the defendant accesses the computer and tampers with programs or data so that graffiti or obscenities subsequently appear on screens. In a 1988 case reported by Davies,[14] a computer manufacturer's electronic mailbox was filled with obscene pictures and in another a council

---

[9] *State* v *Burleson*, unreported, Texas 1988.

[10] S. Schølberg, *Computers and Penal Legislation*, Norwegian Research Centre for Computers and Law, Oslo: Universitetsforlaget, 1983, p. 21.

[11] [1982] 1 All ER 96.   [11a] Though not now: Computer Misuse Act 1990, s. 3(6).

[12] For examples see Schølberg (1983), pp. 27–8; in one case a senior computer operator falsified 22 marks for a student, receiving $300 in return.

[13] [1988] AC 1063; above, Chapter 3, Section 1.

[14] D. Davies, 'Computer Losses During 1988: A Review' (1989–90) 1 *Computer Law and Security Report* 2.

officer was the subject of personal abuse which had been fed into the housing department's computer. In May 1990, at Southwark Crown Court, a hacker who had sabotaged computer held material at universities in London, Bath, and Hull, was convicted on four counts of criminal damage.[15] The hacker, Whiteley, using a home computer in his bedroom, gained access to the university computers through the JANET network and erased data, said to be valued at £25,000, replacing it with various messages of 'schoolboy humour'. The trial is unreported, but it seems from the press reports of the case that the offender's convictions for criminal damage were based upon the erasure of the data; he was acquitted on a charge of criminal damage to the computer hardware itself. Whiteley was sentenced to twelve months imprisonment, with eight months suspended. Although the Jack Committee on Banking has proposed the creation of 'an additional and separate offence'[16] directed at those who corrupt material held on a computer by the introduction of a computer virus, the decision in *Cox* v *Riley* seemed to indicate that there was no need to legislate separately for variations on the method of committing damage to assets held on a computer.

There were always dangers, however, in total reliance upon *Cox* v *Riley*, and the Law Commission's Report and the Computer Misuse Act 1990 have now taken a rather different line. The intended effect of section 3 of the Act is that Whiteley would now be guilty of the new offence under that Act of causing an 'unauthorized modification of computer material', but he could, in consequence, no longer be convicted of criminal damage under the 1971 Act. It is necessary to consider the matter in more depth. The first issue is to determine exactly what is meant by 'damage to property' in the English context. The Act speaks of 'destroys or damages' but it is clear that the latter term must include the former. Property is of such a wide variety that it may be damaged in many different ways, but according to Smith and Hogan[17] damage involves 'some physical harm, impairment or deterioration which can be perceived by the senses'. It is not clear how much physical impairment there must be. An old case holds that grass can be damaged by trampling it down[18] but there is modern, though not high, authority that the mere bending of metal nails is not criminal damage[19] nor is spitting upon a policeman's overcoat.[20] These cases suggest the existence of a *de minimis* rule. Property can also be damaged even though nothing is actually broken, so that a machine may be damaged by removal of an integral part,[21] such as the rotor arm from a car. Perhaps more helpfully, property may be regarded

---

[15] *The Times*, 25 May, 8 June 1990.
[16] Jack Committee, *Banking Services Law*, Cmnd. 622, London: HMSO, 1989, para. 14.53.
[17] J. C. Smith and B. Hogan, *Criminal Law*, 6th edn., London: Butterworths, 1988, p. 678.
[18] *Gayford* v *Choulder* [1898] 1 QB 316.
[19] *Woolcock* [1977] Crim LR 104.
[20] *A (a juvenile)* [1978] Crim LR 689; though see *Samuels* v *Stubbs* (1972) 4 SASR 200, at p. 203.
[21] *Tacey* (1821) Russ & Ry 452.

as damaged if it has been affected in such a way as would require time, effort, and perhaps expense on the part of the owner to put it right, such as where a passenger urinated in a taxi,[22] soil was dumped on land cleared for use as a development site,[23] or graffiti were sprayed on a wall or pavement even though the rain would eventually have dissolved them.[24]

The second question is to determine exactly what was damaged in *Cox* v *Riley*. In theory there are four possible ways of describing this damage. The first is damage to the programs themselves by erasure. It was argued by defence counsel in the Divisional Court that this was the real nature of the damage. The argument was rejected. To have accepted it would have necessitated an acquittal, since the programs were clearly intangible property, not covered by section 10(1). The second is criminal damage to the machine, the saw itself. There are several authorities to the effect that tampering with a machine, involving destruction, removal, or disconnection of a constituent part, involves criminal damage to the machine. One of these authorities, *Fisher*,[25] was cited with approval in *Cox* v *Riley*. In *Fisher* a disgruntled employee who had been employed to operate an agricultural steam engine, had parted company from his employer. He decided, because of a grudge, to put the steam engine out of action. He did various things to disable the machine, including putting a piece of stick up the water feed. Pollock C.B. held in a short judgment of the Court for Crown Cases Reserved that this was criminal damage because some two hours' labour was required to return the machine to working order: 'It is like the spiking of a gun, where there is no actual damage done to the gun, although it is rendered useless.' So the defendant in *Cox* v *Riley* could have been found guilty of causing criminal damage to the machine. But this was not, apparently, the basis of the decision. The third possibility is criminal damage to the card. Stephen Brown L.J. makes it clear that damage to the 'printed plastic circuit card' was the ground for dismissing the appeal. In what way was the card damaged? If the card is viewed as an empty receptacle for the receipt of programs, it is clear that the receptacle itself was not damaged. It may then be argued that since there was no damage to the receptacle, and intangible property cannot be damaged under the Act, there can have been no damage done to 'the printed plastic circuit card'. The fourth possibility which must, then, form the true basis for the decision, is that when programs were written on to the card it became a new item of property being more, in a sense, than the sum of its constituent parts. Perhaps there is an analogy with an oil painting,[26] which may be regarded as an item of property more than the sum of the canvas and the

---

[22] *King* v *Lees* (1949) 65 TLR 21.

[23] *Henderson and Battley*, 1984, unreported, cited in *Cox* v *Riley*, n. 7, above.

[24] *Harden* v *Chief Constable of Avon and Somerset* [1986] Crim LR 330, though see *Fancy* [1980] Crim LR 171.

[25] (1865) 10 Cox CC 146.

[26] Suggested by the Scottish Law Commission, Consultative Memorandum No. 68, *Computer Crime*, Edinburgh: SLC, 1986, para. 3.73.

paint. Thus the application of chemical solvent to the painting would be regarded as criminal damage to the painting rather than to the paint itself, the canvas being undamaged. Of course the analogy is imperfect because there has been damage to the paint, which could form the basis of a conviction.

The immediate implication of *Cox v Riley* is that it is now clear that the damage which has been done to the property need not be tangible in order to qualify under the Act.[27] This is unsurprising since it has always been the case that, for instance, food can be damaged within the meaning of the Act by invisible contamination. The more general significance of the case and the Law Commission's reliance upon it to cover all cases of damage or destruction of data or programs is, however, open to doubt.

The Law Commission suggested in its Working Paper that the case decides that 'any interference with the operation of a computer or its software which causes loss or inconvenience to its legitimate users can probably now be charged as criminal damage'.[28] On the face of it, this goes very wide, encompassing what may be described as 'criminal mischief' as well as criminal damage. The Law Commission's interpretation would include a case where the defendant, who has the only key to the computer room, locks it and hides away the key. This is certainly mischievous, and it might constitute criminal mischief in those jurisdictions where such conduct is an offence,[29] but it would be remarkable if it fell within the scope of the Criminal Damage Act. It is submitted that the case does not go so far, being limited to cases of physical interference with tangible property which brings about some dele-terious change in that property, which requires time, effort, and expense to repair.

Three points may be made about this more qualified interpretation. First, it was possible to obtain a conviction in *Cox v Riley* because there was tangible property which had been impaired by the deletion of the programs. This will almost always be the case. What is crucial is the description of the property. If there has been disruption or erasure of data held on a disk, the prosecution must frame the charge in terms of damage to the disk. Such damage will not always be present, however. Suppose that a person who gains unauthorized access to the computer manages to damage or destroy data which is housed in the memory of the computer, or data which is in the process of being transferred from one medium to another. It seems that such damage, with no impact upon the storage medium such as disk or tape, would not come within the scope of the decision. Second, suppose that a hacker manages to encrypt data in a computer by gaining access and inserting a locking mechanism on the data so that legitimate users cannot gain access to it. This was done in the Canadian case of *Turner*.[30] Perhaps here it could be argued that there was

---

[27] *Contra* Smith & Hogan (1988), p. 678.   [28] Law Commission (1988), para. 3.35.
[29] See below, and M. Wasik, 'Criminal Damage/Criminal Mischief' (1988) 17 *Anglo-American Law Review* 37.
[30] (1984) 13 CCC (3d) 430; see further, below.

damage done to tangible property, but it is interesting that in *Turner* it seems to have been undisputed as a matter of fact that the tapes were undamaged by what the defendant did. In these cases, the prosecution would presumably have recourse to charging damage to the computer itself, in that deletion of the program or data would adversely affect the operation of the machine. This is the view taken by one Australian commentator, who says[31] '... if the property under consideration is described with sufficient generality, there is no real problem in bringing any damaged computer storage media within the definition of property'. Third, the emphasis in *Cox* v *Riley* upon the cost and inconvenience in repairing the damage as forming part of the definition of criminal damage may be unhelpful in the computer context, for in a well-run computerized operation back-up facilities should be readily available, and reconstitution of the data should be simple and inexpensive to achieve. It is suggested, therefore, that there is uncertainty over what the decision stands for, and that it was necessary to clarify the law.

In the light of comment such as this, the Law Commission accepted that reform was necessary. They proposed, accordingly, the introduction of a new criminal offence based upon the 'unauthorized modification of computer material'.[32] This suggestion, representing a striking change from the view taken in the Working Paper, has been incorporated into the Computer Misuse Act 1990 which, by section 3, provides:

3(1) A person is guilty of an offence if—
    (a) he does any act which causes an unauthorized modification of the contents of any computer; and
    (b) at the time when he does the act he has the requisite intent and the requisite knowledge
  (2) For the purposes of subsection (1)(b) above the requisite intent is an intent to cause a modification of the contents of any computer and by so doing—
    (a) to impair the operation of any computer;
    (b) to prevent or hinder access to any program or data held in any computer; or
    (c) to impair the operation of any such program or the reliability of any such data.
  (3) The intent need not be directed at—
    (a) any particular computer;
    (b) any particular program or data or a program or data of any particular kind; or
    (c) any particular modification or a modification of any particular kind.

---

[31] R. A. Brown, 'Computer-Related Crime Under Commonwealth Law, and the Draft Federal Criminal Code' (1986) 10 *Criminal Law Journal* 377, at p. 386.

[32] Law Commission, Report No. 186, *Computer Misuse*, Cm. 819, London: HMSO. See App. 3, below.

(4) For the purposes of subsection (1)(b) above the requisite knowledge is knowledge that any modification he intends to cause is unauthorized.

(5) It is immaterial for the purposes of this section whether an unauthorized modification or any intended effect of it of a kind mentioned in subsection (2) above is, or is intended to be, permanent or merely temporary.

By section 3(7) the offence of unauthorized modification of computer material is made triable either way, punishable on summary conviction with imprisonment not exceeding six months, a fine not exceeding £2000, or both, and on conviction on indictment, to imprisonment for a term not exceeding five years, or a fine, or both. It is apparent from the wording that a wide range of different forms of conduct are included within it.

The central issue of the erasure, falsification, or corruption of data or programs held in a computer is certainly adequately covered by this offence. The drafting avoids the *Cox* v *Riley* problem of requiring proof of damage to a tangible medium, by using the phrase 'contents' of a computer's memory or computer storage medium.[33] This is a better solution than another possible option, that of amending the Criminal Damage Act 1971 to extend the definition of property to include intangible computer-held material. As the Commission said, the Act is not really suitable to deal with non-physical interference with programs or data. A separate provision seems a better approach. The offence does, however, extend further than erasure, falsification, or corruption of data or programs. As we have seen, the introduction of a worm program into a computer will have the effect of using up all the spare capacity of the computer, impairing its operation. This, even where it did not adversely affect the computer-held material as such, would be covered by the wording, since it would 'impair the operation' of the computer. Also covered is the deliberate introduction by a person of a computer virus.[34] If a floppy disk infected with a virus is deliberately introduced into circulation, the person doing so can surely be proved to have intended thereby to impair the operation of a computer or computer program. Viruses are notoriously random in their impact and the drafting is such that it need not be shown that the person had any particular target in mind. It would suffice that they had

---

[33] According to para. 3.68, 'The term "contents" is not used in our proposed offence in any technical sense, but is a way of including, for example, data and programs, while also avoiding the need for a technical explanation of exactly what forms such "information" or "instructions" might take.'

[34] In para. 3.69 the Law Commission says that in order for the deliberate introduction into circulation of a disk contaminated by a virus to come within their definition, the phrase 'causes an unauthorized modification' would have to be extended so that the offence is committed as soon as the disk is put into circulation if the necessary *mens rea* can be established. Otherwise the offence would not be committed until the unauthorized modification actually occurred. In para. 3.70 the Commission states that 'We have been told that the problem of infected disks is substantial and serious, and we consider that the law should make adequate provision to meet that case.'

intended an unauthorized modification to some computer somewhere. Further, passage of an infected disk through the hands of intermediaries, before an eventual unauthorized modification occurred, would not affect liability provided that a causal link could be established between putting the disk into circulation and the eventual modification. The offence is ingeniously drafted in respect of computer viruses. Since it is defined in terms of the impact of a virus, and the term 'virus' does not appear in the proposal, it is not necessary to attempt to define one, surely a task which would be fraught with difficulty.

The offence would not normally extend to an authorized user who misuses computer time or facilities,[35] such as an employee who plays computer games on his employer's computer or uses his employer's computing capacity without permission to run his own business. This conduct could only fall within the proposed offence where an intent thereby to impair the operation of the system could be shown, such as where so much space was consumed by the unauthorized activity that there was a deleterious effect upon other computer operations.

What now is the relationship between the new offence of unauthorized modification of computer material and the offence of criminal damage? It seems that they are intended to be mutually exclusive. Section 3(6) of the Computer Misuse Act seeks to confine the operation of the Criminal Damage Act, in the computer context, to cases where the effect of the damage is to impair the 'physical condition' of the 'computer or computer storage medium', though it does seem strange that this change was not effected by an appropriate amendment to the 1971 Act itself. The result would seem to be, however, that the hacker Whiteley, whose case was mentioned above, would now be convicted of the new offence and would not be guilty of criminal damage. This would also be so if the facts of *Cox* v *Riley* itself were to recur. That case would only give rise to conviction under the 1971 Act if the defendant had tampered with the programs in such a way that, for instance, subsequent use of the saw damaged the window frames while they were being cut. Such a result seems perfectly acceptable. It was argued above, however, that a conviction for criminal damage could have been returned in *Cox* v *Riley* on the basis that the machine itself had been damaged.[36] If so, there seems to be an overlap between the two offences. If there is such an overlap, a prosecutor would take note that recklessness is a sufficient fault element for criminal damage, which also attracts higher maximum penalties on indictment, while proof of intention is required for the offence under the Computer Misuse Act.

How have other jurisdictions tackled these problems? In Scotland, just prior to the case of *Cox* v *Riley*, the Scottish Law Commission expressed the view that existing laws were capable of covering the situation, since 'any

[35] See above, p. 92.
[36] At p. 139. Could it be said that the machine's 'physical condition' was impaired?

corruption of the data is a form of damage to the disk or tape itself'.[37] While the Computer Misuse Act also applies in Scotland, the pre-existing law on criminal damage in Scotland is slightly different from that in England. Scots law recognizes two offences relating to damage to property, the statutory offence of vandalism under section 78 of the Criminal Justice (Scotland) Act 1980 and the common law crime of malicious mischief. Section 78 is virtually identical to section 1(1) of the Criminal Damage Act,[38] but the common law offence has on occasions been described in wider terms. In *Ward* v *Robertson*,[39] for instance, it was 'said that the offence was committed if 'damage is done by a person who shows a deliberate disregard of, or even indifference to, the property or possessory rights of others'. Most striking is the decision in the case of *HMA* v *Wilson*.[40] The defendant in that case was employed at a nuclear power station. He deliberately activated an emergency stop button thereby causing the power station to shut down and remain inoperative for 28 hours. During that time the electricity authorities were obliged to supply the national grid from other sources at a cost of around £147,000. The defendant was charged with malicious mischief but argued that no physical damage to property had been occasioned. This was accepted by the sheriff but rejected by a majority of the High Court. Lord Justice-Clerk Wheatley said,[41]

If the malicious intention improperly to stop the production of electricity is established, and the achievement of that had the effect of rendering inoperative a machine which should have been operating productively and profitably, then, in my view, that is just as much damage to the employer's property as would be the case in any of the more physical acts of sabotage.

The view taken in Australia seems to be much the same, using a broad interpretation of 'damage' to include 'rendered less valuable in an economic sense'[42] and regarding deletion of data as constituting damage to the storage medium.

A survey of developments in other jurisdictions reveals similar problems being tackled somewhat differently elsewhere.[43] There have been two broad approaches. One has been to amend existing criminal damage offence definitions specifically to include intangible property, and the other has been to extend the notion of criminal damage to include criminal mischief directed at the property of others.

As examples of the first approach, in Belgian, French, German, Austrian, and Finnish criminal law the erasure of information without damaging the

---

[37] Scottish Law Commission (1986), para. 3.72.
[38] And see *Black* v *Allan*, 1985, SCCR 11.
[39] 1938 JC 32 at p. 36 *per* L.J.C. Aitchison.   [40] 1984 SLT 117.
[41] At p. 119.
[42] I. Temby and S. McElwaine, 'Technocrime: An Australian Overview' (1987) 11 *Criminal Law Journal* 245.
[43] OECD, Information Computer Communications Policy No. 10, *Computer-Related Crime: Analysis of Legal Policy*, Paris: OECD, 1986, pp. 54–6.

physical medium has been held not to fall within the criminal damage provisions,[44] and there is current law reform pending in several of these jurisdictions to modify the existing statutes or create new provisions against computer sabotage.[45] The German proposal is to add a section 303A to the traditional 'damage to property' provision in section 303 to cover the 'erasure, suppression, rendering useless and modification of data'. Similar developments are in hand in Austria, with the creation of a new section 126A of their Penal Code. Law reform proposals in Finland suggest equating damage to data with damage inflicted on tangible property.

Perhaps the best example of the 'criminal mischief' approach, on the other hand, is that of Canada. The leading case is *Turner*,[46] which came before the Ontario High Court of Justice on an application by the defendants to quash their committal for trial. The undisputed facts were that during the course of telephone connections between Milwaukee and Toronto, lasting a total of ten and a half hours, various computer tapes containing data files of American companies were accessed by the defendants and then encoded or encrypted in such a way that they could not be accessed by anyone other than the encoders. The process of encryption electronically altered the data but did not in any way physically alter the tape itself. The data were still accessible to anyone using the reverse of the encryption program followed by the usual software. The effect of the encryption was, then, to impose a locking mechanism on access to the data. The defendants were charged with the offence of 'mischief' under section 387(1) of the Canadian Criminal Code. This provides as follows:

Every one commits mischief who wilfully
(a) destroys or damages property;
(b) renders property dangerous, useless, inoperative or ineffective;
(c) and without authorisation, express or implied, destroys or damages a computer program or computer data or alters a computer program or computer data in a way that renders it useless or inoperative or diminishes its commercial or scientific value;
(d) obstructs, interrupts or interferes with the lawful use, enjoyment or operation of property, or
(e) obstructs, interrupts, or interferes with any person in the lawful use, enjoyment or operation of property.

Section 385 further declares that:

In this Part, 'property' means real or personal corporeal property, any computer software or program, or copy thereof, in any retrieval computer data or information produced and stored in machine readable form by any means.

---

[44] e.g. Belgian Penal Code, ss. 528, 559.   [45] OECD (1986), p. 55.
[46] (1984) 13 CCC (3d) 430.

It was, of course, argued for the defendants before Gray J. that since the computer tape remained intact and that since its use as a computer tape was unaffected by the encryption there was no evidence that the defendants had obstructed, interrupted, or interfered with the lawful use, enjoyment, or operation of 'property' as defined in these provisions. The judge had no difficulty in finding, however, that in section 387(1)(d) the gist of the offence was not the physical alteration of the property but interference with the lawful use of that property, and he dismissed the application.[47]

At the time of the decision in *Turner* amendments to section 387 were being canvassed, and were noted by Gray J. These amendments are now law, by virtue of the Criminal Law Amendment Act 1985, which by section 58 adds a new subsection 1.1 to section 387 of the Criminal Code, cited above, covering 'mischief in relation to data':

Every one commits mischief who wilfully
(a) destroys or alters data;
(b) renders data meaningless, useless or ineffective;
(c) obstructs, interrupts or interferes with the lawful use of data; or
(d) obstructs, interrupts or interferes with any person in the lawful use of data or denies access to data to any person who is entitled to access thereto.

For the purpose of these provisions, 'data' is defined to mean[48]

... representations of information or of concepts that are being prepared or have been prepared in a form suitable for use in a computer system.

The effect of this change is, for good measure, to make 'data' equivalent to 'property' in the extent of its protection from damage and other varieties of mischief. The resulting law, particularly in (c) and (d), looks very broad indeed. In a recent review of the Canadian Criminal Code,[49] the abolition of the 'mischief' offences is proposed, since the word 'carries too trivial a connotation', but the proposed replacement of 'vandalism' would embrace damaging another's property 'or by physical interference rendering it useless or inoperative', which does not appear to be significantly narrower.

As may be expected, American criminal law is well armed to deal with problems arising in this kind of area. The federal statute, the Computer Fraud and Abuse Act 1984, makes criminal *inter alia* the modification or destruction of only limited types of information (national security, foreign relations, financial, credit) contained in certain computers (operated for or on behalf of the federal government).[50] At the state level many have followed the lead of California in section 502(d) of its Penal Code which provides that:

---

[47] See also *Biggin* (1980) 5 CCC (2d) 408.
[48] Criminal Law Amendment Act, ss. 46, 58; Canadian Criminal Code, ss. 301.2(2), 387(8).
[49] Canadian Law Reform Commission, Report No. 31, *Recodifying Criminal Law*, Montreal: CLRC, 1987.
[50] 18 USC ss. 1029–30 (1984), s. 103(a)(3).

(d) Any person who maliciously accesses, alters, deletes, damages or destroys any computer system, computer network, computer program, or data shall be guilty of a public offence.

Whether or not particular states have computer crime legislation at present, most have other provisions, such as malicious mischief offences[51] under which destruction or damage might be charged. 'Malicious mischief' might be appropriate to deal with a case dubiously cited by Bequai as a computer crime[52] where someone removed all the labels from 1,500 reels of computer tape, causing a firm considerable expenditure of time and money in re-identifying the data. This is theft of the labels, of course, but if the labels had been swapped around rather than taken, it seems that without dishonesty this would not be theft,[53] nor would it be criminal damage under English law.

2. DENIAL OF ACCESS TO AUTHORIZED USERS

Although closely related to the previous topic, this form of computer misuse requires a separate though short discussion. In several of the cases already considered, one effect of the defendant's misuse of the computer has been to prevent authorized users having access to data stored on a computer. This may be done by purely physical means, such as by cutting a wire, in which case the offence of criminal damage has clearly been committed. On occasions, however, it has been achieved by electronic manipulation. The Law Commission identified the following three possibilities:[54]

(a) a computer can only handle a finite number of users at any one time. When all its 'ports' are in use, attempts to log on will be rejected. Thus an unauthorized user may obstruct an authorized user merely by occupying a port;
(b) an unauthorized user may, deliberately or otherwise, activate defensive mechanisms in the computer which cause it to shut down a whole or part of its system;
(c) that part of the computer's software which controls access could be altered, for example, so as to change or delete passwords in order to deny access to some or all legitimate users.

It will be recalled that in the Canadian hacking case of *Turner*,[55] discussed in the last section, the defendant's long-range accessing of the computer effectively and quite deliberately 'locked' the data by encryption. In some of the cases reported to the Audit Commission, this has also been the case, as where the employee's parting gift to the company was to modify the operations software so that it was made difficult to interpret the data.[56] Some of the

---

[51] e.g. Cal Penal Code, s. 594.
[52] A. Bequai, *White-Collar Crime: A Twentieth Century Crisis*, Lexington, Mass.: D. C. Heath, 1978, p. 106.
[53] According to Lord Roskill in *Morris* [1983] 3 All ER 288.
[55] (1984) 13 CCC (3d) 430.   [54] Law Commission (1988), para. 2.18.
[56] Audit Commission for Local Authorities in England and Wales, *Computer Fraud Survey*, London: HMSO, 1984, case 71.

American computer crime literature talks of defendants 'capturing' computer files. Sometimes this seems to indicate the changing of the password to a particular file; sometimes it entails the corruption or deletion of data within that file. Clearly the distinction between denial of authorized access and criminal damage is a fine one and, as we have seen, it is doubtful whether existing English criminal damage provisions would extend to this kind of 'mischief' directed at the victim's property. Denying a person access to his own tangible property, such as by locking it away in a drawer and retaining the key, or deliberately blocking a person's car in a car park by parking in front of it, does not constitute criminal damage. Provided there is no actual damage to the computer or the storage medium then, it is submitted, it is not criminal damage to deny him access to computer data. In an unreported Australian case,[57] a former employee of the Bureau of Statistics wrote a program which had the effect of progressively deleting information from master tapes at Canberra every time there was an attempt made to access the material. The prosecution, rather than bringing a charge of wilful damage,[58] relied upon the offence under section 76 of the Crimes Act, of wilfully obstructing a Commonwealth Officer while engaged in the discharge of his duties of office. The defendant pleaded guilty and was fined $200. The charge was certainly an artificial one and, even though successful here, could only apply in the case of government computers.

In Britain, the possibility of creating a specific offence of intentional or reckless denial of lawful access to data was considered by the Scottish Law Commission, but rejected largely on the ground that 'we have at present no clear information to suggest that it is either a widespread activity or one which is likely to present major problems in the future'.[59] In the United States, precluding an authorized user from gaining access to the computer is a specific offence in several states, including Connecticut, which criminalizes[60] 'interrupting or degrading, or causing a denial of computer service to an authorised user', and such conduct would probably fall within the terms of compendious computer crime legislation adopted in many other states. In Canada the 1985 revision to the Criminal Code created a new section 387(1.1) which covers, *inter alia*, denial of access to data. By subsection (d) of this provision, a person commits an offence of mischief in relation to data if they obstruct, interrupt, or interfere with any person in the lawful use of data, or deny access to data to any person who is entitled to access thereto. The offence, which is punishable with a prison term not exceeding ten years, seems extraordinarily broad. On the face of it, it would cover distracting a

---

[57] Cited in Temby and McElwaine (1987), at p. 253.
[58] Crimes Act 1914 (Queensland), s. 29.
[59] Scottish Law Commission (1986), para. 4.28.
[60] Conn Gen Stat Ann s. 53a–251(d); also Fla Stat Ann s. 815.06(1), La Rev Stat Ann s. 14:73.4, Utah Code Ann s. 76.6.703, Wyo Stat s. 6.3.504(a)(ii).

person who is working at a computer terminal or obstructing a computer programmer on his way to work.[61]

When the English Law Commission, in their Report on Computer Misuse, proposed a new offence of 'unauthorized modification of computer material', they envisaged that it would be capable of extending to cover some instances of denial of access. [62] The new offence in section 3 of the Computer Misuse Act 1990, based squarely on the Law Commission's proposal, was set out and discussed above. One situation in which that offence will be made out is where the defendant intentionally causes an unauthorized modification of the contents of any computer, intending thereby to prevent or hinder access to any program or data held in any computer. It is irrelevant whether this denial of access is intended to be permanent or merely a temporary inconvenience to the user. The wording of this offence would seem to cover the facts of all of the cases where such activity has so far come to light and it avoids the inappropriate breadth of the North American laws.

3. DEATH, PHYSICAL INJURY, AND ENDANGERMENT

It is certainly conceivable that a computer might be used as the means of bringing about a person's death or causing physical injury. As we saw in Chapter 1, computer malfunction, accident, or misuse by computer operators have already created many situations of real physical danger, including the very real risks of responding to a nuclear attack mistakenly reported by a computer. Experts predict that since computers now perform so many safety-critical tasks, in the near future we can expect to see computer malfunctions and misuse as increasingly significant causes of death and injury. In an incident which occurred in January 1979 an aircraft, landing at JFK Airport in New York with the Soviet ambassador on board, was endangered by computer manipulation by an air traffic controller. Terrorist activity is also a real possibility. In 1985 there were terrorist attacks on the computer and communications systems of Tokyo Airport and the Japanese railways.

An area of particular risk is the computerization of hospital records and the increasing use of computers to assist in patient diagnosis. There have been three reported incidents so far in which computerized hospital records have been affected by computer misuse. In the 414 case[63] in the United States hackers accessed the computer but did not alter any data. During 1988 a

---

[61] Scottish Law Commission (1986), para. 4.28.

[62] Law Commission (1989*b*), para. 3.64. The Commission states at para. 3.65(4) that the proposed offence is designed to cover the following case: 'The unauthorized addition of a password to a data file, thereby rendering that data inaccessible to anyone who does not know the password.'

[63] J. J. BloomBecker, 'Computer Crime Update: The View as we Exit 1984' (1985) 7 *Western New England Law Review* 627, at p. 630.

computer virus infected three hospital computers in Michigan.[64] These computers were used in part to assist in diagnosis, and the virus garbled patient names and affected most of the programs. Fortunately, nobody was misdiagnosed or wrongly prescribed in consequence. Nicholson[65] cites a case where the medical records of cancer patients were accessed and altered. If a patient were to die as a result of manipulation of records by a hacker, the use of the computer in this way would provide no special criminal law problem: the machine is merely being used as the instrument to create the risk. The hacker could well be guilty of the murder or manslaughter of that patient, depending upon the hacker's criminal intent at the time of his action.

It may seem very strange to legislate specifically for the risk of death or physical injury resulting from computer misuse, but this has been done in some American state computer crime statutes. In Connecticut[66] the statute penalizes anyone who recklessly engages in computer misuse that creates a risk of serious physical injury to another person, the Wisconsin statute[67] penalizes the creation by computer misuse of any situation of unreasonable risk and high probability of death or great bodily harm to another, and the Virginia statute[68] creates an offence of 'personal trespass by computer', which prohibits the unauthorized use of a computer with the intent to cause physical injury to a person. These statutes are probably best seen as examples of the comprehensive laws of endangerment which exist in the United States but which have no general counterpart in English law.[69] Interestingly, however, one of the few examples of endangerment laws which does exist here is the aggravated form of criminal damage under section 1(2) of the Criminal Damage Act 1971. The section provides that:

A person who without lawful excuse destroys or damages any property, whether belonging to himself or another; and

(a) intending to destroy or damage any property or being reckless as to whether any property would be destroyed or damaged; and

(b) intending by the destruction or damage to endanger the life of another or being reckless as to whether the life of another would be endangered;

shall be guilty of an offence.

The maximum penalty is life imprisonment.

In the discussion of destruction or damage to computers and computer-related material, above, it was explained that the importance of the offence of

---

[64] B. Zajac, 'Virus Hits Michigan Medical Centres' (1989–90) 2 *Computer Law and Security Report* 28.

[65] E. Nicholson, 'Hacking Away at Liberty', *The Times*, 18 Apr. 1989. See also *Hansard*, 9 Feb. 1990, col. 1153.

[66] Conn Gen Stat Ann s. 53a–254(a)(2).

[67] Wis Stat Ann s. 943.70(2)(b)(4).

[68] Va Code s. 18.2–152.7; R. K. Kutz, 'Computer Crime in Virginia: A Critical Examination of the Criminal Offences in the Virginia Computer Crimes Act' (1986) 27 *William and Mary Law Review* 783.

[69] K. J. M. Smith, 'Liability for Endangerment' [1983] *Criminal Law Review* 127.

criminal damage in the computer misuse context has been reduced by the Computer Misuse Act 1990, s. 3(6). Accordingly, the offence under section 1(2) of the 1971 Act can now only be made out where the defendant 'impairs the physical condition' of a 'computer or computer storage medium', intending thereby to endanger life or being reckless whether life would be endangered. Manipulation of data on a hospital computer, rather than damage to the computer itself could not, therefore, fall within the Criminal Damage Act. Section 3 of the 1990 Act is designed to cater for cases of unauthorized modification of computer material. Depending on the precise facts, interference with data on the hospital computer might also be covered quite adequately by the new offence of unauthorized access to computer material (the 'basic hacking offence') under section 1 of the 1990 Act or, where an intention on the part of the offender to commit a 'further offence' (such as an intention to cause injury or death to a patient) could be proved, an offence under section 2 of the 1990 Act would be made out.

4. BLACKMAIL

As we have seen, the valuable assets represented by computer hardware and software are attractive targets for crime. Apart from theft, this value may be exploited by the removal and holding of tangible items such as disks and tapes for ransom, or threatening to destroy intangible programs or data. In an English case,[70] two defendants pleaded guilty to blackmail under section 21 of the Theft Act 1968 after taking disk packs and computer tapes, hiding them, and demanding £275,000 from ICI for their return. The defendants were arrested when they tried to collect the money. While presenting no criminal law problems, the case highlights a particular threat to computer security. There have also been instances of deliberate insertion of logic bombs or viruses into computer systems, with a view to demanding money before information is given on how to remove the threat. One such case is reported from Spain, where two computer technicians infected several municipal computers with a virus and then offered to sell the programmed vaccine to cure it.[71] One security expert, Beker, has spoken of unreported cases in which several hundred thousand pounds have been demanded in this way.[72] A much more ambitious case of computer blackmail came to light in Britain in December 1989. Thousands of computer disks which purported to give advice on AIDS, but which in fact contained a computer virus, were sent from

---

[70] Norman (1983), case 77.101; further details emerge in the appeal against sentence: *Cox and Jenkins* (1979) 1 Cr App R (S) 190. Sentences of 6 years' and 5 years' imprisonment were reduced, in clemency, to 4 years and 3 years.

[71] News item, *The Times*, 6 June 1989.

[72] R. Matthews, 'Computer Viruses Used as Blackmail Says Security Expert', *The Times*, 18 Jan. 1989.

London to addresses in seven different European countries and also to Thailand and Zimbabwe. Companies, including Rolls Royce, Shell, and ICL; charities, including Help the Aged; hospitals, universities, and government offices, were affected. In some cases it was reported that loading of the disks rendered the computer inoperable; in other cases a screen message appeared telling users to send £250 to a post office box address in Panama to receive a decoding disk to allow the computer to be 'unlocked'. In February 1990 it was reported that in the United States the FBI, acting for Scotland Yard, had arrested 'a computer consultant and former medical researcher for the World Health Organization' in connection with this blackmail threat. It seems likely that the defendant will be extradited to Britain.

In two cases cited by Nicholson,[73] blackmail was the motivation for computer eavesdropping, which eventually netted the blackmailer £350,000 when he threatened to reveal certain transactions to the tax authorities, and for a hacker to copy a file of AIDS blood analysis. In these instances the issue is slightly different, for use is being made of unauthorized access to confidential or damaging information as the basis for the blackmail, rather than the threat to destroy tangible items or data. One writer[74] has argued that the computerization of personnel records has provided an 'ideal environment in which blackmail can flourish'. He argues that information technology has made more likely the concept of the full-time criminal blackmailer, previously virtually unheard of.

Some state computer crime statutes address the blackmail issue directly. The North Carolina statute specifies that[75]

> any person who verbally or by a written or printed communication, maliciously threatens to [damage computers and related materials] with the intent to extort money or any pecuniary advantage, or with the intent to compel any person to do or refrain from doing any act against his will

commits a felony. It will be seen that the focus upon the threat of damage to computer materials means that this wording would only cover the first two cases cited above, though alternative unauthorized access provisions would seem to cater for the others. In a Michigan case, the state computer crime statute was held not to cover an example of extortion where a computer programmer refused to tell his former employer how a program which he had written actually worked. He argued that the employer owed him $19,500 for the programming work which he had done.[76] There, the court acquitted the defendant on the basis of lack of proof of criminal intent. In England, too, the

---

[73] Nicholson (1989).

[74] M. Hepworth, cited in a news report, *The Times*, 19 Aug. 1986; see further M. Hepworth, *Blackmail*, London: Routledge, 1975.

[75] NC Gen Stat s. 14–457.

[76] *People* v *Kovar*, Wayne County Recorders Court No. 83–64108 (1983), cited in Bloom-Becker (1985).

law of blackmail provides a defence where the defendant honestly believes that he has reasonable grounds for making the demand and that the use of the threat was a reasonable way of enforcing that demand.[77]

Existing English criminal law would appear to be perfectly adequate to deal with all the examples of computer blackmail which have so far come to light. Apart from the offence of blackmail itself, threats to destroy or damage tangible property are covered by a specific offence under section 2 of the Criminal Damage Act 1971, and an offence is now committed under section 2 of the Computer Misuse Act 1990 where a defendant gains unauthorized access to material held on a computer, with a view to committing a 'further offence', such as blackmail.

5. CORRUPTION

In cases where there exist no criminal law provisions in England capable of dealing directly with a case of unauthorized removal or misuse of computer stored information, it may be that other criminal law provisions will offer an indirect alternative. The activities of the industrial spy, for example, may well involve paid co-operation from an employee of the computer owner, perhaps in revealing the access code. This was so in the Canadian case of *Stewart*,[78] discussed in Chapter 4. If payment can be proved, criminal liability will attach to both the payer and the payee, under the Prevention of Corruption Act 1906:[79]

(1) if any agent corruptly obtains, or agrees or attempts to obtain, for himself or for any other person, any gift or consideration, or

(2) if any person corruptly gives or agrees to give or offers any gift or consideration to any agent,

as an inducement or reward for doing or forbearing to do, or for having done or forborne to do, any act in relation to his principal's affairs, or for showing or forbearing to show favour or disfavour to any person in relation to his principal's affairs

he commits an offence. By section 1(2) the expression 'agent' includes any person employed by or acting for another, and the expression 'principal' includes an employer. A related specific offence, which imposes a duty of secrecy upon Post Office employees in respect of information learned from the operation of data processing services, is provided by the British Telecommunications Act 1981, section 50.

---

[77] Theft Act 1968, s. 21.

[78] (1988) 1 SCR 963.

[79] Section 1 (1); see also Prevention of Corruption Act 1916 and the Public Bodies Corrupt Practices Act 1889. Anomalously low maximum penalties under these provisions were increased to 7 years under the Criminal Justice Act 1988, s. 47.

6. OFFICIAL SECRETS

Some computer data held by government agencies and police forces is protected by the Official Secrets Acts 1911–1989, which make it an offence for any Crown servant or government contractor to reveal to an unauthorized person certain classes of information coming to him in the course of his employment.[80] The recipient of the information, who knows or has reasonable cause to believe that it was given in contravention of the Act is, if he discloses it without lawful authority, also guilty of an offence.[81] Many people are Crown servants or government contractors, including policemen,[82] civil servants, and those who work at the Department of Health and Social Security. Tettenborn[83] points out that prosecution under the Official Secrets Act 1911 was considered for use against policemen who allegedly passed on information held in the Police National Computer as to who owned cars parked outside casino premises, so that a rival casino owner could solicit their custom. Following investigation and numerous allegations of corruption made in a book by Campbell and Connor,[84] the Police Complaints Authority investigated a number of related incidents in 1985, and prosecutions were brought towards the end of 1988 against eight defendants for misuse of information held on the Police National Computer. They were convicted of offences under the Official Secrets Act 1911 and the Prevention of Corruption Act 1906.[85] Some of the defendants were private detectives, and they obtained information relating to people's criminal records and motor vehicle ownership from the other defendants, police officers who had access to the computer records. It emerged during the trial that apart from the surprisingly wide range of groups having legitimate access to the records, many private investigators and other individuals had used police contacts in the past to obtain information from the five million records in the criminal names register and thirty-four million records in the vehicle owners' register stored on the Police National Computer.[86] The outcome of the case has reopened discussion about placing the computer under some form of independent control to monitor access more effectively. Section 2 of the 1911 Act was

---

[80] Section 2 of the Official Secrets Act 1911 has been replaced by the Official Secrets Act 1989 which retains a number of specific offences relating to the disclosure of secret information.

[81] Official Secrets Act 1989, s. 5.

[82] *Lewis v Cattle* [1938] 2 KB 454.

[83] A. Tettenborn, 'Some Legal Aspects of Computer Abuse' (1983) 2 *Company Lawyer* 147, at p. 150; also P. Hewitt, *The Abuse of Power*, London: Martin Robertson, 1982, at p. 50.

[84] D. Campbell and S. Connor, *On the Record: Surveillance, Computers and Privacy*, London: Michael Joseph, 1986; Home Office, *The Police National Computer*, HC 425, London: HMSO, 1986; C. Pounder, 'Police Computers and the Metropolitan Police' (1985) 7 *Information Age* 123.

[85] Press reports in Jan. and Feb. 1989.

[86] T. Dawe and P. Evans, 'The Confidential Police Files That Are Open to Hundreds', *The Times*, 3 Feb. 1989.

notoriously widely drafted, and the scope of the law has been narrowed in its replacement by the Official Secrets Act 1989. Prosecution of the defendants under the 1989 Act would not have succeeded, unless the disclosure of the information had resulted in the commission of an offence or impeded the detection of offences.

7. ASPECTS OF SECONDARY LIABILITY

(i) *Manufacture and Sale of Certain Devices*

A number of special devices are now available for purchase, largely without restriction, which will aid a person in the range of activities described in this book as computer misuse. Examples are modems, required to effect communications between computers, surveillance devices, such as the equipment needed to perpetrate computer eavesdropping, and computer software actually written to assist the hacker by, for example, generating random dialling. Every time a new form of technical protection is devised to assist with computer security, it seems that devices designed to undermine them become available.[87] Bit copiers, for example, are software products designed to overcome or bypass copying protection measures in software products. Such a program will scan a floppy disk track by track and copy the material held there without setting off the security system in place. It is appropriate to consider to what extent a manufacturer or seller of such a device commits a criminal offence or becomes a party to a criminal offence committed by the user of that device. Although there are some articles the possession, making, or supply of which constitutes a criminal offence in itself, none of these are likely to be applicable in the field of computer misuse. There is now, however, under the Copyright, Designs and Patents Act 1988 a specific offence committed where a person[88]

(a) makes an article specifically designed or adapted for making copies of a particular copyright work, or
(b) has such an article in his possession, knowing or having reason to believe that it is to be used to make infringing copies for sale or hire or for use in the course of a business.

This new offence would seem to extend to bit copiers and other similar devices. An example of circumstances in which the new offence would apply are provided by the American case of *Vault Corporation* v *Quaid Software*.[89]

---

[87] See J. Chesterman and A. Lipman, *The Electronic Pirates*, London: Routledge, 1988, ch. 15.

[88] Section 107(2). Further, by s. 296, a civil remedy is provided against a person who manufactures a device to circumvent copy-protection.

[89] 655 F Supp 75; (ED La, 1987).

Certain computer disks were protected by PROLOK and carried physical identification and copy protection software which checked the identification before the principal software could be run. Quaid manufactured a software package specifically to overcome this protection and enable copies to be made.

Apart from the creation of offences aimed at certain articles such as this, criminal liability in general will turn upon accessoryship or the commission of an inchoate offence by the manufacturer or supplier. Neither avenue, of course, is open where the act of computer misuse contemplated does not amount to a criminal offence, although there is the exceptional possibility of charging conspiracy to defraud, which does not require that the conduct envisaged would amount to a substantive crime.[90]

According to *Invicta Plastics* v *Clare*,[91] where the defendants manufactured a device called Radatec which detected police radar speed traps, to advertise an article for sale representing its virtue to be that it may be used to do an act which is a criminal offence is itself an incitement to commit that offence, even where the advertisement is accompanied by a warning that the act is an offence. A comparable example is *Hollinshead*,[92] where defendants were found guilty of conspiracy to defraud where they agreed to manufacture, sell, and put into circulation 'black boxes', which had the sole purpose of causing the unit counter on an electricity meter to move in reverse, thereby defrauding electricity boards. The House of Lords held that it was irrelevant that the black boxes were to be provided for a third party who would resell the devices and not actually use them himself. The difficulty, of course, is that very few articles fall clearly into the same category as black boxes, in being devices that can only actually be used for a criminal purpose. Conversely, most articles can be used for some criminal purpose or another.

A more difficult example, then, arose out of civil litigation in *Amstrad Consumer Electronics* v *British Phonographic Industry*.[93] Here the defendants had manufactured recording equipment with a twin tape cassette deck, capable of copying prerecorded cassettes at twice the normal speed, knowing and intending that many purchasers would use them in contravention of copyright legislation. The models were extensively advertised in the press and on television, stating 'Now thanks to the twin cassette deck you can record from any source and make copies of the tapes in half the time'. At the foot of the published advertisements was a warning: 'NB The recording and playback of certain material may be possible only by permission. Please refer to the Copyright Act 1956.' In the event the Court of Appeal refused to grant Amstrad a declaration that their activities were lawful, and also left open the question of whether putting out their advertising material constituted an

---

[90] See above, p. 114.
[91] [1976] RTR 251.
[92] [1985] AC 975; commentary by Smith at [1985] Crim LR 657.
[93] (1986) 12 FSR 159.

incitement to commit offences under the Copyright Act, on the basis that such a finding by the court would prejudice any later criminal proceedings. In subsequent civil litigation, *CBS Songs Ltd.* v *Amstrad Consumer Electronics*[94] in the House of Lords, it was decided that Amstrad, by producing the machines, did not 'authorize' the breaches of copyright committed by users of the machines, and so the copyright owners were not entitled to an injunction to restrain the sale of the machines, but the issue of criminal incitement was not dealt with. In *IRC* v *Atkinson and Allsop*,[95] however, a first instance decision, two defendants developed and marketed a software package called 'Movieman', which was designed to record rentals and associated VAT payments for video recording hire shops. The software contained within it a secret 'patch' which when activated by a password allowed the shopkeeper to hide a part of what he earned each day so that it reduced his statement of earnings for VAT purposes. Twelve retailers were found to have perpetrated a fraud on the revenue to the extent of £100,000, and the defendants pleaded guilty to charges of conspiracy to incite the commission of false accounting. They were given suspended prison sentences and each fined £1,000. Since this software was in fact being operated without any criminal purpose by many other retailers, who were unaware of the 'patch', the decision is some authority to the effect that a manufacturer or supplier of equipment designed to fulfil more than one purpose, one of which is contrary to the criminal law, may be found guilty of incitement.

In its Working Paper on Conspiracy to Defraud,[96] the Law Commission is considering the possibility of creating a new offence to cover situations where articles are manufactured with a view to their use for a fraudulent purpose, if the offence of conspiracy to defraud were to be abolished. This might be achieved by legislating in respect of specific named devices, such as 'black boxes', or more generally in respect of the making, selling, hiring, or offering for sale of any article which the defendant 'knows or believes is or is likely to be used in the commission of any offence involving fraud'.[97] In the context of computer misuse, the broader provision here would seem to cover the manufacture of computer programs designed to assist those intending to gain unauthorized access to a computer, such as those which enable the random dialling of numbers until a data tone indicates that the number of an on-line database has been located, only if it could be established that the ultimate purpose was a fraudulent one and that the defendant knew that it was. It may be noted that the offence under the Copyright, Designs and Patents Act 1988, in line with other offences in the Act, extends to cases where the defendant

---

[94] [1988] 2 WLR 1191.

[95] Unreported (1986), Derby Crown Court, Judge Davidson; Audit Commission, *Survey of Computer Fraud and Abuse*, London: HMSO, 1987, case 59.

[96] Law Commission, Working Paper No. 104, *Conspiracy to Defraud*, London: HMSO, 1987.

[97] Para. 10.36, and Appendix C of the Working Paper for an alternative proposal.

had 'reason to believe' that the article was to be so used. This lowers the threshold of liability, where formerly 'belief' on the part of the defendant had to be proved.[98]

Another possible approach is through the licensing of articles which may be used for illicit purposes. The government, however, has at least for the moment set its face against the licensing of surveillance or eavesdropping devices since this would[99] 'inevitably involve complex and bureaucratic procedures, requiring invidious judgments to be exercised about whether individuals had established a legitimate use for the device in question, without providing any confidence that those who wanted to acquire and use such equipment would be deterred from doing so in practice'. Despite the existence of much tougher controls in other countries and concern amongst opposition parties in Parliament, a string of debates and Private Members' Bills on such matters have produced no significant legislative change.

(ii) *Bulletin Boards*

A computer bulletin board, of course, bears only a functional resemblance to bulletin boards as they are commonly conceived. They operate by way of a computer system, which stores and displays messages to remote callers who read them on their own VDUs and sometimes make copies of the messages. Bulletin boards are widely used for perfectly legitimate purposes and indeed some users have become victims of hackers who have entered the system and wiped out their database. Some bulletin boards, however, are a prime source of contact for hackers to exchange information. It has never been suggested in this country that any criminal liability might attach to those who organize bulletin boards or exchange information there, though there has been one, unsuccessful, prosecution in the United States.[100] The case, which aroused great controversy, arose when a bulletin board operator had his home searched and equipment seized by the FBI as a result of the posting of a Pacific Telephone credit code number on his board by a subscriber. The defendant was acquitted on the ground that he had not read, and could not be expected to read, all the messages posted on the board and was unaware of the appearance of this particular number. One American commentator on the case[101] questions whether the bulletin board should be regarded as 'akin to a telephone service, where the owner bears no responsibility for the content of calls, or like a radio station, whose content is heavily regulated'. In Britain, computer bulletin boards would appear to be non-licensable cable programme

---

[98] In contrast, the Law Commission recommended that intent should be proved in respect of proposed computer misuse offences (Law Commission (1989b)). This has been accepted in the drafting of the offences in the Computer Misuse Act 1990.

[99] *Hansard*, 13 Mar. 1989, col. 187.

[100] *People* v *Tcimpidis*, Los Angeles Municipal Court No. 900532 (1984).

[101] G. Thackeray, 'Computer Related Crimes' (1985) 25 *Jurimetrics Journal* 300, at p. 312.

services under the Cable and Broadcasting Act 1984.[102] This means that the general provisions concerning obscenity, defamation, and incitement to racial hatred would apply to them. The Home Secretary stated in September 1989 that existing criminal law was adequate to deal with pornography which can be accessed via computer bulletin boards. The difficulty, he said, lay in tracing and obtaining evidence against the suppliers of the material.[103]

Apart from the question of regulation of bulletin boards, however, now that unauthorized access to computer material is a criminal offence under section 1 of the Computer Misuse Act 1990, this raises the real possibility of secondary liability for this offence attaching to anyone who supplies information useful to a hacker, such as computer system passwords, knowing or deliberately closing his mind to the fact[104] that this information was to be used for gaining unauthorized access to material held on a computer, in just the same way that knowingly supplying the combination to a safe would constitute counselling and procuring theft of the contents by another.

[102]　*Hansard*, 24 Apr. 1989, col. 404.
[103]　News item, *The Times*, 14 Sept. 1989.
[104]　Or, perhaps, being reckless: *Carter* v *Richardson* [1974] RTR 314.

6

Detection, Proof, and Prosecution

1. DETECTION AND INVESTIGATION

While there is scope for argument about the extent to which computer misuse presents novel problems for the substantive criminal law, it seems to be universally accepted that the manipulation of computers brings with it substantial problems of detection, proof, and prosecution. A whole catalogue of novel difficulties is set out in the text of a talk given by Trew to the Bramshill Police Staff College:[1]

(E)vidence of abuse, say computer fraud, is very difficult to detect. Electronic finger prints are more easily erased than human prints. Computers can instruct other computers to commit crimes; the only human intervention being the creation of a program, say to transfer funds from one bank to another on a given day. That program may have been written months before, by an employee who has now left the relevant company. His program will not only provide the *actus reus* but also destroy the evidence of the crime . . .

Although there has been much public discussion in recent years about computer misuse, and the extent to which activities such as hacking or unauthorized use of a computer should properly be regarded as criminal, this has tended to distract attention from the question of whether such conduct could be proved successfully in the courts. Sheriff Nicholson, a member of the Scottish Law Commission which recommended in 1987 the creation of new offences tò tackle computer misuse, has subsequently argued before the International Bar Association in Strasburg[2] that the mere existence of criminal offences is unlikely to have more than a minimal impact on the incidence of computer misuse. In this context, there may be some cause for concern that neither the English Law Commission's proposals to create offences of computer misuse, nor the Computer Misuse Act 1990 which was the outcome of those proposals, carry any associated recommendations on improving matters of evidence or proof in this area. Now that computer misuse offences have been enacted in Britain, it will surely be questions of detection, proof, and prosecution which will move to the centre of the stage.

[1] A. Trew, 'Computer Crime: Does Technology Outstrip Enforcement?' (1986) 2 *Computer Law and Practice* 178, at pp. 178–9. The practicality of these problems was confirmed recently by the Director of the FBI, William S. Sessions, in evidence given in May 1989 to a Subcommittee of the United States Senate, where he commented that 'The FBI has found that computer crime is often one of the most elusive crimes to investigate. It may be invisible. It has no geographic limitation, and the entire transaction may last less than one second.'
[2] News item, *The Times*, 5 Oct. 1989.

In Chapter 2, it was explained that many known incidents of computer misuse, including fraud, are not reported to the police. There is also evidence that many more such incidents never come to light at all, the victims remaining in ignorance of their losses. This is most likely to occur where individuals are trusting and naïve, security and audit procedures are slack, or where a large number of victims are losers, each to a relatively small extent, so that individual losses remain unnoticed. The classic 'round-down' or 'salami' fraud could, in principle, remain undetected for a very long time, while the single massive defalcation will be noticed but, for various reasons discussed in Chapter 2, may not be reported. In cases where the public is defrauded by corporate computer misuse, the victims may well tend to attribute discrepancies to human error or computer malfunction, rather than to fraud.

It is instructive to consider how those losses which are uncovered actually come to light. In the Audit Commission's survey[3] in 1987, respondents to the questionnaire were invited to indicate whether the fraud or other misuse was discovered through internal control procedures, internal audit, or other means. Internal control procedures include mechanisms in place to provide a secure environment in which financial processing could be performed safely and accurately, such as separation of employee duties, control over the issue and use of financial stationery and the ordering of goods and certifying of invoices for payment. The results were that of the 118 cases reported to the Audit Commission, 48 were discovered by internal controls and 13 by an internal audit, 13 following the enquiry or complaint of a claimant or customer, 29 as a result of 'information received', and 10 by 'other means'. The Audit Commission expresses concern at the relatively low number of cases discovered by internal control:[4] 'If only 40 per cent of the incidents were discovered by the day to day control procedures, then reliance on them is clearly misplaced . . . If some 44 per cent of all incidents were detected by accident it is a further sad indictment of internal control mechanisms.' In a breakdown of the figures for detection against the type of fraud or misuse committed, the Audit Commission found that whilst internal control procedures detected one-third of input frauds and two-thirds of the incidents of hacking, it was the 'other means' which had to be relied upon for uncovering other forms of fraud and the detection of misuse of computer resources. Further, in the area of computer fraud involving substantial losses, only one in five was discovered through internal control. This survey indicates that the level of awareness of computer fraud and misuse is probably low; quite apart from incidents which are known about and not reported, there are many incidents which simply go unnoticed. Ten of the Audit Commission's reported cases had been continuing for more than three years before they were detected. There does seem to be some difference between the detection pattern here and the pattern for fraud generally. In Levi's study of commercial

---

[3] Audit Commission, *Survey of Computer Fraud and Abuse*, London: HMSO, 1987.
[4] Ibid., pp. 19–20.

fraud,[5] the main difference is that many frauds were discovered by routine internal audits though some others were uncovered as a result of information received or following customer, investor, or other query.

What is the duty of the auditor in fraud detection generally, and particularly in respect of computer misuse? Comer asserts[6] that while most senior managers believe that internal auditors are responsible for most fraud detection, less than 20 per cent of auditors share that view. Traditionally it seems that the auditor's prime duty has been the determination of the fairness of the company's reported financial position, though more recently there has been acceptance of a degree of responsibility in the detection of deceptive financial practices. The 1981 Audit Commission survey[7] drew attention to this matter, commenting that

Auditors are often criticized for failing to discover computer frauds but this fails to recognize that one of the primary duties of auditors is to encourage management to instil and maintain effective internal control mechanisms. The main responsibility to prevent and detect fraud lies with management and there is no measure available of the number of frauds prevented thanks to the imposition of effective controls.

Comer agrees with this,[8] adding that in recent years many internal audit departments have been cut back to save costs and are seldom given the responsibility and authority to detect and investigate fraud. There is no specific reference to the duties of the auditor in relation to fraud detection in the Companies Act 1985. The position is complicated in practice[9] because accountants owe a legal duty of care to their client, the company. An obligation of confidentiality exists in respect of that relationship and an accountant may be sued by his client if he divulges confidences, including his suspicion of fraud, to any third party. The traditional recourse of the accountant has been to resign during his spell of office, but the Companies Act 1985 requires auditors to state the full circumstances connected with that resignation which should be drawn to the attention of shareholders or creditors.[10] Short of resignation the confidentiality obligation remains. The Financial Services Act 1986 and the Banking Act 1987 both now confer qualified privilege on auditors if they choose to pass on information about fraud.

---

[5] M. Levi, *The Incidence, Reporting and Prevention of Commercial Fraud*, Summary of Findings, Cardiff: Dept. of Social Administration, 1986, p. 5.

[6] M. J. Comer, *Corporate Fraud*, 2nd edn., London: McGraw-Hill, 1985, p. 10.

[7] Audit Inspectorate, *Computer Fraud Survey*, London: Department of the Environment, 1981; statement endorsed in Audit Commission (1987), p. 20.

[8] Comer (1985), p. 10.

[9] For a fuller discussion see R. Pennington, *Company Law*, 5th edn., London: Butterworths, 1985, ch. 19, and M. Levi, *Regulating Fraud*, London: Tavistock, 1987, pp. 124 et seq.

[10] Companies Act 1985, s. 390; an auditor will be negligent if he fails to uncover fraud or defalcation which is apparent from the accounts, or which is discoverable by the exercise of normal auditing care and skill: *Henry Squire Cash Chemist Ltd.* v *Ball, Baker & Co.* (1911) 106 LT 197. See further, Pennington (1985), pp. 784–7.

Auditors do have some responsibility for fraud detection. The Code of Local Government Practice for England and Wales, for example, refers specifically to the responsibilities of the auditor in this area, as do the Computer Audit Guidelines issued by the Chartered Institute of Public Finance and Accountancy.[11] These guidelines affirm that 'the integrity of public funds is at all times a matter of general concern and the auditor should be aware that his function is seen to be an important safeguard'. There is increasing awareness of the importance of this issue. In March 1986 it was reported that the government was considering placing a legal duty upon accountants to report cases of fraud, after amendment to the Financial Services Bill which was at that time before Parliament. The idea received strong support from some, but the proposal was dropped soon after the publication of a survey by the Chartered Association of Certified Account-ants[12] which revealed that two-thirds of directors and top executives ques-tioned thought that auditors should be required to report fraud only to their client companies, who would then take any necessary action, rather than to the police. Two-thirds of the respondents, however, thought that it was acceptable for auditors to report such matters to the police as long as the client had already been informed. The general view was that to impose a duty on auditors to disclose information to a third party would destroy trust between auditor and client. In Levi's study,[13] however, no doubt responding to a differently phrased question, two-thirds of respondents advocated that auditors should be obliged by law to report any frauds detected.

There is also the question of expertise amongst auditors in detecting computer misuse. According to the Audit Commission[14] 'it is still surprising how few organizations have sufficiently computerate auditors to assess and advise upon the adequacy of the organization's data processing safeguards'. They also state that

the elements of detection and prosecution are indeed fraught with problems not least because of the necessity in many cases to unravel the technicalities of accounting procedures which have been applied to prevent the possibility of any detection. The additional complications of the accounting process being computerized further hampers the possibility of speedy—or indeed any—detection.

An article in a professional journal on auditing in a computer environ-ment observes that[15] 'many auditors feel uncomfortable when faced with

---

[11] Chartered Institute of Public Finance and Accountancy, *Computer Audit Guidelines*, London: CIPFA, 1987.

[12] Reported in *The Times*, 3 Mar. 1986.

[13] Levi (1986), p. 8. Under the Insolvency Act 1986, s. 218(4) a voluntary liquidator of a company must report to the DPP evidence of offences committed by past or present company officers or members, committed in relation to that company. For consideration of a general duty to report incidents of computer misuse, see Chapter 2.

[14] Audit Commission, *Computer Fraud Survey*, London: HMSO, 1984, p. 6.

[15] J. K. Loebbecke, J. F. Mullarkey, and G. R. Zuber, 'Auditing in a Computer Environment' (1983) *Journal of Accountancy* 68, at p. 70.

performing a study and evaluation of internal accounting control in a computer environment . . . the basic difference between a manual system and a computer system is that the computer system contains more points at which errors and irregularities can occur'.

The role of the police in the investigation of fraud is of long standing. As Levi points out,[16] however, the history of fraud detection shows that such investigation has largely been conducted by detectives who had a special interest in the subject but little specialized training. A more specialized Company Fraud Department was established within the Metropolitan and City police forces in 1946. Gradually since then Fraud Squads have been formed in all British police forces, though some remain very limited in manpower and specialism. There are few career specialists: officers in the CID generally spend a relatively short period of time assigned to a Fraud Squad and then move on to a different area of policing. It was not until the establishment of the Fraud Investigation Group (FIG) by the Director of Public Prosecutions in 1985 that accountants were formally brought in to co-operate with the police in the investigative process and the police were able to receive such advice at an early stage. Because of lack of resources and the pressure of many other commitments, the police approach to fraud offending is still generally reactive, in the sense of responding to reports from victims, rather than being concerned with launching investigative operations themselves. Specialism in the area of computer fraud and misuse is even more rare. Indeed Comer comments that 'the police may not be overjoyed at receiving a call for assistance, particularly where the facts are complicated, the accounting system confused or the proof of loss unclear'.[17] There is a single Computer Fraud Squad Division in the Metropolitan Police, established in 1985 and headed by Detective Inspector John Austen. The Bramshill Police Staff College has introduced some intensive four-week Computer Crime Investigation Techniques courses for officers from all fraud squads from England and Wales and elsewhere. The first Interpol Training Seminar for Computer Crime Investigators was held in Paris in December 1981. Other forms of fraud squad training have been amended in the light of criticisms made in the Roskill Committee Report.[18] There is still considerable evidence, however, that business has little confidence in the ability of police fraud squads to investigate cases of computer fraud or misuse, because of the relative lack of experience of the police in dealing with such cases and their relative complexity. The various considerations which will weigh with a corporate victim in deciding whether to report suspected computer fraud or misuse to the police were discussed in Chapter 2.

In the United States, which has had the greatest experience in investigating computer misuse, the FBI has, since 1976, offered specialized training for investigators of computer misuse at their training academy in Quantico,

---

[16] Levi (1987), pp. 136 et seqq.   [17] Comer (1985), p. 282.
[18] Roskill Report, *Report of the Fraud Trials Committee*, London: HMSO, 1986.

Virginia. By mid-1989, over five hundred FBI special agents and numerous local and foreign law-enforcement officers had graduated from an intensive three-week course. The Director of the FBI, in comments to a Senate subcommittee in 1989, stressed the importance of a 'team approach' to computer misuse investigation, drawing specialists together from different disciplines. In Britain, the setting up of the Serious Fraud Squad[19] under powers provided in the Criminal Justice Act 1987 also reflects an attempt to integrate specialists from different backgrounds, and is a significant new development in this area. This innovation followed the recommendations of the Roskill Report on Fraud Trials which highlighted the weaknesses in the existing investigation system. The Serious Fraud Office is now made responsible for the investigation and prosecution of serious fraud cases. Among its immediate declared objectives are the development of an interdisciplinary team approach to the investigation of serious fraud which, it is hoped, will be more coherent, speedier, and more effective than the previously fragmented efforts of different investigative groups, and to develop greater expertise in specialist areas such as computer fraud.

The SFO is headed by a director and will eventually comprise some 80–100 staff, including administrative support. The deputy director and legally qualified staff are broadly responsible for the overall conduct of cases including their prosecution, while the chief accountant and his team handle investigative functions. The stress is upon the use of interdisciplinary teams of lawyers, accountants, and others with relevant expertise. It will work closely with the police and other investigative authorities. The SFO complements rather than supersedes existing fraud investigative agencies, and expects to handle only about 60 cases at any one time. The criteria for selection of these cases are that the facts or law involved are very complex, the sums of money at risk are substantial, and that there is considerable public interest or concern in the case.[20] On the subject of investigation of computer fraud, the Director of the SFO has commented that[21]

The SFO has computer experts who are available to assist in unravelling computer fraud, as well as to advise institutions whose computers may have been attacked, particularly to ensure that internal enquiries do not prejudice the criminal investigation and the presentation of evidence in court.

A recent article by a member of the SFO staff indicates[22] that it will be SFO policy to protect the victim as far as possible from disclosure of details about the precise method of perpetration of a computer fraud. Whilst the police remain the primary channel for complaints regarding fraud the SFO, when

[19] See J. Wood, 'The Serious Fraud Office' [1989] *Criminal Law Review* 175, and S. Street, 'The Serious Fraud Squad' (1988–9) 1 *Computer Law and Security Report* 6.
[20] Street (1988–9), at p. 7.
[21] Wood (1989), at p. 179.
[22] M. Tantum, 'The Serious Fraud Office Approach to Computer Fraud' (1988–9) 3 *Computer Law and Security Report* 13.

called, will assume overall control of the investigation. The constitutional position of the police, their accountability, and their command and control structure, however, remain unaltered by the setting up of the SFO.

2. GATHERING OF EVIDENCE

The gathering of evidence in cases of computer misuse can often be a very delicate matter. This is for several reasons. First, some forms of computer misuse are, by their nature, virtually invisible. Computer espionage committed by the copying of files or programs will leave no trace. Program manipulation by a skilled fraudster may be very difficult for an investigator to detect. The unauthorized use of computer time or services may well not be apparent to the victim. Computer sabotage may sometimes be put down to system failure or to accident or mistake rather than malice. Privacy infringements may never be discovered. Second, some forms of computer misuse are likely to be concealed by the perpetrator, perhaps in ingenious ways. Computer fraud, as we have seen, is often concealed by manipulation of output, and audit trails may be much harder to follow. The origin of a computer virus is normally impossible to ascertain from the virus itself, and requires some extrinsic evidence. Third, the perpetrator may well be in a position to erase evidence of the defalcation. This may be a very simple matter for an employee, and erasure can be explained away as an accident. A more sophisticated device was employed in a reported Dutch case,[23] where the defendant had stored evidence of his illegal arms deals on computer. He had programmed it in such a way that the input of a 'copy' or 'print' command by an investigator would execute the erasure of all the data. Similarly, Sieber reports a West German case[24] where a perpetrator had constructed a data safe which was built to erase all data by an electric field when opened by an investigator.

These difficulties highlight the importance of having specialist investigators where computer misuse is suspected, who are able to act promptly and without alerting the suspicion of the fraudster, thereby giving him time to delete evidence or otherwise cover his tracks. Old-fashioned methods may well be ineffective. In a 1971 case,[25] 300,000 customer addresses stored on magnetic tape had been stolen from a mail-order firm in West Germany. The firm obtained a court injunction for the restoration of the tapes but the court officer, when confronted with a multitude of magnetic tapes and disks the contents of which he could not discover, had no idea how to seize the proper material. Sieber suggests that many instances of stayed proceedings and case dismissals can be explained by lack of experience in the investigating authorities.[26] In the Dutch case mentioned above the police, employing computer

---

[23] Cited in U. Sieber, *The International Handbook on Computer Crime*, New York: John Wiley, 1986, p. 141.
[24] Ibid., p. 141.   [25] Ibid., pp. 140–1.   [26] Ibid., p. 142.

specialists, realized that something had been changed in the computer's operating system and avoided the trap by the simple expedient of producing copies of the incriminating data on their own computer. In a case reported in the press in 1988, the Scotland Yard Fraud Squad deployed great ingenuity and manpower in trapping an ATM fraudster whose targets were two building societies.[27] The fraud itself was a relatively simple one, relying on making large unauthorized withdrawals during Christmas and Easter holiday periods when the machines were off-line and withdrawals were not being verified. The investigation and arrest involved the use of computer technology and several police arrest teams positioned to cover virtually the whole of London, when the fraudster made his next attempt at withdrawal. The defendant was subsequently convicted of theft.

The first step is the gathering of reliable information that computer misuse is occurring and the second step is identifying the perpetrator. Of course detection techniques will vary depending upon the kind of misuse suspected. As we have seen, in the majority of cases the misuse will be perpetrated by an insider, such as an employee. In all but the most sophisticated computer frauds, there will be some evidence that fraud is taking place. Techniques of detection in cases of suspected computer fraud lie outside the scope of this book, but several specialist works are available on the topic.[28] The question of the motivation of computer fraudsters was discussed in Chapter 2. Suffice it to say here that management initially, and then investigators, should be vigilant in noticing the alteration or loss of documentary or computerized records, shortages of stock or cash, complaints from staff or customers, members of the staff living beyond their legitimate means, or showing signs of personal problems, such as drug or alcohol abuse, gambling, financial problems, marital difficulties, or dissatisfaction with personal promotion and so on. Immediate action to stop the fraud may then be necessary, but before the allegation is made all relevant data should be copied to thwart destruction of the evidence. In other cases it may be preferable to allow the fraudster to continue, under discreet observation, until adequate evidence can be assembled. In this situation a conflict of interests can arise between a victim organization, whose primary concern will be to identify and remove the perpetrator, and the investigators, who will prefer not to make a move before obtaining sufficient evidence for a conviction. Some writers advocate the setting of 'traps' for the fraudster, but English rules of evidence may result in material obtained in such a manner being excluded by the court.[29]

Police powers of arrest, search, and seizure are laid down in the Police and Criminal Evidence Act 1984 and the accompanying Codes of Practice. The

---

[27] Described in Y. Henniker-Heaton, 'Fraud Investigation: A Perspective on the Role of the Police' (1988–9) 1 *Computer Law and Security Report* 7, at p. 8.

[28] e.g. J. Krauss and A. MacGahan, *Computer Fraud and Countermeasures*, New York: Englewood Cliffs, 1979; Comer (1985), chs. 6 & 7.

[29] See Section 3 below.

detailed operation of this law lies outside the scope of this book, but it is worth noting that the powers are not confined to search and seizure of tangible objects, but extend to any 'material',[30] and that the Code of Practice for the Searching of Premises and the Seizure of Property[31] makes special provision for requiring relevant information held in a computer to be supplied in a visible and legible form.[32] As far as the new offences under the Computer Misuse Act 1990 are concerned, it will be recalled that both the offences under section 2 and section 3 are made punishable on indictment with a maximum prison term of five years. The selection by the legislature of the period of five years is no accident, since this means that the offences qualify as arrestable offences under the Police and Criminal Evidence Act 1984. This entails that they attract powers of arrest without warrant, entry in order to arrest, and search of the accused person's premises for material of evidentiary value in relation to the offence for which the person was arrested.[33] The offence under section 1 (the basic hacking offence) is triable only summarily, but special provision has been made in section 14 of the Computer Misuse Act for the issue of a search warrant[34] by a circuit judge where there are reasonable grounds for believing that an offence under section 1 has been or is about to be committed in particular premises and that evidence relating to that offence can be found on those premises. Other jurisdictions have recently introduced similar provisions. Canadian law, for instance, now permits search for 'any data contained in or available to the computer system'[35] and law reform proposals in the Netherlands will permit the seizure of data 'stored, processed or transferred by means of a computerised device'.[36] The English law powers do not extend to members of the

[30] Police and Criminal Evidence Act 1984, s. 8. In order to avoid unacceptable inconvenience to business, the police are obliged to comply with any request of the occupier of premises to have access to or to copy material seized: s. 21.

[31] Home Office, *Police and Criminal Evidence Act 1984, Codes of Practice*, London: HMSO, 1985, made under s. 66 of the Act. Evidence obtained in breach of the provisions may be excluded at trial, in the court's discretion; see Section 3 below.

[32] Police and Criminal Evidence Act 1984, s. 19(4), which specifically mentions the danger of evidence contained in a computer being 'concealed, lost, tampered with or destroyed' and Code of Practice B, para. 6.5: 'Where an officer considers that a computer may contain information that could be used in evidence, he may require that information to be produced in a form that can be taken away and in which it is visible and legible.' By s. 20, a similar rule applies in respect of a power to seize conferred by other statutes, such as the Interception of Communications Act 1985.

[33] Police and Criminal Evidence Act 1984, s. 32.

[34] Contrary to the views of the Law Commission.

[35] e.g. Environmental Protection Act 1988, s. 100(6) and s. 101(5) and Mutual Legal Assistance in Criminal Matters Act 1988, s. 18(2). Other developments are detailed in U. Sieber, 'Collecting and Using Evidence in the Field of Information Technology' in A. Eser and J. Thormundsson (eds.), *Old Ways and New Needs in Criminal Legislation*, Freiburg, 1989, pp. 203, 218.

[36] Supplementing the Dutch Code of Criminal Procedure. In West Germany the Federal Criminal Court has held that the right to inspect seized 'papers' under s. 110 of the Criminal Procedural Code extends to films, magnetic tapes, diskettes, and the CPU of a computer: Sieber (1989), p. 213.

Serious Fraud Office, though a member of the SFO would probably accompany the police when engaged on a search and seizure operation, in order to help identify the relevant documents, software, or data. The Director of the SFO has extensive investigative powers, and these may be delegated as appropriate to other persons, but not to the police, to investigate the affairs of any person. These powers include serving a written notice on a person under investigation or believed to have relevant information, requiring them to answer questions or produce documents. It is a criminal offence to fail to comply with the SFO requirement, to give false or misleading statements, or to destroy or conceal relevant material. Additionally, the Secretary of State is empowered under the Companies Act 1985 to order an investigation into the affairs of any company upon receiving evidence of fraud or misconduct.[37] It is a criminal offence to obstruct an appointed investigator or to destroy, mutilate, or falsify any relevant material.[38]

An issue which is likely to be of increasing importance in the future is the obtaining of evidence of computer misuse through surveillance and tapping of communications. A recent survey of this area of law[39] has found great differences of approach amongst different European countries. In Britain there is so far very little authority on the matter. The Interception of Communications Act 1985 deals with the interception of all forms of communication, including the electronic transmission of computer data.[40] While the Act creates a general criminal offence of unlawful interception, it also provides that there is no offence committed where the person making the interception has reasonable grounds to believe that either the sender or the receiver of the communication has consented to the interception or that interception of that communication has been authorized by a warrant issued by the Secretary of State.

The first of these exceptions, permitting 'participant monitoring',[41] would, of course, allow the police or other investigative agency to monitor a hacker's attempts to access a computer system, where the system owner had agreed to such monitoring. This might enable the police to trace the origin of the electronic signal and hence identify the person seeking to make the unauthorized access. Where, as in the majority of cases, this involves tracing of signals being carried on lines owned by British Telecom or Mercury, the co-operation of such bodies would be essential.[41a] In its recent Report on

[37] Companies Act 1985, ss. 431 and 432.

[38] Ibid., ss. 448(5) and 450(1), as amended by Companies Act 1989, s. 66.

[39] Sieber (1989), pp. 221–6.

[40] See .R. Wacks, *Personal Information, Privacy and the Law*, Oxford: Clarendon Press, 1988, pp. 285–91.

[41] Ibid., pp. 267–9 and see generally I. D. Elliott, 'Listening Devices and the Participant Monitor: Controlling the Use of Electronic Surveillance in Law Enforcement' (1982) 6 *Criminal Law Journal* 327.

[41a] Such co-operation is not always forthcoming. See N. Nuttall, 'BT Policy on Hacking Criticised by Police', *The Times*, 28 May 1990, stating that senior police officers have found that 'requests to trace cases are being ignored and some are taking a very long time to process'.

Computer Misuse, the Law Commission summarizes the present position as follows:[42]

Provided that the owner of the computer under attack gives the full co-operation to the authorities that they are entitled to expect, it is possible first to identify the line down which the unauthorized signals are being passed to the computer, and then for the authority running the public telephone system to monitor the time, duration and destination of calls on that line, with a view to comparing the pattern with the traffic arriving at the attacked computer. Such monitoring is not 'telephone tapping' because no attempt is made to intercept the calls themselves, or to scrutinize their content.

In the Commission's view this procedure falls outside the scope of the 1985 Act and no warrant would be required from the Secretary of State. Further, the Commission argues that where a hacker communicates with a target computer by means of a modem, that initiates an 'echo' from the target computer which returns through the communication link to appear on the hacker's screen. Monitoring of this echo, with the consent of the computer owner is, in the view of the Commission, 'a perfectly legitimate procedure'[43] which would not require authorization under the Act.

The second option would involve the obtaining of a warrant for interception. Such a warrant may be obtained from the Secretary of State or in some circumstances from an official of his Department, where he considers it necessary in the interests of national security, safeguarding the economic well-being of the United Kingdom, or for the purpose of preventing or detecting the commission of serious crime.[44] This arrangement may be compared with that which exists in most other European countries, where interception of communication requires judicial authorization.[45] A warrant normally lasts for two months, but may be renewed for up to six months. The Act establishes a Tribunal[46] to oversee the operation of the Act, but the Tribunal's powers are limited to dealing with the investigation of complaints about unauthorized tapping. In the case of a wrongly authorized tap, the Tribunal can quash the warrant, destroy any intercepted material, and award compensation to the complainant, but where the tapping was never authorized

---

[42] Law Commission, Report No. 186, *Computer Misuse*, Cmnd. 819, London: HMSO, 1989b, para. 2.20.

[43] Law Commission, Report No. 186, *Computer Misuse*, Cm. 819, London: HMSO, 1989b, para. 2.21.

[44] Defined in s. 10(3) to include violent crime, crime resulting in substantial financial gain, conduct by a large number of persons in pursuit of a criminal purpose, or an offence which carries, for an adult first offender, a reasonable expectation of a minimum prison sentence of 3 years.

[45] See Council of Europe, Legislative Dossier No. 2, *Telephone Tapping and the Recording of Telecommunications*, Strasburg: Council of Europe, 1982. United States law also requires judicial authorization and Belgian law makes all tapping, including that performed by the authorities, illegal: Wacks (1989), pp. 290–1; Sieber (1989), p. 223.

[46] By s. 7.

at all the Tribunal has no power to investigate the circumstances. It can offer no further assistance to the complainant and there is no right of appeal against its decision.[47]

The Scottish Law Commission, when recommending the creation of a new offence of obtaining unauthorized access to a computer, felt that the new offence should be subject to a special provision for official authorization, so that investigative officers conducting remote accessing of a computer for surveillance purposes would not come within the definition of that offence.[48] They suggested a procedure analogous to that under the Interception of Communications Act 1985, with the grant of a warrant upon similar grounds. The Private Member's Bill sponsored by Emma Nicholson MP in 1989 proposed substantially increased powers for the police in investigating computer misuse cases.[49] The English Law Commission, however, in making comparable proposals for the introduction of new offences to cater for computer misuse, felt that the existing law was adequate and recommended no increase in the powers of investigative agencies dealing with computer misuse.[50]

3. PRESENTATION OF EVIDENCE

The parties to any litigation involving computer misuse will clearly be subject to the normal panoply of rules of evidence in criminal cases. It is likely that some of the evidence to be presented will be in the form of computer documentation such as print-outs, which may be the only record of the facts contained therein. This can give rise to problems of hearsay. Traditionally in criminal trials the hearsay rule, which says that the original maker of a particular statement should be called as a witness wherever possible, rather than the court having to rely on the testimony of some other person, has been of great importance.[51] In recent years, however, inroads have been made into the hearsay rule in criminal cases, reflecting its virtual abandonment in civil cases. Particularly in the case of documentary evidence, it has at last been recognized that a rejection of evidence other than that of the original maker of the statement will often be unrealistic, unnecessary, and may produce unjust results. The Criminal Law Revision Committee, in its Eleventh Report on

---

[47] Criticized by Wacks (1989), p. 287. See also P. Fitzgerald and M. Leopold, *Stranger on the Line: The Secret History of Phone Tapping*, London: Bodley Head, 1987.

[48] Scottish Law Commission, *Report on Computer Crime*, Cm. 174, Edinburgh: HMSO, 1987, paras. 5.4–5.7 and draft Bill.

[49] In clause 3, providing for the monitoring by electronic means or other forms of surveillance, equipment which the police have reasonable cause to believe may be used to obtain unauthorized access to a computer. The Bill was withdrawn in Aug. 1989.

[50] Law Commission (1989b), paras. 4.4–4.13 on search warrants, see p. 166, above.

[51] C. Tapper, *Cross on Evidence*, 6th edn., London: Butterworths, 1985, ch. 15; A. Keane, *The Modern Law of Evidence*, 2nd edn., London: Butterworths, 1989, ch. 9.

Evidence in 1972, commented that[52] 'The increasing use of computers by the Post Office, local authorities, banks and business firms to store information will make it more difficult to prove certain matters such as cheque frauds, unless it is made possible for this to be done from computers'. A substantial and increasing amount of documentary evidence coming before the courts will have been generated by a computer. The almost universal use of computerized word-processing systems for the production of documents and the widespread use of computers in the office and at home means that many more documents presented to the court will fall into this category. In 1980 the Court of Appeal took the initiative in deciding that the definition of 'bankers' books' within the Bankers' Books Evidence Act 1879 must be updated to include computerized records[53] to take account of such records being a virtually universal feature of modern banking practices, and a subsequent statutory change to the same effect[54] was implemented from 1982. Nevertheless, special concern over the accuracy and reliability of statements in documents generated by computers has led to the legislature catering for this type of evidence alongside but separately from other documentary evidence. While, as we shall see, there is arguably no need to make any separate provision for computer generated evidence at all, the Civil Evidence Act 1968 created three new principal routes by which evidence which would previously have been excluded by the hearsay rule might now become admissible in civil cases, of which section 5(1) caters specifically for the admissibility of statements produced by computers. The relevant sections have together been described as 'complex and Byzantine provisions . . . of needless complexity'.[55]

The relevant law in criminal cases is also complex. Two fairly distinct routes for admissibility of computer-generated evidence in criminal cases have been developed, where the evidence is admissible either (i) as real evidence or (ii) under statutory provisions in the Police and Criminal Evidence Act 1984 and the Criminal Justice Act 1988.

(i) *The 'Real Evidence' Route*

It is now well established in the case-law that where a computer is being used as a 'recording device' or 'calculator' and not, in the peculiar terminology

[52] Criminal Law Revision Committee, 11th Report, *Evidence*, Cmnd. 4991, London: HMSO, 1972, para. 259. See also the comment of Steyn J. in *Minors and Harper* [1989] 2 All ER 208 at p. 210: 'If computer output cannot readily be used as evidence in criminal cases, much crime (and notably offences involving dishonesty) will in practice be immune from prosecution '

[53] *Barker* v *Wilson* [1980] 2 All ER 81; see also *Buckingham* v *Shackleton* (1981) 79 LGR 484, where the Divisional Court construed 'accounts' to include computer print-outs. The Patents, Designs and Marks Act 1986 enables registers of patents, designs, and trade marks to be held on computer. Sched. 1, s. 1(10) of the Act provides that the admissibility of such matters in evidence in a criminal case is then subject to Police and Criminal Evidence Act 1984, s. 69. On this, see further below.

[54] Banking Act 1979, Sched. 6, providing a new definition section, s. 9.

[55] Tapper (1985), p. 497.

which has been used in the cases, 'contributing to its own knowledge', then a computer print-out is a piece of 'real' or 'original' evidence and admissible as such in a criminal case. No hearsay problem arises, since the print-out is itself tendered as the fact to be proved. In *Wood*,[56] Lord Lane C.J. commented that

Witnesses, and especially expert witnesses, frequently and properly give factual evidence of the results of a physical exercise which involves the use of some equipment, device or machine. Take a weighing machine; the witness steps on the machine and reads off the dial, receives a ticket with the weight on or, even, hears a recorded voice saying it. None of this involves hearsay evidence. The witness may have to be cross-examined as to whether he kept one foot on the ground; the accuracy of the machine may have to be investigated. But this does not alter the character of the evidence which has been given.

In *Wood*'s case, where the defendant was charged with handling stolen metal, samples of metal found in the defendant's possession were compared, by detailed scientific analysis, to metal taken from the stolen consignment, and the results were then processed mathematically so that the percentage of various metals in the samples could be stated as figures. That process was undertaken by a computer, operated by scientists. At the trial, detailed evidence was given as to how the machine had been programmed and used. The judge ruled that the evidence was real evidence rather than hearsay. A similar result was reached in *Ewing*[57] in respect of bankers' computer print outs of account statements and, in *Castle* v *Cross*[58] it was held by the Divisional Court that an Intoximeter 3000 breath-test machine produced a print-out which, in the absence of any evidence that the machine was defective, was admissible as real evidence. All of these cases were decided before the coming into force of the Police and Criminal Evidence Act 1984, section 69 of which will now be relevant to them, that section being applicable to all cases of computer generated evidence, not just those where hearsay is in issue. For section 69, see further, below.

Of course real evidence tendered in these and similar cases is always open to challenge on the basis of malfunction, unreliability, or improper use of the computer. Lord Lane C.J., in *Wood*, said that:[59]

Virtually every device will involve the persons who made it, the persons who calibrated, programmed or set it up ... and the person who uses or observes the device. In each case how many of these people it is appropriate to call must depend on the facts of, and the issues raised and concessions made in, that case.

---

[56] (1982) 76 Cr App R 23 at p. 26. A similar route to admissibility has been established in the United States: *State* v *Armstead* 432 So 2d 837 (La 1983).

[57] [1983] 2 All ER 645; commentary by Professor Smith at [1983] Crim LR 473. See also the decision in *Pettigrew* (1980) 71 Cr App R 39, criticized in J. C. Smith, 'The Admissibility of Statements by Computer' [1981] Crim LR 387.

[58] [1985] 1 All ER 87.

[59] (1982) 76 Cr App R 23 at p. 27.

Evidence that the computer was not working properly would entitle the court to attach little or no weight to the evidence but, it seems, this would not render it strictly inadmissible.[60] The presumption of fact which states that mechanical instruments are presumed to have been working properly should be applicable here, but for so long as computers continue to be regarded by the courts as new and unfamiliar, something more may still be required in the way of foundation testimony to establish the ordinary working of the device.[61]

(ii) *The Statutory Route*

The starting-point for the modern law of hearsay is the case of *Myers* v *DPP*,[62] where the issue was whether microfilm records, on which the employees of a motor car manufacturer had recorded the numbers cast into the cylinder blocks of cars, were admissible in a criminal case. The House of Lords held that they were not admissible, that the hearsay rule required the original maker of the record to be called as a witness, and refused to create a further exception to the hearsay rule to cover the facts of the case. The outcome is clearly unfortunate, since the microfilm records were the best available evidence of the matter, and were almost certainly reliable. The person who originally recorded the number on the record, even if traceable, would clearly have no recollection of the recording of an individual number. The decision in *Myers* was quickly reversed by Parliament in the Criminal Evidence Act 1965, which was passed as an interim measure and was restricted to records 'relating to any trade or business' and itself gave rise to anomalies where apparently perfectly reliable records were excluded because they were, for instance, immigration records held by the Home Office, which was not operating a business.[63] There was no express reference in the Act to computer-generated documents. The statute was replaced by sections 68 to 72 and Schedule 3 of the Police and Criminal Evidence Act 1984. Section 68 in effect extended the scope of the 1965 Act, so as to render admissible statements in documents which were or which formed part of 'any record', whether or not they were related to a trade or business. The section was wide enough to cover computer-generated documents but these, exceptionally, were made subject to the additional hurdle of section 69 of the Act. Section 68 has now been replaced, in its turn, by sections 23 to 28 and Schedule 2 of the

---

[60] *Fawcett* v *Gasparics* [1986] RTR 375.

[61] Tapper (1985), p. 44, discussed in *Castle* v *Cross*, above. See also the comment of Steyn J. in *Minors and Harper* [1989] 2 All ER 208 at p. 210 that 'realistically . . . computers must be regarded as imperfect devices'. Compare the more generous approach of American courts, as in *People* v *Gauer* 7 Ill App 3d 512, 288 NE 2d 24 (1972), where it was stated that '(T)he scientific reliability of such machines can hardly be questioned.'

[62] [1965] AC 1001.

[63] *Patel* [1981] 3 All ER 94.

Criminal Justice Act 1988. Section 69 survives the 1988 Act, and will be considered in a moment.

Where it is argued that a computer print-out is inadmissible hearsay, apart from the possibility of the evidence being admissible under one of the older established common law hearsay exceptions,[64] the most likely route for admissibility now is under section 23 or section 24 of the 1988 Act which in turn allow, with various conditions and safeguards and with the leave of the court, the admission of first-hand documentary hearsay and hearsay in trade, business, and related documents. These provisions are complex but in the main create no special difficulty for computer-generated documents. Although there are as yet no relevant cases on the operation of these sections, it seems that they would extend not only to material held on paper, such as input data or computer output, but also data held on computer disks,[65] and documents received by a computer via a telecommunications link. The original document, or an authenticated copy of it, may be received.[66] The criminal court retains under section 25 of the 1988 Act a discretion to exclude the evidence, having regard *inter alia* to its nature and source, its likely authenticity, its relevance, and the extent to which it provides information not readily available from any other source. The document may also be excluded on the more general ground that its admissibility would have such an adverse effect on the proceedings that the court ought not to admit it.[67] While 'computer' is not defined in the 1988 Act as such, it seems that the pre-existing definition from the Civil Evidence Act 1968 may have been incorporated inadvertently.[68] If so, a computer is very broadly defined as 'any device for storing and processing information'.[69]

It is crucial to note, however, that these provisions render admissible statements made by a 'person', even though these now appear in computer-generated form, and that neither section will operate if the statement is based on information which has been automatically selected, recorded, or processed by the computer. Hearsay evidence always relates to information which has

[64] Such as a computer print-out of a university record of a degree result, admissible at common law as a statement in a public document: *Collins* v *Carnegie* (1834) 1 Ad & El 695; Criminal Justice Act 1988, s. 28, preserves the existing common law hearsay exceptions, but the print-out in this example would probably be admissible under s. 24 in any event; other possibilities are discussed by C. Tapper, *Computer Law*, 4th edn., London: Longman, 1989, pp. 379–80.

[65] Criminal Justice Act 1988, Sched. 2, para. 5.

[66] Ibid., s. 27; a copy may be received whether or not the original is still in existence.

[67] Ibid., s. 25; s. 28(1)(b) makes it clear that the court's discretionary powers at common law to exclude evidence the propative value of which is outweighed by its prejudicial effect and under Police and Criminal Evidence Act 1984, s. 78, are retained; see, further on this, below.

[68] D. J. Birch, 'Documentary Evidence' [1989] *Criminal Law Review* 15, at p. 30, pointing out that Sched. 2 of the 1988 Act says that 'expressions' used in Part II of the Act are to be construed in accordance with the definitions in s. 10 of the Civil Evidence Act 1968. Section 23 of the 1988 Act uses the expression 'computer', and s. 10 of the 1968 Act defines that by reference to s. 5 of that Act.

[69] Civil Evidence Act 1968, s. 5(6).

passed through a human mind. If the input to the computer would have fallen foul of the hearsay rule, the output will be similarly tainted, but the computer cannot convert original evidence into hearsay evidence. Section 23 only renders admissible by way of an exception to the hearsay rule a statement made by a person in a document as evidence 'of any fact of which direct oral evidence by him would be admissible' and section 24 similarly requires that the original supplier of the information contained in the document must have had, or be reasonably supposed to have had, 'personal knowledge of the matters dealt with'. It follows that in those cases discussed under Section (i) above, where the computer itself has observed a fact and recorded it by way of the print-out, there is no hearsay issue and hence no need to rely upon section 23 or section 24. Take as an illustration the case of the putting in evidence of a computer-generated bank account statement. If the receipt is tendered in order to show that X paid £100 into Y's account, this is hearsay, because the print-out is being tendered as evidence of the fact stated by X. The receipt is admissible as an exception to the hearsay rule only if sections 23 or 24, or some other exception to the hearsay rule, applies. If, however, the receipt is tendered as evidence that Y's account has been credited with £100, this is not hearsay.[70]

Any statement which satisfies the requirements of section 23 or section 24, however, must still fulfil the additional conditions of section 69 of the Police and Criminal Evidence Act 1984. Section 69 of that Act provides:

(1) In any proceedings, a statement in a document produced by a computer shall not be admissible as evidence of any fact stated therein unless it is shown—
    (a) that there are no reasonable grounds for believing that the statement is inaccurate because of improper use of the computer
    (b) at all material times the computer was operating properly, or if not, that any respect in which it was not operating properly or was out of operation was not such as to affect the production of the document or the accuracy of its contents . . .

Section 69(1)(c) provides that as a further condition of admissibility, compliance may be required with certain rules of court made under section 69(2), such as giving notice of the intention to rely upon section 69, but no such rules have yet been made. It is important to notice that no statement is made admissible by virtue section 69 which would not have been admissible otherwise. The section is negative in form, and hence provides in the case of computer-generated statements additional obstacles[71] to those which apply

---

[70] See commentary on *Minors and Harper* [1989] Crim LR 360 by Professor Smith. In that case Steyn J. commented that 'there will be much scope for serious argument whether a particular print-out does amount to real evidence and the usefulness of this exception is therefore limited': [1989] 2 All ER 208 at p. 212.
[71] See Tapper (1985), p. 560; confirmed in *Minors and Harper*, above.

in relation to the admissibility of other documents. Whilst it is clear that the requirements of section 69 must be fulfilled every time it is sought to introduce computer-generated evidence under either section 23 or section 24 of the 1988 Act, it appears that notwithstanding the clear words of section 69, a statement in a document produced by a computer 'shall not be admissible as evidence' unless that evidence complies with section 69, there is some doubt over its application to the 'real evidence' route mentioned under (i) above. In *Minors and Harper*[72] it was said that section 69 had no relevance where a computer print-out is admissible as real or original evidence. More dubiously in *Sophocleus* v *Ringer*,[73] however, the Divisional Court held that section 69 had no application in a case where a laboratory scientist gave evidence of analyses of a blood sample by gas chromatography carried out by a computer which printed the results in graph and tabulated form. While there is certainly no hearsay problem here, the computer print-out does appear to be tendered as evidence of facts stated therein, the reliable operation of the computer needs to be established, and hence section 69 should apply. So, while section 69 is not relevant where the print-out is itself tendered as the fact to be proved, or as an item of real evidence, if the print-out is tendered as evidence of a fact observed by the computer, then section 69 must surely still be satisfied.

Under section 69 the evidence is only admissible if the court is satisfied that the computer was working properly or that, if it was not, any malfunction did not affect the statement in the document under consideration. For these purposes the court may draw reasonable inferences from the circumstances in which the statement was made and from any other circumstances, including the 'form and contents of the document'[74] in question. This provision has been little explored by the courts, but in *Minors and Harper*[75] it was established by the Court of Appeal that where there was a disputed issue as to the admissibility of a computer print-out, the issue should be resolved by the judge on a trial within a trial. Where the prosecution seeks to introduce the statement, the standard of proof beyond reasonable doubt would apply.[76]

---

[72] [1989] Crim LR 360, and commentary by Professor Smith; the case was decided before the coming into force of the relevant sections of the Criminal Justice Act 1988, and so is also concerned with the application of s. 68 of the Police and Criminal Evidence Act 1984, repealed by the 1988 Act. *Minors and Harper* was, apparently, followed on this point, in *Spiby, The Times*, 16 Mar. 1990.

[73] [1987] Crim LR 422, and commentary by D. J. Birch; Keane (1989) contends at p. 264 that s. 69 'has no application to computer-produced documents admissible at common law', and would include the computer print-out in *Sophocleus* v *Ringer* in that category; both Birch [1987] Crim LR 423 and Smith [1989] Crim LR 361–3 appear to argue that in that case the requirements of s. 69 should have been fulfilled.

[74] See Police and Criminal Evidence Act 1984, Sched. 3, para. 14, preserved by the 1988 Act, and Keane (1989), p. 264; even so, its admissibility may be challenged on grounds of unreliability or improper use.

[75] See above.

[76] Where the defence introduces the evidence, presumably the standard required is the balance of probabilities.

There has, however, been considerable litigation in the comparable area of the reliability of print-outs from Intoximeter machines, and it seems likely that a similar approach will be taken. The courts have held in that context that oral evidence may be received from an operator to explain an error in the print-out,[77] or to trace the error to a human operator rather than to the machine,[78] and that even if the machine is shown to have malfunctioned the print-out may still be relied upon if it can be shown that the malfunction could not have affected the document in issue.[79] If the statement in the computer-generated document is held to be admissible in accordance with section 69, paragraphs 11 and 12 of Schedule 13 to the 1988 Act indicate that in estimating the weight to be attached to such a statement, regard should be had 'to all the circumstances', but in particular whether the information contained in the statement was supplied to the computer contemporaneously with the occurrence of the facts dealt with in that statement, and whether the person supplying the information to or operating the computer had any incentive to conceal or misrepresent the facts.

Two research studies carried out by the Central Computer and Tele-communications Agency during 1987 and 1988, codenamed VERDICT (the Verification of Electronically Reproduced Documents in Court) and APPEAL, have provided a commentary on the practical problems faced by the parties seeking to rely on computer-generated evidence in a criminal court.[80] It was suggested in the course of the VERDICT research that section 69 of the Police and Criminal Evidence Act should be abolished and replaced by non-statutory guidelines reflecting the weight to be attributed to particular pieces of computer-generated evidence. The abolition of section 69 also has the powerful advocacy of the British Computer Society and a leading author in the field of evidence, Tapper, who argues that it is 'unnecessary', and says that documents generated by computers should be subject to exactly the same regime as any other documents.[81]

The statute lays stress on the computer operating properly at all material times, and this requirement is further elaborated in Schedule 3 of the Police and Criminal Evidence Act.[82] The problem identified by some writers is that a

---

[77] *Fawcett v Gasparics* [1986] RTR 375.

[78] *Burditt v Roberts* [1986] RTR 391.

[79] *Wright v Taplin* [1986] RTR 388.

[80] Summarized by S. Castell, 'The Legal Admissibility of Computer Generated Evidence' (1989–90) 2 *Computer Law and Security Report* 2.

[81] Tapper (1985), p. 560. The law in Scotland is still governed by the Criminal Evidence Act 1965. In Scottish Law Commission, Discussion Paper No. 77, *Criminal Evidence*, Edinburgh: SLC, 1988, para. 5.26, the Scottish Law Commission is 'unpersuaded that there is any need for special rules on the admissibility of computer evidence'. This is also the line taken in the United States, where the Federal Rules of Evidence have been amended to include 'data compilations, in any form', but the courts have otherwise dealt with the admissibility of such evidence without the need for special provision; see *Westinghouse Electric Supply Co. v B. L. Allen*, 138 Vt 84, 413 A 2d 122 (1980).

[82] Sections 8–12.

computer malfunction, or an act of unauthorized tampering, may be almost impossible to detect by all but experts in the field. How then can a court be assured of the accuracy of the statement contained in a computer document? According to Kelman and Sizer,[83]

> The Data Processing Manager, when producing, as evidence, a print-out from the computer he is in charge of, frequently says in a deposition that the computer was working properly. This is an opinion and, with a large and complex computer system, it is doubtful whether such a manager could have sufficient knowledge about the computer system to be capable of forming such an opinion based on fact.

One of the conclusions of the VERDICT report was that if defence lawyers begin to challenge computer-generated evidence in a determined fashion, requiring the prosecution to prove accuracy beyond reasonable doubt in each case, legal proceedings would come to a halt. The only solution proposed in the reports is to abandon the attempt to legislate separately for computer evidence and to concentrate on achieving detailed guidelines and codes of practice to ensure a very high standard of computer system reliability and security. While there is some merit in this argument, and steps are being taken both in the computer industry and at government level to achieve greater consistency and reliability of operation, overall the APPEAL report is pessimistic:[84] '(W)hatever candidate technologies and techniques there may be available for achieving this legally acceptable status they are not yet of proven performance; nor, if dependence on intrinsically insecure machine architectures is continued, are they ever, perhaps, likely to be.'

A more particular problem in cases of computer misuse, however, is that important documentary evidence about the misuse may have been generated by the very computer which, it is alleged, has been the subject of the unauthorized access or other tampering. Some respondents to the Law Commission's Working Paper on Computer Misuse felt that there was an unsurmountable problem in proving facts necessary to demonstrate that the computer was working properly. The Law Commission, which dealt 'quite shortly' with this specific evidential point in its subsequent Report, disagreed, since[85]

> ... those facts will be data at present contained within the computer. We see no reason in such a case for exempting the prosecution from the general requirement imposed by section 69 of showing that the computer was, apart from the alleged interference of which evidence will be given, otherwise operating properly.

The Court of Appeal in *Minors and Harper*[86] has taken a similar line, with Steyn J. stating that a judge should 'examine critically a suggestion that a prior malfunction of the computer . . . has any relevance to the reliability of

---

[83] A. Kelman and R. Sizer, *The Computer in Court*, Aldershot: Gower, 1982, p. 19.
[84] Castell (1989–90), p. 8.
[85] Law Commission (1989*b*), para. 4.9.
[86] [1989] 2 All ER 208 at p. 214.

the particular computer record tendered in evidence'. Where a computer which is the target of unauthorized access logs the time and extent of such access, that computer-held information may be valuable prosecution evidence. It would seem that the evidence would not be rendered inadmissible by section 69 if it could be shown that the misuse occasioned to the computer was not such as to affect the reliability of that log.

Another area in which challenge to computer-generated evidence is likely to increase, however, is where the defence argues that evidence should be excluded on the ground of unfairness to the defendant. *Gold and Schifreen*[87] was one of the first cases in which such a challenge was brought, the defence arguing that much of the computer evidence upon which the prosecution was based should be excluded in the judge's discretion under section 78 of the Police and Criminal Evidence Act 1984. This section provides that the court may disallow prosecution evidence where, having regard to all the circumstances, including the circumstances in which the evidence was obtained, the admission of the evidence would have such an adverse effect on the fairness of the proceedings that the court ought not to admit it. The defence claimed that British Telecom's detection methods, by which they had kept a check on the defendants' unauthorized accesses of Prestel, particularly the use of a Data Monitor Device and the Miracle Call Logger, which had eventually identified the two defendants, were objectionable. It was further suggested that British Telecom had themselves committed an offence in the course of assembling the evidence.[88] The arguments were, however, rejected by the trial judge Butler J. The matter was not pursued on appeal and so unfortunately there was no opportunity for appellate consideration of the question.

In the United States, the use of informants and various undercover operations have been a key means of obtaining information necessary to prosecute computer hackers under state legislation. Law enforcement officers have made use of established hacker bulletin boards, or have set up their own, to obtain intelligence about hacker activity. In one case information about a supposed computer telephone access code was left by the authorities on a bulletin board, and then the telephone numbers of all those who called the supposed access code were logged and traced.[89] In England, section 78 of the

---

[87] [1988] AC 1063.

[88] Though this seems untenable: s. 45 of the Telecommunications Act 1984, as substituted by s. 11(1) and Sched. 2 of the Interception of Communications Act 1985 provides that the authorities running a public telecommunications system commit no offence if they disclose information for the purposes of the prevention or detection of crime, or for the purposes of criminal proceedings.

[89] J. J. BloomBecker, 'Computer Crime Update: The View as we Exit 1984' (1985) 7 *Western New England Law Review* 627, at p. 634. See also U. Wuermeling, 'New Dimensions of Computer Crime: Hacking for the KGB' (1989–90) 4 *Computer Law and Security Report* 20, discussing the gathering of evidence by Clifford Stoll of the United States Lawrence Berkeley Laboratory, in conjunction with United States and German authorities, against German hackers thought to be working for the KGB. At one point Stoll provided the hacker with a lengthy text of bogus information as a 'bait', and while the hacker copied it he was traced, with the assistance of the German telecommunications authorities, to a computer base at the University of Bremen and

Police and Criminal Evidence Act 1984 is being used to exclude evidence in cases where the police have been responsible for some illegality, impropriety, or unfairness in obtaining the evidence, including stepping outside the Codes of Practice issued under the Act.[90] In some of the decided cases it seems that a reason for excluding the evidence has been to discipline the police.[91] In others it has been said that whether the impropriety was wilful or committed through ignorance is irrelevant.[92] Whilst the operation of section 78 would not impinge directly upon police undercover or surveillance methods the section, as currently interpreted, is capable of resulting in the exclusion of any evidence which may be described as having been obtained by a trap. In *R v H*,[93] for example, the police bugged a rape complainant's telephone, with her consent. She instigated telephone conversations with the defendant, who was suspected by the police of having committed the offence but had been released by them pending further enquiries. The conversations were recorded and contained material damaging to the defendant. The judge held that the tapes had been obtained by a trap, and excluded them.

(iii) *The Expert Witness*

An expert witness may be called to give evidence in any matter which calls for expertise and where the triers of fact are not able to rely upon their own knowledge and experience.[94] The testimony of an expert witness is likely to carry considerable weight and very high standards of accuracy and objectivity are insisted upon.[95] Such evidence is commonly given in cases involving scientific issues and, increasingly, where the operation or misuse of computers is in issue. An expert on computing may be called upon to help the court by explaining computing practices, to assist the prosecution with the provision of technical evidence, or to consider possible defences for the defendant. In practice it seems that in every case where computer-generated evidence is crucial to the case an expert witness will be required to testify under section 69 of the Police and Criminal Evidence Act that there are no reasonable grounds for believing that improper use of the computer has adversely affected the print-out. The same witness will be required to identify the actual

eventually to the hacker's own home computer. Recorded tapes of the hacker's activities were, however, inadmissible at trial because the German authorities omitted to obtain the necessary judicial authorization. In Aug. 1989 a number of charges were dropped by the Federal Public Prosecutor. See further C. Stoll, *The Cuckoo's Egg*, London: The Bodley Head, 1990.

[90] See Keane (1989), pp. 42–4, and R. May, 'Fair Play at Trial: An Interim Assessment of Section 78 of the Police and Criminal Evidence Act 1984' [1988] *Criminal Law Review* 722. In *Deacon* [1987] Crim LR 404 it was said that a mere technical breach of the Codes was irrelevant.

[91] *Mason* (1988) 86 Cr App R 349 (though the court, at p. 352, denied that it was doing so).

[92] *Samuel* [1988] 2 WLR 934; *Foster* [1987] Crim LR 821.

[93] [1987] Crim LR 47.

[94] Tapper (1985), pp. 440–3.

[95] The duties of the expert witness are summarized by Lord President Cooper in *Davie v Edinburgh Magistrates* [1953] SC 34; see also *Preece v HM Advocate* [1981] Crim LR 783.

computer which has produced the print-out.[96] This may be technically very difficult where the operation has not been logged by the computer itself, and will be most difficult in cases of 'one-off' fraud rather than a continuing series of computer manipulations or unauthorized accesses. According to Kelman and Sizer,[97] 'In an exhaustive analysis, different aspects of the computer may need to be considered, and a series of independent experts on hardware, software and communications may be required.' In *Minors and Harper*[98] it was held that the evidence of an experienced auditor in the audit investigation department of a building society, who had worked regularly with the computer in question, was properly qualified to testify as to the reliability of that computer, but that the evidence of a revenue protection official who was not a computer technologist, but who regularly relied on print-outs from the computer in question and had no reason to doubt its accuracy, was not so qualified. Before the case comes to court there must be mutual disclosure of expert evidence between the parties where that evidence is to be relied upon at trial at Crown Court.[99]

The British Computer Society and the Association of Professional Computer Consultants have both created registers of expert witnesses, which are available to members of the legal profession and the public.[100] The BCS criteria for including someone on their register is that they should be Fellows of the Society, have a minimum of ten years' experience in the computer industry, and have knowledge and experience of legal practice and proceedings. In the United States, as might perhaps be expected, a considerable market for computer security specialists who can provide expert evidence has developed. Numerous professional bodies and other organizations provide lists of approved individuals and a Computer Crime Expert Witness Manual is published.[101]

4. MEASURES TAKEN AGAINST PERPETRATORS

Of the 118 cases of computer fraud and computer misuse discovered by the Audit Commission[102] in 1987, action was taken by employers as follows: prosecution (38 cases), resignation (14), dismissal (14), and no action (6). In the remaining 46 cases the action taken was not disclosed but we may well

---

[96] Police and Criminal Evidence Act 1984, Sched. 3.
[97] Kelman and Sizer (1982), pp. 19–20.
[98] [1989] 2 All ER 208 at pp. 215–16.
[99] Crown Court (Advance Notice of Expert Evidence) Rules 1987, made under Police and Criminal Evidence Act 1984, s. 81.
[100] J. J. P. Kenny, 'The Expert Witness Register of the British Computer Society' (1988) 4 *Computer Law and Practice* 92; C. Berman, 'Hi-Tech Experts Who Get the Call into Court', *The Times*, 19 Jan. 1988.
[101] BloomBecker (1985), p. 635.
[102] Audit Commission (1987), p. 21.

infer from this lack of detail that prosecution was not brought. Thirty-two per cent of the total number of incidents ended in prosecution; this was a decline from the 1984 survey where the figure was 47 per cent of the total. While there is some evidence that American companies are more inclined to seek prosecution against computer misusers,[103] in the American Bar Association survey, where one-third of the respondents who had reported a computer crime said that they did not report it to the law enforcement agencies and a third chose to report only some of the offences, a substantial number of perpetrators who were identified were dealt with by disciplinary action rather than prosecution.

It was one of Sutherland's contentions that white-collar offending is dealt with leniently, and while there is little hard evidence on the matter, penalties imposed for white-collar crime do seem to be low when compared to more traditional categories of crime. Levi[104] has compiled a body of material on sentencing levels for fraud and notes the generally low incidence of immediate imprisonment for fraud offending and the relatively short length of sentence, notwithstanding a guideline judgment of the Court of Appeal in *Barrick*[105] on sentencing for cases of theft in breach of trust committed by employees and professional persons. The amount of information available on sentencing for computer fraud or, indeed, any other form of computer misuse, is too sparse to make any meaningful assessment. There is no reason to think, however, that sentencing levels for computer fraud would be significantly different from those where no computer was involved. The Audit Commission survey was able to provide details of sentences received in only a handful of computer misuse cases and the information even in those cases is far from comprehensive.[106] There were six immediate prison sentences imposed, ranging from two years up to five years, and six non-custodial sentences. A case of unauthorized alteration of input by a clerk involving a loss of £400 was dealt with by way of a probation order for two years, a similar case where the loss was £1,290 incurred 240 hours community service, and a third involving £54,000 attracted a two-year suspended sentence. Other similar cases were dealt with by way of a suspended sentence together with a fine pitched at a level to remove profit associated with the offence.

Apart from the imposition of imprisonment and fines, several other measures are available to the criminal courts which might prove appropriate in particular cases of computer misuse. One is the compensation order, where a criminal court may require the offender to pay compensation to the victim of the offence where that victim has suffered 'injury, loss or damage' resulting from the offence.[107] Compensation powers have been used in some computer ·

---

[103] See Chapter 2.

[104] M. Levi, 'Suite Justice: Sentencing for Fraud' [1989] *Criminal Law Review* 420.

[105] (1985) 7 Cr App R (S) 142.

[106] Audit Commission (1987), p. 22; the distinction drawn there between 'committal' sentences and 'suspended' sentences is obscure.

[107] Powers of Criminal Courts Act 1973, s. 35.

misuse cases to compensate victims for physical damage to their property and for expense occasioned in the loss of computer time and services. The powers to compensate are limited to cases where there is no dispute over the quantum of damage and where the defendant can realistically afford to pay, though payment of a lesser sum or payment by instalments lasting for up to two or three years may be ordered.[108] Another option is the forfeiture order,[109] a measure recently revised in the Criminal Justice Act 1988. The court may order that any property which was used by the offender in the commission of the offence is to be forfeited. Clearly this could, in an appropriate case, extend to forfeiture of the offender's computer and related equipment. Such an order may be made by the court in respect of conviction for any of the offences in the Computer Misuse Act 1990.[110] An important limitation on the use of these powers is that a forfeiture order is regarded as a form of fine, constituting part of the punishment for the offence, so that the value of the property seized must not be out of proportion to the seriousness of the crime committed.[111] Also, there would be no objection in principle to a criminal court inserting a condition into a probation order that the offender refrain from hacking activities, subject to such a condition being regarded by the courts as enforceable. In the United States one well-known hacker was required by the sentencing court, after completion of a six-month term of imprisonment, to spend a further year under supervision in a rehabilitation centre, to be treated for his 'computer addiction'.[112]

There are also important provisions in the Company Directors Disqualification Act 1986, which permit the court, in addition to sentencing for the offence, to disqualify a person from acting as a company director for a period of up to fifteen years, where they have been convicted of an indictable offence 'in connection with the promotion, formation, management or liquidation of a company'.[113] In *Re Dawson Print Group Ltd.*,[114] Hoffman J. said that disqualification required 'some conduct which if not dishonest is at any rate in breach of the standards of commercial morality, or some really gross incompetence which persuades the court that it would be a danger to the public if he were to be allowed to continue to be involved in the management of companies'. In theory such disqualification is regarded as preventive rather

---

[108] *Olliver* (1989) 11 Cr App R (S) 10.

[109] Criminal Justice Act 1988, s. 69, amending Powers of Criminal Courts Act 1973, s. 43.

[110] See Law Commission (1989*b*), para. 4.12.

[111] *Buddo* (1982) 4 Cr App R (S) 268; Powers of Criminal Courts Act 1973, s. 43(1A).

[112] The hacker in question was Kevin Mitnick. Tapper cites an unreported English case where refraining from hacking was made a condition of a defendant's bind over to keep the peace: Tapper (1989), p. 293. Such a course would appear to be unlawful, since a bind over may not include specific conditions: *Randall* [1987] Crim LR 254.

[113] Sections 2–5, s. 2(1) was widely construed in *Georgiou* (1988) 10 Cr App R (S) 137, approving *Corbin* (1984) 6 Cr App R (S) 17, to cover cases where the defendant's conduct displayed gross negligence, incompetence, or a lack of commercial probity.

[114] [1987] BCLC 601.

than punitive, but a mixture of penal objectives, including retribution and deterrence, probably underlie their use in individual cases. It seems that some proportion should be maintained between the length of the period of disqualification and the seriousness of the offence.[115] A contravention of a disqualification order is in itself a criminal offence punishable with up to two years' imprisonment.[116]

---

[115] *Re Civica Investments Ltd.* [1983] BCLC 456; *Re Stanford Services Ltd.* [1987] BCLC 607.

[116] By s. 13.

7

The International Dimension

The increasingly international nature of offending, particularly large-scale fraud, much of it computer-related, involving the transfer of assets or the proceeds of crime from one jurisdiction to another, or the interception of money in the process of being transferred from one country to another, has important implications for the scope and operation of the criminal law.[1] The detection and prosecution of fraud is often complicated by the existence of the international dimension and fraudsters will make use of weak links on the international stage: they will transfer money to countries where financial controls are lax or where the banking laws hamper the investigations of police or fraud squad officers. They will prefer those countries for their operations where the fraud laws are outdated and adhere to rigid and technical requirements before courts can proceed to try the offence. They will prefer countries where security controls are weak, evidence of offending is easy to cover up, and where there are tight restrictions on admissibility of evidence of fraud. They will prefer countries which are weak in their record of mutual assistance with other countries in the detection of fraud and which have restrictive laws on extradition.

The Roskill Committee on Fraud Trials[2] noted the vital importance of international co-operation if serious fraud offences were to be discovered and the offenders brought to justice. Both the OECD[3] and the International Chamber of Commerce Working Party on Computer Crime,[4] which produced reports on the subject of computer-related crime and the criminal law in 1986 and 1988 respectively, have stressed the particular importance of the international dimension of computer misuse. They mention in particular the need to strengthen both the general legislative environment and to reform the rules of jurisdiction concerning, especially, the international transfer of money.

---

[1] See B. A. K. Rider, 'Combating International Commercial Crime' (1985) *Lloyds International and Maritime Law Quarterly* 217.

[2] Roskill Report, *Report of the Fraud Trials Committee*, London: HMSO, 1986.

[3] OECD, *Computer-Related Crime: Analysis of Legal Policy*, Paris: OECD, 1986.

[4] International Chamber of Commerce, Commission on Computing, Telecommunications and Information Policies, *Computer Related Crime: An International Business View*, Paris: ICC, 1988.

1. INTERNATIONAL CO-OPERATION

Several improvements have been made in these areas recently in English law and more changes are likely. The Criminal Justice Act 1987 implemented many of the Roskill Committee's proposals for improving the detection and prosecution of fraud cases by the creation of the Serious Fraud Office, with special expertise and a range of investigative powers.[5] In particular, the Act gives the Director of the Serious Fraud Office powers to make agreements with investigative agencies abroad regarding the exchange of information about international fraud. There is now, for instance, a memorandum of understanding between the Department of Trade and Industry and the Securities and Exchange Commission and the Commodity Futures Trading Commission in the United States which establishes a framework for the exchange of information relating to suspected breaches of legal rules in the securities and futures sector.[6] Quite apart from the new machinery, many steps are being taken to improve international police, fraud squad, and international agency co-operation, an area of difficulty in the past.[7]

Again implementing the Roskill proposals, the Criminal Justice Act 1988 has made the reception of documentary evidence from abroad simpler, section 29 of the Act assisting either prosecution or defence to obtain evidence from a witness abroad after the issuing of a letter of request, the document then being admissible under sections 23 or 24. By section 32 a witness from abroad, whether a British subject or a foreign national, may be examined on commission abroad and give their evidence by means of a video-link to the courtroom in Britain.

The Extradition Act 1989 improves extradition arrangements where, it seems, 'the United Kingdom has always been a long step behind other European countries'.[8] The law and procedure have been updated to allow the United Kingdom to ratify the European Convention on Extradition, concluded on 13 December 1957. Parties to the Convention, which include most European states and some others, may enter into a 'general extradition agreement' or a 'special extradition agreement' made pursuant to the 1989 Act, which has swept away the previous arrangements under the Extradition Act 1870 and the Fugitive Offenders Act 1967. The most important change made by the Act is to confer on the government the power to enter into such agreements with foreign states which will not require the requesting state to demonstrate a prima-facie case against the fugitive, previously a cornerstone of English law. This change was thought necessary both to allow ratification

---

[5] See Chapter 6.

[6] J. Wood, 'The Serious Fraud Office' [1989] *Criminal Law Review* 175, at p. 183.

[7] Rider (1985), commenting on the 'built-in opposition within many organisations to share information'.

[8] C. Warbrick, 'The New Law on Extradition' [1989] *Criminal Law Review* 4, at p. 4.

of the convention and to counter the argument that, in spite of a judicial trend towards construing extradition legislation in favour of the requesting state rather than the fugitive in recent years,[9] the United Kingdom's requirements for extradition were so much more difficult to overcome than those of other states that it was becoming regarded internationally as a haven for fugitives. There was considerable opposition to this move in Parliament, and further opposition is anticipated when the government seeks to implement new extradition arrangements by way of Orders in Council.

Another amendment is the replacement of the notion of 'extradition crime' as it was understood in the Extradition Act 1870. Rather than detailing individually those crimes in England for which extradition may be granted,[10] as was done in Schedule 1 of the 1870 Act, the 1989 Act defines 'extradition crime' as 'conduct' in the territory of a foreign state which, if it occurred in the United Kingdom, would constitute an offence punishable with imprisonment for a term of twelve months or more, and which is similarly punishable in the state seeking extradition, however the offence is there defined.[11] Prior to the Computer Misuse Act 1990, in cases involving computer misuse, such conduct would have been extraditable provided that it could have been prosecuted under the Theft Acts or other legislation appearing in the comprehensive list of offences in Schedule 1 of the Extradition Act 1870.[12] In a recent case under that statute, for example, it was argued unsuccessfully that a conviction in the United States for 'wire fraud' would not have amounted to the offence of either theft or obtaining property by deception in England.[13] Similarly, it seems that in the case described in Chapter 5, of the person charged with putting the AIDS disks containing a computer virus into general circulation, the defendant may be extradited to this country from the United States since his conduct, if proved, would clearly constitute blackmail. Those extradition rules, however, would not have permitted the extradition of a hacker so long as hacking itself remained outside the criminal law of England and no other substantive offence listed in the Schedule had been committed. Now, the offences under section 2 and section 3 of the Computer Misuse Act 1990 (though not hacking *per se* under section 1) are made punishable with a maximum sentence in excess of 12 months and would, therefore, be extraditable under the general provision in section 2 of the Extradition Act 1989. Section 15 of the Computer Misuse Act, however, also brings these offences within the ambit of Schedule 1.

[9] *Government of Belgium* v *Postlethwaite* [1987] 2 All ER 985, *per* Lord Bridge; Warbrick (1989), at p. 6.

[10] Criminal Justice Act 1988, Sched. 1, para. 4 added insider dealing under the Company Securities (Insider Dealing) Act 1985 to the list of extradition crimes under the 1870 Act. The general provision in Extradition Act 1989, s. 2, would now apply.

[11] Section 2.

[12] For discussion, see *Jennings* v *US Government* [1982] 3 All ER 154; Orders in Council made under the 1870 Act remain valid notwithstanding its repeal: Extradition Act 1979, s. 36(3).

[13] *Re Bruce Parkyn Jackson* [1988] Crim LR 834.

The extradition issue arose in the case of *Osman*.[14] This was a case where the defendant had been committed to custody in England to await return for trial in Hong Kong in respect of forty-two charges of conspiracy to defraud, conspiracy to steal, bribery, theft, and false accounting, involving hundreds of millions of dollars. One alleged incident concerned the sending of a telex by the defendant's company in Hong Kong to its bank in New York, instructing it to effect an electronic transfer of funds above the authorized amount to the New York account of a Hong Kong company, from whom the defendant was to receive corrupt payments in return. The defendant argued that the Hong Kong courts lacked jurisdiction to try the offences since they occurred in New York. The case before the Divisional Court turned upon the wording of the Fugitive Offenders Act. The Court said that in a case where acts constituting the offence took place in two or more countries, as here, the question was whether the acts which had occurred in Hong Kong, if they had occurred in England, would have amounted to an offence in England. It was held that the defendant's conduct would have amounted to the offence of theft in England, and so he could be returned to Hong Kong. The decision in *Osman*, as we shall see, required a controversial interpretation of the English law of theft to reach this view.

On international mutual assistance in criminal matters which concerns, *inter alia*, search and seizure, service of documents, and taking the statements or testimony of persons abroad, the Home Office has issued a Discussion Paper,[15] which comments that in the past the United Kingdom's record 'has earned us a poor reputation, even in the event of entirely reasonable and proper requests; it has also caused serious problems for our own prosecution authorities as other states may refuse to render assistance because of lack of reciprocity'. The Paper concludes that there is a strong case for the United Kingdom to enter into formal arrangements for mutual assistance in criminal matters, initially by full participation in the 1959 European Convention on Mutual Assistance in Criminal Matters. In the Commonwealth, the Commonwealth Scheme for Mutual Assistance in Criminal Matters is dependent on the enactment of broadly similar reciprocal domestic legislation in participating countries, and would probably require some changes to United Kingdom law. Both these international Schemes require the existence in each participating state of a central authority to process requests. The Paper recommends the setting up of such an authority by the early 1990s and concludes that the main benefits from membership of such Schemes would be 'the speedier and more efficient prosecution of offences which otherwise would not come to court'. Numerous other treaties or bilateral agreements have been entered into, creating additional obligations of mutual assistance,

---

[14] [1988] Crim LR 611.
[15] Home Office, *International Mutual Assistance in Criminal Matters*, London: Home Office, 1988, at p. 3.

between countries such as Germany and France in 1974, the United States and Switzerland in 1977, and the United States and Canada in 1985. In the Queen's Speech in November 1989 outlining the government's proposed legislative programme, a Bill was foreshadowed which would 'improve the ability of the United Kingdom to co-operate with other countries in the investigation of crime' and the resulting Criminal Justice (International Co-operation) Act 1990 makes a number of modest improvements in this area, in respect of the mutual provision of evidence, transfer of persons overseas to give evidence or assist in criminal investigations, and powers of search for evidence in this country in connection with criminal inquiries being pursued overseas. There are, however, no specific changes to improve international co-operation in fraud or computer misuse cases.

2. JURISDICTION

The basic principle applied by English courts in this area, derived from common law, is that English law is territorial in extent, though there are a few offences which also have extra-territorial effect.[16] 'Abroad' for these purposes includes Scotland and Northern Ireland. In implementing this principle, a crime is regarded as having been committed only where the last act or event necessary to its completion took place. Where the definition of a crime specifies a particular result, such as obtaining property by deception, English courts do not have territorial jurisdiction if the conduct necessary for the offence occurs here but no part of the prohibited result occurs in this county, but they do have such jurisdiction if some part of that result occurs here.[17] There are relatively few English appellate decisions on jurisdiction, though it is generally accepted that these are difficult to reconcile with one another and that the law is in an unsatisfactory state. These rules can operate very capriciously, particularly in relation to offences involving dishonesty.

In *Harden*,[18] for example, a deception was contained in documents posted in England by the defendant to a company in Jersey. Because he invited the company to send cheques by post, the Court found on the facts that the offers in the defendant's letters could be accepted by the sending of a cheque for the appropriate amount. He was held to have obtained them, for the purpose of section 15 of the Theft Act 1968, when they were posted in Jersey; consequently the English courts did not have jurisdiction and he could not be found guilty. Apparently, no general rule about the time and place of

---

[16] See Offences Against the Person Act 1861, s. 9.
[17] See generally A. Arlidge and J. Parry, *Fraud*, London: Waterlow, 1985, ch. 11; Law Commission, Report No. 180, *Jurisdiction Over Offences of Fraud and Dishonesty With a Foreign Element*, London: HMSO, 1989a; L. H. Leigh, 'Territorial Jurisdiction and Fraud' [1988] *Criminal Law Review* 280.
[18] [1963] 1 QB 8.

'obtaining' was laid down in this case, for in *Tirado*[19] the Court of Appeal interpreted *Harden* restrictively. The defendant, based in Oxford, fraudulently induced a number of Moroccans to send him money in the belief that he would find them jobs. He suggested that the money could be posted to him or transferred via a Moroccan bank, which would send him a draft drawn on a London bank. The Court of Appeal said that the English courts did have jurisdiction, reiterating 'as a matter of first principle' that a person does not obtain property sent to him until it reaches him, and that *Harden* was a limited exception to that principle. This last statement is, however, inconsistent with another decision, *Baxter*,[20] which adopts and purports to extend to a general principle the view taken in *Harden*.

In another example, *Bevan*,[21] the defendant, who had a bank account in England, presented cheques abroad which he supported by his cheque card at a time when he was not authorized by his bank to overdraw. The English court was held to have jurisdiction, because the obtaining of a pecuniary advantage under section 16 of the Theft Act 1968 occurred in England. Similarly in *Beck*,[22] where the defendant used forged traveller's cheques in France, the Court of Appeal dismissed the defendant's appeal against his conviction for procuring the execution of valuable securities by deception. Although the immediate effect of his deception was operative in France, when the bank honoured the cheques in England the defendant procured their execution within the jurisdiction.

The Law Commission,[23] in its 1978 Report on the topic, concluded that no universal rules of jurisdiction could be recommended to deal with every offence of which some elements had taken place within, and others outside, England and Wales and that, instead, the question should be considered in the context of individual offences. In 1986, however, the Roskill Fraud Trials Committee drew attention to the special jurisdictional problems in relation to fraud. The Law Commission was asked to reconsider the question of fraud jurisdiction in 1987, and produced a further report and a Draft Bill in 1989.[24]

It is accepted now by the Law Commission that law reform in the area of jurisdiction over fraud offences is required as a matter of some urgency:[25]

International fraud is a serious problem that is practised in many different and ingenious forms. It is essential that persons who commit frauds related to this country should not be able to avoid the jurisdiction of this country's courts simply on outdated or technical grounds, or because of the form in which they cloak the substance of their fraud . . . (I)t is particularly important that this country, as a leading international

---

[19] (1974) 59 Cr App R 80.   [20] [1972] 1 QB 1.
[21] (1986) 84 Cr App R 143.   [22] [1985] 1 All ER 571.
[23] Law Commission, Report No. 91, *The Territorial and Extraterritorial Jurisdiction of the Criminal Law*, London: HMSO, 1978. Sections of the Report dealing with cross-border offending were described as 'superficial and misleading' by M. Hirst [1979] Crim LR 355, 356.
[24] Law Commission (1989a).
[25] Law Commission, Consultation Paper, *Jurisdiction Over Fraud Offences With a Foreign Element*, London: Law Commission, 1987, para. 2.7.

financial centre, should have and should be seen to have effective means of taking action against fraudulent conduct connected with this country.

As we have seen, fraudsters setting up machinery here to obtain property by deception abroad cannot be tried for the offence here. This, according to the Law Commission, creates anomalous results, seems to reflect an indifferent and insular attitude to the property of people outside the jurisdiction, and is almost an invitation for fraudsters to set themselves up here. The unsatisfactory jurisdictional rules are compounded by modern technology, particularly cross-border offending inherent in the misuse of computers and electronic funds transfer. Determining the geographical site where an 'obtaining' of property has taken place seems very artificial in the light of the modern electronic means of transferring money.

The very rapid development of computer technology over the last twenty years or so has raised to a different level of risk the opportunities for massive frauds committed across national and international borders.[26] It is difficult to exaggerate these potential risks. The opportunities for the largest losses lie in the rapid growth of network and communication facilities between computers, particularly electronic funds transfer. In the United Kingdom, in the course of an average day, some £30–40 billion is transferred between the UK clearing banks using CHAPS (Clearing Houses Automated Payments System). It has been estimated that a fraud linking CHAPS with SWIFT, the international financial switching service, could empty the UK of sterling in fifteen minutes.

In one of the earliest and most famous cases which have come to light, in 1978, *Rifkin*,[27] the defendant managed to get $10.2 million transferred from the Security Pacific National Bank in Los Angeles to a New York bank account by impersonating a bank official and making a single telephone call. Subsequently he transferred most of the funds to a Swiss bank account. The fraud was undetected for eight days, apparently because the transaction was small by banking standards. Rifkin was charged and convicted of various offences, based on 'wire-fraud'. While on bail for this offence he was arrested in connection with a second computer-based scheme involving an accomplice. An undercover FBI man, who had learned of the scheme from Rifkin, said that Rifkin had told him his intention was to 'do it right the second time'. In September 1987 two British-born defendants were given prison sentences of three years and eighteen months in the United States after admitting a conspiracy to defraud Prudential Bache Securities of New York of £5.15 million by initiating the unauthorized transfer of eighteen Eurobonds through the Morgan Guaranty Trust's Euroclear account in London. The crime was uncovered when a supervisor noticed that the wrong reference numbers for

---

[26] See Chapter 1.
[27] Unreported; see J. A. Becker, 'Rifkin: A Documentary History' (1980) 2 *Computer and Law Journal* 471.

the transfers had been keyed in.[28] In 1988 seven people in the United States were charged with participating in a scheme to embezzle no less than $70 million from the First National Bank accounts of United Airlines, based in Chicago, Merrill Lynch, based in New York, and Brown Forman, based in Kentucky. Using three wire transfers, the money was transferred to two Australian banks via the Chase Manhattan bank in New York. The scheme was discovered before any of the money was drawn upon.[29]

There have been a handful of English appellate cases where issues of jurisdiction in relation to computer-assisted international fraud have been considered. In *Thompson*,[30] a case discussed earlier in a different context, the defendant was a computer programmer employed by a bank in Kuwait. He opened accounts at Kuwaiti branches and programmed the bank's computer to credit those accounts with amounts debited from accounts belonging to other customers. This manipulation went undetected. He then returned to England and wrote asking for his credit balances to be telexed to accounts at English banks. The Kuwaiti bank telexed the so-called balances. The defalcation was then detected and the defendant was convicted of obtaining property by deception, though there is some doubt about the correctness of this decision. The Court of Appeal held that the defendant had 'obtained' the property in England, when he managed to get the Kuwaiti bank to transfer the amount falsely standing to his credit, to his account in England. This decision has been much criticized, however. It is difficult first of all to identify the property which was so obtained. The court seems to have proceeded on the basis that the property took the form of a thing in action, a bank credit. Here, however, there was only the illusion of a bank credit, created by the defendant's computer manipulation, and such an illusion surely cannot be stolen or obtained by deception. If, however, there was a bank credit, then it would seem that it was obtained in Kuwait.[31] Another reported English case is *Tomsett*,[32] where the London branch of a Swiss bank transferred $7 million to New York, to earn interest overnight. The money should have been returned to London the next day but a telex was sent by the defendant, a telex operator employed by the bank, to divert the money plus interest to a co-defendant's bank account in Geneva. That telex did not take effect, so the defendants were charged with conspiracy to steal. Their appeal was allowed. In this case, the Court of Appeal appeared to hold that the sending of the telex from London intending to divert the funds to the fraudster's account in Switzerland was not sufficient to amount to an appropriation of those funds, so that the sender could not be tried here. The theft would have occurred in

---

[28] Reported in *The Times* during Sept. 1987.
[29] D. Davies, 'Computer Losses During 1988: A Review' (1989–90) 1 *Computer Law and Security Report* at 2, p. 4.
[30] [1984] 3 All ER 565, and see Chapter 4.
[31] See further Smith at [1984] Crim LR 428 and Law Commission (1989a), para. 2.9.
[32] [1985] Crim LR 369.

New York, and there was no jurisdiction to try the conspiracy unless the theft would have been completed here. This case, too, has been criticized by Professor Smith, who argues that all the elements of theft were made out at the time the telex was sent, thus giving the English court jurisdiction.[33] In *Osman*,[34] however, the Divisional Court said that this precise issue had not been resolved in *Tomsett*, and, in agreeing with Professor Smith's analysis, went on to hold that the sending of a telex in these circumstances did amount to an appropriation, the theft being triable here. The court interpreted the offence of theft such that the sending of the telex was itself an appropriation, even though at that stage the account had not been debited.

Whether or not it is desirable to develop the law of theft in this way, the Law Commission says that 'technical arguments of this kind do not go to the merits of the case or enhance respect for the law'[35] and argues that the need for more satisfactory rules on jurisdiction is obvious. Specifically, the Law Commission proposes that, in relation to certain fraud offences, including theft, false accounting, and all the main deception offences under the Theft Acts 1968 and 1978, the current jurisdictional rules should be abolished and replaced with a rule whereby the courts of England and Wales would have jurisdiction to try a charge of one of the listed offences, if any event that is required to be proved in order to obtain a conviction for that offence takes place in England and Wales.[36] This, if implemented, would have the effect that in a case like *Thompson* it would not matter whether the defendant could be said to have 'obtained' the property in this country or Kuwait, so long as an event necessary for proof for conviction took place in England and Wales, which clearly on the facts it did. Such a reform would effect a great simplification and improvement in the law.

There is also proposed a special rule in relation to jurisdiction over inchoate offences, conspiracy in particular. Currently, in relation to conspiracies, conspiracy to murder excepted, an agreement in England and Wales to do an act abroad that is an offence there is nevertheless not triable here. That was the central problem in *Tomsett*. The agreement occurred in England but, according to the decision in that case, the theft was to take place in either New York or Geneva. The Commission proposes a new and much wider rule of jurisdiction. Provided the offence which is the object of the conspiracy would be triable here under the rules just mentioned, any conspirator will be triable here, whether or not the conspiracy is formed here or abroad, and whether or not anything is actually done within England and Wales to further that conspiracy.[37] The Law Commission proposes parallel changes to the rules in respect of attempt and incitement. It regards the implementation of these

---

[33] [1985] Crim LR 370.
[34] [1988] Crim LR 611.
[35] Law Commission (1989*a*), para. 2.10; also *Nagdhi* [1989] Crim LR 825.
[36] Law Commission (1989*a*), Part II (E).
[37] Ibid., Part IV.

changes, both on substantive offences and on inchoate offences, as a matter of some urgency.

The Law Commission reviewed the position in various other countries. European civil law countries, whose laws are based on Roman law, have a different approach to laws governing jurisdiction, treating nationality as a crucial element.[38] The Commission regarded this as 'particularly inappropriate in the present context'.[39] The rules of several common law states were considered to be better models, being generally wider than those operating in England. In Canada the test of jurisdiction is whether a significant proportion of the activities constituting the offence took place in Canada.[40] The rules are also wider in Australian states and in New Zealand. The OECD Report on computer-related crime found that the territorial principle was the most usual determinant of jurisdiction for member states of that organization, in that the applicable law 'is that of the country in which the offence, or one of the elements of the offence, is alleged to have taken place'.[41] The New Zealand provision, under section 7 of the Crime Act 1961, forms the basis for the Law Commission's own proposal in Clause 2 of the Draft Bill attached to its report, that

> A person may be guilty of a listed offence if any relevant event occurred in England and Wales

'Relevant event' is defined to mean 'any act or omission or other event proof of which is required for conviction of an offence' and the 'listed offences', which include theft, obtaining property by deception, false accounting, forgery, blackmail, conspiracy or incitement to commit a listed offence, and conspiracy to defraud are set out in Clause 1 and the Schedule to the Draft Bill.

In the United States, questions of jurisdiction have also given rise to difficulties over the years, and the resulting law is complex.[42] As far as federal jurisdiction is concerned, the common law rule is the same as that in England, based on territoriality and the view that every crime has only one '*situs*', generally where the defendant's acts take effect, even though the acts themselves occurred elsewhere or the ultimate consequences happened elsewhere. It would follow from this that in the absence of a statute enlarging federal jurisdiction to cover crimes only partly committed within the United States, the American federal courts would not have had jurisdiction in the case of

---

[38] Ibid., para. 2.14, citing West German Penal Code, s. 8(1); see also U. Sieber, *The International Handbook on Computer Crime*, New York: John Wiley, 1986, p. 113, and OECD (1986), pp. 66–7.

[39] Law Commission (1989*a*), para. 2.15.

[40] *Libman* v *The Queen* [1985] 2 RCS 178; Law Commission (1989*a*), para. 2.15.

[41] OECD (1986), p. 66.

[42] W. R. La Fave and A. W. Scott, *Criminal Law*, 2nd edn., St Paul, Minn.: West Publishing, 1986, pp. 118 et seq.

Turner,[43] discussed above, where a computer in Canada was accessed without authorization, and data encrypted to deny authorized users access to it, by defendants situated in Milwaukee. Problems of jurisdiction arise more frequently in respect of individual states. Again the common law is territorial in scope and applies the general principle that the offence takes place at only one site. Many states, however, have adopted a provision of the Model Penal Code provision, section 1.03(1)(a) which states that:

> . . . a person may be convicted under the law of this State of an offence . . . if . . . either the conduct which is an element of the offence or the result which is such an element occurs within this State.

In the context of computer-related crime, this has been interpreted in the Pennsylvanian case of *Commonwealth* v *Kastafansas*[44] to mean that if the computer is instrumental to the offence, the location of the computer is one of the places where venue lies. State computer crime legislation propounds variants on this general theme. Delaware[45] exercises jurisdiction if it was (a) the place where an act occurred or (b) where the computer system or part of it was located. New Jersey[46] specifies (a) the location of the accessed computer, (b) the place of terminal use, or (c) the place of actual damage. Somewhat wider is Kentucky,[47] which specifies (a) any county in which the act was performed, (b) where any violator had control or possession of proceeds of violation or anything used in furtherance of violation, or (c) from, to, or through which any access to a computer, computer system, or computer network was made in any way. Widest of all, perhaps, is Virginia,[48] which specifies (a) where any act was performed in furtherance of the criminal act, (b) where the owner had his principal place of business in the state, (c) where the offender had control or possession or proceeds of violation or any equipment etc. used in furtherance of violation, (d) from which, to which, or through which access to a computer or computer network was accomplished, whether by wires, electromagnetic waves, microwaves, or any other means of communication, or (e) where the offender resides.

In 1987 the Scottish Law Commission suggested[49] that in cases where two jurisdictions are involved, their proposed offence of obtaining unauthorized access to a computer should be triable in Scotland, when at the time of the offence was committed either the accused was in Scotland or the computer in relation to which the offence was committed was in Scotland. Subsequently, the English Law Commission produced their Report on Computer Misuse[50]

---

[43] (1984) 13 CCC (3d) 430.
[44] 318 Pa Super 143, 464, A. 2d 1270 (1983).   [45] Del Code Ann, s. 938.
[46] NJ Stat Ann s. 2C:20–34.   [47] Ky Rev Stat s. 434.860.
[48] Va Code s. 18.2–152.10.
[49] Scottish Law Commission, *Report on Computer Crime*, Cm. 174, Edinburgh: HMSO, 1987, para. 5.15.
[50] Law Commission, Report No. 186, *Computer Misuse*, Cm. 819, London: HMSO, 1989*b*.

advocating the creation of three new offences of computer misuse. The Commission was well aware that computer misuse is often committed across national and international boundaries:[51]

A hacker, with or without dishonest intentions, may for instance sit in London and, through an international telephone system, enter or try to enter a computer in New York, or vice versa. More complex 'chains', involving computer systems in a number of countries before the 'target' computer is accessed, are entirely possible.

The Law Commission therefore proposed that, in relation to all three proposed offences, courts in this country should have jurisdiction to entertain proceedings if at the time at which the offence was committed either the offender or the computer concerned was located in this country.

Effect is given to the Law Commission proposals by the Computer Misuse Act 1990. In a complex set of provisions,[52] the statute provides new rules whereby courts in the United Kingdom will have jurisdiction in respect of the three new offences of computer misuse created by the Act (together with their equivalent inchoate offences), whether the computer misuse originates in the home country or is directed against a computer located within it. For these purposes Scotland and Northern Ireland are regarded as separate home countries from England and Wales, so that these more generous rules of jurisdiction would apply to a hacker in England who gained unauthorized access to a computer in Scotland: he could be tried in either England or Scotland. It should be emphasized that while the Law Commission's Report on Jurisdiction recommended a change in jurisdictional rules in respect of all offences involving fraud or dishonesty, the changes in the Computer Misuse Act anticipate a more general amendment to these rules, which has not yet taken place. Jurisdiction in computer misuse offences is made subject to the principle of double criminality. This means that where a hacker is operating within England, but the further offence envisaged by him, and which must be proved by the prosecution on a charge under section 2 of the Act, will take place abroad, the English courts will only have jurisdiction where the contemplated conduct is a criminal offence in that other country as well as in England.

3. HARMONIZATION

While the approach of different countries may well be very comparable in respect of well-established areas of criminality, there is bound to be divergence from one country to another in the ways in which new problems raised by computer-related crime are being tackled. The diversity of existing laws in different jurisdictions has been discussed in earlier chapters. The OECD

[51] Para. 4.1.
[52] See App. 4, below, for details.

Report[53] in 1986 examined some of the differences to be found in the laws of member states, and concluded that:[54] 'international co-operation requires clear definitions of what is criminal at the national level as well as what are the relevant sanctions attached to a given offence. This is not yet the case in this specific field . . .' While the most significant impression gained from the study is the similarity of the problems being confronted in so many different jurisdictions, there is, as we have seen, considerable divergence in the methods employed in tackling them, from those countries who are treating computer misuse as *sui generis* and legislating comprehensively, to those countries who in general prefer to leave it to the judges to develop existing offence categories as and when necessary.

Whilst general harmonization of the criminal law is perhaps both unnecessary and unattainable, there is much to be said for neighbouring states and member states of international organizations such as the OECD to develop their laws on computer misuse in comparable ways. Several such attempts are being made. The EC Green Paper on Copyright and the Challenge of New Technology,[55] for instance, envisages harmonization of legal protection for computer software, including the laying down of European minimum requirements for criminal sanctions. The establishment of an International Software Protection Federation has been proposed, to co-ordinate software protection on an international level, including criminal penalties. The International Chamber of Commerce has produced a report on the international perspective on computer-related crimes,[56] urging that states should broaden existing jurisdictional rules and extradition arrangements and establish a 'minimum set' of internationally agreed practices to achieve co-operation in this area. Most recently, in 1989, the Council of Europe's European Committee on Crime Problems adopted a Report on Computer Crime prepared by a Select Committee of Experts on Computer Related Crime.[57] This Report has drawn up guidelines for national legislatures for the harmonization of criminal laws to combat computer misuse. It provides draft definitions for a 'minimum list of offences', a list which comprises computer fraud, computer forgery, damage to data or programs, computer sabotage, unauthorized access or interception, and program piracy. There is a further 'optional list' of draft offence definitions, which includes computer espionage and unauthorized use of a computer or computer program.

Despite these various initiatives, there are many practical difficulties in the way of harmonization of the criminal law. The English and Scottish Law Commissions in formulating their proposals for change were, perhaps understandably, more concerned with justifying their proposed new offences in the context of existing English or Scottish criminal law, and paid little attention

---

[53] OECD (1986).
[54] Ibid., 67.
[55] COM 1988 172 Final, 7 June 1988.
[56] ICC (1988).
[57] Not yet published; summarized by N. G. Nilsson, 'The Council of Europe Fights Computer Crime' (1989) 6 *Computer Law and Practice* 8.

to substantive law reform developments elsewhere in Europe, Australia, or North America. The problems are strikingly illustrated by the diverse approaches taken in Australia to reforming their state laws and Commonwealth law on computer misuse. The Australian Capital Territory and the Northern Territory have made small changes to their laws, in the first case directed mainly at automatic teller machine abuse and in the second to cater for unauthorized access to confidential information. In Queensland it has been decided that, for the moment, no change to its Code is necessary. Victoria has legislated more generally, creating an offence of 'computer trespass'. The New South Wales Crimes (Computers and Forgery) Amendment Act 1989 has gone further, and introduced a number of computer-related offences, catering for unlawful access to data, with penalties increased upon proof of intent to commit a further offence, and damage to data. South Australia now proposes to introduce an offence to criminalize unauthorized access into a computer system, but only where that system has a security device in place. One commentator, Hughes, laments this lack of a uniform approach, arguing that it is bound to leave gaps in jurisdiction to try computer-related offences.[58] The Queensland Green Paper on computer-related crime referred to the issue of jurisdiction as 'one of great complexity involving a detailed consideration of the existing laws of each Australian jurisdiction as well as international considerations',[59] but the Victoria Crimes (Computers) Act 1988 has taken the step of replacing the traditional 'final element' test in respect of theft, fraud, and blackmail offences committed in relation to computers, and has provided that a prosecution may be commenced in Victoria if there is 'a real and substantial link' with that state. It had been hoped that the meeting of the Standing Committee of Attorneys-General in 1987 would recommend harmonization of the rules relating to transborder computer-related offending within Australia, but this has not happened. Hughes questions the likelihood of 'adequate international regulation of some of the more common forms of computer abuse when well informed federations cannot, internally, evolve any semblance of uniformity'.[60]

The question of harmonization arises indirectly from the Law Commission's reform proposals on jurisdiction, implemented in the computer misuse context by the Computer Misuse Act 1990. In its consultation paper the Commission has said that[61] 'It seems to us that in almost all cases the conduct in question is likely to be a crime (or a fraud for the purposes of conspiracy to defraud) both here and in the relevant overseas country'. It none the less accepted that the 'double criminality' principle should operate.[62] At first the

---

[58] G. Hughes, 'Queensland Computer Crime Report' (1988) 4 *Computer Law and Practice* 100; G. Hughes, 'Disjointed Australian Attack on Hackers' (1989) 6 *Computer Law and Practice* 28.
[59] Queensland Government Department of Justice, *Green Paper on Computer Related Crime*, Queensland: Government Printer, 1987, p. 55.
[60] Hughes (1989), p. 31.   [61] Law Commission (1987), para. 3.24.
[62] Law Commission (1989a), paras. 5.23 et seq.

Commission suggested that the burden of proof should be on the defendant to establish that what he planned to do was not an offence in the country where he planned to do it, but they subsequently proposed that the existence of double criminality should be presumed unless the defendant had given notice that he required it to be established by the prosecution.[63] This proposal was implemented, in some detail, by section 8 of the Computer Misuse Act 1990. It does seem that there are more likely to be problems of non-coincidence of criminal laws in the computer misuse context, given the divergent approaches within national laws and national law reforms which have been described in earlier chapters of this book.

Rules of admissibility of computer-generated evidence in criminal cases also vary considerably from one jurisdiction to another. A broad distinction has been identified[64] between Continental law countries and others, such as Japan, where there appears to be no hesitation in allowing the admissibility of computer-generated evidence, subject only to the question of its weight, determined by the judge. In Britain, as was explained in Chapter 6, there is more reluctance to allow such evidence, and this is a stance mirrored in other common law jurisdictions. Some countries have extended their 'business record' exception to the hearsay rules;[65] others have created special provisions for computer evidence.[66] The Council of Europe's Select Committee of Experts in Computer-Related Crime recommended in 1989 that international harmonization of the rules of evidence was highly desirable in criminal proceedings.[67]

It seems clear that the problems outlined in this chapter must be tackled on two fronts, first within individual state legislatures, to improve domestic laws and procedures, and internationally, through greater harmonization of law and through mutual co-operation between computer security experts and investigative agencies of different countries, to frustrate the operations of fraudsters generally and computer fraudsters and misusers in particular. So far, in spite of the various initiatives outlined above, progress has been slow.

---

[63] Ibid., para. 5.28.

[64] Sieber (1986), pp. 139 et seqq.

[65] As in the United States: see M. D. Scott, *Computer Law*, New York: John Wiley, 1985, ch. 10, reporting a 'refinement' rather than 'a wholesale revision of the laws of evidence'. See also E. W. Cleary, *McCormick on Evidence*, 3rd edn., St Paul, Minn.: West Publishing, 1984, pp. 885–7.

[66] R. A. Brown, 'Computer Produced Evidence in Australia' (1984) 8 *University of Tasmania Law Review* 342; H. Staniland, 'Computer Evidence in South Africa' (1985) 2 *Computer Law and Practice* 21.

[67] Discussed in U. Sieber, 'Collecting and Using Evidence in the Field of Information Technology' in A. Eser and J. Thormundsson (eds.), *Old Ways and New Needs in Criminal Legislation*, Freiburg: University of Freiburg, 1989, p. 203.

Appendix 1

COMPUTER CRIME (SCOTLAND) BILL

1.—(1) A person commits an offence if, not having authority to obtain access to a program or data stored in a computer, or to a part of such program or data, he obtains unauthorised access in order to inspect or otherwise to acquire knowledge of the program or the data or to add to, erase or otherwise alter the program or the data with the intention—

    (a) of procuring an advantage for himself or another person; or

    (b) of damaging another person's interests.

(2) A person commits an offence if, not having authority to obtain access to a program or data stored in a computer, or to a part of such program or data, he obtains such unauthorised access and damages another person's interests by recklessly adding to, erasing or otherwise altering the program or the data.

(3) For the purposes of this section, a person does not have authority to obtain access to a program or data stored in a computer, or to a part of such program or data, if he does not have the authority of a person entitled to control such access.

(4) Notwithstanding the foregoing provisions of this section, a person shall not commit an offence under this section if he obtains such access as aforesaid in pursuance of a warrant issued by the Secretary of State under section 2 of this Act.

2.—(1) Subject to the provisions of this section, the Secretary of State may issue a warrant requiring the person to whom it is addressed to obtain access to a program or data stored in a computer, or to any part of such program or data, for the purpose of acquiring information; and such a warrant may also require the person to whom it is addressed to disclose any information so acquired to such persons and in such manner as are described in the warrant.

(2) The Secretary of State shall not issue a warrant under this section unless he considers that the warrant is necessary—

    (a) in the interests of national security;

    (b) for the purpose of preventing or detecting serious crime; or

    (c) for the purpose of safeguarding the economic well-being of the United Kingdom

(3) The matters to be taken into account in considering whether a warrant is necessary as mentioned in subsection (2) above shall include whether the information which it is considered necessary to acquire could reasonably be acquired by other means.

(4) A warrant shall not be considered necessary as mentioned in subsection (2)(c) above unless the information which it is considered necessary to acquire is information relating to the acts or intentions of persons outside the British Islands.

(5) A warrant under this section shall specify or describe an address or addresses, being an address or addresses used, or likely to be used, to accommodate a computer containing a program or data the examination of which the Secretary of State considers necessary as mentioned in subsection (2) above.

(6) Sections 4 to 10 of the Interception of Communications Act 1985 and Schedule 1 to that Act shall, subject to the adaptations set out in the Schedule of this Act, apply in relation to a warrant under this section. 1985 c. 56

3.—A person guilty of an offence under this Act shall be liable— Penalties.

    (a) on summary conviction, to imprisonment for a term not exceeding 6 months or to a fine not exceeding the statutory maximum, or both; or

    (b) on conviction on indictment, to imprisonment for a term not exceeding 5 years or to an unlimited fine, or both.

4.—A court in Scotland shall have jurisdiction to entertain proceedings for an offence under this Act if at the time the offence was committed— Jurisdiction.

    (a) the accused was in Scotland; or

    (b) the program or the data in relation to which the offence was committed was stored in a computer in Scotland.

5.—(1) This Act may be cited as the Computer Crime (Scotland) Act 1987. Short title commencement and extent.

(2) This Act shall come into force at the end of the period of 2 months beginning with the day on which it is passed.

(3) This Act extends to Scotland only.

EXPLANATORY NOTES

Clause 1 implements the general policy of the Report that there should be new offences to penalise the unauthorised obtaining of access to a program or data stored in a computer. See recommendations 1, 6 and 7.

Subsection (1) implements Recommendations 5, 6, 8 and 10. It makes it an offence to obtain access to a program or data stored in a computer, or to a part of such program or data, (not having authority to do so) in order to inspect or otherwise to acquire knowledge of the program or data, or to add to, erase or otherwise alter the program or data with the intention of procuring an advantage or of damaging another person's interests. Expressed in this way the offence will not be committed by a person who obtains unauthorised access to a program or data but who does so without the stated purpose or intention.

Subsection (2) implements Recommendations 5, 7 and 10. It creates a parallel offence to deal with the situation where a person obtains unauthorised access to a program or data without the purpose or intention in the offence in subsection (1), but who damages another person's interests by recklessly adding to, erasing or otherwise altering the program or data.

Subsection (3) implements Recommendation 9, and in effect defines the words "not having authority" as used in subsections (1) and (2).

Subsection (4) implements Recommendation 12. It provides that neither of the offences in subsections (1) and (2) will be committed by a person who obtains access to a program or data in pursuance of a warrant issued by the Secretary of State. The circumstances in which such a warrant may be granted are dealt with in clause 2 and in the Schedule annexed to the Bill. See discussion in paragraphs 5.4 and 5.5.

Clause 2 sets out the circumstances in which the Secretary of State may grant a warrant for the obtaining of access to a program or data stored in a computer. The provisions in the clause are modelled on those in the Interception of Communications Act 1985 (the 1985 Act), and much of that Act will, with modifications, apply to warrants issued under this clause.

Subsection (1) implements Recommendation 13, and permits the Secretary of State to issue a warrant requiring the person to whom it is addressed to obtain access to a program or data stored in a computer, or to any part of such program or data, for the purpose of acquiring information. This is analogous to section 2(1) of the 1985 Act.

Subsection (2) implements Recommendation 14, and sets out the grounds upon which a warrant may be issued. These are the same as the grounds expressed in section 2(2) of the 1985 Act.

Subsections (3) and (4) are in further implementation of Recommendation 13, and apply to the issuing of a warrant on the same considerations as are to be found in section 2(3) and (4) of the 1985 Act.

Subsection (5) provides that a warrant must specify or describe an address or addresses used, or likely to be used, to accommodate a computer containing a program or data the examination of which the Secretary of State considers necessary. This subsection is intended to perform a limiting function in relation to the scope of a warrant comparable to that achieved by section 3 of the 1985 Act.

Subsection (6) applies sections 4 to 10 and the Schedule of the 1985 Act to a warrant issued under subsection (1) above, subject to the adaptations set out in the Schedule to the Bill.

Clause 3 implements Recommendation 11, and prescribes the maximum penalties which may be imposed on summary conviction, and conviction on indictment, in respect of the offences in clause 1(1) and (2).

Clause 4 implements Recommendation 17. It provides that a court in Scotland is to have jurisdiction in respect of an offence under the Bill if, at the relevant time, the accused was in Scotland, or the program or data in relation to which the offence was committed was stored in a computer in Scotland.

Section 2(6)   SCHEDULE   ₒ

Adaptations of provisions of the Interception of Communications Act 1985 in their application to warrants under section 2 of this Act.

1. Any reference to a warrant under section 2 of the Interception of Communications Act 1985 shall, unless the context otherwise requires, include a reference to a warrant under section 2 of this Act.

2. In section 5—

    (a) in subsection (1)(a) after the word 'above' there shall be inserted the words 'or which he considers is used, or is likely to be used, as mentioned in section 2(5) of the Computer Crime (Scotland) Act 1987';

    (b) in subsection (2) after the word 'above' there shall be inserted the words 'or is no longer used, or is no longer likely to be used, as mentioned in section 2(5) of the Computer Crime (Scotland) Act 1987'.

3. In section 6—

    (a) in subsection (1)(a) after the word 'material' there shall be inserted the words 'or, as the case may be, the information acquired in pursuance of the warrant under section 2 of the Computer Crime (Scotland) Act 1987';

(b) in subsections (2) and (3)—

    (i) after the words 'intercepted material' there shall be inserted the words 'or acquired information';

    (ii) after the words 'the material' wherever they occur there shall be inserted the words 'or information'.

4. In section 7—

(a) after subsection (2) there shall be inserted the following subsection—

    '(2A) Any person who believes that access has been obtained to a program or data stored by him in a computer may apply to the Tribunal for an investigation under this section.';

(b) at the end of subsection (3)(b) there shall be added the words 'or, as the case may be, of section 2 of the Computer Crime (Scotland) Act 1987 or sections 4 or 5 above in relation to the warrant.';

(c) in subsection (4) after the word 'certificate' there shall be inserted the words 'or, as the case may be, of section 2 of the Computer Crime (Scotland) Act 1987 or sections 4 or 5 above in relation to a relevant warrant';

(d) at the end of subsection (5)(b) there shall be added the words 'or of copies of the information acquired in pursuance of the warrant under section 2 of the Computer Crime (Scotland) Act 1987';

(e) at the end of subsection (7) there shall be added the words 'or, as the case may be, of section 2 of the Computer Crime (Scotland) Act 1987 or section 4 or 5 above in relation to a relevant warrant.';

(f) at the end of subsection (9) there shall be added the following paragraph—

    (c) a warrant under section 2 of the Computer Crime (Scotland) Act 1987 is a relevant warrant in relation to an application if an address used by the applicant to accommodate a computer is specified or described in the warrant.'.

5. In section 8—

(a) in subsection (1)(a) after the words 'sections 2 to 5 above' there shall be inserted the words 'and by section 2 of the Computer Crime (Scotland) Act 1987';

(b) in subsection (5)(a) after the words 'sections 2 to 5 above' there shall be inserted the words 'or, as the case may be, of section 2 of the Computer Crime (Scotland) Act 1987 or section 4 or 5 above'.

6. In section 9, in subsections (1)(a), (3)(b) and (4)(a) after the word 'above' there shall be inserted the words 'or under section 1 of the Computer Crime (Scotland) Act 1987'.

7. In section 10(1) in the definition of 'copy'—

(a) after the words 'intercepted material' there shall be inserted the words 'or information acquired in pursuance of the warrant';

(b) after the words 'the material' in both places where they occur there shall be inserted the words 'or information'.

EXPLANATORY NOTE

The *Schedule* is provided for in clause 2(6). It set out the adaptations which are necessary so that sections 4 to 10 of the Interception of Communications Act 1985 will apply to a warrant issued under clause 2 of the Bill.

Appendix 2

BILL ON COMPUTER MISUSE (THE ANTI-HACKING BILL) (1989)

This Bill was sponsored by Miss Emma Nicholson, Member of Parliament for Torridge and West Devon, in April 1989, but withdrawn in August 1989 when the government promised to legislate on the matter in the near future, in the light of the Law Commission's then forthcoming Report on Computer Misuse.

Offences

(1)(1)(a) A person who effects unauthorized access to a computer or computer system either
    (i) to his own or another's advantage; or
    (ii) to another's prejudice;
  or
(b) being reckless as to whether his action would result in
    (i) his own or another's advantage; or
    (ii) another's prejudice;
shall be guilty of an offence.

(2) A person who without lawful authority or reasonable excuse has in his custody or under his control anything with the intention of effecting unauthorized access to a computer or computer system to enable some act to his own or another's advantage or to another's prejudice, shall be guilty of an offence.

(3) A person who, without lawful authority or reasonable excuse, transmits, receives or causes to be transmitted or received by means of wire, radio or electromagnetic waves, any writing, signals, signs, pictures or sound
(a) with the intention of committing an act
    (i) to his own or another's advantage; or
    (ii) to another's prejudice; or
(b) being reckless as to whether his action would result in
    (i) his own or another's advantage; or
    (ii) another's prejudice;
shall be guilty of an offence.

(4) A person commits an offence if he effects unauthorized access to the computer of another for an unauthorized purpose.

(2) [sets out penalties for offences under Clause 1(1)–(3). These range from up to ten years' imprisonment for acts committed with intent, and up to five years for acts committed recklessly; the penalty for an offence under Clause 1(4) is a fine of up to £2,000]

(3) [provides for the issues of warrants to permit the seizure, confiscation and destruction or other disposal of equipment, documentation or anything else used to commit offences under the Act. Where another person's equipment has been used, he would have the right to be heard by the court before the order to destroy or otherwise dispose of it were made. It also provides for monitoring by electronic means or other forms of surveillance of equipment which the police have reasonable cause to believe may be used to obtain unauthorized access to a computer]

Interpretation

4(1) In this Act—

'computer' includes any device for storing and processing information or communications facility directly relating to, or operating in conjunction with, such a device

'wire' includes any wire, cable, printed circuit, or any other means by which communications can be transmitted.

'unauthorized access' includes access by a person who is authorized to have access to a computer, but who exceeds the terms of such authorization.

'another' includes any person, body corporate, institution, firm, association trust or any other body of persons.

'prejudice' is caused if, and only if, an action leads to—

   (i) the temporary or permanent loss of property or information; or

  (ii) the deprivation of an opportunity to earn remuneration or greater remuneration; or

 (iii) the deprivation of an opportunity to gain financial advantage otherwise than by way of remuneration

(2) In this section 'loss' includes not getting what one might get as well as parting with what one has.

(5) [states that English courts shall have jurisdiction if at the time the offence was committed, the accused was in England and Wales, the computer was in England and Wales, a communications link was used in England and Wales, or the proceeds of the offence was 'deposited, processed or transferred from within England and Wales'. The Act would not extend to Scotland or Northern Ireland.

Appendix 3

LAW COMMISSION REPORT NO. 186, COMPUTER MISUSE
RECOMMENDATIONS 1989

This important document was published in October 1989. It followed the publication of a Working Paper on Computer Misuse (No. 110, 1988). The Law Commission has proposed the creation of three new offences to tackle the problem of computer misuse. Because of a very tight time schedule imposed upon the Commission, to leave open the possibility of legislation in the new session of Parliament, no Draft Bill is attached to the Report nor are the proposed offences precisely defined by the Commission. The definitions given below reflect the Commission's wording in the Report. Following the three proposed offences, the summary of conclusions and recommendations in Part V of the Report are set out.

(1) The proposed offence of 'unauthorized access to a computer' (the basic hacking offence).

A person is guilty of an offence if, knowing that his access was unauthorized, he causes a computer to perform any function with intent to secure access to or obtain information about a program or data held in a computer. (Based on Report, para. 3.14)

According to the Commission, this offence should be triable summarily only, and be punishable with a maximum of three months' imprisonment or a fine of up to level 4 on the standard scale.

(2) The proposed offence of committing the basic hacking offence, 'with intent to commit or facilitate the commission of a serious crime' (the ulterior intent offence).

A person is guilty of an offence if, knowing that his access was unauthorized, he causes a computer to perform any function with intent to secure access or to obtain information about a program or data held in a computer with intent to facilitate the commission by the accused or by any other person of an offence for which the maximum penalty is five years' imprisonment or more, whether or not that further offence would involve the use of a computer. (Based on Report, para. 3.49)

This offence should be triable either way, and should carry a maximum penalty on conviction on indictment, of imprisonment for five years.

(3) The proposed offence of 'unauthorized modification of computer material'.

A person is guilty of an offence if he does an act which causes an unauthorized modification of the contents of any computer's memory or the contents of any computer storage medium, with intent thereby to impair the operations of any computer or computer program, or to destroy, or to impair the reliability or accessibility of, any data stored or otherwise held in any computer. (Based on Report, para. 3.64).

This offence should be triable either way, and should carry a maximum penalty, on conviction on indictment, of imprisonment for five years.

In addition (Report, paras. 5.3–5.6):

We recommend, in relation to three new offences, that there should be wide provisions conferring jurisdiction on the courts of England and Wales, similar to those recommended in the case of fraud in our recent report. [Law Commission Report No. 180,

Jurisdiction Over Offences of Fraud and Dishonesty With a Foreign Element, London: HMSO, 1989.]

We do not, in this report, make any recommendation as to the reform of the law of deception, reserving that matter for further report.

We recommend that use by an authorized user of a computer for an unauthorized purpose should not, in itself, be a criminal offence.

We make no recommendation as to alterations of the law of evidence or procedure in relation to crimes of computer misuse.

Appendix 4

COMPUTER MISUSE ACT 1990

The Computer Misuse Act 1990 gives effect, with some modifications, to various changes to the substantive law recommended by the Law Commission's Report No. 186, *Computer Misuse* (*see* Appendix 3) and jurisdictional changes which are in line with those advocated by the Commission in respect of fraud offences in their Report No. 180, *Jurisdiction over Offences of Fraud and Dishonesty with a Foreign Element*, discussed in Chapter 7, above. A Private Member's Bill, sponsored by Mr Michael Colvin, was designed to give effect to the Law Commission's recommendations and this Bill, with some amendments, now takes the form of the Computer Misuse Act 1990. The Parliamentary Debates may be found at *Hansard* HC vol. 166, cols. 1134–84; vol. 171, cols. 1287–339 and HL. vol. 519, cols. 230–47. The Bill was considered in Standing Committee C from 14 March to 28 March 1990.

Computer misuse offences

1.—(1) A person is guilty of an offence if—

Unauthorised access to computer material

    (a) he causes a computer to perform any function with intent to secure access to any program or data held in any computer;

    (b) the access he intends to secure is unauthorised; and

    (c) he knows at the time when he causes the computer to perform the function that that is the case.

(2) The intent a person has to have to commit an offence under this section need not be directed at—

    (a) any particular program or data;

    (b) a program or data of any particular kind; or

    (c) a program or data held in any particular computer.

(3) A person guilty of an offence under this section shall be liable on summary conviction to imprisonment for a term not exceeding six months or to a fine not exceeding level 5 on the standard scale or to both.

EXPLANATORY NOTES

A number of terms are defined in section 17, but 'computer', 'data' and 'program' are not defined in the Act and should, therefore, be given their ordinary meaning by the courts.

Section 1 creates a new offence triable summarily in a magistrates' court in England (for proceedings in Scotland see s. 13 and for Northern Ireland see s. 16). The new law is discussed in the context of the debate over criminalizing hacking in Chapter 3(1), above. The *actus reus* of the offence requires the defendant to 'cause a computer to perform any function'. This is meant to exclude mere physical contact with a computer and the scrutiny of data without any interaction with a computer (thus the reading of confidential computer output, the reading of data displayed on the screen, or 'computer eavesdropping', are not covered). See further on this, Chapter 3(3), above. On the other hand, the offence does not require that the defendant must succeed in obtaining access to the program or data, or be successful in subverting computer security measures in place. A remote hacker would, thus, 'cause a computer to perform any function' if he accessed it remotely and the computer responded, such as by activating a computer security device or by offering a log-on menu. An employee would 'cause a computer to perform any function' as soon as he switched on the computer, and would be guilty of the offence if the requisite *mens rea* could also be proved. The substantive offence is thus drafted in such a way as to include conduct which might usually be thought to fall within the scope of the law of attempt. There are two limbs to the *mens rea* of the offence. The first limb is the 'intent to secure access to any program or data held in any computer'. The word 'any' makes it clear that the intent need not relate to the computer which the defendant is at that time operating. Subsection (2) explains that the defendant's intent need not be directed at any particular program or data, so as to include the hacker who accesses a computer without any clear idea of what he will find there. Recklessness is insufficient; still less would careless or inattentive accessing of the computer suffice for liability. The second limb is that the defendant must know at the time when he causes the computer to perform the function that the access which he intends to secure is unauthorized. The prosecution must prove both limbs.

Since this offence is summary only, there can be no charge of an attempt in respect of it. There is, however, the possibility of secondary liability arising in accord with Magistrates' Courts Act 1980, s. 44(1), where, for example, a person supplies a hacker with information which would assist him, such as a confidential computer password. The operator of a computer-hacker 'bulletin board' might, therefore, come within the reach of such an offence. See, further, Chapter 5(7), above.

The Law Commission recommended that the penalties available in respect of this offence should be 3 months' imprisonment and a fine of up to Level 4 on the standard scale (i e. £1,000), but these penalties were doubled when the Bill was first introduced by Mr Colvin. The Law Commission also drew attention to the courts' general powers to award compensation under Powers of Criminal Courts Act 1973, s. 35, as amended by the Criminal Justice Acts of 1982 and 1988, and to the courts' powers to forfeit property used or intended for use in committing offences (e.g. hacking equipment) under Criminal Justice Act 1988, s. 69(1). See Chapter 6(4), above.

2.—(1)　A person is guilty of an offence under this section if he commits an offence under section 1 above ("the unauthorised access offence") with intent—

　　(a)　to commit an offence to which this section applies; or

　　(b)　to facilitate the commission of such an offence (whether by himself or by any other person);

and the offence he intends to commit or facilitate is referred to below in this section as the further offence.

Unauthorised access with intent to commit or facilitate commission of further offences.

(2)　This section applies to offences—

　　(a)　for which the sentence is fixed by law; or

　　(b)　for which a person of twenty-one years of age or over (not previously convicted) may be sentenced to imprisonment for a term of five years (or, in England and Wales, might be so sentenced but for the restrictions imposed by section 33 of the Magistrates' Courts Act 1980).

(3)　It is immaterial for the purposes of this section whether the further offence is to be committed on the same occasion as the unauthorised access offence or on any future occasion.

(4) A person may be guilty of an offence under this section even though the facts are such that the commission of the further offence is impossible.

(5) A person guilty of an offence under this section shall be liable—

    (a) on summary conviction, to imprisonment for a term not exceeding six months or to a fine not exceeding the statutory maximum or to both; and

    (b) on conviction on indictment, to imprisonment for a term not exceeding five years or to a fine or to both.

EXPLANATORY NOTES

Section 2 creates an offence triable either way, of committing the unauthorized access offence under section 1 with intent to commit or facilitate the commission of a more serious 'further' offence. It is not necessary to prove that the intended further offence has actually been committed. The offences in section 1 and section 2 are hierarchical, with the section 2 offence catering for the defendant who gains unauthorized access to computer-held material with serious criminal intentions. Where a charge is brought under section 2, a conviction may be returned for the section 1 offence if this further intention is not proved: see section 12, below. The new offence is discussed in the context of the criminalizing of hacking generally in Chapter 3(2), above.

A person will be guilty of the section 2 offence in a range of situations. Obtaining the unauthorized access may, for example, be done with the intention of committing theft, such as by diverting funds which are in the course of an electronic funds transfer to the defendant's own bank account, or to the bank account of an accomplice. It would also cover the case where the defendant gained unauthorized access to sensitive information held on computer with a view to blackmailing the person to whom that information related. For discussion of such cases see Chapters 4, 5(4), and 7(2), above.

Subsection (2) explains what qualifies as a further offence for the purposes of the section 2 offence. The main example of an offence the sentence for which is fixed by law is murder (life imprisonment). Most offences of fraud and dishonesty are punishable with at least 5 years' imprisonment. Such offences are 'arrestable offences' for the purposes of the Police and Criminal Evidence Act 1984 and attract prescribed powers of arrest, search, and seizure. See further explanatory note to section 14, below and Chapter 6(2), above.

Subsection (3) makes clear that the defendant may intend to commit the further offence on the same occasion as the unauthorized access offence (as in the theft example just given) or on a future occasion (as in the blackmail example).

Subsection (4) makes it possible to convict a person who intended to commit the further offence even if, on the facts, that would be impossible (e.g. where the intended blackmail victim was, unknown to the defendant, dead). This rule is analogous to that in Criminal Attempts Act 1981, section 1(2), as applied in *Shivpuri* [1987] AC 1.

The penalties available in respect of this offence are in accord with the Law Commission's recommendation. Since this offence is punishable on indictment with imprisonment for a term of 5 years, the offence is an arrestable offence for the purposes of the Police and Criminal Evidence Act 1984: see explanatory note to section 14, below and Chapter 6(2), above.

3.—(1) A person is guilty of an offence if—   Unauthorised modification of computer material.

    (a) he does any act which causes an unauthorised modification of the contents of any computer; and

    (b) at the time when he does the act he has the requisite intent and the requisite knowledge.

(2) For the purposes of subsection (1)(b) above the requisite intent is an intent to cause a modification of the contents of any computer and by so doing—

  (a) to impair the operation of any computer;
  (b) to prevent or hinder access to any program or data held in any computer; or
  (c) to impair the operation of any such program or the reliability of any such data.

(3) The intent need not be directed at—

  (a) any particular computer;
  (b) any particular program or data or a program or data of any particular kind; or
  (c) any particular modification or a modification of any particular kind.

(4) For the purposes of subsection (1)(b) above the requisite knowledge is knowledge that any modification he intends to cause is unauthorised.

(5) It is immaterial for the purposes of this section whether an unauthorised modification or any intended effect of it of a kind mentioned in subsection (2) above is, or is intended to be, permanent or merely temporary.

(6) For the purposes of the Criminal Damage Act 1971 a modification of the contents of a computer shall not be regarded as damaging any computer or computer storage medium unless its effect on that computer or computer storage medium impairs its physical condition.

(7) A person guilty of an offence under this section shall be liable—

  (a) on summary conviction, to imprisonment for a term not exceeding six months or to a fine not exceeding the statutory maximum or to both; and
  (b) on conviction on indictment, to imprisonment for a term not exceeding five years or to a fine or to both.

EXPLANATORY NOTES

Section 3 creates an offence triable either way. When read in the context of section 17, it is clear that a wide range of different forms of conduct are included within its scope. It would cover all cases involving deliberate (recklessness is insufficient) alteration or erasure of any program or data held on a computer (s. 17(7)(a)), where the defendant intended thereby to impair a computer's operation, hinder access to computer material by a legitimate user, or impair the operation or reliability of computer-held material, and where he knew that the intended modification was unauthorized. It does not have to be proved that the defendant had any specific target computer, program, or data in mind.

The section would also extend to a case where the defendant intentionally introduced a computer 'worm' program into a computer system, where such a program uses up all the spare capacity on the computer by adding programs or data to the computer's contents (s. 17(7)(b)), thereby impairing its operation (s. 3(2)(a)). A likely effect of the introduction of a 'worm' is to prevent or hinder access to a legitimate user (s. 3(2)(b)). For discussion of such cases see Chapter 5(1) and (2), above.

Also within the section is the intentional introduction of a computer 'virus' into a computer system. Where X deliberately introduces into circulation a floppy disk contaminated with a computer virus and Y, an innocent party, uses the disk on his computer, impairing its operation, it seems that X would be guilty of the offence at the time he introduced the disk into circulation, since section 17(7) states that any act which contributes towards causing such a modification shall be regarded as causing it. The liability of X would be unaffected by Y passing the disk, unused, to another innocent party, Z, who uses the disk and impairs the operation of Z's computer, since X's intent need not be directed at any particular computer, program, or data (s. 3(3)). See, further, Chapter 5(1) and (2), above.

The offence under section 3 would also cater for a case where the defendant intentionally causes an unauthorized modification of the contents of a computer, intending thereby to prevent or hinder access by legitimate users to any data or program held on the computer (see e.g. *Turner* (1984) 13 CCC (3d; 430, considered in Chapter 5(2), above, where a hacker placed a 'locking device' on computer-held data, rendering the data inaccessible to users). By section 3(5) it is immaterial whether this modification or its intended effect is, or is intended to be, permanent or temporary.

Subsection (6) deals with the relationship between this offence and the offence of criminal damage under the Criminal Damage Act 1971. In *Cox v Riley* (1986) 83 Cr App R 54, discussed at length in Chapter 5, the defendant's conviction was approved by the Divisional Court on the basis that the card itself had been damaged (the programs themselves, being intangible property, fell outside the scope of the Criminal Damage Act, by virtue of s. 10(1)). Section 3(6) now declares that the scope of the 1971 Act in computer cases is confined to circumstances where the physical condition of the computer or computer-storage medium has been impaired. The intended effect of this, it seems, is that were the facts of *Cox v. Riley* to recur, the defendant would not now be guilty of criminal damage, but would be guilty of the offence under section 3 of the Computer Misuse Act. It seems surprising that this change to the law was not achieved by amendment to the 1971 Act.

The penalties for this offence are the same as for the offence under section 2. See the explanatory notes on penalties in relation to section 2.

Jurisdiction

4.—(1) Except as provided below in this section, it is immaterial for the purposes of any offence under section 1 or 3 above— *Territorial scope of offences under this Act.*

    (a) whether any act or other event proof of which is required for conviction of the offence occurred in the home country concerned; or

    (b) whether the accused was in the home country concerned at the time of any such act or event.

(2) Subject to subsection (3) below, in the case of such an offence at least one significant link with domestic jurisdiction must exist in the circumstances of the case for the offence to be committed.

(3) There is no need for any such link to exist for the commission of an offence under section 1 above to be established in proof of an allegation to that effect in proceedings for an offence under section 2 above.

(4) Subject to section 8 below, where—

    (a) any such link does in fact exist in the case of an offence under section 1 above; and

    (b) commission of that offence is alleged in proceedings for an offence under section 2 above;

section 2 above shall apply as if anything the accused intended to do or facilitate in any place outside the home country concerned which would be an offence to which section 2 applies if it took place in the home country concerned were the offence in question.

(5) This section is without prejudice to any jurisdiction exercisable by a court in Scotland apart from this section.

(6) References in this Act to the home country concerned are references—

(a) in the application of this Act to England and Wales, to England and Wales;

(b) in the application of this Act to Scotland, to Scotland; and

(c) in the application of this Act to Northern Ireland, to Northern Ireland.

EXPLANATORY NOTES

'Home country' is explained in section 4(6) and 'significant link with domestic jurisdiction' in section 5. The purpose of this section, taken together with sections 5–9 and section 16, is to introduce new rules whereby courts in the United Kingdom will have jurisdiction over the offences of computer misuse set out in sections 1–3 of this Act, whether that computer misuse originates from this country or is directed against a computer or computers located within it. The changes to jurisdiction are in line with the recommendations of the Law Commission's Report No. 186, discussed in Chapter 7(2). The extension of the new rules to all offences involving fraud or dishonesty, as the Commission proposed, has not yet been acted upon.

Subsection (3) provides that jurisdiction to prosecute an offence under section 2 is not dependent on the existence of a 'significant link' for the unauthorized-access offence under section 1 (the offences under section 1 and section 2 are hierarchical). It is sufficient that the accused intended to carry out the further offence in that home country and that there would be jurisdiction under the current rules to try that offence. The circumstances where that would be relevant are when unauthorized access to a computer is achieved abroad with the intent to commit the further offence in that home country, for example to carry out a fraud.

Subsection (4) explains that an offence under section 2 will be triable in a home country where the accused committed an offence under section 1 within that home country with intent to commit abroad an act which would have amounted to the further offence if it had been committed in that home country. Thus an offence under section 2 would be triable in England where an accused hacked into a computer in England in order to obtain information with a view to blackmailing someone in the United States. This provision is subject to the 'double criminality' test, in section 8(1).

The common law jurisdiction of the courts in Scotland already extends to offences of fraud which take place partly in one country and partly in another, provided that a significant part of the conduct takes place in Scotland. For the avoidance of doubt, however, sections 4 and 5 are extended to apply to Scotland.

5.—(1) The following provisions of this section apply for the interpretation of section 4 above.

Significant links with domestic jurisdiction.

(2) In relation to an offence under section 1, either of the following is a significant link with domestic jurisdiction—

(a) that the accused was in the home country concerned at the time when he did the act which caused the computer to perform the function; or

(b) that any computer containing any program or data to which the accused secured or intended to secure unauthorised access by doing that act was in the home country concerned at that time.

(3) In relation to an offence under section 3, either of the following is a significant link with domestic jurisdiction—

    (a) that the accused was in the home country concerned at the time when he did the act which caused the unauthorised modification; or

    (b) that the unauthorised modification took place in the home country concerned.

EXPLANATORY NOTES

This section determines, for the purposes of the offences under section 1 and section 3 of this Act, what constitutes a 'significant link' with a home country. The test for founding jurisdiction is, in the case of an offence under section 1, if *either* the accused was in that country when he secured unauthorized access to a computer *or* if any computer to which the accused secured or intended to secure unauthorized access was in the home country at that time and, in the case of an offence under section 3, if *either* the accused was in the home country concerned when he did the act which caused the unauthorized modification *or* if any computer whose contents were modified was in the home country at that time. See further Chapter 7(2), above.

6.—(1) On a charge of conspiracy to commit an offence under this Act the following questions are immaterial to the accused's guilt— *Territorial scope of inchoate offences related to offences under this Act.*

    (a) the question where any person became a party to the conspiracy; and

    (b) the question whether any act, omission or other event occurred in the home country concerned.

(2) On a charge of attempting to commit an offence under section 3 above the following questions are immaterial to the accused's guilt—

    (a) the question where the attempt was made; and

    (b) the question whether it had an effect in the home country concerned.

(3) On a charge of incitement to commit an offence under this Act the question where the incitement took place is immaterial to the accused's guilt.

(4) This section does not extend to Scotland.

EXPLANATORY NOTES

This section, together with section 7, makes changes to the jurisdictional rules relating to conspiracy, attempt, and incitement in respect of the offences under section 1 and section 3 of this Act, which are parallel to the changes made by sections 4 and 5 in respect of the substantive offences. Section 6 deals with cases where the conduct takes place abroad but is targeted on a computer situated in a home country (or takes place in one home country and is targeted on a computer in a different home country). Conduct which takes place in a home country and which is targeted on a computer situated abroad or in a different home country is catered for in section 7. These changes are in line with the Law Commission recommendations in its *Report on Computer Misuse*, para. 4. 3.

Subsection (2) is confined to an attempt to commit the offence under section 3 of the Act, whilst subsections (1) and (3) apply to all three offences. This is because the offences under section 1 and section 2 are already drafted in such a way as to penalize attempts to gain unauthorized access.

This section does not extend to Scotland because the jurisdiction of the Scottish courts over inchoate offences flows from their jurisdiction over the substantive offences. See explanatory note to section 4(5), above.

7.—(1) The following subsections shall be inserted after subsection (1) of section 1 of the Criminal Law Act 1977—

> "(1A) Subject to section 8 of the Computer Misuse Act 1990 (relevance of external law), if this subsection applies to an agreement, this Part of this Act has effect in relation to it as it has effect in relation to an agreement falling within subsection (1) above.

> (1B) Subsection (1A) above applies to an agreement if—
>
> > (a) a party to it, or a party's agent, did anything in England and Wales in relation to it before its formation; or
> >
> > (b) a party to it became a party in England and Wales (by joining it either in person or through an agent); or
> >
> > (c) a party to it, or a party's agent, did or omitted anything in England and Wales in pursuance of it;

and the agreement would fall within subsection (1) above as an agreement relating to the commission of a computer misuse offence but for the fact that the offence would not be an offence triable in England and Wales if committed in accordance with the parties' intentions."

(2) The following subsections shall be inserted after subsection (4) of that section—

> "(5) In the application of this Part of this Act to an agreement to which subsection (1A) above applies any reference to an offence shall be read as a reference to what would be the computer misuse offence in question but for the fact that it is not an offence triable in England and Wales.

> (6) In this section "computer misuse offence" means an offence under the Computer Misuse Act 1990."

(3) The following subsections shall be inserted after section 1(1) of the Criminal Attempts Act 1981—

> "(1A) Subject to section 8 of the Computer Misuse Act 1990 (relevance of external law), if this subsection applies to an act, what the person doing it had in view shall be treated as an offence to which this section applies.

> (1B) Subsection (1A) above applies to an act if—
>
> > (a) it is done in England and Wales; and
> >
> > (b) it would fall within subsection (1) above as more than merely preparatory to the commission of an offence under section 3 of the Computer Misuse Act 1990 but for the fact that the offence, if completed, would not be an offence triable in England and Wales."

(4) Subject to section 8 below, if any act done by a person in England and Wales would amount to the offence of incitement to commit an offence under this Act but for the fact that what he had in view would not be an offence triable in England and Wales—

Territorial scope of inchoate offences related to offences under external law corresponding to offences under this Act.

(a) what he had in view shall be treated as an offence under this Act for the purposes of any charge of incitement brought in respect of that act; and

(b) any such charge shall accordingly be triable in England and Wales.

EXPLANATORY NOTES

This section provides for the prosecution of an inchoate offence in England and Wales to commit elsewhere the equivalent of the computer-misuse offences. These provisions are subject to the principle of 'double criminality' established in section 8(1). These provisions apply to Northern Ireland by virtue of section 16 of the Act, but not to Scotland.

Subsections (1) and (2) relate to conspiracy and amend section 1 of the Criminal Law Act 1977. Subject to the double-criminality principle (s. 8(1), below), they provide that every party to a conspiracy to perform abroad an act, which if performed here would constitute a computer-misuse offence, will be triable in England and Wales if at least one conspirator became a party to it in England and Wales, or if he did anything there relating to the conspiracy or in pursuance of it.

Subsection (3) relates to attempt and amends section 1 of the Criminal Attempts Act 1981. Subject to the double-criminality principle (section 8(1), below), it provides that every attempt in England and Wales to perform abroad an act, which if performed in England and Wales would be an offence under section 3, will be triable in England and Wales. This subsection is confined to an attempt to commit the offence under section 3 of the Act, whilst subsections (1), (2), and (4) apply to all three offences. This is because the offences under section 1 and section 2 are already drafted in such a way as to penalize attempts to gain unauthorized access.

Subsection (4) makes similar provision for the law of incitement, and is similarly subject to the double-criminality principle (s. 8(1), below).

8.—(1) A person is guilty of an offence triable by virtue of section 4(4) above only if what he intended to do or facilitate would involve the commission of an offence under the law in force where the whole or any part of it was intended to take place. Relevance of external law.

(2) A person is guilty of an offence triable by virtue of section 1(1A) of the Criminal Law Act 1977 only if the pursuit of the agreed course of conduct would at some stage involve—

(a) an act or omission by one or more of the parties; or

(b) the happening of some other event;

constituting an offence under the law in force where the act, omission or other event was intended to take place.

(3) A person is guilty of an offence triable by virtue of section 1(1A) of the Criminal Attempts Act 1981 or by virtue of section 7(4) above only if what he had in view would involve the commission of an offence under the law in force where the whole or any part of it was intended to take place.

(4) Conduct punishable under the law in force in any place is an offence under that law for the purposes of this section, however it is described in that law.

(5) Subject to subsection (7) below, a condition specified in any of the subsections (1) to (3) above shall be taken to be satisfied unless not later than rules of court may provide the defence serve on the prosecution a notice—

(a) stating that, on the facts as alleged with respect to the relevant conduct, the condition is not in their opinion satisfied;

(b) showing the grounds for that opinion; and

(c) requiring the prosecution to show that it is satisfied.

(6) In subsection (5) above "the relevant conduct" means—

(a) where the condition in subsection (1) above is in question, what the accused intended to do or facilitate;

(b) where the condition in subsection (2) above is in question, the agreed course of conduct; and

(c) where the condition in subsection (3) above is in question, what the accused had in view.

(7) The court, if it thinks fit, may permit the defence to require the prosecution to show that the condition is satisfied without the prior service of a notice under subsection (5) above.

(8) If by virtue of subsection (7) above a court of solemn jurisdiction in Scotland permits the defence to require the prosecution to show that the condition is satisfied, it shall be competent for the prosecution for that purpose to examine any witness or to put in evidence any production not included in the lists lodged by it.

(9) In the Crown Court the question whether the condition is satisfied shall be decided by the judge alone.

(10) In the High Court of Justiciary and in the sheriff court the question whether the condition is satisfied shall be decided by the judge or, as the case may be, the sheriff alone.

EXPLANATORY NOTES

This section applies to those cases where, under the provisions of the Act, a court in a home country would have jurisdiction to try someone for acts which took place in the home country but which were directed at committing the computer-misuse offence abroad. As we have seen, if there is a significant link with the domestic jurisdiction, the offence is triable in the relevant home country. Where, however, in respect of an offence under section 2 the offence is triable in the home country (see s. 4(3) and (4) above), or where the offence charged is a conspiracy, attempt, or incitement to commit a computer-misuse offence abroad (see section 7, above), section 8 provides that, in addition, any such offence can only be prosecuted in the home country if, in respect of the section 2 offence, the further offence contemplated, if carried out, would be both punishable in the home country and in the relevant country abroad or, in respect of an inchoate offence to commit a computer-misuse offence abroad, that any such inchoate offence can only be prosecuted in the home country if the acts contemplated, if carried out, would be punishable both in the home country and in the relevant country abroad. These provisions apply to England and Wales, Scotland, and, by virtue of section 16, to Northern Ireland.

Subsections (1) to (3) apply the double-criminality principle to cases where an accused is charged with a section 2 offence triable by virtue of section 4(4), and to cases where an accused is charged with conspiracy, attempt, or incitement to commit a computer-misuse offence abroad.

While several foreign countries have enacted computer-misuse offences, their existence is not universal. See further Chapters 3, 4, 5, and 7(3), above. Subsection (4) provides that if the conduct is punishable in the foreign country in question, it is not relevant how the offence is described in that law.

Subsections (5) to (9) provide that it should be presumed that the condition of double criminality is satisfied unless the defence serves a notice on the prosecution stating that it is, in their opinion, not satisfied, and setting out the associated procedural matters.

9.—(1) In any proceedings brought in England and Wales in respect of any offence to which this section applies it is immaterial to guilt whether or not the accused was a British citizen at the time of any act, omission or other event proof of which is required for conviction of the offence. British citizenship immaterial.

(2) This section applies to the following offences—

(a) any offence under this Act;
(b) conspiracy to commit an offence under this Act;
(c) any attempt to commit an offence under section 3 above; and
(d) incitement to commit an offence under this Act.

EXPLANATORY NOTES

Under this Act, jurisdiction is not limited to those who hold British citizenship, since the offences are designed to include computer misuse which takes place abroad but is targeted at a computer in this country. Subsection 2(c) is confined to an attempt to commit the offence under section 3 of the Act since offences under section 1 and section 2 are already drafted in such a way as to penalize attempts to gain unauthorized access. It does not apply to Scotland as the Scottish courts have jurisdiction at common law to try any person charged with an offence triable in a Scottish court.

Miscellaneous and general

10.—Section 1(1) above has effect without prejudice to the operation— Saving for certain law enforcement powers.

(a) in England and Wales of any enactment relating to powers of inspection, search or seizure; and
(b) in Scotland of any enactment or rule of law relating to powers of examination, search or seizure.

EXPLANATORY NOTES

A number of enactments provide various authorities with powers of access, under certain circumstances, to computer records. Examples are Police and Criminal Evidence Act 1984, sections 19 and 20 (see above, p. 166), Finance Act 1985, section 10, and Children Act 1989, section 63. Where these authorities gain access to a computer in pursuance of their statutory powers they, by virtue of section 10 of this Act, commit no offence.

11.—(1) A magistrates' court shall have jurisdiction to try an offence under section 1 above if— Proceedings for offences under section 1.

(a) the accused was within its commission area at the time when he did the act which caused the computer to perform the function; or
(b) any computer containing any program or data to which the accused secured or intended to secure unauthorised access by doing that act was in its commission area at that time.

(2) Subject to subsection (3) below, proceedings for an offence under section 1 above may be brought within a period of six months from the date on which evidence sufficient in the opinion of the prosecutor to warrant the proceedings came to his knowledge.

(3) No such proceedings shall be brought by virtue of this section more than three years after the commission of the offence.

(4) For the purposes of this section, a certificate signed by or on behalf of the prosecutor and stating the date on which evidence sufficient in his opinion to warrant the proceedings came to his knowledge shall be conclusive evidence of that fact.

(5) A certificate stating that matter and purporting to be so signed shall be deemed to be so signed unless the contrary is proved.

(6) In this section "commission area" has the same meaning as in the Justices of the Peace Act 1979.

(7) This section does not extend to Scotland.

EXPLANATORY NOTES

In respect of the offence under section 1 of the Act, section 11 provides that a magistrates' court shall have jurisdiction if either the accused or the affected computer was in its commission area at the relevant time. The section also defines time-limits for prosecution for this offence. An exception is made here to the normal rule, set out in Magistrates' Courts Act 1980, section 127, that a prosecution for a summary offence must be brought within 6 months of the date of commission of the offence. Instead, for this offence, summary prosecution must be brought within 6 months of the date on which evidence sufficient in the opinion of the prosecutor to justify prosecution came to his knowledge and, in any event, not later than 3 years after the offence was allegedly committed. Corresponding provisions for Scotland are contained in section 13.

12.—(1) If the trial on indictment of a person charged with—

    (a) an offence under section 2 above; or

    (b) an offence under section 3 above or any attempt to commit such an offence;

the jury find him not guilty of the offence charged, they may find him guilty of an offence under section 1 above if on the facts shown he could have been found guilty of that offence in proceedings for that offence brought before the expiry of any time limit under section 11 above applicable to such proceedings.

Conviction of an offence under section 1 in proceedings for offence under section 2 or 3.

(2) The Crown Court shall have the same powers and duties in relation to a person who is by virtue of this section convicted before it on an offence under section 1 above as a magistrates' court would have on convicting him of the offence.

(3) This section is without prejudice to section 6(3) of the Criminal Law Act 1967 (conviction of alternative indictable offence on trial on indictment).

(4) This section does not extend to Scotland.

EXPLANATORY NOTES

In many cases the commission of an offence under section 2 or section 3 of this Act will entail commission of an offence under section 1. This section provides for the possibility of conviction of an offence under section 1 where the accused is found not guilty of an offence under section 2 or section 3, or an attempt to commit an offence under section 3. Special provision is made for this in section 12, since the general provision in Criminal Law Act 1967, section 6(3) enabling an alternative conviction to be returned is inapplicable where offences are triable only summarily. If, by section 12, the offender is convicted of a section 1 offence in the Crown Court, that court is restricted to the powers of a magistrates' court when dealing with such a case. The normal time-limits for prosecution of an offence under section 1 (see s. 11, above) will not operate to debar conviction of a section 1 offence on a charge brought for an offence under section 2 or section 3. Corresponding provisions for Scotland are set out in section 13.

13.—(1) A sheriff shall have jurisdiction in respect of an offence under section 1 or 2 above if— *Proceedings in Scotland.*

    (a) the accused was in the sheriffdom at the time when he did the act which caused the computer to perform the function; or

    (b) any computer containing any program or data to which the accused secured or intended to secure unauthorised access by doing that act was in the sheriffdom at that time.

(2) A sheriff shall have jurisdiction in respect of an offence under section 3 above if—

    (a) the accused was in the sheriffdom at the time when he did the act which caused the unauthorised modification; or

    (b) the unauthorised modification took place in the sheriffdom.

(3) Subject to subsection (4) below, summary proceedings for an offence under section 1, 2 or 3 above may be commenced within a period of six months from the date on which evidence sufficient in the opinion of the procurator fiscal to warrant proceedings came to his knowledge.

(4) No such proceedings shall be commenced by virtue of this section more than three years after the commission of the offence.

(5) For the purposes of this section, a certificate signed by or on behalf of the procurator fiscal and stating the date on which evidence sufficient in his opinion to warrant the proceedings came to his knowledge shall be conclusive evidence of that fact.

(6) A certificate stating that matter and purporting to be signed shall be deemed to be so signed unless the contrary is proved.

(7) Subsection (3) of section 331 of the Criminal Procedure (Scotland) Act 1975 (date of commencement of proceedings) shall apply for the purposes of this section as it applies for the purposes of that section.

(8) In proceedings in which a person is charged with an offence under section 2 or 3 above and is found not guilty or is acquitted of that charge, he may be found guilty of an offence under section 1 above if on the facts shown he could have been found guilty of that offence in proceedings for that

offence commenced before the expiry of any time limit under this section applicable to such proceedings.

(9) Subsection (8) above shall apply whether or not an offence under section 1 above has been libelled in the complaint or indictment.

(10) A person found guilty of an offence under section 1 above by virtue of subsection (8) above shall be liable, in respect of that offence, only to the penalties set out in section 1.

(11) This section extends to Scotland only.

EXPLANATORY NOTES

This section makes very similar provision in respect of proceedings in Scotland as sections 11 and 12 make in respect of proceedings in England. See explanatory notes on sections 11 and 12, above.

14.—(1) Where a circuit judge is satisfied by information on oath given by a constable that there are reasonable grounds for believing— *Search warrants offences under section 1.*

    (a) that an offence under section 1 above has been or is about to be committed in any premises; and

    (b) that evidence that such an offence has been or is about to be committed is in those premises;

he may issue a warrant authorising a constable to enter and search the premises, using such reasonable force as is necessary.

(2) The power conferred by subsection (1) above does not extend to authorising a search for material of the kinds mentioned in section 9(2) of the Police and Criminal Evidence Act 1984 (privileged, excluded and special procedure material).

(3) A warrant under this section—

    (a) may authorise persons to accompany any constable executing the warrant; and

    (b) remains in force for twenty-eight days from the date of its issue.

(4) In executing a warrant issued under this section a constable may seize an article if he reasonably believes that it is evidence that an offence under section 1 above has been or is about to be committed.

(5) In this section "premises" includes land, buildings, movable structures, vehicles, vessels, aircraft and hovercraft.

(6) This section does not extend to Scotland.

EXPLANATORY NOTES

This section provides the police in England and Wales with a power, on obtaining a search-warrant from a Circuit Judge, to enter and search premises and seize evidence (though not extending to privileged, excluded, and special-procedure material under the Police and Criminal Evidence Act 1984) if there are reasonable grounds to show that an offence under section 1 has been committed or is about to be committed. A power of search in respect of a summary offence is unusual, though a similar power is provided by section 109 of the Copyright, Designs and Patents Act 1988. The computer misuse offences under section 2 and section 3 of the Act are arrestable offences, being punishable with 5 years imprisonment on indictment, so that a power of search already exists in relation to them by virtue of sections 17 and 18 of Police and Criminal Evidence Act 1984 and in some circumstances under section 8 where an arrestable offence qualifies as a 'serious arrestable offence' within the meaning of Police and Criminal Evidence Act 1984, s. 116(2). See Chapter 6(2), above.

This section does not apply to Scotland, since common law powers of search in Scotland may extend to any offence and can be invoked by a warrant.

15. The offences to which an Order in Council under section 2 of the Extradition Act 1870 can apply shall include—

   (a) offences under section 2 or 3 above;

   (b) any conspiracy to commit such an offence; and

   (c) any attempt to commit an offence under section 3 above.

Extradition where Schedule 1 to the Extradition Act 1989 applies

EXPLANATORY NOTES

The Extradition Act 1989 provides that conduct is extraditable if it is both an offence here and in the other country and the conduct would, on conviction, attract a maximum sentence of 12 months or more in custody. The offences under section 2 and section 3 of the Computer Misuse Act are, therefore, extraditable on those grounds. The 1989 Act, however, by Schedule 1, retains in force the 1870 extradition regime which continues to apply in respect of countries with which Britain has negotiated extradition treaties. These are given effect by Orders in Council made under section 2 of the 1870 Act. Section 15 of the Computer Misuse Act brings the offences under section 2 and section 3 within the ambit of that Schedule. It also includes conspiracy in relation to a section 2 or section 3 offence and an attempt to commit an offence under section 3. There is no reference to an attempt to commit an offence under section 2 since that offence is defined in such a way as to include an attempt to commit it. Incitement is not included in the offences listed in Schedule 1. See also Chapter 7(1), above.

16.—(1) The following provisions of this section have effect for applying this Act in relation to Northern Ireland with the modifications there mentioned.

Application to Northern Ireland.

   (2) In section 2(2)(b)—

      (a) the reference to England and Wales shall be read as a reference to Northern Ireland; and

      (b) the reference to section 33 of the Magistrates' Courts Act 1980 shall be read as a reference to Article 46(4) of the Magistrates' Courts (Northern Ireland) Order 1981.

   (3) The reference in section 3(6) to the Criminal Damage Act 1971 shall be read as a reference to the Criminal Damage (Northern Ireland) Order 1977.

   (4) Subsections (5) to (7) below apply in substitution for subsections (1) to (3) of section 7; and any reference in subsection (4) of that section to England and Wales shall be read as a reference to Northern Ireland.

   (5) The following paragraphs shall be inserted after paragraph (1) of Article 9 of the Criminal Attempts and Conspiracy (Northern Ireland) Order 1983—

"(1A) Subject to section 8 of the Computer Misuse Act 1990 (relevance of external law), if this paragraph applies to an agreement, this Part has effect in relation to it as it has effect in relation to an agreement falling within paragraph (1).

(1B) Paragraph (1A) applies to an agreement if—

(a) a party to it, or a party's agent, did anything in Northern Ireland in relation to it before its formation;

(b) a party to it became a party in Northern Ireland (by joining it either in person or through an agent); or

(c) a party to it, or a party's agent, did or omitted anything in Northern Ireland in pursuance of it;

and the agreement would fall within paragraph (1) as an agreement relating to the commission of a computer misuse offence but for the fact that the offence would not be an offence triable in Northern Ireland if committed in accordance with the parties' intentions."

(6) The following paragraph shall be inserted after paragraph (4) of that Article—

"(5) In the application of this Part to an agreement to which paragraph (1A) applies any reference to an offence shall be read as a reference to what would be the computer misuse offence in question but for the fact that it is not an offence triable in Northern Ireland.

(6) In this Article "computer misuse offence" means an offence under the Computer Misuse Act 1990."

(7) The following paragraphs shall be inserted after Article 3(1) of that Order—

"(1A) Subject to section 8 of the Computer Misuse Act 1990 (relevance of external law), if this paragraph applies to an act, what the person doing it had in view shall be treated as an offence to which this Article applies.

(1B) Paragraph (1A) above applies to an act if—

(a) it is done in Northern Ireland; and

(b) it would fall within paragraph (1) as more than merely preparatory to the commission of an offence under section 3 of the Computer Misuse Act 1990 but for the fact that the offence, if completed, would not be an offence triable in Northern Ireland."

(8) In section 8—

(a) the reference in subsection (2) to section 1(1A) of the Criminal Law Act 1977 shall be read as a reference to Article 9(1A) of that Order; and

(b) the reference in subsection (3) to section 1(1A) of the Criminal Attempts Act 1981 shall be read as a reference to Article 3(1A) of that Order.

(9) The references in sections 9(1) and 10 to England and Wales shall be read as references to Northern Ireland.

(10) In section 11, for subsection (1) there shall be substituted—

"(1) A magistrates' court for a county division in Northern Ireland may hear and determine a complaint charging an offence under section 1 above or conduct a preliminary investigation or preliminary inquiry into an offence under that section if—

(a) the accused was in that division at the time when he did the act which caused the computer to perform the function; or

(b) any computer containing any program or data to which the accused secured or intended to secure unauthorised access by doing that act was in that division at that time.";

and subsection (6) shall be omitted.

(11) The reference in section 12(3) to section 6(3) of the Criminal Law Act 1967 shall be read as a reference to section 6(2) of the Criminal Law Act (Northern Ireland) 1967.

(12) In section 14—

(a) the reference in subsection (1) to a circuit judge shall be read as a reference to a county court judge; and

(b) the reference in subsection (2) to section 9(2) of the Police and Criminal Evidence Act 1984 shall be read as a reference to Article 11(2) of the Police and Criminal Evidence (Northern Ireland) Order 1989.

EXPLANATORY NOTES

While the foregoing provisions of the Act apply to Northern Ireland, section 16 modifies them in a number of ways in respect of their application to Northern Ireland.

17.—(1) The following provisions of this section apply for the interpret-   Interpretation.
ation of this Act.

(2) A person secures access to any program or data held in a computer if by causing a computer to perform any function he—

(a) alters or erases the program or data;

(b) copies or moves it to any storage medium other than that in which it is held or to a different location in the storage medium in which it is held;

(c) uses it; or

(d) has it output from the computer in which it is held (whether by having it displayed or in any other manner);

and references to access to a program or data (and to an intent to secure such access) shall be read accordingly.

(3) For the purposes of subsection (2)(c) above a person uses a program if the function he causes the computer to perform—

(a) causes the program to be executed; or

(b) is itself a function of the program.

(4) For the purposes of subsection (2)(d) above—

    (a) a program is output if the instructions of which it consists are output; and

    (b) the form in which any such instructions or any other data is output (and in particular whether or not it represents a form in which, in the case of instructions, they are capable of being executed or, in the case of data, it is capable of being processed by a computer) is immaterial.

(5) Access of any kind by any person to any program or data held in a computer is unauthorised if—

    (a) he is not himself entitled to control access to the kind in question to the program or data; and

    (b) he does not have consent to access by him of the kind in question to the program or data from any person who is so entitled.

(6) References to any program or data held in a computer include references to any program or data held in any removable storage medium which is for the time being in the computer; and a computer is to be regarded as containing any program or data held in any such medium.

(7) A modification of the contents of any computer takes place if, by the operation of any function of the computer concerned or any other computer—

    (a) any program or data held in the computer concerned is altered or erased; or

    (b) any program or data is added to its contents;

and any act which contributes towards causing such a modification shall be regarded as causing it.

(8) Such a modification is unauthorised if—

    (a) the person whose act causes it is not himself entitled to determine whether the modification should be made; and

    (b) he does not have consent to the modification from any person who is so entitled.

(9) References to the home country concerned shall be read in accordance with section 4(6) above.

(10) References to a program include references to part of a program.

EXPLANATORY NOTES

It will be noticed that there is no definition of 'computer', 'program', or 'data' in this Act, since it was felt that the pace of technological change would soon render such definitions outdated. This is in accord with the recommendation of the Law Commission. At the Committee Stage, however, the following definition of 'computer' was tabled as an amendment to the Act, by Mr Harry Cohen MP: 'A computer means equipment which can, in the form of one or more continuous variables, accept data, store data or programs in a storage medium, process data by means of a program, and provide for the output of data. Where a computer is embedded within other equipment, the computer shall form a unit which can be (a) identified as being a distinct part of the equipment and (b) routinely accessed in order to allow modifications to programs or data to be made.' The amendment was unsuccessful. For discussion of matters of definition see Chapter 1(1), above.

18.—(1) This Act may be cited as the Computer Misuse Act 1990.

(2) This Act shall come into force at the end of the period of two months beginning with the day on which it is passed.

(3) An offence is not committed under this Act unless every act or other event proof of which is required for conviction of the offence takes place after this Act comes into force.

Citation, commencement, etc.

EXPLANATORY NOTES

The Act comes into effect on 29 August 1990.

Bibliography

American Bar Association, Task Force on Computer Crime, *Report on Computer Crime*, Washington, DC: Government Printer, 1984.

American Institute of Certified Public Accountants, EDP Fraud Review Task Force, *Report on the Study of EDP Related Fraud in the Banking and Insurance Industries*, 1984, cited in United States Congress, Office of Technology Assessment.

Arlidge, A., and Parry, J., *Fraud*, Criminal Law Library No. 1, London: Waterlow, 1985.

Audit Inspectorate, *Computer Fraud Survey*, London: Department of the Environment, 1981.

Audit Commission for Local Authorities in England and Wales, *Computer Fraud Survey*, London, HMSO, 1984.

—— *Survey of Computer Fraud and Abuse*, London: HMSO, 1987.

Bainbridge, D. I., 'Hacking: The Unauthorized Access of Computer Systems: The Legal Implications' (1989) 52 *Modern Law Review* 236.

Beale, I., 'Computer Eavesdropping: Fact or Fantasy?' (1986–7) 4 *Computer Law and Security Report* 14.

Becker, J. J., 'Rifkin: A Documentary History' (1980) 2 *Computer and Law Journal* 471.

Bell, D., *The Coming of Post-Industrial Society*, New York: Basic Books, 1976.

Bequai, A., *White-Collar Crime: A Twentieth Century Crisis*, Lexington, Mass.: D. C. Heath, 1978.

—— *Technocrimes*, Lexington, Mass.: D. C. Heath, 1987.

Berman, C., 'Hi-Tech Experts Who Get the Call into Court', *The Times*, 19 Jan. 1988.

Bigelow, R., 'Crime and High Technology' (1985) 1 *Computer Law and Practice* 81.

—— 'Computer Security, Crime and Privacy — US Status Report' (1988–9) 6 *Computer Law and Security Report* 10.

Birch, D. J., 'Documentary Evidence' [1989] *Criminal Law Review* 15.

Birkinshaw, P., *Freedom of Information*, London: Weidenfeld, 1988.

BloomBecker, J. J., 'Computer Crime Update: The View as we Exit 1984' (1985) 7 *Western New England Law Review* 627.

—— *Computer Crime, Computer Security, Computer Ethics*, Statistical Report of the National Centre for Computer Crime Data, Los Angeles: NCCD, 1986.

Bolter, J. D., 'The Computer in a Finite World' (1985) 6 *Computer and Law Journal* 349.

Bone, J., 'Computer Virus Invades Pentagon', *The Times*, 5 Nov. 1988.

Box, S., *Power, Crime and Mystification*, London: Tavistock, 1983.

Bremner, C., 'Virus Plague Wreaks Havoc with Computers', *The Times*, 1 Jan. 1988.

—— 'Friday 13 Virus Bugs The Times', *The Times*, 14 Oct. 1989.

—— 'Death to the Hackers', *The Times*, 16 Oct. 1989.

British Institute of Management, *Managers and IT Competence*, London: British Institute of Management, 1988.

Brown, R. A., 'Crime and Computers' (1983) 7 *Criminal Law Journal* 68.

—— 'Computer Produced Evidence in Australia' (1984) 8 *University of Tasmania Law Review* 342.

—— 'Computer-Related Crime under Commonwealth Law, and the Draft Federal Criminal Code' (1986) 10 *Criminal Law Journal* 377.

Campbell, D., and Connor, S., *On The Record: Surveillance, Computers and Privacy*, London: Michael Joseph, 1986.

Canadian Law Reform Commission, Report No. 31, *Recodifying Criminal Law*, Montreal: CLR, 1987.

Castell, S., 'The Legal Admissibility of Computer Generated Evidence' (1989–90) 2 *Computer Law and Security Report* 2.

Caulfield Institute of Technology, Computer Abuse Research Bureau (CIT/CARB), 'Computer Related Crime in Australia' (1984) 6 *Computer Fraud and Security Bulletin* no. 12, 1.

Central Statistical Office, *Social Trends*, vol. 19, London: HMSO, 1989.

Chapman, J., 'Computer Misuse: A Response to Working Paper No. 110' (1989) 5 *Computer Law and Practice* 115.

Chartered Institute of Public Finance and Accountancy (CIPFA), *Computer Audit Guidelines*, London: CIPFA, 1987.

Chesterman, J., and Lipman, A., *The Electronic Pirates*, London: Routledge, 1988.

Christensen, K., 'Home PC: People Don't Need it, But they Fear Life Without it', *Wall Street Journal*, 13 Aug. 1985.

Cleary, E. W., *McCormick on Evidence*, 3rd edn., St Paul: West Publishing, 1984.

Clinard, M. B., and Quinney, R., *Criminal Behaviour Systems: A Typology*, New York: Holt, Rinehart & Winston, 1967.

Cohen, S. (ed.), *Images of Deviance*, London: Pelican Books, 1971.

—— 'Property Destruction: Motives and Meanings' in Ward (1973).

—— and Young, J. (eds.), *The Manufacture of News*, London: Constable, 1981.

Coleman, A., 'Trade Secrets and the Criminal Law: The Need for Reform' (1989) 5 *Computer Law and Practice* 111.

Comer, M. J., *Corporate Fraud*, 2nd edn., London: McGraw-Hill, 1985.

Confederation of British Industry (CBI), 'Submission to the Law Commission on Working Paper No. 110 on Computer Misuse', summarized at (1989–90) 1 *Computer Law and Security Report* 14.

Cornish, D. B., and Clarke, R. V. (eds.), *The Reasoning Criminal*, New York: Springer-Verlag, 1986.

Cornwall, H., *The Hacker's Handbook*, London: Century Hutchinson, 1985, 1986, 1989.

—— *Datatheft*, London: Heinemann, 1987.

Council of Europe, Legislative Dossier No. 2, *Telephone Tapping and the Recording of Telecommunications*, Strasburg: Council of Europe, 1982.

Cressey, D., *Other People's Money*, New York: Patterson Smith, 1973.

Criminal Law Revision Committee, 11th Report, *Evidence*, Cmnd. 4991, London: HMSO, 1972.

—— 18th Report, *Conspiracy to Defraud*, Cmnd. 9873, London: HMSO, 1986.

Data Protection Registrar, *Fourth Annual Report*, London: HMSO, 1988.

—— *Fifth Annual Report*, London: HMSO, 1989.

Davies, D., 'Computer Losses During 1988: A Review' (1989–90) 1 *Computer Law and Security Report* 2.

Dawe, T., and Evans, P., 'The Confidential Police Files That Are Open to Hundreds', *The Times*, 3 Feb. 1989.

Doherty, G., 'Stewart: When Is a Thief Not a Thief? When He Steals the Candy But Not the Wrapper' (1988) 63 *Criminal Reports* 3d, 322.

Doswell, R., and Simons, G. L., *Fraud and Abuse of IT Systems*, Manchester: National Computing Centre Publications, 1986.

Dunning, M., 'Some Aspects of Theft of Computer Software' (1983) *Auckland University Law Review* 273.

Dworkin, G., and Taylor, R., *Blackstone's Guide to the Copyright, Designs and Patents Act 1988*, London: Blackstone Press, 1989.

Dyer, J., Williams, F., and Haynes, D., 'Gauging Public Attitudes Towards Science and Technology' in F. Williams (1988).

Edlehertz, H., *The Nature, Impact and Prosecution of White-Collar Crime*, Washington, DC: US Government Printing Office, 1970.

—— and Rogovin, C., *A National Strategy for Containing White-Collar Crime*, Lexington, Mass.: D. C. Heath, 1980.

Edmonton Institute of Law Research and Reform, Report No. 46, *Trade Secrets*, Edmonton: Government Printer, 1988.

Ericson, R. V., Baranek, P. M., and Chan, J. B. L., *Visualising Deviance*, Milton Keynes: Open University, 1987.

Eser, A., and Thormundsson, J. (eds.), *Old Ways and New Needs in Criminal Legislation*, Freiburg: University of Freiburg, 1989.

Essinger, J., *Computers in Financial Trading*, London: Elsevier Advanced Technology Publications, 1988.

Estes, N., and Williams, V., 'Computers in Texas Schools' in F. Williams (1988).

European Community Information Technology Task Force, *The Vulnerability of the Information Conscious Society: European Situation*, unpublished, cited in Levi (1987).

Everson, S. L., *Computer Crime*, London: ELS Services, 1987.

Farr, R., *The Electronic Criminals*, New York: McGraw-Hill, 1975.

Federation Against Software Theft (FAST), *Thou Shalt Not Cheat*, publicity material, London: FAST, 1986.

—— 'Submission to the European Commission on the Software Piracy Implications of the E.C. Green Paper on Copyright' (1989) 5 *Computer Law and Practice* 94.

Finn, P., and Hoffman, A. R., *Prosecution of Economic Crime*, Washington, DC: US Government Printing Office, 1976.

Fishlock, T., 'Schoolboy Hackers Crack Pentagon Telephone Codes', *The Times*, 18 July 1985.

Fites, P., Johnston, P., and Kratz, M., *The Computer Virus Crisis*, New York: Van Nostrand Reinhold, 1989.

Fitzgerald, P., and Leopold, M., *Stranger on the Line: The Secret History of Phone Tapping*, London: Bodley Head, 1987.

Gait, J., 'Security of Electronic Fund Transfer Systems' (1981) 32 *Journal of Systems Management* 6.

Gans, H. J., *Deciding What's News*, New York: Pantheon Books, 1979.

Geddes, D., 'Computer Pirates Raid Stuns Paris', *The Times*, 19 July 1986.

Geis, G., and Stotland, E. (eds.), *White-Collar Crime: Theory and Research*, Beverly Hills, Calif.: Sage Publications, 1980.

George, B. J., 'Contemporary Legislation Governing Computer Crimes' (1985) 21 *Criminal Law Bulletin* 389.

Gold, S., 'Hackers: Are They a Threat to World Peace?' *Computer Talk*, 28 Nov. 1988.

Griew, E. J., *The Theft Acts 1968 and 1978*, 5th edn., London: Sweet and Maxwell, 1986*a*.

—— 'Stealing and Obtaining Bank Credits' [1986b] *Criminal Law Review* 356.

Hadden, T., 'Fraud in the City: The Role of the Criminal Law' [1983] *Criminal Law Review* 500.

Hamilton, P., *Espionage and Subversion in an Industrial Society*, London: Hutchinson, 1967.

Hammond, G., 'Theft of Information' (1984) 100 *Law Quarterly Review* 252.

—— 'Electronic Crime in Canadian Courts' (1986) 6 *Oxford Journal of Legal Studies* 145.

Hansen, A. C., 'Criminal Law; Theft of Use of Computer Services' (1985) 7 *Western New England Law Review* 823.

Hayes, D., *Behind the Silicon Curtain*, London: Free Association Books, 1989.

Henniker-Heaton, Y., 'The Human Risks: An Auditor's Point of View' (1986–7) 3 *Computer Law and Security Report* 21.

—— 'Fraud Investigation: A Perspective on the Role of the Police' (1988–9) 1 *Computer Law and Security Report* 7.

Hepworth, M., *Blackmail*, London: Routledge, 1975.

Hewitt, P., *The Abuse of Power*, London: Martin Robertson, 1982.

Hochman, M., 'The Flagler Dog Track Case' (1986) 7 *Computer and Law Journal* 117.

Hochstedler, E. (ed.), *Corporations as Criminals*, Beverly Hills, Calif.: Sage Publications, 1984.

Hodkinson, K., and Wasik, M., *Industrial Espionage: Protection and Remedies*, London: Longman Intelligence Reports, 1986

Hogg Robinson, *Computer Security in Practice*, London: Hogg Robinson, 1986.

Home Office, *Statement on the Recommendations of the Security Commission*, Cmnd. 8539, London: HMSO, 1982.

—— *British Crime Survey*, Home Office Research Study No. 76, London: HMSO, 1983.

—— Consultation Paper, *Trespass on Residential Premises*, London: HMSO, 1983.

—— *Police and Criminal Evidence Act 1984, Codes of Practice*, London: HMSO, 1985.

—— *The Police National Computer*, HC 425, London: HMSO, 1986.

—— *International Mutual Assistance in Criminal Matters: A Discussion Paper*, London: HMSO, 1988.

Hughes, G., 'Mindless Computers in Australia' (1987–8) 2 *Computer Law and Security Report* 25.

—— 'Queensland Computer Crime Report' (1988) 4 *Computer Law and Practice* 100.

—— 'Disjointed Australian Attack on Hackers' (1989) 6 *Computer Law and Practice* 28.

Ingraham, D. G., 'On Charging Computer Crime' (1980) 2 *Computer Law Journal* 429.

Institute of Electrical Engineers, *Software in Safety-Critical Systems*, London: IEE, 1989.

International Chamber of Commerce, Commission on Computing, Telecommunications and Information Policies, *Computer Related Crime: An International Business View*, Paris: ICC, 1988.

Jack (Chairman) Committee, *Banking Services Law*, Cmnd. 622, London: HMSO, 1989.

Johnson, D. G., 'Should Computer Programs be Owned?' (1985) 16 *Metaphilosophy* 276.

Keane, A., *The Modern Law of Evidence*, 2nd edn., London: Butterworths, 1989.

Keith (Chairman) Committee, *Enforcement Powers of the Revenue Departments*, Cmnd. 8822, London: HMSO, 1983.

Kelman, A., and Sizer, R., *The Computer in Court*, Aldershot: Gower, 1982.

Kenny, J. J. P., 'The Expert Witness Register of the British Computer Society' (1988) 4 *Computer Law and Practice* 92.

Kling, R., 'Computer Abuse and Computer Crime as Organisational Activities' (1980) 2 *Computer and Law Journal* 403.

Kramer, R. C., 'Corporate Criminality' in Hochstedler (1984), p. 13.

Krauss, J., and MacGahan, A., *Computer Fraud and Countermeasures*, New York: Englewood Cliffs, 1979.

Kutz, R. K., 'Computer Crime in Virginia: A Critical Examination of the Criminal Offences in the Virginia Computer Crimes Act' (1986) 27 *William and Mary Law Review* 783.

La Fave, W. R., and Scott, A. W., *Criminal Law*, 2nd edn., St Paul, Minn.: West Publishing, 1986.

Lane, V. P., *Security of Computer-Based Information Systems*, London: Macmillan, 1985.

Law Commission, Report No. 55, *Forgery and Counterfeit Currency*, London: HMSO, 1973.

—— Report No. 76, *Conspiracy and Criminal Law Reform*, London: HMSO, 1976.

—— Report No. 91, *The Territorial and Extraterritorial Jurisdiction of the Criminal Law*, London: HMSO, 1978.

—— Working Paper No. 104. *Conspiracy to Defraud*, London: HMSO, 1987.

—— Consultation Paper, *Jurisdiction Over Fraud Offences With a Foreign Element*, London, Law Commission, 1987.

—— Working Paper No. 110, *Computer Misuse*, London, HMSO, 1988.

—— Report No. 180, *Jurisdiction Over Offences of Fraud and Dishonesty With a Foreign Element*, London: HMSO, 1989*a*.

—— Report No. 186, *Computer Misuse*, Cm. 819, London: HMSO, 1989*b*.

Leigh, L. H., *The Control of Commercial Fraud*, London: Heinemann, 1982.

—— 'Territorial Jurisdiction and Fraud' [1988] *Criminal Law Review* 280.

Levi, M., *The Phantom Capitalists*, London: Heinemann, 1981.

—— *The Incidence, Reporting and Prevention of Commercial Fraud*, Summary of Findings, Cardiff: Dept. of Social Administration, 1986.

—— *Regulating Fraud*, London: Tavistock, 1987.

—— 'Suite Justice: Sentencing for Fraud' [1989] *Criminal Law Review* 420.

—— and Jones, S., 'Public and Police Perceptions of Crime Seriousness in England and Wales' (1985) 25 *British Journal of Criminology* 234.

Levy, S., *Hackers: Heroes of the Computer Revolution*, New York: Doubleday, 1984.

Lindop (Chairman) Committee, *Report of the Committee on Data Protection*, Cmnd. 7341, London: HMSO, 1978.

Lloyd, I., 'Computer Abuse and the Law' (1988) 104 *Law Quarterly Review* 203.

Loebbecke, J. K., Mullarkey, J. F., and Zuber, G. R., 'Auditing in a Computer Environment' (1983) *Journal of Accountancy* 68.

Loeffler, R., *Report of the Trustee of Equity Funding Corporation of America*, Report to the United States District Court for the Central District of California, 1974.

Loeschmann, D. C., 'Computers and the Management of a Law Practice' (1987) 3 *Yearbook of Law, Computers and Technology* 68.

Magnusson, D., 'Using the Criminal Law against Infringement of Copyright and the Taking of Confidential Information' (1983) 35 *Criminal Reports* (3d) 129.

Mandell, S. L., *Computers, Data Processing and the Law*, St Paul, Minn.: West Publishing, 1984.

Marcuse, H., *One-Dimensional Man*, Boston: Beacon Press, 1964.

Mattera, P., *Off the Books*, London: Pluto Press, 1985.

Matthews, R., 'Computer Viruses Used as Blackmail Says Security Expert', *The Times*, 18 Jan. 1989.

—— 'Psychology to Beat the Hackers', *The Times*, 2 Feb. 1989.

—— 'New Light on Problems', *The Times*, 13 July 1989.

May, M., 'How a Hacking Law Could Weaken Security', *The Times*, 20 Apr. 1989.

May, R., 'Fair Play at Trial: An Interim Assessment of Section 78 of the Police and Criminal Evidence Act 1984' [1988] *Criminal Law Review* 722.

Miers, D., *Responses to Victimisation*, London: Professional Books, 1978.

Moger, A., 'A Hacker's Electronic Voyage Around the World', *The Times*, 28 Oct. 1988.

Moskoff, F. R., 'The Theft of Thoughts: The Realities of 1984' (1985) 27 *Criminal Law Quarterly* 226.

Nicholson, E., 'Hacking Away at Liberty', *The Times*, 18 Apr. 1989.

Nilsson, H. G., 'The Council of Europe Fights Computer Crime' (1989) 6 *Computer Law and Practice* 8.

Nimmer, R. T., *The Law of Computer Technology*, New York: John Wiley, 1985.

Norman, A. R. D., *Computer Insecurity*, London: Chapman and Hall, 1983.

Nuttall, N., 'Idealistic Hackers a Global Threat', *The Times*, 21 Sept. 1989*a*.

—— 'Fear Proves More Infectious Than Software Disease', *The Times*, 14 Oct. 1989*b*.

—— 'BT policy on Hacking Criticised by Police', *The Times*, 28 May 1990.

Organization for Economic Co-operation and Development (OECD), *Banking and Electronic Fund Transfers*, Paris: OECD, 1983.

—— Information Computer Communications Policy No. 10, *Computer-Related Crime: Analysis of Legal Policy*, Paris: OECD, 1986.

—— *Internationalisation of Software and Computer Services*, Paris: OECD, 1989.

—— *Electronic Funds Transfer: Plastic Cards and the Consumer*, Paris: OECD, 1989.

Parker, D. B., Stanford Research Institute Report, *Computer Abuse Assessment*, Menlo Park, Calif.: Stanford Research Institute, 1975.

—— *Crime by Computer*, New York, Scribner, 1976.

—— 'Computer-Related White-Collar Crime' in Geis and Stotland (1980), p. 199.

—— 'Computer Abuse Research Update' (1980) 2 *Computer and Law Journal* 329.

—— *Fighting Computer Crime*, New York: Scribner, 1983.

—— and Nycum, S., *Computer Crime: Criminal Justice Resource Manual*, Washington, DC: National Criminal Justice Resource Service, 1979.

—— —— and Aura, S., *Computer Abuse*, Menlo Park, Calif.: Stanford Research Institute, 1973.

Pearce, F., *Crimes of the Powerful*, London: Pluto Press, 1976.

Pennington, R., *Company Law*, 5th edn., London: Butterworths, 1985.

Phillips, J., *An Introduction to Intellectual Property Law*, London: Butterworths, 1986.

Potts, R., 'Emission Security' (1988–9) 3 *Computer Law and Security Report* 27.

Pounder, C., 'Police Computers and the Metropolitan Police' (1985) 7 *Information Age* 123.

Price Waterhouse, *Information Technology Review, 1988/89*, London: Price Waterhouse Publications, 1989.

Public Accounts Committee, 25th Report, *Computer Security in Government Departments*, HC 291, London: HMSO, 1988.

Queensland Government Department of Justice, *Green Paper on Computer Related Crime*, Queensland: Government Printer, 1987.

Rider, B. A. K., 'Combating International Commercial Crime' (1985) *Lloyds International and Maritime Law Quarterly* 217.

Roskill (Chairman) Report, *Report on the Fraud Trials Committee*, London: HMSO, 1986.

Rowell, R., *Counterfeiting and Forgery*, London: Butterworths, 1986.

Saunders, M., *Protecting Your Business Secrets*, London: Gower, 1985.

Saxby, S., 'EFT Fraud Report' (1986–7) 3 *Computer Law and Security Report* 2.

Schølberg, S., *Computers and Penal Legislation*, Norwegian Research Centre for Computers and Law, 1983. Oslo: Universitetsforlaget.

Schrager, L., and Short, J., 'How Serious a Crime? Perceptions of Common and Organisational Crimes' in Geis and Stotland (1980).

Scott, M. D., *Computer Law*, New York: John Wiley, 1985.

Scottish Law Commission, Consultative Memorandum No. 68, *Computer Crime*, Edinburgh: SLC, 1986.

—— *Report on Computer Crime*, Cm. 174, Edinburgh: HMSO, 1987.

—— Discussion Paper No. 77, *Criminal Evidence*, Edinburgh: SLC, 1988.

Shotton, M., *Computer Addiction? A Study of Computer Dependency*, London: Taylor & Francis, 1989.

Sieber, U., *The International Handbook on Computer Crime*, New York: John Wiley, 1986.

—— 'Collecting and Using Evidence in the Field of Information Technology' in Eser and Thormundsson (1989), p. 203.

Sizer, R., and Clark, J., 'Computer Security: A Pragmatic Approach for Managers' (1989) 11 *Information Age* 88.

Smith, A. T. H., 'Conspiracy to Defraud' [1988] *Criminal Law Review* 508.

Smith, D., 'White-Collar Crime, Organised Crime and Business Establishment' in Wickham and Dailey (1982).

Smith, J. C., 'Some Comments on Deceiving a Machine' (1972) 69 *Law Society Gazette* 576.

—— 'Theft, Conspiracy and Jurisdiction: Tarling's Case' [1979] *Criminal Law Review* 220.

—— 'The Admissibility of Statements by Computer' [1981] *Criminal Law Review* 387.

—— *The Law of Theft*, 6th edn., London: Butterworths, 1989.

—— and Hogan, B., *Criminal Law*, 6th edn., London: Butterworths, 1988.

Smith, K. J. M., 'Liability for Endangerment' [1983] *Criminal Law Review* 127.

Soble, R. L., and Dallas, R. E., *The Impossible Dream: The Equity Funding Story: The Fraud of the Century*, New York: Putnam, 1975.

Sparks, R., Genn, H., and Dodd, D., *Surveying Victims*, Chichester: John Wiley, 1977.

Spencer, J. R., 'The Metamorphosis of Section 6 of the Theft Act' [1977] *Criminal Law Review* 653.

—— 'The Theft Act 1978' [1979] *Criminal Law Review* 24.

Staniland, H., 'Computer Evidence in South Africa' (1985) 2 *Computer Law and Practice* 21.

Stoll, C., *The Cuckoo's Egg*, London: The Bodley Head, 1990.

Stotland, E., 'White Collar Criminals' (1977) 33 *Journal of Social Issues* 179.

Street, S., 'The Serious Fraud Office' (1988–9) 1 *Computer Law and Security Report* 6.

Sullivan, C., 'The Response of the Criminal Law in Australia to Computer Abuse' (1988) 12 *Computer Law Journal* 228.

Sullivan, G. R., 'Fraud and the Efficacy of the Criminal Law: A Proposal for a Wide Residual Offence' [1985] *Criminal Law Review* 616.

Sutherland, E. H., 'Is "White Collar Crime" Crime?' (1945) 10 *American Sociological Review* 132.

—— *White-Collar Crime*, New York: Holt, Rinehart & Winston, 1949.

Taber, J. K., 'On Computer Crime' (1979) 1 *Computer and Law Journal* 517.

—— 'A Survey of Computer Crime Studies' (1980) 2 *Computer and Law Journal* 275.

Tantum, M., 'The Serious Fraud Office Approach to Computer Fraud' (1988–9) 3 *Computer Law and Security Report* 13.

Tappan, P., 'Who is the Criminal?' (1947) 12 *American Sociological Review* 96.

Tapper, C., *Computer Law*, 3rd edn., London: Longman, 1983.

—— *Cross on Evidence*, 6th edn., London: Butterworths, 1985.

—— 'Computer Crime: Scotch Mist?' [1987] *Criminal Law Review* 4.

—— 'Copyright in Databases' (1988) 5 *Computer Law and Practice* 20.

—— *Computer Law*, 4th edn., London: Longman, 1989.

Tasmanian Law Reform Commission, Report No. 47, *Computer Misuse*, Tasmania: Government Printer, 1986.

Taylor, L., and Walton, P., 'Industrial Sabotage: Motives and Meanings' in Cohen (1971), p. 219.

Temby, I., and McElwaine, S., 'Technocrime: An Australian Overview' (1987) 11 *Criminal Law Journal* 245.

Tettenborn, A., 'Some Legal Aspects of Computer Abuse' (1980) 2 *Company Lawyer* 147.

Thackeray, G., 'Computer Related Crimes' (1985) 25 *Jurimetrics Journal* 300.

Tompkins, J. B., and Mar, L. A., 'The 1984 Federal Computer Crime Statute: A Partial Answer to a Pervasive Problem' (1985) 6 *Computer and Law Journal* 459.

Trew, A., 'Computer Crime: Does Technology Outstrip Enforcement?' (1986) 2 *Computer Law and Practice* 178.

United States Congress, Office of Technology Assessment, *Management, Security and Congressional Oversight*, Washington, DC: Federal Government Publication, 1987.

United States Department of Commerce, Bureau of the Census, *Computer Use in the United States*, Washington, DC: Federal Government Publication, 1988.

United States Department of Justice, *Criminal Justice Resources Manual*, Washington, DC: Federal Government Publication, 1979.

Van Eck, W., *Electronic Radiation from Video Display Units*, Netherlands: PTT dr Neher Laboratories, 1985.

Vaughan, D., *Controlling Unlawful Organisational Behaviour*, Chicago: University of Chicago Press, 1983.

Volgyes, M. R., 'The Investigation, Prosecution and Prevention of Computer Crime: A State-of-the-Art Review' (1980) 2 *Computer and Law Journal* 385.

Wacks, R., *Personal Information, Privacy and the Law*, Oxford: Clarendon Press, 1988.

Walker, N., and Marsh, C., 'Do Sentences Affect Public Disapproval?' (1984) 24 *British Journal of Criminology* 1.

Walsh, M. E., and Schram, D. D., 'The Victim of White-Collar Crime: Accuser or Accused?' in Geis and Stotland (1980).

Warbrick, C., 'The New Law on Extradition' [1989] *Criminal Law Review* 4.

Ward, C., *Vandalism*, London: The Architectural Press, 1973.

Wasik, M., 'Surveying Computer Crime' (1985) 1 *Computer Law and Practice* 110.

—— 'Criminal Damage and the Computerised Saw' (1986) 136 *New Law Journal* 763.

—— 'Computer Crime: Recent Legal Developments' (1987) 3 *Yearbook of Law, Computers and Technology* 195.

—— 'Scottish Law Commission: Report on Computer Misuse' (1987–8) 4 *Computer Law and Security Report* 20.

—— 'Criminal Damage/Criminal Mischief' (1988) 17 *Anglo-American Law Review* 37.

—— 'Law Reform Proposals on Computer Misuse' [1989a] *Criminal Law Review* 257.

—— 'Tackling Technocrime: The Law Commission Report on Computer Misuse' (1989b) 6 *Computer Law and Practice* 23.

—— 'Crime' in S. Saxby (ed.), *Encyclopedia of Information Technology Law*, London: Sweet and Maxwell, 1990, ch. 12.

Webber, C., 'Computer Crime, or Jay-Walking on the Electronic Highway' (1984) 26 *Criminal Law Quarterly* 217.

Weeramantry, C. G., *The Slumbering Sentinels*, Middlesex: Penguin Books, 1983.

Weinrib, E., 'Information and Property' (1988) 38 *University of Toronto Law Journal* 117.

Wickham, P., and Dailey, T. (eds.), *White Collar and Economic Crime*, Lexington, Mass.: D. C. Heath, 1982.

Williams, F., 'The Information Society as a Subject of Study' in F. Williams (1988).

—— (ed.), *Measuring the Information Society*, Beverly Hills, Calif.: Sage Publications, 1988.

Williams, G. L., 'Temporary Appropriation Should Be Theft' [1981] *Criminal Law Review* 129.

—— *Textbook of Criminal Law*, 2nd edn., London: Stevens, 1983.

Wines, M., 'FBI Investigates Network Crash', *The Times*, 9 Nov. 1988.

Wolfgang, M., Figlio, R., Tracy, P., and Singer, S., *The National Survey of Crime Severity*, Washington, DC: Department of Justice, 1985.

Wong, K., *Computer Crime Casebook*, London: BIS Applied Systems, 1983, 1987.

—— and Farquhar, B., *Computer-Related Fraud Casebook*, London: BIS Applied Systems, 1983, 1987.

Wood, J., 'The Serious Fraud Office' [1989] *Criminal Law Review* 175.

Wood, M. B., *Computer Access Control*, Manchester: National Computing Centre, 1985.

Wuermerling, U., 'New Dimensions of Computer Crime: Hacking for the KGB' (1989–90) 4 *Computer Law and Security Report* 20.

York, C. M., 'Criminal Liability for the Misappropriation of Computer Software Trade Secrets' (1986) 63 *University of Detroit Law Review* 481.

Younger (Chairman) Committee, *Report of the Committee on Privacy*, Cmnd. 5012, London: HMSO, 1972.

Zajac, B., 'Computer Viruses: The New Global Threat' (1988–9) 1 *Computer Law and Security Report* 3, 31.

—— 'Computer Viruses: Can They Be Prevented?' (1989–90*a*) 1 *Computer Law and Security Report* 18.

—— 'Virus Hits Michigan Medical Centres' (1989–90*b*) 2 *Computer Law and Security Report* 28.

Index